P9-CKQ-741

Jesse H. Jones

By the Same Author:

Garner of Texas

Portrait of an American: Charles Gates Dawes

Jesse H. Jones

Jesse H. Jones

THE MAN AND THE STATESMAN

by Bascom N. Timmons

ILLUSTRATED WITH PHOTOGRAPHS

NEW YORK • HENRY HOLT AND COMPANY

Published by Owl Publications, Inc.

In Canada, George J. McLeod, Ltd.

First Edition

Library of Congress Catalog Card Number: 56-10519

88461—0216

Printed in the United States of America

To Mary Gibbs Jones

Contents

PART I

The School of Experience

1

A Boy and His Forebears

TO forty-four-year-old William Hasque Jones, farmer and tobacco dealer, the spring of 1874 held the brightest prospect in the life of that amiable, hard-working man. The panic of 1873, precipitated by the failure of the banking house of Jay Cooke and Company in Philadelphia, had caused the closing of banks as far away as Tennessee. The depression that followed the panic gripped the nation.

The effects of that catastrophe had touched William Hasque Jones hardly at all. In the summer of 1873, as mines, mills, and manufacturing companies closed their doors, banks fought for their lives, and, on the nation's stock exchanges prices plunged to a new low, planter Jones had harvested a bountiful tobacco crop on his Robertson County, Tennessee, farm. Miraculously, too, the scourge of Asiatic cholera that swept Tennessee that year had not touched him or his family.

In this spring of 1874 there had been increasing prosperity in Tennessee, which had been the last state to leave the Union and the first to be readmitted and which had escaped the military occupation and carpetbag rule that was to be the lot of the other Confederate states.

In his little factory, dealer Jones saw hogshead after hogshead of tobacco packed for shipping; and in the first week of April the nearby Nashville market reported the arrival of a greater quantity of tobacco than in any week since the war.

As William Hasque Jones made his trips to the busy market, there was more political talk than there had been for years. Around the Maxwell House in Nashville, Jones heard the guests wonder what would happen to Charles Sumner's civil-rights bill now that death had vacated the New Englander's Senate seat; and they gabbled about Grant's support of an inflation bill, which most certainly meant that the old soldier wanted to puff up the nation into prosperity and try for a third term as President. Parson Brownlow, finishing his Senate term in Washington, had written to friends in the State House at Nashville that it undoubtedly was Grant's intention.

For nine years the guns of the War Between the States had stood mute; and now the Nashville *Republican Banner*, stanchly Democratic despite its name, proclaimed:

> Recent elections have settled many questions which grew out of the war. . . . Emancipation is settled; enfranchisement is settled; amnesty is settled; and the reconciliation of the sections is settled. But many new questions will arise in their place: The relations of the states to the Federal Government; the extinction of the debt; the currency; the best modes of taxation; freedom of trade; the reformation of abuses in war, and the administration of them.

But the new questions that would arise could be discussed calmly. Indeed, so firmly established was the era of good feeling that the *Republican Banner* noted a movement, with strong bipartisan support, to send Andrew Johnson back to the United States Senate to represent Tennessee in the last years of his life.

And so the big talk around the Maxwell House was that Andrew Johnson, just recovered from his cholera siege at Greeneville, had come to Nashville in his Senate canvass, had there met General Nathan Bedford Forrest and received a pledge of support from the redoubtable former Confederate cavalryman—a consummation that meant almost certainly that Uncle Andy would go back to the Senate, the first former President to be thus honored.

Bustling Nashville stores sought some of the ready money of the tobacco boom, advertising English walking coats for men "who have escaped the prostrating effects of the great financial crisis." Postwar finery for Southern women, from faraway Paris, was again appearing on the shelves of the city's shops. On the big board at the Maxwell House were posted the winners of the Louisville lottery.

But William Hasque Jones took no interest in the lottery, little part in the political conversation, and made no purchases of the alluring finery in the Nashville stores. His consuming interest at the moment was centered in an event soon to occur in the Jones home.

There on the Robertson County farm on April 5, 1874, the day tobacco hit its highest quotation on the Nashville market, a son was born to William Hasque and Anne Holman Jones. He was the fourth of the five children they were to have, three girls and two boys. The infant was promptly named Jesse Holman, after his mother's brother. Except for the middle name of Holman, there had been at least three Jesse Joneses before him in the family.

Artisans, tradesmen, merchants, and men who till the soil leave few records. Preachers, teachers, lawyers, keep written chronicles of their families. There apparently was no family historian in the William Hasque Jones kin.

That the family came from Wales about 1656 and settled in Virginia is established. In 1660 they moved on to help form a colony on the Chowan River in North Carolina. By 1760 the most westward branch of the family was near Raleigh, and in 1768 John Jones was with James Robertson in the adventurous group that crossed the mountains and formed a settlement on the Watauga River, and John Jones became a commissioner of the Watauga Association. About 1778 a group from the Watauga settlement led by two Jones brothers, Eli and Jesse, moved westward. They halted at a point that became known as Jones Settlement, and later Jonesboro, in what is now Washington County, Tennessee.

The first recorded Jesse Jones became a warm personal friend and backer of John Sevier, who had commanded the over-the-mountain men at the Battle of King's Mountain, and was one of the leaders in the movement to elect him governor of the proclaimed state of Franklin. But Sevier was hardly established in his governorship in the frontier town of Jonesboro when the Jones brothers banded together a group of about 125 men, women, and children and trekked west to join John Donelson and James Robertson in what is now Davidson County, Tennessee. The new settlement successively bore the names of French Lick, the Bluffs, Nashborough, then Nashville.

Still the Jones brothers had not quite found the place they wanted. They drove their oxen northward forty miles and became homesteaders between Springfield and Pleasant View, in what became Robertson County, Tennessee, named after James Robertson, with whom the

Joneses had been associated ever since the days of the Watauga Association in North Carolina. They had found a rich jewel of unclaimed land in the new West.

Eli and Jesse Jones put up stout log houses, broke the fertile sod, and planted crops of tobacco, corn, and wheat. By 1796 they were prospering from the providence of their fields in Robertson County and had added a grist mill to their belongings. In that year, too, Tennessee became a state and their old friend, John Sevier, was its first governor.

Both Joneses continued to live in Robertson County until Jesse died. His widow then moved southward to Maury County. Eli Jones, farmer and part-time preacher, died in Robertson County in 1819.

While Jesse and Eli Jones were pushing on to Robertson County, Tennessee, another branch of the family in which there was a younger Jesse Jones, left the Watauga River area, turned southwestward to the Creek Indian country near what is now Tuscaloosa County, Alabama, giving the settlement the name of Jones Valley.

Methods of communication being difficult, the two Jones brothers who went west to middle Tennessee heard little from their kinsmen in Alabama. The Alabama Joneses prospered, too, and when Davy Crockett and three of his neighbors in the autumn of 1817 went to explore the new Alabama country taken over by treaty from the Creek Indians, they visited Jones Valley, which Crockett described as "a large, rich one." Here Crockett fell ill and was near death in the home of Jesse Jones.

Seventeen years later in his autobiography the frontiersman, expansionist, and sometimes Congressman paid tribute to the Joneses. He also used the incident to ridicule President Jackson's methods of political patronage and some of the men and women who had the run of the White House. And he betrayed the fact that he did not regard the Presidency as out of his own reach.

> I knew but little that was going on for about two weeks [Crockett wrote of the incident in his autobiography], but the family treated me with every possible kindness in their power, and I shall always feel thankful to them. The man's name was Jesse Jones. At the end of two weeks, I began to mend without the help of a doctor or any doctor's means.
>
> Perhaps [Davy soliloquized], Mrs. Jones, who had a bottle of Batesman's draps and gave me the whole bottle in a single dose, will someday be spoken of as the kind woman who saved President Crockett's life.

Crockett was not to go to the White House, but was to occupy a quite different niche in American annals, along with Travis, Bowie, and Bonham, among the heroic dead of the Alamo. And he came to be better known to American children than any of the Presidents of Crockett's time.

John Jones, born in Robertson County in 1797, was the son of Eli, the farmer and preacher. To John and Elizabeth Price Jones were born Milton, William Hasque, Eli, Arch, Martin Tilford, and Nancy. Only William Hasque and Nancy remained in Tennessee, the other four sons emigrating to Ocenee, Shelby County in Illinois.

On October 31, 1867, in his thirty-eighth year, William Hasque Jones was married to Laura Anna Holman, in a ceremony performed by the Reverend R. S. Blakenship. The bride was a tall, slender, dark-haired, blue-eyed, twenty-year-old beauty, the daughter of Mr. and Mrs. J. C. Holman. The families lived on adjoining farms. The Holmans, like the Joneses, were almost exclusively farmers.

Because his father's brothers had moved to Illinois, Jesse Jones was to know more of the Holmans than the Joneses, but he actually knew little of the early history of the Holman kin. He was to say later, "I figured a man had to make his own record; and, if it was a good one, it made no difference whether he knew much about who his ancestors were."

Of his immediate family he was to say, "We were a congenial family but not a clannish one."

Jesse's mother died on April 22, 1880, two days after her thirty-third birthday. Jesse had just reached his sixth birthday. She had been ill for two or three years. Jesse's Aunt Nancy, widow of a Confederate sharpshooter, was living in the Jones home with her own two children. Neither William Hasque Jones nor Nancy Hurt ever remarried. Aunt Nancy was mother to her own two children and foster mother to her brother's five—Elizabeth, Ida, John T., Jesse Holman, and Carrie.

Nancy Hurt, the diminutive only sister of the five huge and muscular Jones brothers, was a remarkable woman with little education, who said that she "never read anything I did not have to." She was the only mother Jesse ever knew, so young was he when his mother died, and she proved to be one of the greatest influences in his life. She was guide, physician, and clothes-maker of all the Jones children, who paid her the tribute of saying no children ever had a better mother. She was a famous cook, preparing all sorts of edibles without benefit of cookbook; set a much-talked-of table for the family and friends who dropped in; and exported the products of her culinary art to neighbors for miles around when sickness overtook them.

The home where Jesse Jones was born and lived for the first nine years of his life had four rooms. Its living room had a large fireplace and served as the father's bedroom. It also accommodated some of the children. There were two bedrooms and a kitchen. The 100 acres of farmland were none too fertile; but Billy Jones had been able to make a living on it and, even in the worst years, to save a little money. He became the most prosperous farmer in the neighborhood.

The first of the Jones kin to reach a state of affluence was Jesse's uncle, Martin Tilford Jones, who went from Tennessee to Illinois in his youth.

Martin Tilford Jones, a twenty-one-year-old, six-foot, 200-pound hard-muscled, steel-gray-eyed farmer, enlisted in the 115th Illinois Infantry at Camp Butler, Illinois, on August 12, 1862, and fought through such bloody battles as Chickamauga, Wilson Creek, Rocky Face, Resaca, and Nashville.

Though battle casualties had decimated his regiment, Martin Tilford Jones, upon his discharge at Camp Harker, Tennessee, on June 11, 1865, quietly noted that he had received not so much as a scratch in battle.

After the war M. T. Jones married Louise Wollard. He tried farming in Illinois until falling farm prices following the panic of 1873 forced him to look elsewhere for a livelihood. He then moved to Texas to engage in the lumber business, of which he knew practically nothing; and he had very little capital. He arrived in Texas in 1875 and located in Terrell, using his scant resources to open a small lumber yard. A decade later he organized the M. T. Jones Lumber Company, of which he was the principal owner. He had moved to Houston in 1883. Texas was growing fast and M. T. Jones grew with it, expanding his company with more lumber yards scattered over the state. He also built two sawmills.

Although M. T. Jones had fought in the Union Army and his older brother, William Hasque Jones, had espoused the Southern cause, they never discussed the war. Years later the famous son of William Hasque Jones wrote:

> I do not know what, if any, interest Father took in politics, since it was never discussed at home. However, he must have taken a normal citizen's interest, since he was prominent in the community. Also, I never heard him mention the war. This was probably natural, since he was a Southerner and his brothers, all living in Illinois, were Unionists and Republicans. When I grew up, I assumed that Father was a Democrat, and I became one.

Jesse Jones eventually was to deal almost casually in millions; but his first experience with money, which came very early in life, was extremely modest and far from casual. Of this tingling money episode, he wrote:

When I was five years old, I fell out of the loft of our stable and fractured my skull. Country doctors in those days were none too well equipped, and had few opiates except possibly a little morphine.

The necessary operation and repair job was severe and very painful. A neighbor gave me a silver dollar to quit crying during the operation; and I did. When it was over, he took the dollar back. I thought he was the meanest man in the world.

As a child, I sensed the value of money. I would save nickels and dimes throughout the year, getting together maybe as much as a dollar. A few days before Christmas, we children would be taken to town to buy what we wanted. I would usually spend 15 or 20 cents and bring the balance back home.*

Jesse had plenty to do, both inside and outside the house; and his life on the first 100-acre farm where his family lived was similar to that of other farm boys, with the usual endless chores. He wrote:

My jobs included looking after the chickens and turkeys, feeding the pigs, wiping the dishes, helping with the churning, bringing in wood and kindling, building fires, taking out the ashes, sweeping and doing generally the things necessary to farm life where there was no hired help for housework.

My best friends were two Negro boys, just about grown, who lived in a cabin in the corner of our yard and I was happiest with them. Their names were Neil and Albert. I do not remember their surname.

Six years old and small for his age, wearing brass-toed shoes and stockings knitted by Aunt Nancy, young Jesse began such education as he was to get at old Howard School, a one-room, log schoolhouse attended by children of all ages. The school was something over a mile from the Jones home. Jones' recollections of the schoolhouse included a potbellied stove that burned wood ravenously in the wintertime, for he helped to carry the fuel that kept it going.

We carried our lunches [he wrote]. (It was dinner in those days.) I attended Howard School one session, then old Hopewell, another one-room school near home, for two years. I did not learn very easily. The children were punished for slight infractions of the rules, sometimes with the switch but more often by standing in the corner of the schoolroom, facing the wall. I had my share of this kind of punishment, largely as a result of playing pranks on the other children when I should have been studying.

J. B. Farthing, one of his earliest teachers, who was to know him for forty years after he left the little school, gave this version:

* Never at any time in his life was Jesse Jones a diary-keeper; he made no ventures in autobiography although, on occasion, he buttressed his remarkable memory with some carefully preserved memoranda of events. The nearest to memoirs he attempted was in recollections of his childhood, written at intervals. These memoranda and some recollections by his sister Ida, who was five years older, are the best history of his childhood.

Jesse Jones in school was not particularly bright; nor did he differ greatly from the other boys of the countryside. He never seemed to study very hard; his lessons were only fair. But his grades averaged high enough not to cause him any worry from me. In short, he was just the average rural schoolboy of his time, and not without a goodly amount of devilment in him.

He studied the old *Blue Back Spelling Book* and the *Appleton Reader*, and had geography and arithmetic. He liked arithmetic better than any other study, and got good grades in it. So far as I have been able to learn, he missed grammar and its use entirely. Later he was to develop the art of self-expression to a fine degree. This was done before he reached the mark of twoscore years. That which he lacked as a young man, he seemed to master before he reached forty.

The things he learned in his maturity, he learned with a conscious recognition of their value, and made full use of. I doubt if he would have done as well as he has if he had had a more extensive formal education. I do not know of any other man about whom I could say that.

In some recollections of life in rural Tennessee in the 1880's Jesse wrote:

In summer we liked to "go washin"—more properly stated "in swimming." We also went barefoot in summer; and the woe of my existence was having to wash my feet every night before going to bed. I would sit up as long as I could, because I liked to hear the grown people talk. There were no bathtubs in the country homes, and all the bathing we got was in washtubs or in large wash pans. By the time I was ready to go to bed, I was usually sleepy enough to try to skip the foot-washing chore, and sometimes succeeded, only to get a scolding next day from Aunt Nancy.

My father and most other men shaved only once or twice a week, and father used ordinary home-made soap for shaving and for brushing his teeth. When he died at sixty-three, he still had every one of his teeth, and every tooth was a sound one.

Many legends were built around Jesse Jones. One of the most repeated of them was that, when he was young, he wanted a horse. As the recital goes, his father did not believe in giving children everything they wanted, so he gave his son a small pig instead. Jones, the narrative continued, raised the pig until it was ready to be a brood sow, traded it for a yearling calf, and raised that to a milch cow, then traded the cow for a horse.

The trouble with the story was that, while Jesse was to be a trader most of his life, he got no further in the supposed parlay than the pig. After it had been disposed of, he found that it was so entwined in his affection that he made a decision more clearly indicative in his career than the pig-cow-horse story. Jones himself told the episode:

When I was nine, my father sold the little farm for, I think, about $5000, and took the family to Dallas, Texas. He thought the five children could get better schooling there than in the country schools where we lived. Moreover, M. T. Jones had been urging my father to come to Texas and go into business with him.

When the man who bought Father's farm went with him around the fence lines to see where the boundaries were, I went along. There were no abstracts of title in those days in the country where we lived. When we got back to the house, my pet pig greeted us as he always did when I came into the yard.

Father said to the man: "I cannot sell you the farm unless you buy Jesse's pig." The man looked at the pig, then looked at me and asked: "What do you think your pig is worth?" I told him, "About $4.25." He then asked what I thought it would weigh, and I told him, "About eighty-five pounds." The market price of hogs was five cents a pound, that made $4.25. The gentleman replied: "I think you are about right, and I will buy your pig."

It was my biggest money transaction up to that time. I was very proud to have $4.25 all my own. But a great shock and sorrow came to me when I realized that the friendly pig had gone from me forever.

After letting the companionable little pig go, he resolved never again to sell anything he liked; and, for a man who built so many business buildings for investment—more than any other man in the United States—no man ever signed fewer property deeds.

While the Jones children entered the public schools at Dallas, with Aunt Nancy making a home for them, William Hasque (Billy) Jones, who had invested 2000 dollars of the proceeds of his farm sale in stock of the M. T. Jones Lumber Company, went to Terrell, thirty miles east of Dallas, and was manager of the Jones lumber yard there.

In the Cumberland Hill public school in Dallas, Jesse had trouble keeping up with his classes in the third and fourth grades. He was keenly disturbed at his lack of scholastic progress there, but the friendship he formed for his teacher became one of the great compensations of his life. Of her he wrote:

My teacher, Miss Blanche Aldehoff, was a strict disciplinarian and did not hesitate to use the switch; except that, in my case, it was a flat ruler which she seemed to delight in punishing me with, slapping the palms of my hands with it. I would infuriate her by smiling when she was punishing me.

She was a beautiful woman. I suppose it is natural for a boy to think his teacher beautiful; but there is no doubt that this medium-sized, auburn-haired Miss Blanche was good-looking. She later married and lived to be ninety, and thought the New Deal a travesty on democracy. We corresponded as long as she lived, and I still regarded her as my teacher.

The end of school meant no vacation for young Jesse. This was from choice. With him it was school or work.

One of the two summers when we lived in Dallas, I worked in cotton fields near town, and got 50 cents a day for chopping the weeds. However, in picking cotton, we were paid by the pound, and I was able to make as much as a dollar a day.

During the next summer, when I was twelve, I herded and looked after a small bunch of cattle, between thirty and forty head, on a small ranch about thirty miles from Dallas. At the ranch, I lived alone in a one-room ranch house most of the time, and did my own cooking, which was not much—meat, bread, and coffee. Aunt Nancy had taught me a little; but my enthusiasm for it was not very strong, and I have never cooked anything since.

It was a dry summer, and the creek which furnished water for the cattle went dry. With the help of a Negro man from an adjoining small ranch, we dug a well in the bed of the creek to get water for the small herd. This kept me drawing water all day. Finally, the cattle, not getting enough, became restless.

I had heard that animals could find water if there was any near. So, one morning, I saddled my pony, cut the fence, and let the cattle out, following them. They ran almost in a stampede for seven or eight miles, and found water in the bed of a nearly dry creek which I did not know was there.

I let the cattle graze in that vicinity for a couple of weeks, until we had a good rain, then drove them back to the ranch. There was a small shack not far from this water hole, where a young man and his wife lived. They were kind enough to give me a place to sleep, and also food. They charged me nothing. I got $50 for that summer's work.

2

Free Enterprise at Fourteen

AGRICULTURE was a complete and satisfactory mode of life to William Hasque Jones. His days on the farm had been ordered and natural. To him hard work, the outdoors, and the feel of the earth underneath were solid realities of daily existence. Although he did well in his two years in Terrell, he did not like the lumber business. When in 1886 a 600-acre farm on the Kentucky-Tennessee line not far from the old Jones home went on the market, he bought it, partly on credit, and took the family there.

It was a farm he had long wanted. The land, 500 acres of which lay in Kentucky and 100 in Tennessee, was more fertile than the old Jones farm. The ten-room brick house, which was on the Tennessee side of the state line, when erected just before the Civil War, was the finest outside of Nashville. It was still a showplace as it neared its one hundredth anniversary in 1956.

Dr. J. S. Brown, a whisky distiller, had built it for his bride, the daughter of a wealthy tobacco planter. The mantels were of marble, the doorknobs of silver, and the other construction in keeping. A tapestry of multicolored maples threw a cooling shade over the house and the two-acre yard. The house stood on the eminence of a hill, at the foot of which was a hydraulic pump that brought spring water to the house. In the rear was a poplar-thick sash of timber, marking the farm's boundary line.

The house was modern, with the exception of plumbing and electricity [Jesse Jones wrote in his description of it]. All the outbuildings, servant quarters, barns, stables, and the like were brick. It was one of the few homes which had an icehouse. The icehouse was in reality a roof over a large hole in the ground, about the size of an ordinary living room, and some ten or twelve feet deep. In the wintertime it was filled with ice bedded in sawdust and straw. This kept the ice through the summer.

Father unfailingly had a plentiful supply of meat in the smokehouse, from which less-thrifty neighbors would borrow a ham or a side of bacon during the summer months. There were always ample fruits, vegetables and berries in season, and they were canned and preserved for the winter. We had a good table.

The post office, two miles from the new Jones home, was Adairville, Kentucky, a town of about 500 people. The five Jones children attended school there. Jesse, whose last formal schooling was at Adairville, in recollections of his childhood wrote of the days there and of his views on education then and in later life:

We rode horseback to Adairville, carrying our lunches with us. At this school, I had a man teacher who employed the switch often, and occasionally would throw a book at me or some other boy whom he might catch up to some prank. I was frequently punished by my teachers, even after I was twelve and thirteen. Being kept in after school or part of the lunch hour was a common occurrence. I was always getting in scraps with boys my own age, and sometimes a little bigger. I seemed to think they were always teasing me or picking on me. Very likely it was my own fault. Anyhow, there was usually plenty of fighting among teen-age boys in school, and doubtless still is.

My brother, John, who was two years my senior, could whip most of the boys of our age. He always came to my rescue when the battle was going against me.

At school, except business college, I did not learn easily. I was fairly good in arithmetic, but that was all. I did not like school, and would frequently absent myself. I quit at fifteen, at the end of the ninth grade. Father asked me if I wanted to go to college; I told him I did not, that I wanted to work. I really had no conception of college or what college life was like. I thought, if a boy did not intend to be a professional man (that is, a doctor, a lawyer, a teacher, or a preacher), he need not waste a lot of time going to school after he had learned to read, write, and figure.

In 1912-13, Laurette Taylor, always a favorite actress with me, had a line in her play, "Peg o' My Heart," which impressed me, and which I have always remembered. Laurette, acting the part of a young girl in school, and finding it difficult to learn, threw her geography down and remarked: "Oh, well, what's the use of learning the height of a lot of mountains you never expect to climb?"

I thought that was sensible but nevertheless, I have often wished that I had learned in school the height of some mountains which I have had to climb since.

At the family home on the Kentucky-Tennessee line, after two years in Texas, Jesse Jones, thirteen years old, was told by his father that he might choose any two acres of land on the 600-acre farm, for a tobacco crop of his own. He selected his land adjoining the yard, and it actually measured close to three acres. It was necessary to pick worms off the growing tobacco at least once a week to keep them from ruining many of the leaves. He said he chose his plot near the yard because he wanted the chickens and turkeys to help eliminate the worms; but it might well have been because he would be less lonesome there than farther from the house.

Giving an account of this episode, Jones wrote:

Father had said that I could have what I made on the crop; but he stipulated that I was to do the work and pay for any hired help I might have. I would be strictly on my own. He took me to town and told the general store of his arrangement with me, and said that, if I needed any credit, to give it to me.

One nice spring morning, Father told me I should hitch up two of our old, gentle mules and start breaking the ground for my tobacco crop. Normally, it would take something more than a day to do the job. Father went to town, and, when he got back home about four in the afternoon, I was just finishing the entire plot in a little more than half the required time. I had been plowing in a semi-trot most of the time instead of a slow, steady walk, as is customary; and the mules were white with lather.

Actually, I did not go in a trot because I wanted to get through in a hurry. The reason was that an old mule seems to know when a man is handling him and when a boy is handling him; consequently, I was fighting with the mules all the time, throwing gravel and clods of dirt at them, which would make them walk at double speed, or even sometimes in a slow trot.

That tobacco patch furnished the basis for the origin of the saying, "Don't be deceived by Jesse Jones' calm casualness; he always plows in a trot."

As long as I lived on the farm [Jones continued], that was the last time I was allowed to plow. I could work the farm hands as hard as I could but not the animals. Father had good stock and did not allow it to be abused by anyone. While there were riding plows at that time, Father did not allow them on his farm. He did not want his mules to have to haul a lazy man, he said, in addition to pulling the plow.

The following spring, when I sold and delivered my tobacco crop, I received $120 for it. I went straight to the general store and paid my account. Then I went to the hardware store and bought a double-barreled, breech-loading shotgun. I already had a single-barreled muzzle loader, a .32 Winchester rifle, and a .22 rifle. Then I went to the post office, got a money order, and sent it to Louisville for a pearl-handled Smith and Wesson pistol. I invested most of the balance of my proceeds in ammunition.

I had not intended to tell Father about the pistol; that is, not right off. But, a few days later, when he got the mail, it included a postal card acknowledging receipt of my order for the pistol. That night after supper, he handed me the post card and said in a perfectly normal voice, with no indication of reprimand or question: "If you will leave it in my top drawer I will pay for it." The top drawer of Father's bureau was a catch-all; it was in the living room, which was also his bedroom.

I was greatly relieved when he treated it that way; and the matter was never mentioned between us again. Upon reflection, I have assumed that, when my father gave me the use of the land to grow a crop of my own under the conditions he imposed, his purpose must have been to start me out thinking for myself and making my own decisions in my own way, and to run my own affairs. There was perfect sympathy between my father and me, and I would not have offended him for anything. For some reason, he must have thought I needed special attention, for I do not recall that he ever scolded me or even corrected me; and, certainly, I was by no means a model boy. He was not as considerate of my brother, although he was not severe with him. I think my father spoke very few cross words to his family or to anyone else in his life.

In illustration of consideration for and attitude toward me, one Sunday afternoon when I was six or seven years old, my brother and I, together with an older boy, raided the watermelon patch of one of the sharecroppers. Father happened to be walking over the farm and saw us; but, because of some timber, we did not see him.

That night at supper, I did not eat much, and remarked at the table that I was not hungry. Father, in a perfectly natural tone, with no apparent sting whatever, remarked: "Did the watermelon make you sick?" There was no reprimand in his tone, but one could not have been more effective. Of course, I was greatly embarrassed, and it was a good lesson. I guess Father just understood.

The tall, slender Jones boy, who in school still had trouble keeping up with other pupils, was launched on a business career when he was fourteen years old, by the father who never scolded or punished him.

William Hasque Jones by now had several sharecroppers on his Kentucky-Tennessee farm. He was buying most of the tobacco raised by other farmers in his neighborhood, and operating what was called a tobacco factory. His factory being in the dark-tobacco area, most of the product was prized about 2000 pounds to the hogshead, and shipped to market. Ultimately it went to Italy, Germany, and England.

When Jesse's father, in partnership with two other men, opened another branch factory under the firm name of Jones, Holman and Armstrong to care for the expanding business, Jesse was put in charge as manager, with complete responsibility.

The elder Jones took Jesse to the bank in Springfield, Tennessee, and opened a bank account for him so that he could pay for the tobacco when delivered. There was to be plenty of grief for young Jesse in his first managerial capacity, a very responsible position for a boy.

It was a proud day but a serious one for me when Father took me to the bank in town, where I left my signature and was told that my checks would be honored there, and that I had the sole responsibility of running this factory [Jones wrote of this experience].

When Father told me he was going to put me in charge of the factory, I asked him if he thought I could do it. He replied that I could do it as well as he could; that I knew tobacco, knew how to order and grade it and how to put it up and ship it. I, of course, knew that I could not do the job as well as Father; but, when he told me I could do it, I felt I could.

There are two or three grades of tobacco on the same stalk, and it must be carefully classed, which is not difficult if you know tobacco. We made our own hogsheads from green staves sawed at a nearby sawmill, with hoops rived from green, flexible young timber on the place.

Tobacco can only be delivered in a rainy season, when there is moisture in the air, so as to make it pliable enough not to break and crumble. Sometimes, a farmer would bring his tobacco to the factory when it was "too high"—that is, when it had too much moisture in it. Always, before unloading it, we would draw samples to see if it was in proper order. When it was found to contain too much moisture, the farmer would have to take it back home, dry it out, and deliver it the next rainy spell, in proper shape.

There were no hard-surfaced roads in those days; and most country roads were very bad in the rainy season. To require a farmer to take his tobacco back home, hang it up in the barn to dry, and deliver it the next rainy spell, would of course make the farmer very mad.

Not to be overlooked was the fact that the more moisture the tobacco contained, the more it would weigh; and it was paid for by the pound. It was to the interest of the farmer to deliver it with all the moisture it could stand. The farmers for the most part were men in their 40's, 50's and 60's. I had to take many a severe tongue lashing when it was necessary for me to tell such a man to take his tobacco home and deliver it in proper order the next rainy season. Yet, if I accepted it damp it would spoil and be a total loss; so I had no choice but to refuse it.

Sometimes, after one of these tongue lashings, I would go out behind the factory and have a cry. My help was all Negroes and all of them were my good friends. I was ashamed to have these helpers see me cry, and I was too young to talk back to the men as I would have liked to do; but I was determined to do my job. I would not report these things to Father, for fear he might be bothered about it and maybe put some grown man in my place.

Tobacco buying and shipping was speculative. Most seasons, there would be some little profit; occasionally, there would be a small loss. Father was very meticulous in having it properly graded and packed for shipment; and a hogshead of tobacco bearing his mark always brought top price for the grade, whether in a local or foreign market.

This branch factory was on the farm of Josephus Armstrong, a member of the firm. I stayed in his home while on this job. Living with his family meant very early rising. Mr. Armstrong, a hard-working farmer, would get up every morning long before daybreak, and feed the livestock. His wife, who was my mother's sister, would prepare the breakfast, and Mr. Armstrong would be in the field plowing at the break of day. He lived a hard life and was a good man, very kind and gentle.

When Jones was Secretary of Commerce and Federal Loan Administrator and the world's most famous moneylender, he was to recall this early experience. On October 10, 1940, in a telegram to Mayor E. A. Covington of Springfield, he said, in declining an invitation to the town's tobacco festival:

My first work on the farm was in a tobacco patch, and my first work in a factory was "handing" tobacco. I remember well that the packer would frequently slap me with a hand of tobacco when I did not drop it to suit him.

I got my first business training and business principles from my father in the tobacco business; and his standards and principles have been my guiding influence in all my business and public life.

These two years with his father, the last two years of close association they were to have, were decisive ones in molding the kind of man Jesse Jones was to be. His father's example and precept promoted in the son a standard of good business conduct that was to remain through life.

Among his neighbors Billy Jones was considered a benign and tactful man of irreproachable character and high business ideals. Years later Jesse Jones was to write:

I have known a great many of the leading men of my generation in all lines of endeavor, and I have sometimes tried to think whom I considered the ablest man I have ever known. I think my father was the gentlest man I ever knew, and the ablest for his occupation, that of farmer and tobacco merchant. He was never in big business, but had a very successful life. I have always thought that he would have been a success in any business he might have entered.

Those two years with his father on the Kentucky-Tennessee farm were pleasant ones for Jesse in many ways. He fished for trout and perch in the East Fork of the Red River, which was sometimes a rollicking river and sometimes a gently flowing rivulet; and took part in the social affairs of the countryside. But most of the time father and son were together.

> Father usually walked over his Kentucky-Tennessee farm every day, visiting and advising with the sharecroppers [Jones wrote], I went with him when not in school, and on Saturdays and Sundays. Father had an old cur dog named Bruno, which always went with him. When Father died in 1893, Bruno quit eating and, in a few weeks, died of starvation and a broken heart.

At thirteen Jesse joined the Oak Grove Baptist Church in Logan County, Kentucky, which was near his home. Later he felt he was a backslider from the rigid teaching of the church because he was good with marbles and, along with other boys, played for keeps.

That last summer on the farm decided Jesse that he wanted something more out of life than raising tobacco. Quint Fuqua, a friend of William Hasque Jones, whose son later owned the principal Jones home, related this incident to his son Garner:

> Jesse came over to my place with a repeating rifle, the first I had ever seen in the neighborhood. He told me he did not intend to do any more tobacco raising. I said to him: "Any man who don't work tobacco in this section of the country is on a doggone good road to the poorhouse." Jesse raised his rifle and shot a grasshopper some distance away, a remarkable feat of marksmanship. Then he replied: "I think I can find a better way to make a living."

It was to be some years and after many unsuccessful tries before he was to find that way.

3

A Bit of Wandering

IN 1891 Jesse Jones went with his father and the rest of the family back to Texas in order that the children might complete their education. Jesse, then seventeen, entered Hill's Business College in Dallas for a course that included bookkeeping and a short form of commercial law.

Here was something to his liking. The course usually was completed in three or four months. Jesse learned all there was to learn in four or five weeks. He was then given a place as a paid instructor in the school. He stayed on as instructor for a short time, until one day, at the noon hour, a rather old, one-legged man came in and offered to teach the boys a new method of detecting errors and keeping books in balance. The price would be fifty cents to each student, and he would return the next day to see how many would join his class.

Jesse knew figures. He spent most of the night trying to reason out the process used. When the man returned the next day, Jesse told him he believed he knew what the method was. The seedy-looking old man hooted any such idea, whereupon Jesse told him what he thought it was. "That's it," the old gentleman said, "but, if I had not come here, you would never have thought of it." Jesse paid him the fifty cents.

Deeply impressed with the method, Jesse left the business college and started on the road, teaching bookkeepers "Proofs on How to Keep Books in Balance." He would gauge his charges on what he thought the customer might pay, anywhere from two to ten dollars. After working three or four towns between Dallas and Denison, Texas, Jesse woke up to the realization that what he was teaching was, in fact, worthless. He took the first train for Dallas and started looking for a new job.

The three years that followed, which in many youngsters' lives are spent in college, were for Jesse Jones experimental, restless, and not altogether happy. His nature barred any impulse to settle down. He was certainly not seeking a mediocre security. Nor were the various trials at jobs that mostly proved to be errors a planned effort to prepare for a specific career. And he was certainly not seeking adventure for its own sake. Somehow his movements indicate an effort not altogether conscious to find a spot where he could flex the muscles of his mind and win by his own efforts substantial material satisfactions.

One opportunity came when he saw an advertisement in a newspaper for a cigar salesman, or "drummer" in the jargon of that day. Jesse applied for the job, found that it was on a commission basis and that he would have to buy his samples. He sold a few cigars but soon decided he was a failure as a cigar salesman. He smoked up his samples and quit.

About this time Jesse developed a cough. It caused great concern to his father; for Jesse's mother and two of her brothers had died of tuberculosis in their early thirties. Before returning to Kentucky his father took Jesse to west Texas and arranged with a sheep rancher to take his son as a boarder for the summer. Then, again leaving the other children with Aunt Nancy and planning to visit them once or twice a year, William Hasque Jones returned to Tennessee to live on the big farm.

Jesse spent the summer in the land of sheep, jackrabbits, and coyotes; riding, fishing, and getting well. He was always to remember the rancher's wife as "a perfect mother to me. She fixed me a pallet on a fruit-drying table in the yard, and I slept in the open. The helpers on the sheep ranch were Mexicans, and I enjoyed mixing with them."

Jesse had told Quint Fuqua he could find a better way of making a living than tobacco raising. But he still had not found the way. The job he needed for that test showed up with M. T. Jones Lumber Company at Hillsboro. The town, which had a population of 2500, was situated where the rolling Black Land Prairies meet the east Texas Cross Timbers. The starting pay of the job would be twenty-five dollars a month.

Jesse Jones arrived in the little north central Texas town from nearby Dallas, bringing along the wardrobe he had accumulated; and he liked nice clothes. Joe Didiot, a young Frenchman employed then in a rival lumber yard, but who was several years later to go into the employment of Jesse Jones and remain with him until well past the middle of the next century, remembered the youthful Jones as "slender, if not already almost six feet tall and of commanding appearance."

What Joe Didiot held in his memory most distinctly was the Jones garb. Jesse arrived wearing a tweed suit with a double-breasted coat, known to the fancy youth of that day as a lounge coat, with notched lapels. The vest was single-breasted; a bow tie was unshaped and tied so as to give a flat appearance. The cuffless trousers were the kind the Texans wore to prevent the collection of black dust that cuffs invited. His shoes were square-toed, giving a boot appearance. From the bottom hole of his vest was looped a long, heavy, gold watch chain; and in the pocket was what, if not the biggest gold watch in all Texas, must have been the second biggest. He topped off his fancy apparel with a tall derby with a broad, thick, rolling brim.

Young Jesse took off the fine regalia and began his job of unloading lumber from freight cars, stacking it, then loading it onto farmers' wagons.

> But, the next Sunday [Didiot said], he appeared at the Baptist Church wearing a black Prince Albert coat with cream-colored pants of figurative design; a long, pointed, turn-down collar; and the small and short black bow tie of that era, suspended by a small rubber loop. Nobody else there had clothes like that; but his dudish appearance did not militate against him, and he became very popular.

In Hill County, as elsewhere in his increasing lumber business, M. T. Jones had chosen his location well. From the rich Brazos bottoms on the west side of the county, to the Trinity Basin to the east, farmers came to settle and plant cotton, corn, wheat, sorghums, and peanuts in the black, waxy soil. M. T. Jones sold them the lumber for their new homes.

After a few months Jesse's salary went up to forty dollars. He continued to unload freight cars, stack lumber, and load farmers' wagons, but also took over the duties of bookkeeper and salesman.

Jesse, at the end of a year on the job, in weather torpid in the summer heat and cold and disagreeable in winter, decided that the economics of a job in which he was paying twenty-two of his forty dollars for table board, leaving eighteen dollars for all other purposes, was not sound. He saved on room rent, for he slept in a small room over the office and made his own bed. Necessarily, he had to have some spending money, particularly since he was known to be the nephew of the owner of the business, who was recognized to be a wealthy man.

He wrote to his uncle, asking that his salary be raised to sixty dollars a month. He explained that he was busy at the lumber yard all day, and kept the books at night, and could not quite make ends meet on forty dollars. In reply M. T. Jones not only declined to raise his nephew's salary but said there was not enough work at the lumber yard to keep him so busy. Young Jesse deeply resented this.

It was all right for him not to raise my salary; for that was his privilege [Jesse wrote in his recollections]. But I did not like what he said about the amount of work I was doing; and, if that was the way he felt toward me, and all he was willing to pay, I decided to quit and go back home. Furthermore, I was not getting along well with the manager.

He had another lumber yard at Waxahachie, thirty miles away, and wrote me that he would be there in a few days and would like for me to meet him there. When I met him, he insisted that it would be a great disappointment to my father if I quit.

I then told him that, if he would transfer me to another lumber yard and give me a week or two to go home and see Father, I would continue to work for him.

He then made me tell him my real reason for wanting to quit, which was that there were certain irregularities in the business at Hillsboro. He countered that with the argument that it was my duty to him and to my father to go back to Hillsboro and prevent the irregularities.

This, of course, created an impossible situation; but, being an eighteen-year-old boy, I did not know any better than to try. However, the relationship between the manager and me soon became very strained, and I decided definitely to quit and go home.

I had a few debts at the stores; so I went to the bank and borrowed $150 to pay my bills and buy a ticket home. The bank required me to get two endorsers on my note, which I had no trouble in doing.

I paid my bills, packed my valise, and bought my ticket home. It was Saturday, and I had not told the manager I was leaving.

Having completed my arrangements, and with the books posted up to date, I went to the manager to tell him I was quitting, but he beat me to the draw by telling me he had been instructed to discharge me.

I have never known whether he had actually been so instructed or whether he did it because I was in his way.

My father died on March 13, while I was en route home. I had not been told he was ill; in fact, neither the family nor the doctor had known how sick Father was.

A week after his father's death Jesse was in the field of the Tennessee-Kentucky farm, preparing the land for a crop of tobacco.

In that spring of 1893 all the nation was talking about the Columbian Exposition World's Fair being readied for a summer opening in Chicago.

Perhaps no World's Fair had ever been so ballyhooed and attracted so much attention.

In April, as Jones worked in his tobacco field, dark clouds appeared on the country's financial horizon. The year before Jesse's birth, the panic of 1873, precipitated by the failure of Jay Cooke and Company in Philadelphia, had prostrated the country.

Now, on May 6, 1893, National Cordage, a speculative stock on the New York Stock Exchange, which had risen to 147 a share and only recently declared a 100 per cent dividend, mysteriously tumbled to almost nothing and carried every other stock with it. At first only the speculators were hurt, but the calamity soon fell on every segment of the country's economy. Business and banking leaders everywhere felt that the country was in for a depression far worse than that which followed the panic of 1873.

But, panic or no panic, Jesse Jones wanted to see the World's Fair. In August he borrowed sixty dollars on his growing crop and told his Negro friends on the farm that, if they would work his patch for two weeks while he was gone, he would tell them all about the Fair when he came back. The bargain was made.

> I bought a round-trip ticket to Chicago for $10 [Jesse recorded]. I sewed $10 in the waist band of my trousers, just in case I got robbed or an emergency, and spent the other $40 for the expenses of my trip and seeing the Fair. I took an old telescope valise filled with food prepared for me by Aunt Nancy; a boiled ham, several baked chickens, preserves, and light bread; and an extra shirt or two. My room in Chicago cost me $1 a day, and I had to buy coffee for breakfast if I wanted it.
>
> The hotel where I stopped was improvised from a warehouse, with temporary partitions making rooms about six by eight feet. There were no windows; but the walls did not go to the ceiling, thus giving ventilation. There were no facilities in the rooms; but it was a place to sleep and keep my valise.

Young Jesse stayed in Chicago two weeks and thought he saw the Fair as thoroughly as anyone could. He put down indelibly in his memory most of the things he saw: the majestic and artistic array of buildings; the colonnades, pillars, and statues of colossal size with the lakes of clear water surrounding many of the buildings. Along the Midway Plaissance he saw foreign people living exactly as they lived in Europe, Asia, or Africa. He carefully inspected the architecture of the Chinese Theater, spent hours in the realistic German and Irish villages, even saw the shocking "hootchy-kootchy" danced by girls in abbreviated pants. He saw the daddy of all the Ferris wheels, with its capacity of

1440 persons, which was causing almost as much talk as the Eiffel Tower had at the just-completed Paris Exposition.

Among crowds that spent money with gay disdain despite the atmosphere of national panic and despair, Jesse's budget permitted only one show, and he studied the marquees of the theaters. Sol Smith Russell was appearing in *April Weather*, a new play written by Clyde Fitch; buxom Lillian Russell in *Girofle-Girofla*; Marie Tempest in *The Fencing Master*; at Schiller's Opera House was *The Girl I Left Behind Me*. One theater showed William De Mille's great spectacle, *Paradise Lost*; another, *The Bohemian Girl*.

Young Jesse chose the Columbian Theater, where crowds stood outside every night to catch a glimpse of Lillian Russell as she arrived in a carriage drawn by her own team of fancy bays.

He joined with the audience inside as it clapped and roared its approval as she sang the arias of *Girofle-Girofla* and everything else the lyric songstress did. He bought his ticket outside from a scalper, "75 cents for the dress circle." The "dress circle" turned out to be the peanut gallery, but Jesse did not mind.

Black headlines in Chicago newspapers brought the news that in Washington, President Grover Cleveland had called a special session of Congress to deal with the critical plight of the nation; but that information made little impression on Jesse Jones. For one dollar he bought a round-trip ticket on a whaleback lake boat to Milwaukee, which allowed several hours to see the city. The jammed boat was no great shakes of a vessel; but to young Jesse it seemed sleek and grand and luxurious. The Milwaukee trip enhanced his good opinion of money. A single dollar that could buy a trip like that was something to be respected.

In the Loop area of Chicago, young Jesse saw sights that to him were almost as wondrous as the Fair. Rising from the ashes of its great fire that had all but destroyed it, and the panic of 1873 that had hit it harder than perhaps any other American city, Chicago, building for the Columbian Exposition, had become the cradle of the skyscraper.

The heat of 3000 degrees, which the city's great fire had generated, melted most of the cast-iron buildings which had been believed fireproof. Chicago architects had, by the mid-eighties, invented and mastered steel framing and made possible the modern office building, hotel, and apartments.

Young Jones gazed in wonder at the Monadnock Building, a masonry structure on Jackson Boulevard resting on walls seventy-two inches thick at the base; wandered through the lobbies but did not become acquainted with the cuisine of such hotels as the Great Northern, the Congress, and the Plaza; or thrilled at the opulence and ostentation of the massive Auditorium Hotel and Theater.

But wonder of wonders was the Masonic Temple at the corner of State and Randolph Streets, twenty-two stories high, the tallest building in the world at that time.

"Toward the end of my stay," Jones wrote, "the food I had brought from home got a little moldy, and I finally had to buy some ham and eggs."

Back home in Tennessee, he told his incredulous colored friends of such things as the Hagenbeck animal exhibition, where a lion rode horseback just as an equestrian might have done; of other lions harnessed to a chariot by their keepers and driven around the ring, three abreast; how he himself had ridden through downtown Chicago on the first elevated electric train.

To the simple Tennessee farm boys, to whom a city was a general store, a blacksmith shop, a schoolhouse, a church, and a few residences, the tales of the skyscrapers seemed unbelievable, something which only the most powerful prevaricator could conjure up. But Mr. Jesse was telling them, and Mr. Jesse would not fool them!

Jones wrote, "Seeing Chicago, the tall buildings, so many people, and the World's Fair, gave me an ambition to get out into the big world."

Sixty years later Jones still considered that trip to Chicago the greatest adventure of his life; and there is no doubt that what the Robertson County, Tennessee, farm boy experienced during the two weeks he spent there so stimulated his ambition as to affect the course of his life.

He had made the trip from Chicago back to Tennessee with his valise empty, but the ten dollars was still sewed in his pants.

At his father's death Jesse had felt it his responsibility to look after the family, a role he never relinquished. He was deeply devoted to his sister Ida. When he came back from Chicago she told him that she was going to marry Daniel E. Garrett, a rising young Springfield lawyer, later to be a long-time member of Congress from Texas. Jesse was greatly upset—so much that he borrowed forty dollars from Aunt Nancy and started for Texas. When he got as far as Nashville, where he was to take the train, he saw a furniture store, regretted his plan, and used the forty dollars to buy some furniture for Ida.

Jesse now turned to the task of getting his father's estate settled.

Jesse and his brother John had each inherited in their father's will 1000-dollar stock in the Waxahachie bank of which Royal A. Ferris was president, and 1000 dollars in the M. T. Jones Lumber Company. John had used his 2000 dollars to enter business.

William Hasque Jones, in the last years of his life, had been setting up three well-improved farm homes, one for each of his three daughters. The big farm on the Tennessee line he cut in half and erected buildings and equipment for a second self-sustaining farm home. He bought some adjoining land for a third set of improvements, which were under way at the time of his death.

There had been two executors of the estate. They were not very businesslike and had not done a good job in completing the third farm and paying the few remaining debts. Jesse sold his stock in the bank and in the lumber company and used most of the proceeds to pay the remaining obligations so there would be no debts against his sisters' homes. With little more than his railroad fare he set out for Texas the third time.

4

Years in the Lumber Business

THE Texas to which Jesse Jones returned in 1894 was still predominantly a cattle empire and farm domain. Its population divided, according to the census of 1890, into 1,886,016 rural and 349,511 urban.

The great names in Texas were those of the cattle kings, led by Charles Goodnight, the most noted of them all, far out in the high Texas Panhandle. Next to him ranked Captain James King, part of whose million acres lay near the rolling Rio Grande, a good 800 miles away from Goodnight's vast grazing land. The King Ranch remained intact a good half-century after Goodnight's broke up. Dan Waggoner and a dozen more were almost as famous as Goodnight and King.

The biggest ranch in all Texas or the nation, the 3,000,000-acre XIT in the Texas Panhandle, was not the creation of one of the renowned individual cattle kings, but of a syndicate that had built the state capitol at Austin. In payment for that capitol the state of Texas had written the Capitol Freehold Syndicate a quitclaim to 3,000,000 of the state's 168,732,160 acres. Texas was a "state full of grass," and the grass was full of cattle.

Although the 1890 census takers had found a human population of only 2,235,527 compared to the 8,543,635 cattle that nibbled its rich and nutritious grass, four Texas towns had aspirations to be centers of teeming city thousands. The same 1890 census takers also found that industrialization was raising its not unanimously applauded head in Texas and that Dallas led these aspirants, with 38,967 people within its corporate limits. Immediately some lusty Dallasite, quick on the trigger, attached to it the appellation, "Big Dallas," to which it was forever afterward to cling proudly.

San Antonio in 1890 had 37,789 people; Galveston 29,084; and Houston completed the "Big Four" with 27,557. In the light of subsequent events these relative figures were to assume considerable importance.

Jones had no aspirations to be a cattle king. He had been a cowboy one summer, a cowboy with a *remuda* of one horse. He was a dude cowboy who disdained boots and wore high-button shoes, but whose solution of the problem of finding water for his cattle on a dehydrated ranch won the profound admiration of the owner of the little herd for the youthful Tennessee-born cowhand.

Nor did the oil business attract him, although a year later a development took place at Corsicana, a few miles from Dallas, that resounded all over the Lone Star State. Some Corsicana people formed a partnership that produced a small amount of oil. But the next year the discovery of more productive wells brought oil scouts, geologists, and speculators from Pennsylvania and Ohio whom Jones could hear talking excitedly in the lobbies of the Oriental, the McCloud, the St. George, and other Dallas hotels. Jones, however, took as little personal interest in that talk as he did in the tales of rich gold discoveries on Bonanza Creek, a tributary of the Klondike River in faraway Yukon Territory.

The boy rapidly growing into manhood came back to Texas with ideas of connecting himself in some way with the industrialization of the state about which the newspapers and chambers of commerce talked so glibly. His ideas of how he was to make the connection or what it was to be were very hazy. "Big Dallas" certainly was not making urgent calls for manpower in its industries; indeed, it was pretty certain that San Antonio had again passed it in population. At any rate, the depression following the 1893 panic had clasped Dallas strongly in its embrace.

Elsewhere in the broad expanse of the state, crop failure was complete and the spirits of the people drooped. Savage winds and smoldering heat lashed humans, animals, and vegetation. Congress, taking heed of the devastation, passed a Texas Farm Relief Bill. When it reached

President Cleveland's desk in Washington, old Grover, although expressing sympathy for the drought sufferers, fired back to Congress a veto and a message, as fast as a fast bicyclist could take it to the Capitol saying that "though the people support the government, the government should not support the people."

Young Jesse thought he could always find a place with the M. T. Jones Lumber Company. The year before, after his father's death in Tennessee, M. T. Jones had written Jesse that, when he was ready to come back to Texas, "I will have a job for you."

When Jesse arrived in Dallas, M. T. Jones, a man certain of Texas' future despite the troubles through which it was passing, was setting up the largest of all his lumber yards, the location of which was one day to be the center of the Dallas skyscraper area.

Jesse walked in confidently and told his uncle he was ready for a job. M. T. Jones icily informed his nephew that he had nothing to offer him. This rebuff was a shock and a great surprise to Jesse, who knew that the personnel for the new yard had not been completed. But he soon discovered that the man from Hillsboro who had been his boss there was helping to put the new yard in operation. This former boss, who had fired him in Hillsboro, would be in the Dallas management; so the cards were stacked against Jesse.

> I later learned [he wrote] that this man had poisoned my uncle's mind against me, telling him that, when at Hillsboro, I gambled and drank, and that there were some irregularities in the cash account and he finally had to discharge me.
>
> There were some irregularities; but the shoe was on the other foot. It is true that I took an occasional drink, played a little penny-ante poker, and did most of the things an eighteen-year-old boy living away from home is likely to do, but nothing dishonorable or really to my discredit. I could not have been very bad on $40 a month, even if I did go into debt a little.

Having been refused a job by his uncle, Jesse went elsewhere looking for one, and found it as a laundry wagon driver. The pay would be ten dollars a week; but Jesse never went to work for the laundry. As he was ready to start on this stopgap job, C. T. Harris, the general manager of the M. T. Jones Lumber Company, asked him to help out for a week or two, keeping the books and running the office at the lumber yard while Harris took a trip to some of the company's other yards. For this Jesse received fifteen dollars a week.

When Harris returned from the second of these trips and found everything in good order, he offered Jesse the job as bookkeeper at sixty dollars a month. Jesse thanked him but declined. Harris, a kindly gentleman who took a deep interest in young Jesse, could not understand why he would not take the job; so Jesse finally told him:

> There is one man in the world I will not work for; that is my uncle. I was willing to help YOU temporarily; but my uncle believed things which were told him about me in Hillsboro, which were not true. He doesn't trust me; and I won't work for him.

Harris talked with Jesse for two or three days and finally persuaded him that there must be some misunderstanding. "Your uncle is a good man," he argued. "You come in here and make good, and everything will clear up."

Jesse then told him there was another reason why he would not take the job; that he would not be associated with the man who had been his boss at Hillsboro who, while not manager of the Dallas yard, was in the management. He simply would not work with him, and there was no use talking any more about it.

This last statement caused Harris more worry, and he asked Jesse to stay while he took one more trip, as it was necessary for him to go immediately to another yard. Jesse agreed.

When Harris returned, Jesse was able to show positive proof that the "leopard had not changed its spots." Harris fired the man who had been Jesse's boss in Hillsboro, and Jesse took the job at sixty dollars a month.

Six months later Harris summarily discharged his manager and, having no one else available, made Jesse Jones his successor. When Harris told M. T. Jones what he had done, Jesse's uncle fumed: "You might as well have set fire to the blankety-blank yard and have been done with it!"

Had Jesse heard this remark at the time, instead of years later, his connection with the company would have ended there.

M. T. Jones was what was known in the lumber trade as a "double-ender." He owned both lumber yards and sawmills. This made him a competitor not only of other sawmills but of retail lumber dealers as well. His entry into Dallas set off a bitter lumber war. But the difficulties in no way awed Jesse. He had been manager of a tobacco factory at fourteen and now, at Christmas, 1894, still four months away from his twenty-first birthday, he was not afraid of rough competition in the lumber business. He accepted the job at 100 dollars a month although he realized as Harris fixed the salary that the two managers who had been discharged in less than a year had received 150 dollars.

He saw to it that under the block-long sign, M. T. JONES LUMBER COM-

PANY, there appeared another line, *Jesse H. Jones, Manager,* in letters almost as large as the firm name.

Another fight faced the young manager, however. The lung ailment, which had sent him seeking recovery on a sheep ranch three years before, reappeared.

I consulted a doctor [he said in writing of his early experiences], who told me he could straighten me out if I would follow his instructions, but that it would probably take a year. I asked him what he would charge me, and he said, "$75 a month."

But, I was only earning $100 a month, so I looked for another doctor and found one, a delightful, good-natured, sympathetic, and understanding gentleman. He told me what to do generally in taking care of my health, and gave me a prescription which was easy to take. It consisted of bourbon whisky with enough rock candy and glycerin added to make a sort of syrup. He told me to take a swallow three or four times a day. I liked his medicine and took more, some days, than was prescribed. My doctor's bill was $5.

Either through the pleasant medicine or the care I took of myself, or both, I got rid of my cough, and it never returned.

Under orders from Houston headquarters to "sell lumber, profit or no profit, but to sell lumber," Jesse was soon not only getting more than his share of the business in the newest yard in Dallas, but was making a profit. However, no words of commendation came from Houston. Evidently it was no secret at the head office that M. T. Jones put no high value on his nephew; moreover, it would have pleased the force in the Houston office if there were no Jones kinsmen in the organization. There was more than one man, including the vice-president of the company, who aspired to top rank in the growing M. T. Jones operations, whose estimates of the young man's ability were higher than his uncle's.

For four months Jesse had nothing but fault-finding letters from the Houston office. He hung on until two weeks past his twenty-first birthday; then, tired of the continued heckling, he sent his resignation to his uncle.

"You will need the best man you can find to handle the job," Jesse wrote M. T. "The circumstances here are generally unfavorable and unfriendly to you. I will continue until July 1, and help the new manager get started."

The temerity of his nephew in stating that his successor must be unusually capable irritated the big lumberman. He lost no time in sending a new manager. The successor was a man much older than Jones and had been manager of another of the company's lumber yards. He arrived and informed Jesse that he had been sent under orders to keep the books and act as assistant for two months, then take over the management.

This chosen successor had been in Dallas only two or three weeks when he saw that he faced a tough job, with all of his competitors hating and fighting the M. T. Jones Lumber Company. He tried to persuade Jesse to remain as manager and let him be the assistant and keep the books; but Jesse had resigned effective the 30th of June and was determined not to reconsider, even if his uncle had wanted him to, of which there was no indication.

On June 30, the date of his departure, Jesse asked his successor to invoice the lumber yard with him and check the books and bank account. When this was done he turned the business over. The inventory and book balance showed that Jesse had been making a good profit for the company, something that the Houston office had considered impossible because of the lumber war and the instructions to sell with or without profit.

And now, out of a job and with no plans for another job or business, but feeling proud that he had made money for the company under such difficult circumstances, Jesse decided to go to Houston and visit the home of his uncle. This was not the first time he had been there because M. T. Jones had children of his own age for whom Jesse had a real affection.

After a few days during which he made several visits to the company office he found his uncle in a more genial mood.

"Jesse," said M. T., "I am going to do something nice for you. I am going to raise your salary to 100 dollars a month."

"I am not working for you any more," was the reply. "And besides I have been getting 100 dollars a month for six months."

"I did not know it," exploded M. T. "Or you would not have been getting it."

"I can believe that," said the nephew, "but your general manager fixed the salary when I accepted the job as manager of the yard. He believes in paying better salaries than you do."

Jesse wrote later that he remained a guest in his uncle's home for several days.

> He insisted that I go back to Dallas and run the yard. At first I refused but then it occurred to me that maybe I was making a mistake, since during my first six months as a manager I had been able to make a profit against tough competition.
>
> I decided to do a little trading with my uncle. One morning, I told him I would go back to Dallas and run the yard at a salary of $150 a month and

6 per cent of the profits of the business. He stormed and stormed, and I left the office. The next morning at the breakfast table, he said to me: "Go on back and have your way." But he was still mad. I went back and ran the yard successfully for him until his death three years later.

When Jesse returned to Dallas, he was to learn why his uncle had changed his mind so suddenly. In the course of his visit M. T. had sent auditors to check the books and reinvoice the lumber yard to find out if Jesse had actually made the profit he had reported when the Houston office thought he was losing money. When the auditors confirmed the reported profit, the shrewd uncle decided that Jesse should continue to work for him.

Jesse left Houston firmly resolved on one point: he would take no more bully-ragging from the Houston office. Two years before, he had gone back to Hillsboro at his uncle's urging, and had been rewarded by getting fired. Later he had gone to work in Dallas at the urgent request of Mr. Harris, general manager of the company, after M. T. Jones had refused him the job. Now, dubious of the final outcome, he was in the employ of his uncle again. If anyone was to give ground hereafter it would not be Jesse.

As a restored manager Jesse Jones found the Dallas lumber war increasing in intensity. So bitter was the feeling against M. T. Jones, the "double-ender," that Jesse Jones, as a representative of his uncle, was refused admittance to the State Lumbermen's Convention. As the battle continued, railroads were active in the background, for there was strong rivalry between railroads at such competitive points as Dallas. At these important centers the competing carriers gave rebates to large shippers.

George J. Gould's Texas and Pacific brought lumber from east Texas and Arkansas. The Southern Pacific, along which M. T. Jones' mills were situated, annually loaded thousands of cars of lumber in southeast Texas and Louisiana.

The freight rebates had been the reason for instructions to Jesse to sell lumber, profit or no profit. If he sold it for what it cost him at Dallas, the company would still make money from the freight rebate, and also a profit from the sawmill. There was the added fact that the rail lines would sometimes carry the freight bill until the fall of the year, when the farmers sold their cotton and could pay their debts. These matters were handled at the Houston office, and Jesse knew nothing about them. He was charged the full freight rates.

But a new order was dawning; the Texas legislature soon passed an act creating the Texas Railroad Commission, and gave it power to "prevent discriminations against persons or places." Doughty old John H. Reagan resigned his seat in the United States Senate to be chairman of this Texas Railroad Commission. There were no more rebates.

Finally, to stop the lumber fight in Dallas, Harris, the general manager for M. T. Jones, worked out an arrangement with all the other lumber yards, whereby they would all sell lumber at the same price. They employed a secretary to look over the books of all the yards, to see that they were keeping faith. Harris did not tell Jesse about the particulars of this arrangement, but did tell him not to cut the established price. The agreement finally became known, the grand jury called the lumbermen to testify, and promptly indicted them for violating the Antitrust law.

At the time of the grand-jury investigation the retail price of lumber in Dallas was not much, if any, greater than its current cost to the yards. The dealers thought that if they were frank with the grand jury and gave it the facts the investigation would be dropped. But, naturally, the members of the grand jury or the trial jury refused to believe that the dealers were doing business without a profit, and each lumber yard was fined 100 dollars.

Jones extended credit freely to farmers, expecting payment when they sold their cotton in the autumn. When one such farmer failed to pay, and ignored all letters sent to him, Jesse Jones filed his first lawsuit.

With his 150-dollar-a-month salary and 6 per cent of the profits, he was dressing better than ever before. On the day of the trial Plaintiff Jones walked into the Dallas County Courthouse, the best-dressed man in it. He wore a morning coat with peak lapels, with a braid of silk around the lapels. The vest was a fancy one. He also wore a straight, stiff collar, two inches high, and a wide-looped four-in-hand tie, held in place by a small diamond stick pin. His shoes were patent leather.

Barry Miller, later to be one of the state's most noted trial lawyers and powerful public figures, but then a young man little older than Jones, was the farmer's attorney. He and Jones were friends.

There was no doubt the farmer owed the bill; Miller never claimed otherwise. He did not even question Jones, but he did interrogate the farmer. Then he addressed the jury with all the ridicule and sarcasm of which he was master:

I want you gentlemen of the jury to observe this dude who has taken my hard-working client away from the toils in his fields so necessary if he is to support his family [Miller began, to a jury made up mostly of farmers]. Note that jacket. No, it is not a vest; it is a waistcoat, or a weskit. I do not know which; I do not read the fashion magazines any more than you gentlemen of the jury do. But this I know: That waistcoat—or maybe it's a weskit—cost more money than you could get for the best cow or horse on your farm.

Look at those shoes. He does not have to black them like you black yours when you go to church. They are patent leather; they shine like that all the time.

Look at that shiner he is wearing in his pretty necktie. That's a diamond! That pin cost more than all the money my client will receive for his labor from daylight to dark in the field in a year.

Gentlemen of the jury, I especially want you to look how this dude parts his hair, right down the middle.

Miller used all of his time before the jury with this sort of inimical discourse; and, although Jones' attorney pleaded eloquently that his client's apparel and the merits of the lawsuit were two unrelated subjects, and the judge admonished the jury to disregard the prejudicial argument, the damage was done. The jury found for the farmer.

"It taught me a valuable lesson," Jones related. "I gave the diamond to my sister for a ring; began parting my hair on the side, where I should have parted it all the time; and quit wearing patent leather shoes and my best clothes, except on Sunday."

By the year 1897, at the age of twenty-three, Jesse Jones seemingly firmly entrenched in his uncle's organization, had made its Dallas outlet by far the most profitable in M. T. Jones chain. But two credits that Jesse had extended brought Uncle M.T. to Dallas to remonstrate against his "recklessness."

Jesse was a bicyclist; and cyclomania (the bicycle craze) was sweeping the country. Dallas had its full share of addicts. The wheelmen were organized into companies. On Sundays battalions of pedaling wheelmen, heads low over their handle bars, practiced fancy formations. The Dallas wheelmen were perhaps the very first advocates of good roads in Texas, for they sought matches with teams from Fort Worth, San Antonio, Houston, and Galveston. Good roads were required for the contests.

Jones was a thorough believer in the future of the bicycle. Even as conservative a man as President McKinley had said: "In this country of inventions, I doubt if any means of rapid-transit locomotion was ever so favorably received. . . . Eight hundred thousand bicycles are being produced ever year. . . . The bicycle has beaten the best time ever made by a running horse."

When two promoters went to Jesse Jones with plans to build a half-mile circular bicycle-race track out of lumber, their proposal fell on receptive ears. The track was to be adjoining the state fairground. The promoters planned that they would bring to Dallas such celebrities in the world of whirling wheels as William Martin. In his familiar Irish flag and green-harp colors, doing unbelievable things on a high-wheeler, Martin alone guaranteed big crowds. They would also bring Major Taylor, who had shattered most of the bicycle records, and even the most spectacular and popular of them all, Albert Schock, of Chicago, the cycling king. Wearing his black jacket and old-gold sleeves, with the horseshoe on his back, and to the stirring notes of "Ta-Ra-Boom-de-Aye," Schock, in the Madison Square Garden six-day "go-as-you-please" race, had beaten the world record, completing 1600 miles plus one lap.

In addition to the gate receipts for the bicycle races, the fees Dallas wheelmen were willing to pay for their fancy-practice didoes and matches with rival cities would seem to go a long way toward maintaining the plant.

Jones let the promoters have the material, believing that the project would be a paying investment. In the early spring of that year Captain Sidney Smith, manager of the Texas State Fair Association, came to see Jesse and said: "Boy, if you will sell me as much lumber as I want, and not require the directors of the Fair Association to guarantee the bills personally, I will put on the greatest fair we have ever had; and you can come out there and take in the gate receipts until your bill is paid. The other lumber dealers in the city will not sell us lumber without the personal guarantee of the directors of the Association; and they hold me down on expenditures."

Jesse knew that collecting the gate receipts would not be practical; yet it was a good argument for the credit. As a result, Jesse was hauling and shipping lumber to the fairground all summer. When the fair opened, Smith owed Jesse more than the value of his lumber yard. It was much the biggest credit risk he had ever taken; but Jesse felt that the people of Dallas would not allow the Fair Association to fail, even if it had a bad year. He thought he would finally get his money.

To help out the fair, remembering that railroads had given rebates prior to the establishment of the Railroad Commission in Texas, Jesse went to the Railroad Commission at Austin, of his own volition, and got the commission to authorize a half-freight rate on lumber shipped for the Fair Association. That helped the fair by reducing the price of the lumber.

All the lumber had been delivered and put to the use for which it was bought when M. T. Jones heard of the big transaction. He forthwith set out for Dallas. The day of his arrival was the opening day of the fair.

Jesse suspected that his uncle's visit had two purposes; the first was to investigate the two large credits which had been extended without security. Jesse also felt certain that M. T. had been listening to rumors as to his general conduct, since he had sent a man from the Houston office some months before, to help him; and this man, only a few years older than Jesse, divulged that he was there principally to report on Jesse's conduct. Jesse knew what some of the tales were, and that they were coming largely from his competitors.

In the office that day M.T. took Jesse severely to task about the two credits. Jesse insisted he would get his money. After a few hours of quizzing and criticism the uncle suggested that they take a ride and see something of the city. Jesse had a horse and buggy which he kept in the lumber company's stables, along with the company's wagons and teams.

It was a hot, early-autumn afternoon; soon they were passing a beer garden. "Jesse," said M.T., "I would like a glass of cold beer; would you?" Jesse replied that he certainly would. They had it, got back in the buggy, and continued their drive.

Approaching the fairground an hour or so later, they passed a saloon and M.T. said: "Jesse, I feel like a toddy. Would you like one?" Jesse replied that he would, and they had them.

Jesse did not want the drinks and knew that his uncle seldom took one of any kind, that he was just testing him. He decided to give M.T. all the evidence he wanted.

By this time they had reached the gates of the fairground and drove in. The good, if somewhat warmish, weather had brought out a large crowd. All day long the turnstiles had been clicking—Jesse left his uncle in the buggy for a few minutes to go into the fair office and look for Captain Smith. He found the captain in high spirits because of the good weather and big crowds the first day.

"Give me the biggest check you can," Jones said to Captain Smith.

"Bless your heart; I will," exclaimed the captain and proceeded to write him a check for a substantial amount on account, which was more than Jesse expected out of the first day's receipts.

Jesse put the check in his pocket, joined his uncle in the buggy, and they saw the fair, including all the company's beautiful lumber, for which M.T. thought he was not going to get paid!

Jesse said nothing about the check. They sat through the horse races and returned to the lumber yard about six o'clock. Jesse made an entry on the books and put the check in the safe. His uncle asked what it was. Jesse took the check out of the safe and handed it to him.

"Why didn't you tell me you had that?" exclaimed M.T. in anger. Jesse calmly replied, "I wanted you to continue to enjoy your peeve." M.T. handed the check back to his nephew without comment, but he still had more questioning about Jesse's personal habits.

"I understand you gamble," he said. Practically everyone in Texas was exposed to gambling in those days. There were gambling houses in most of the cities, where cards, dice, roulette, chuck-a-luck, and farobank were readily available; and there were some big gamblers such as Riley Grannen, Dan Stewart, and Luke Short, with an occasional visit to Dallas from John W. (Bet-a-Million) Gates in his pipe-organed private railroad car. But young men like Jesse Jones, without the means for big-time gambling, had their sport at the Dallas Club, where the stakes were within their limits.

So Jesse said, "Yes, I play poker in moderation; but my playing is on my time and not yours, and I play with my money, not yours."

M.T. went through the same specific questioning as to drinking and other habits. Finally Jesse said, "Whatever my vices may be, they are normal, and I have never neglected the business."

His uncle replied, "You will have to mend your ways if you want to remain with the company. We cannot allow our employees to drink and gamble."

"Then," said Jesse, "you will have to get someone to take my place. I would like very much to keep my job; but I will not be continually questioned and criticized."

M. T. Jones made no reply and offered no comment; but it was the last word of criticism Jesse ever heard from his uncle.

The Fair Association paid its bill in full before the fair was over; and, while the bicycle track was a failure, its bill was also paid.

Years later and after my uncle's death, I was to learn why I was never criticized by him after this visit [Jones related].

After his visit with me that day, he talked with Royal A. Ferris, the banker, about me. Mr. Ferris was in his late fifties, and certainly a good friend of mine. He knew my habits and how I lived; he also knew human nature better than my uncle. I recall one occasion when the vice-president of his bank criticized a small loan that Mr. Ferris had made me. This gentleman made the criticism at a bank-board meeting, stating that I was an inveterate poker player at the Dallas Club. Mr. Ferris replied, "Yes, I know; and I understand he is a pretty good player."

After my uncle's visit with Mr. Ferris, his attitude toward me was entirely changed. This impressed me with the fact that two of the greatest assets anyone can have are a good record and friends willing to speak up for him when occasion requires.

His constant bickering with his uncle had always puzzled Jesse, who got along well with everyone else. It was all the more baffling because M. T. Jones bore a reputation of being a fair man, who got along well with other people.

"Perhaps his criticism over what seemed to me so long a period was just his natural interest in me, a nephew; and a fear that so young a man as I, with no restraining home influence, might get out of bounds," Jesse wrote years later.

On June 20, 1898, a benign M. T. Jones, now on excellent terms with his nephew, walked into the Dallas office. He was just fifty-seven, apparently in excellent health, and ready for the biggest venture of his life. He had bought a large tract of timber in east Texas and Louisiana and wanted to build some sawmills. He said to Jesse, "I want you to take charge of the enterprise. Move to the woods, build and operate the mills. I will give you one fourth of the net profits for your compensation."

"This was a very generous offer," Jesse wrote, "and I, of course, readily agreed."

The manager of another one of his yards, J. M. Rockwell, of Sherman, Texas, was to go to Houston and run the headquarters office. Rockwell was also to have a fourth of the profits.

M.T. had finally learned that competent men were cheaper at a high price and an occasional pat on the back than incompetent men at low salaries. He left the company office and went to his room at the Oriental Hotel. That night Jesse boarded a train to Tennessee for a visit with Aunt Nancy before moving into the woods.

The next day M. T. Jones became ill and on June 22, 1898, died at St. Paul's Hospital. The project he had outlined for Jesse was never undertaken.

The reading of his will disclosed that M. T. Jones had made Jesse Jones and J. M. Rockwell, the two men he had chosen to run his business, among the five executors of his estate.

In August, Jesse Jones closed his desk in Dallas and went to Houston as general manager of the M. T. Jones lumber yards, sawmills, and timberland.

PART II

A City Is Born

5

Mr. Jones Goes to Houston

JESSE JONES arrived in Houston, which was to be his home the remaining fifty-eight years of his life, on a languorous August day in 1898.

South Texas had been tortured by drought that summer, and the harsh sun beat down like a huge blowtorch as Jones rode in a horse-drawn cab from the railroad station to the venerable five-storied Rice Hotel, where he was to live.

Houston, then about to celebrate its sixtieth birthday as an incorporated place, gave the impression of utter flatness. The elevation at the Rice Hotel was fifty-four feet above sea level, and there were not many places more than a few feet higher or lower anywhere in the purlieu of the town.

The town, which later was to grow like Jonah's gourd in a night, lagged behind San Antonio and Dallas in population, and had barely passed Galveston. The tempo of its life was slow, gentle, and easy. Horses and mules pulled commercial drays and also were the motive power for some streetcars in its outlying areas, and the city seemed perfectly satisfied with its poky public transportation. Its fine ladies and gentlemen rode in victorias and landaus, their horses' hoofs clip-clopping over the cobblestoned streets.

While Houston had few natural endowments of beauty, with a business section nondescript and unkempt, there was a certain charm and romance in its drowsy residential streets. Creamy white blossoms hung from the tops of lacy locusts, a shawl of weeping Spanish moss from the live oaks. Cape jasmines grew wild, and the night-blooming jasmines and magnolias made the night air fragrant. But, in that summer of 1898, on no days—and only a few nights—did a halfhearted Gulf breeze cut the heavy, warm air.

Jones was twenty-four when he arrived in Houston, but he still appeared to be a rangy, slow-spoken youth. He was two inches over six feet in height and he weighed close to 200 pounds. He had a profusion of dark hair, keen blue-gray eyes, and a firm mouth. His features were regular, his face mobile. In Dallas he had been conspicuous for the elegance of his dress, but it was more conservative now. His taste ran to dark blue cheviot suits, double-breasted and three-buttoned. A turn-down collar replaced the earlier stiff, stand-up type. A tie with a high, tight loop replaced the four-in-hands. This summer he was wearing the McKinley tower hat, gray with a broad band, a top piece made popular by the nation's well-liked President.

The day after his arrival in Houston he took over his new office in the six-story Binz Block, then the highest building in the city. It stood near a mosquito-infested bog called the Buffalo Bayou. There had been a yellow fever scare only a short time before, and Houston newspapers carried advertisements of cures for that dread disease.

The new manager's entire personal assets amounted to from 3000 to 5000 dollars. In his last years in Dallas he had been receiving a salary of 3000 dollars per year, and he had made a little money in real estate.

He was a man of companionable warmth who made friends easily, but he seemed in no hurry to break the ice in Houston. He had been unexpectedly pitchforked into the job of general manager of a company operating several yellow-pine sawmills and many retail lumber yards in Texas and New Mexico, and he was feeling his way.

T. W. House, a banker, the senior and most prominent of the executors, was elected president of the M. T. Jones Lumber Company; and J. M. Rockwell, who had come on from north Texas, was elected vice-president. However, as general manager and a member of the family, Jesse was to have more to do with administering his uncle's estate than any of the executors.

It was a considerable advantage to Jesse to be under House's auspices in his first days in Houston. House came from what was undoubtedly Houston's most representative family. It had come to Houston in the first year of the life of that village. The father, Thomas William House, had fought under General Edward Burleson and helped make Texas a republic. He married Mary Elizabeth Shearn, to unite two of the oldest Texas families.

The sons, T. W. House, the banker, and Edward Mandell House, inherited substantial fortunes. A very rich man for his day, T. W. House had a fine Houston home and a big plantation. His private bank was one of the biggest in Houston at the turn of the century, and he was part owner of the profitable gas company. His brother, E. M. House, later to be the adviser of Woodrow Wilson, lived in Austin and was not active in Houston business, but took care of his inheritance and was able to live well without paying much attention to his investments.

No particularly big names glittered in Houston in 1898, Jones' first year there. T. W. House symbolized the Houston that was a neighborly place, that did not particularly care whether it ever grew much larger.

The other most outstanding citizen was John Henry Kirby, who had sometimes appeared to have aspirations to be the panjandrum of a lustier Houston. He had organized the Kirby Lumber Company and acquired vast acres of pine timber, with much the same idea M. T. Jones had when he died. Kirby was the closest friend of United States Senator Joseph Weldon Bailey, a brilliant and highly controversial political figure.

In the spin of the wheel of fortune, bankruptcy was to come to both of these Houston nabobs of the gaslight age. The wealth of House, the cautious conservative, went swiftly within a few years and that of Kirby, the plunger, was drained away in the next three decades. But in that autumn of 1898 no Houstonian could have believed that T. W. House and John Henry Kirby could ever be pushed off the stage. It is certain that diffident Jesse Jones would never have been imagined as their successor. His name was printed along with those of the other four men whom the M. T. Jones' will revealed as the executors of his estate, and was not to be seen again in Houston newspapers for some years.

The young manager was, however, alert to every event and circumstance that might promote his legitimate interests, and in little more than a year an opportunity appeared that placed him on the threshold of fortune.

On a Sunday evening in the spring of 1900 Jones overheard a conversation in the lobby of the old Rice Hotel. Two men who were in the logging business in east Texas were going to Austin to buy stumpage—timber-cutting rights—from the state's school land. The timberland thus to be opened was in great quantity; there would be many bidders. It would be sold, in allotted amounts, to the highest bidder, who would remove the timber; but title to the land would remain in the state.

Two years before, Jesse's uncle had proposed the deal for the establishment of sawmills in east Texas and Louisiana, with Jesse as the manager; and the death of M. T. Jones had prevented the consummation of this project. The average selling price of lumber at that time was about 18 dollars per thousand feet. Of that 18 dollars, the man who owned the tree from which the lumber was cut got fifty cents. Jesse was convinced that the sure way to make money would be to buy timber and hold it for better prices. The sale of this stumpage by the state looked like the very thing of which he had dreamed.

However, to accomplish this deal he would need money far beyond his modest capital.

His foresight five years before opened his way to a solution to his present problem. Back in Dallas, while working on a very uncertain footing with his uncle, he had to establish his credit, in case he should later decide to enter business on his own. He went to see Royal A. Ferris, president of the National Exchange Bank in Dallas, and asked him for a loan of 500 dollars. He had no security, but Ferris knew M. T. Jones and had known Jesse's father to have been a sound man. So he made the requested loan.

Jones put the 500 dollars away and paid it back when due, losing the interest. Then some months later he asked for and received a loan for 2000 dollars, which he also put away. "A week or two before the note fell due," Jones told of the transaction, "I asked the banker if I could pay him $1300 and renew $700. He readily agreed and I paid accordingly. I then felt that I could go to him when and if I had a real opportunity." *

Now, in 1900, with his mind on the timberland that offered such a golden chance for a profit, Jones decided to use the gilt-edged credit he had established with Ferris. He went to Dallas and spent the greater part of a day trying to persuade the banker to lend him 10,000 dollars

* Ferris was a calm, mild-mannered man but one of the geniuses in Texas' banking history. At the time when Jones made his acquaintance, he had Hetty Green as a depositor, and the famous woman financier made Ferris the mentor of her son, Colonel E. H. R. Green. Later Ferris was to guide his bank through its nationalization as the National Exchange Bank, its merger with the American National Bank, and consolidation with the Trinity National Bank and the City National Bank of Dallas, out of which came the First National Bank of Dallas.

for the timber. He had no security, but he told Ferris that he could not lose.

The amiable banker listened with relaxed friendliness, but finally said, "I admire your enthusiasm, but we cannot make a loan of that size without collateral. There are very few people to whom this bank would lend that amount without security."

Jones admitted that, for a person of his age and means, it might seem presumptuous to expect such a loan, but he explained to Ferris that, if he should lose on the timber, he could work the loan out in four or five years.

At three o'clock in the afternoon, with Jones still arguing, Ferris in all kindliness said to Jesse that he would have to be excused, since he was leaving town for Waxahachie, thirty miles away, where he had another bank. So far as Ferris was concerned, the matter was at an end.

At eleven o'clock the next morning Jesse walked into the Ferris office at Waxahachie. Surprised at the visit and probably in admiration at Jones' persistence, even though somewhat annoyed, Ferris asked pleasantly, "What are you doing here?"

"I am here to get that loan," Jones replied.

Again Ferris said he could not make the loan and, after a while, told Jesse he had to go down the street. Jesse went with him. It was about twelve o'clock, and soon they were passing a saloon, of which there were then plenty in Waxahachie—and all Texas towns. Ferris remarked, "Jesse, I usually have a toddy about this time of day. Would you join me?"

Jones replied that he would.

As the two men were enjoying their toddies, Ferris said, "I suppose I will never get rid of you, Jesse, until I lend you that 10,000 dollars."

"I don't believe you will, Mr. Ferris," Jesse replied.

"All right, I suppose I will have to let you have it."

Jones asked how he could get the money, since it was necessary for him to be at Austin, the state capital, the next morning to bid for the timber.

"Just check on the bank at Dallas," Ferris replied.

In Austin, Jones found that there was strong competition for the timber, and that a section of 640 acres was the smallest amount he could buy. It would cost 17,000 dollars. Without hesitation, he made his bid and drew a check for that amount on the Ferris bank. He then telegraphed Ferris what he had done, and told him he would be in Dallas the next morning to see him.

Ferris, evidently convinced by now that Jones was making no mistake, made the loan for the full 17,000 dollars, and carried it three or four years until Jesse was able to pay it.

Returning from Austin, Jones found a letter from a member of the little neighborhood church in Robertson County, Tennessee, the one of which most of the Jones family were members. The congregation was putting a new roof on the building. They had the boards but had to employ carpenters to put them on.

They probably expected a gift of five or ten dollars at the most; but Jones figured about what he thought the labor would cost them, and sent a check for the entire amount, 100 dollars.

A week later he received a letter from one of the church deacons, returning the check and stating that the board felt he could not have made enough money properly in so short a time to give so much.*

Jesse now celebrated his propertied dignity by sending off to Chicago for a huge roll-top desk, which was to go down through the years with him, as a sort of connecting link with his business beginnings. It sat in the corner of his office in the last years of his life, back of a finely carved modern one. He would not have parted with the ancient roll-top under any circumstances. Although its only practical use was that of a backrest, it was a sentimental reminder of the past.

Three events, seemingly far removed from the concerns of a young man in a new job in a city more or less strange to him, were to profoundly affect the course of Jones' life and fortune.

The first was a routine report of the census of 1900, which told that Houston, with no visible great civic effort, had passed Dallas in population. The flat city on the bayou now had 44,633 people. It ranked next to San Antonio's 53,321 and well outdistanced Galveston's 37,789. The city of Jones' choice apparently was on the march.

Two other events were deeply tragic but in the strange interrelations of human affairs ultimately beneficial to Jones.

On September 8 of that year, with little warning, a tropical hurricane struck Galveston. The loss of life was never exactly known, but it ranged between 5000 and 8000. That great storm was to determine forever which was to become the major Gulf port city. Before Galveston could build a sea wall to protect it from future attacks from the sea, Houston had clinched supremacy.

Next there came to Houston in the same month as the Galveston

* Fifty-five years later the citizens of Robertson County named a new hospital the Jesse Holman Jones Memorial Hospital in recognition of the county's most noted son. Jones was the largest individual donor. It was one of the few things that ever bore his name. Wherever he could control he refused to allow memorials to himself.

disaster the shocking news from New York that William Marsh Rice had been found dead, with strong evidence that he was murdered.

Rice, who was eighty-four years of age at his death, had gone to Houston in 1838 when the hamlet was only two years old. He began as a clerk in a mercantile house, then was senior partner in the firm of Rice and Nichols, exporters, importers, and wholesale grocers. Later he had large interests in other businesses, including a stagecoach line to Austin and a railroad to Dallas.

At the end of the Civil War, Rice went to New York City, where he was financial and purchasing agent for the Houston and Texas Central Railroad which he had helped to build. At the time of his death he owned many thousands of acres of land in Texas and Louisiana. His estate was estimated to be worth 10,000,000 dollars.

He had long been regarded as an eccentric and, a widower, he had been a recluse during the last years of his life. His only companion was his valet, Charles F. Jones, and his only visitor, his New York lawyer, Albert T. Patrick.

Some years before his death Rice had created the corporate structure of a William M. Rice Institute for the Advancement of Literature, Science, and Art, and to this he had transferred much of his property.

A sensational series of events after the death of Rice ended with the institute receiving practically the entire estate. Rice's affairs had been handled so well by Captain James A. Baker, Rice's principal lawyer and chairman of the board of the institute, that the investments were large enough to permit the construction of the buildings at once.*

Some years later Jones was to acquire the site of the Rice Hotel from the Rice estate. This location was, from the days of the Lone Star Republic, the most important historic site in the city. On it he built what was then the tallest building in Texas.

On January 10, 1901, still another event took place that was to affect the world greatly and might bring greater direct benefit to Houston than to any other city, depending upon how quickly it comprehended its significance and moved to take advantage of it. Ninety miles away,

* After the death of Rice but before it was known, Patrick appeared at a New York bank with a check purportedly signed by Rice. Because of the size of the check and some doubt about the authenticity of the signature, the bank refused to cash it, and in an effort to reach Rice discovered that he was dead. Later the police halted the funeral services and took the body to a morgue for investigation. It was discovered that there was a new will for the benefit of Patrick. Subsequently the valet confessed that he had entered into a plot with Patrick in which the will and other papers were forged and that he had participated in the chloroform murder of Rice. The valet, having given this evidence, was set free, but Patrick was sentenced to death. Eventually he was reprieved and finally pardoned.

on a small rise in the swampy prairie, a few miles north of the Gulf of Mexico, the world's first great oil gusher made its advent with a mighty roar. It was the Lucas discovery at Spindletop, near the town of Beaumont.

Jones, like most people, gave little thought to Spindletop as the harbinger of a liquid-fuel age. In fact, except that petroleum gushing high over the oil derrick was spectacular in contrast to the discovery at Corsicana a few years earlier, he gave little attention to it.

Finally he did join in the crowds pushing their way toward Beaumont. It was winter weather, even if mild, when he arrived. In the lobbies of the hotels he found that the prospectors, whether brown-derbied drummers or big-hatted Texans, were seemingly as much interested in finding a place to sleep as in acquiring the sudden wealth they had come seeking. No rooms were to be had.

Jesse decided on an expedient. Surely in one of the hotels someone had forgotten to lock his door. He went to a top floor and worked down, trying all the doors until he came to one that was unlocked, and walked in. There was no one in it at the time, so he undressed and went to bed. Some time later, when the rightful tenant returned, he found Jesse sleeping soundly, tried to awaken him, but could not; so he too crawled into bed.

When they awoke the next morning, Jesse told him why he had taken over the room. The man thought anyone that ingenious would be a good one to tie to. He proposed that they go into partnership. Jesse suggested that for a week or so the partnership be limited to the joint occupancy of the bed; and that was agreed to.

In his week in Beaumont, trading in oil leases, he made something like 25,000 dollars, but decided to stick to his lumber business. "If a man wants to get rich, he can do it with things on the face of the earth, which can be plainly seen, without speculating on what is hidden underneath," he told his prospector-bedfellow.

His judgment was soon temporarily vindicated; for there were so many gushing oil wells, with much of the flow going to waste, that crude oil was selling as low as three cents a barrel. Except for a short period when he joined in organizing the Humble Oil Company—one day to be the largest in the Southwest—Jones was never again in the oil business.

Jones was still convinced that there was plenty of money to be made in the lumber business, if he could buy enough timber. He knew that the Santa Fe Railroad was financing John Henry Kirby in buying timber; perhaps E. H. Harriman would be interested in a similar arrangement.

So in the summer of 1902 he went to New York to see Judge Robert S. Lovett, who had recently moved from Houston to New York, where he was general counsel for Harriman's Southern Pacific and Union Pacific Railroads.

Jones' mode of traveling had undergone a great change in the time that had elapsed since his memorable trip to the Chicago World's Fair. In New York he stopped at the then-fashionable Empire Hotel. He went to Louis Martin's exclusive Café Martin where Lillian Russell often dined with Diamond Jim Brady; to Rector's, Delmonico's, and Bustanoby's Beaux Arts; and to the theaters.

A cablegram reached Jones in New York from Mrs. Louisa Jones who, with her three children, had inherited the M. T. Jones fortune of a little over 1,000,000 dollars, including the lumber business of which Jesse was manager. She was in Europe with her daughters, Augusta and Jeanette, and would like to see him if it was convenient for him to come over.

It was very convenient for Jesse. Ever since his arrival in New York the newspapers had been filled with news of the preparation for the coronation of King Edward VII, and he wanted to see the ceremony. Ships were crowded with Americans crossing for the event, but Jones managed to get passage.

All the way over most of the voyagers lived in joyful anticipation of celebrating the coronation. When the bus carrying Jesse and the other boat train passengers from railroad station to hotel reached Pall Mall in London, they found a tremendous congestion of persons and vehicles. The excited crowd had been stricken with horror at the announcement in the *Official Gazette* that the popular son of old Queen Victoria was the victim of a sudden illness and that the most eminent surgeons of the realm were assembling at Buckingham Palace to perform an operation to save his life. The coronation was off, at least for a time.

During the remainder of the distance to the hotel the bus passed crowds wandering aimlessly through the gorgeously decorated streets. The long faces of the drivers of omnibuses, brakes, hansom cabs, and other trade vehicles betrayed not only their anxiety for the monarch but the realization that their dreams of a golden stream of money from the celebrators had vanished. To caterers and to speculators in seats along the coronation procession from Buckingham Palace to Westminster Abbey, the sudden turn of events meant bankruptcy.

In the hotel, Jesse found the lobbies filled with Americans and other visitors, shocked by the event that threatened the sovereign's life.

Around Buckingham Palace thousands kept vigil, many kneeling to utter a prayer for the royal patient inside.

Jones went on to Paris for a visit with Mrs. M. T. Jones and her daughters; then, with his cousin Augusta, he set out to see the Continent. They visited Monte Carlo, Naples, Rome, Venice, Geneva, Berlin, Dresden, Munich, Vienna, Amsterdam, The Hague, Brussels, and Antwerp.

Jones' sole attempt toward becoming a linguist in the countries he visited was to learn four or five words in connection with his personal comfort.

My face was very tender, and I wanted to find how to tell the barbers, in their own language to be careful in shaving me [he wrote]. Few men shaved themselves in those days.

In Monte Carlo, I learned how NOT to play roulette. There were many other kinds of games in the casinos, some of which I never heard of. In Naples, the housewives milked their goats in the streets; anybody's goat, it seemed. We were amused to see a milkman lead a cow around from house to house. A woman would come out with a small vessel, take such milk as she desired, and pay the cow's owner.

The Jones cousins saw the art galleries of Dresden, the parks and gay restaurants of Vienna, and attended the opera there.

Riding in an open landau in Rome, Jesse passed King Victor Emmanuel in a similar vehicle. He was greatly surprised and pleased when the young monarch doffed his hat. In a park in The Hague, he saw Queen Wilhelmina of the Netherlands. He bowed, and the queen acknowledged the greeting.

The twenty-eight-year-old Jesse was struck by the youthful appearance of Victor Emmanuel and Wilhelmina, and asked their ages. When Cousin Augusta told him Victor Emmanuel was thirty-three and Wilhelmina twenty-two, Jesse replied, "People seem to get along faster over here than they do in Texas."

In Berlin, Jesse's good luck at running into royalty out for an airing continued. He saw Kaiser Wilhelm, with his withered arm. But, never a man to throw money around needlessly, the thing he remembered most was that he paid twenty-five cents for an Oregon Delicious apple in the German capital city.

On August 9 Jesse was back in London for the delayed coronation. He sat in a good seat to watch Edward, showing hardly a trace of his illness, riding with the stately Alexandra from Buckingham Palace to Westminster Abbey, to be crowned Edward VII, R.I., by the Grace of

God, of the United Kingdom of Great Britain and Ireland and of the British Dominions Beyond the Seas, King, Defender of the Faith, Emperor of India.

The royal procession, the scarlet lines of British uniforms, Indian rajahs, colonial premiers, princes of the royal houses of Europe, the dazzling array of diplomatic uniforms, the horse guards, made a spectacle of such splendor as he had never imagined; and he thrilled at the sight of Joseph Choate, the American Ambassador, wearing a plain black coat in the midst of a blaze of color and glitter of gold lace.

At the Carlton he saw such American figures as Chauncey Depew and Justice Henry Billings Brown, of the United States Supreme Court, and heard General Joseph E. Wheeler tell his fellow Americans that they had witnessed the most brilliant pageant since the coronation of Napoleon Bonaparte a century before.

"The next night," he wrote, "I went to the theater and sat in the highest balcony, and met many Americans there who were doing the same thing I was."

In the autumn of that year when he had seen so much European royalty, Jesse Jones was designated King Nottoc IV, for Houston's Not-Su-Oh carnival. Nottoc was cotton spelled backward. Not-Su-Oh was a reversal of the spelling of Houston. Not-Su-Oh was Houston's first big effort to draw attention to itself. It was a week-long festival that its promoters had hoped would reach the proportions of the Mardi gras in New Orleans. Although it never fulfilled these aspirations it was a successful event in advertising the city as a cotton mart, and it continued for fifteen years.

Begun in 1898, the festivities included a parade down Main Street, with floats of many descriptions depicting scenes of mythology. The week ended with a grand ball, over which Jesse presided the night of November 20. His consort was Clara Robinson, daughter of a leading family, and an outstanding beauty who later became Mrs. James House Bute. Houston newspapers said Jesse made a handsome king.

The first King Nottoc had been A. C. Allen, a descendant of the city's founder, the second had been John Henry Kirby, and the third Dennis Call, all meaningful names in Houston. Jesse's choice as close up as the fourth King Nottoc was a token of the eminence he had quietly attained in Houston in so short a time.

The glitter of the British coronation and the pomp of his own King Nottoc enthronement had been interesting and novel interludes for Jesse. But he had no towering ambition for a gay-blade career. For the next decade he was to be deep in his own business interests and was called upon many times to lend a hand to other people's problems and projects—even was to take a city's destiny in his hands. All of which, he being of a joyous nature, were to be happy adventures for him.

Jones Weathers a Storm

WHILE Jones was in Paris he had broken the news to Mrs. Louisa Jones that he would continue to manage her husband's estate as long as necessary but he intended also to go into business for himself.

The business he had intended to enter was lumber. But as he could not at this juncture detach himself from the M. T. Jones management he was prepared to wait for an auspicious occasion to enter upon a venture of his own. The trip he was finishing had been unexpectedly broadened to include Europe. At the outset he had intended to present the lumber proposal to Judge Lovett and, however that came out, to remain in New York long enough to get as good an insight into the way business was transacted in that great city as was possible for a young man who had virtually no acquaintance there.

Back in New York and with no urgent reason to immediately return to Houston, he decided to carry out the original purpose of his trip. He established himself at the old Waldorf-Astoria Hotel. On the following day he went to the Bank of America for the purpose of cashing a draft. William Bennett, the cashier, seemed surprised that so promising a man had no bank account in the city of New York. Jones calmly said in reply:

"I have no money to deposit. I am a borrower."

"Well," replied Bennett, "we will lend you money."

"How much will you lend me?" Jones asked.

"How much would you like to borrow?"

Jones thought for a few minutes, adding up in his mind how much he owed all together. It amounted to about 20,000 dollars, so he told Bennett he could use that much. Bennett wrote out a note for the amount; Jones signed it and received credit for the money. No security was asked and none given.

When I got out of the bank I pinched myself to see if I was awake [Jones wrote]. I then decided to try another bank. I went to the National City, which was the country's biggest bank at the time, introduced myself to the cashier, and told him what I wanted. He took me to G. S. Whitson, a vice-president. I told Mr. Whitson I would like to borrow some money. He asked how much. I told him $200,000. He called another vice-president. They took me into a private office and talked to me quite a while, and finally said: "When you get home, send us a statement of your affairs, and we will give it consideration."

My reply was: "Give me a piece of paper, and I will give you a statement now."

"We want a statement from your books," Whitson said.

"I have no books," I answered.

"In that case, you had better borrow at home," Mr. Whitson told me. I replied that I did not come for advice, and left.

Before he went to Europe, Jones had visited Judge Lovett, presented his ideas, and asked whether Lovett thought Harriman would finance him in the same manner in which the Santa Fe was backing John Henry Kirby. Lovett asked how much money Jones wanted to borrow from the Harriman railroads.

"As much as they will lend," replied Jones, "it could run up to as much as 25 to 50 million dollars, maybe even 100 million, depending upon how much timber I can buy and how many sawmills."

Jones had been one of Lovett's clients in Houston when he was dealing in thousands, and the older man could hardly comprehend these new and greatly enlarged plans. He offered the opinion that such a proposition need not even be mentioned to Harriman.

However, just as Jones was preparing to leave for Houston, he received a telegram saying that Judge Lovett wanted to see him.

In Lovett's office, the judge informed him that he had told Harriman about Jones' wish to borrow money to buy timber and that Harri-

Above: William Hasque and Anne Holman Jones, parents of Jesse Holman Jones (*Underwood & Underwood*). *Below left:* Jesse at the age of five. *Below right:* Jesse at 17 and his brother John, 19.

Above: Childhood home of Jesse near Springfield, Robertson County, Tennessee. *Below:* Hopewell School, which Jesse, his brother, and three sisters attended.

At left: Jesse Jones, at 18, was an unsuccessful cigar "drummer." Jones said the retail selling end of the tobacco industry suffered no appreciable loss when he left. *Below left:* This picture was taken at the Columbian Exposition in Chicago in 1893. *Below right:* Jesse, not yet 21, became manager of his uncle's lumber yard in Dallas in 1895.

Dallas Texas 1894

Jany 1895 I was promoted to manager
Jesse H Jones

#1- Jesse H Jones - Bookkeeper
#2- C. B. Martin Yard man
#3 a-teamster-

Above: In this lumber yard Jones started his business career—as a bookkeeper. *Below left:* More firmly entrenched as manager, Jesse parted his hair in the middle and dressed snappily. *Below right:* M. T. Jones, who had to admit reluctantly his nephew's business acumen.

At left: In 1898 Jones went to Houston as an executor of his uncle's estate and general manager of a lumber and sawmill empire. *Above:* This is Jesse's first private office. The desk, though no longer used, went with him to more modern offices. *Below:* The M. T. Jones mansion, at 2908 Main Street.

Jones went to London in 1902 for the coronation of King Edward VII. *At left:* Dapper and silk-hatted, he attended an Embassy reception. *Below:* He relaxed in his room at the Carlton.

At right: Jesse (with cane) vacationed at Hot Springs, Arkansas, with his brother John in 1909. *Below:* Jesse spent the summer of 1917 at the summer home of Mrs. M. T. Jones (at right) in New Hampshire. Seated on the ground (at left) is Mary Gibbs Jones, later to become his wife.

In 1902 Jones was selected as King Nottoc of the Not-Su-Oh Festival in Houston. In this year he entered business for himself.

man looked upon it with favor, believing that it would develop a profitable lumber haul for the Southern Pacific. Harriman had authorized him to get negotiations with Jones under way immediately, Lovett said.

If you can work out a satisfactory plan, Mr. Harriman will see that you get as much money as you can use [Lovett said]. He will charge you 4 per cent for the money, and divide the profits fifty-fifty. The Southern Pacific will furnish the funds and, of course, handle and route the lumber. This would be its purpose in making the loan.

Jones thought it over and, the next morning, saw Lovett and asked what the procedure would be in handling the matter. The judge told him to go to Kansas City and work out the details with Stewart R. Knott, of the Harriman railroad management, and submit them to Attorney Jesse Andrews, of the law firm of Baker, Botts, Baker, and Lovett, of Houston, representing the railroad. The money would be available on the approval of Andrews.

Jones went to Kansas City and with Knott he drew up a plan that from a partnership standpoint was very satisfactory to both parties. He then returned to Houston and, on further consideration, advised Judge Lovett that he would not undertake the enterprise. He had reached that conclusion, he told Judge Lovett, because he had never been in partnership with anyone, and had decided it might not be advisable to go partners with a man so much richer and more powerful than he was.

Jones was soon to start his own business, and the beginning would be modest. He had realized a substantial profit on the timber he had bought with the money loaned by Royal A. Ferris,* he had the money made in the trading at Spindletop and some savings. But at the beginning of his own business in 1902 he was at first to deal in thousands instead of the millions that would have been involved in the Harriman deal; and he was to remain as general manager of the M. T. Jones Company.

In launching this undertaking Jones demonstrated the first of his innumerable examples of shrewd judgment of men. A man named R. M. Farrar, who was employed in a lumber yard in Houston at 100 dollars a month and who had gone broke and made assignments to his creditors on two previous adventures in the lumber business, came to

* He never forgot Ferris. In a speech in Dallas in 1928 he was to say that this banker was responsible for his getting a substantial start. Still later, when he began to establish chairs and scholarships in many colleges throughout the United States, one of the first was the Royal A. Ferris Scholarship at Southern Methodist University in Dallas. An enlarged photograph of Ferris always hung in Jones' office.

Jones with a proposition. He suggested that Jones acquire a small lumber yard in Houston worth about 8000 dollars and that he would manage it.

Jones knew that despite the disasters encountered by Farrar in his own enterprises he was a man of great energy and that he was not interested in anything but work. Jones decided to embark on the enterprise with Farrar.

Jones bought the lumber yard suggested by Farrar and incorporated it as the South Texas Lumber Company. The capital stock was 20,000 dollars. Jones put in 15,000 dollars and lent Farrar 3000 dollars to buy stock for himself. Mrs. Farrar took the remaining 2000 dollars with her own money.

Under Farrar's management and Jones' general guidance the firm made 25,000 dollars in its first year.

The South Texas Lumber Company gradually accumulated a number of yards in Texas, Oklahoma, and New Mexico, and also bought out another yard in Houston, which was named the Jesse H. Jones Lumber Company. It was located on the site where Jones was later to erect the sixteen-story Lamar Hotel, on the top of which he built his penthouse home; and the Commercial and Industrial Life Insurance Company's twenty-two-story building, the home of another Jones enterprise.

Operating his own growing business, Jones was now working a thirteen- to fourteen-hour day. Always a man to take his job seriously, he was likely to follow the line of most resistance. "Nothing which is not difficult is very satisfying to do," he wrote. On another occasion he said, "I never spent much time doing things I could get someone else to do. After I really got going, I always had a responsible managing head for every business I owned."

Calm of temperament, Jones displayed no visible sign of fatigue on the days when he did the most prodigious amounts of labor. He usually worked from seven o'clock in the morning to one in the afternoon, had lunch, took a nap, then worked from two to seven. He always considered that he got the most out of the second of these two days in one. Sometimes he worked a few hours in the evening. A bachelor until 1920, he had no home responsibilities. At one time he had two part-time shifts of employees in his office and worked with both.

In the early part of the century he drove around Houston behind Money Bags, a handsome, sentient, sixteen-hands-high bay trotting horse, for which he had great admiration and affection. "We gave him this name because he had so much sense; and we often talked of making him manager of a lumber yard," Jones wrote in whimsical tribute.

So strong-willed was Money Bags that no one but Jones could drive him, and even he had difficulty. That was before the automobile days, and young men took their young lady friends buggy riding. Always, after one of these rides, when Jones had taken the young lady home and started for the livery stable where Money Bags lived, he would have trouble holding him.

On one of these occasions Money Bags was going at about a three-minute gait when suddenly one side of the shaft of the buggy came loose from the axle and fell to the ground, hitting his heels. The horse stopped instantly and stood perfectly still, except that he was trembling with fear.

Ordinarily, so spirited a horse would have run away. Jones spoke to him, got out of the buggy, patted him, then got the hitch rein out of the buggy, tied it to the shaft, which had fallen to the ground, got back into the buggy, and held the shaft up with the hitch rein. He then spoke to Money Bags, and the intelligent horse walked quietly through the city to the livery stable a mile away.

On another occasion, when Jones was returning to the livery stable a child ran across the street immediately in front of the horse. Money Bags, of his own accord, stopped so suddenly that Jones went over the dashboard.

When Money Bags had passed from the earthly scene and automobiles came along, Jones drove one for a while, but barely missed an accident on one or two occasions, after which he delegated automobile driving to others.

Jesse Jones and J. M. Rockwell continued to operate the M. T. Jones Lumber Company for seven years, from the time Jesse was twenty-four until he was thirty-one; and then, under the terms of the will, they wound it up. Under their management the company had been very successful and had increased the estate from about 1,000,000 dollars when M. T. Jones died, to more than 3,000,000 dollars, exclusive of a large tract of land on Buffalo Bayou, which M.T. had left to his son.

This land had cost M. T. Jones very little and was not considered of any great value. But when Buffalo Bayou was deepened and became the Houston Ship Channel, thus making Houston a deep-water port, the land became of greater value than the remainder of the estate. The property was inherited by the great-granddaughter of M. T. Jones, a young matron of Houston.

"M. T. Jones never liked real estate, and I have often wondered why he bought that land," Jesse Jones said, "unless he in fact foresaw the possibility of Buffalo Bayou someday becoming a ship channel, and Houston a world port."

In 1903 Jesse's physician told him that he was subjecting himself to such enormous strains of work as to jeopardize his health, and urged him to take up horseback riding as a relaxation. Jesse doubted the need of it, but complied. The regimen was to be a profitable one. He did his doctor-directed riding in the early morning when, as he said, "the world always looks best." He saw a great deal of vacant property and, since he was in the lumber business, decided it would be a good idea to build some houses for sale.

Jones' building operations began with Edgewood addition, in the section around Hamilton and McGowen Streets in Houston. The houses were in the 3000-to-5000-dollar class, and sold for a small down payment, with monthly installments for the balance, much the same method as the federal government adopted in the 1930's.

The first one he built was for Aunt Nancy, who had raised all the Jones children after their mother died, when the oldest of the five was twelve, along with her own son and daughter. With all of the children now grown and on their own, Jesse brought Aunt Nancy to Houston (and with her a man and his wife, a couple of whom she was very fond, to live with and make a home for her).*

During the first years of the 1900's Jones' activities began to indicate the place he would eventually take in civic affairs. One day a group of prominent citizens called on him for a contribution of 500 dollars for some civic enterprise, when a more appropriate assessment would probably have been twenty-five or fifty dollars. Jones agreed to make the contribution.

Later in the day another young businessman, somewhat older than Jones and substantially better off financially, with offices in the same building (which was the only office building in the city), came to see Jones, complaining about the amount the committee had asked and,

* Jesse frequently went to see Aunt Nancy on his way to work; occasionally, he would slip a twenty-dollar gold piece into her hand as he left. He never knew what she was doing with the gold; but he had heard her preach that "willful waste makes woeful want" so long that he knew she was not squandering it. One day her house burned, and Jesse hurried to the scene of the fire. He found Aunt Nancy at the home of a neighbor across the street; she was crying and very much excited. Finally, when no one was in the room with them, she whispered, "My gold!"

She told Jesse that the gold was in a small tin box behind a picture that was hanging in the dining room. Jesse went across the street and found that the only part of the house that had not burned down was the wall upon which the picture was still hanging. He climbed through the charred ruins and found the tin box with the gold, exactly where Aunt Nancy said she had kept it.

saying that it was much too large for his circumstances. He was also down for 500 dollars, the amount the committee had asked from Jones.

He said to Jones, "They have us in the wrong class, and we have to do something about it."

Jones replied, "Yes, we must. The thing to do is to get into the class they think we're already in."

Jones operated on borrowed capital most of the time. He usually borrowed two dollars when he needed one dollar. If he borrowed 60,000 dollars from a bank, he made the notes payable 10,000 dollars a month for six months. When the first note matured he would extend it six months. In this way he always had six months to liquidate any particular line if the bank wanted it paid. He figured that, since he would be carrying balances of approximately half the amount of his borrowings (which was his practice), his account would be so profitable that the bank would not be likely to ask him to pay. He wrote:

> I was borrowing from two or three banks in Houston, as well as one each in Dallas, New York, and Chicago. I never had any trouble getting money from banks. In a few cases where one bank would not lend what I wanted I found another that was glad to. To protect my credit, I carried a substantial amount of life insurance. Generally, when I increased my bank obligations, I increased my life insurance; and the banks knew it.

The real test of Jones' financial stability came in the panic year of 1907. Knowing that he was operating heavily on credit, and had been for several years, many people had watched his activities with apprehension. It was freely predicted that, if a period of extreme money stringency hit the country, he would not be able to weather the storm.

There was no doubt in Jones' own mind that in any rough going, the system of long maturities he had worked out would prove helpful; and he actually bounced higher and remained higher while others were falling in the autumn of 1907. He credited this to what seemed to him the premonition of stormy economic weather ahead, and to his long maturities.

> Suddenly, one day in early June, 1907, while I was lunching alone, it came to me that there was going to be a financial panic [he wrote]. Why I had that hunch, I never had the slightest idea; but I did, very definitely.
>
> That afternoon, I called to my office R. M. Farrar, vice-president of our company, N. E. Meador, general manager, and Harry Hurt, auditor, and told them we were in trouble, that there was going to be a panic. I likened our situation to that of being in a small boat in the middle of the ocean, with a storm approaching, and told them we should pull for the shore as hard as ever we could; that we must crowd collection at our lumber yards; that we must push sales for cash; and that we must not buy any lumber which we could not get on eight-to-twelve-month credit.

Jones' principal Houston borrowings were from the T. W. House bank. Another Houston banker who had come to have the greatest faith in Jones' farsightedness was A. P. Root, president of the First National Bank, who had once refused Jesse credit, telling him, "You have gone crazy buying real estate. You would buy the Courthouse if you could get it for a dollar down." But Root by February, 1907, had seen every one of the Jones real estate ventures work out so well that he was willing to lend Jesse any amount he wished.

Jones had taken no vacation for five years but had committed himself to take one at Mrs. M. T. Jones' New Hampshire summer home before he had the premonition of a financial panic. Although he was comfortable as far as his bank debts in Houston were concerned and had safeguarded the banks against loss from his loans, he decided to attempt other precautionary lines of credit that summer. He stopped in Chicago and arranged one for 75,000 dollars.

In New York he visited the Hanover Bank and met William Woodward, a young Harvard-educated lawyer of about his own age. Woodward had served a year under Joseph H. Choate in the American Embassy in London and had just been brought back into the bank as executive vice-president by his uncle, James T. Woodward, its president.

Jones had never before met William Woodward, and Woodward had never heard of Jones; but one of the banks in Houston with which Jones was associated had an account with the Hanover. Jones introduced himself to Mr. Woodward, showed him a statement of his principal lumber company, and said he would like to borrow some money. Woodward studied the statement a few minutes and asked Jones how much he wanted. "As much as you will lend me," Jones replied.

Woodward pushed a button and, when a junior officer came to him, said, "Mr. Jones wants some money. Lend him 200,000 dollars."

Although Jones never actually needed the money, it was a factor in bracing him for whatever might happen.*

* Strangely the paths of Woodward and Jones did not cross again for thirty-nine years. Entering the president's room at Belmont Park between races one day in 1946, the only man Jones found in the room was Woodward. By that time Jones was back in private life, after a public career that saw him the grandee of all moneylenders; and Woodward was paying less attention to banking and more to the breeding and ownership of thoroughbred race horses, having won the Kentucky Derby, the Preakness, and Belmont Stakes with such outstanding horses as Gallant Fox, Omaha, and Johnstown.

Woodward was sipping a highball. Jones went over to him, shook hands, and sat down. Woodward asked, "What will it be, Scotch or Bourbon?" then said, "Do you remember that 200,000 dollars I loaned you in 1907?"

Jones replied that he had never forgotten it; that he had no more vivid recollection of anything in his life and no greater appreciation; that while, as it turned out, he did not need the money, it was good to have it.

Having taken care of his personal affairs that summer of 1907, Jones had one other matter of business that needed attention before he went on to New Hampshire. He telephoned to T. C. Dunn, managing vice-president of the Union Bank and Trust Company in Houston, of which Jones was a director and large stockholder, and asked him if the bank was likely to need any money to handle the cotton crop. Dunn said he would like to arrange for 200,000 dollars each at the Citizens Central National Bank and National Park Bank.

I went downtown in New York and stopped first in the Citizens Central [Jones related] and spoke to the president, Edwin S. Schenck, telling him that our bank (the Union) would probably need some money to handle the cotton crop, and would like to know if it could have a loan of $200,000. He said it could, at any time.

I then went to the National Park Bank and spoke to Richard Delafield, the president. He also said the Union could have $200,000 whenever it needed it.

I advised Mr. Dunn in Houston about the arrangement with these two banks, then left for New Hampshire.

When I returned to New York on October 17, there were evidences of panic. I first went to the Citizens Central National and told Schenck the Union National would like to have the $200,000 which had been arranged for, since cotton had begun to move. He denied having made the commitment. He was probably frightened by the gathering financial storm.

I reminded him that I had telegraphed to Mr. Dunn from his office the day the arrangement was made, and gave the telegram to his secretary, which he could confirm by speaking to her. He insisted that he had not made any such commitment. At this I told him I did not know just what the custom was in New York in such circumstances, but that, if we were in Texas, I would know what to do.

I went on to the other bank, the National Park, and the money was available as promised.

Then I went to the Fourth National Bank, introduced myself to the president, James Graham Cannon, and told him my story about Schenck. He said: "Your bank can have all the money it wants." I was so pleased with his attitude that I had the Union National not only transfer our account from the Citizens Central to it, but made the Fourth National our principal New York correspondent.

That night Jones went to the theater. When he returned to the St. Regis Hotel, the clerk gave him a handful of telegrams. The first one he opened informed him that the T. W. House bank in Houston had failed. The House bank was a private one, and one of the oldest and largest in the city.

As far as Jones was concerned, *that* was real panic; for he owed the T. W. House bank a large amount of money. What might be in the other telegrams Jesse was not to know until he got to his room; but they were all about the House bank failure and its possible effect on the whole situation in Houston.

> The House failure was about the worst thing which could happen to me; or so I thought [he wrote]. The next morning, I went downtown and called on the two banks where the T. W. House bank had its accounts, the Chemical National Bank and the Bank of America. William H. Porter was president of the Chemical Bank.
>
> I introduced myself to Mr. Porter, told him who I was and that, if he cared for me to look over their account with the T. W. House bank, including their collateral, I would be glad to give him such information as I could. He appreciated the offer; and, after studying the collateral, it appeared to me that he would suffer no loss. I told him so. It turned out that way; and Mr. Porter and I became good friends. He was later a partner in J. P. Morgan and Company.

Jones then went to see William H. Perkins, president of the Bank of America, and made the same suggestion. Jones looked over their files on the House bank and told Mr. Perkins he would probably have a small loss. They did.

In the course of his examination of the Bank of America files Jones found his own notes made out to the House Bank to the amount of 500,000 dollars. He already had a line of credit with the Bank of America so that caused him no great concern. But he knew the House Bank failure would have serious repercussions in Houston, so he prepared to leave for home.

On Monday night was to be the American opening of the Viennese opera, *The Merry Widow* and it offered the promise of a diversion from the gloomy events of the moment. Jones sat in the audience at the New Amsterdam Theater that notable first night, the biggest and gayest New York had seen since the turn of the century.

Beautiful Ethel Jackson sang the lead role of Sonia, Donald Brian, light of voice and lighter of foot, sang and danced the role of Prince Danilo. An audience that sat enthralled by the insinuating waltz themes, rattling march tunes, sentimental lyrics, and the great scene of the Café Maxim filed into Forty-second Street, whistling the tunes of the operetta and sounding the praises of Franz Lehar, the composer.

But the next morning, October 22, there was more bad news. The Knickerbocker Trust Company failed. This was the city's "society bank," and many of those who had gaily attended the debut of the tuneful Widow show a few blocks away the previous night were in the despairing lines in front of the tellers' windows that Tuesday morning. By noon most of the bank's cash had been paid out and the windows slammed shut.

The Knickerbocker had been involved in the efforts of F. Augustus Heinze to corner the copper market; and, when copper dropped from twenty-six cents to twelve cents a pound in six months, the fate of the bank was sealed. On the Stock Exchange, on that Terrible Tuesday, prices skidded to a new low. There was a run on the Trust Company of America in New York. Banks closed elsewhere in the nation. At Pittsburgh, Westinghouse Electric failed; the Southern Steel Company at Birmingham shut down. Business houses all over the country toppled. Panic was upon the land.

Jones left gloomy New York and in Houston found the same squally financial weather. But nowhere did he encounter a more doleful spot than in his own business. The three top men in his business (R. M. Farrar, N. E. Meador, and Harry A. Hurt) whom in June he had told to pull for the shore as rapidly as possible, asked for a meeting with him. Farrar, acting as spokesman said, "We are broke and might as well admit it."

Jones took no such melancholy view and asked cheerfully, "Have you told the newspapers about it?"

His frightened associates were in no mood for levity. Jones sought by every means to raise the drooping morale of the three. Conditions would be tough for some time, he agreed; but they would come out of it. The three men, in unison, insisted that they were in an inextricable situation.

When he could not convince his associates that they could survive, he asked each of them what they would take for their stock in the company, and he immediately bought it, on the condition that they continue in their jobs, with some increase in their salaries.

"Now, gentlemen, you are working for me," he told them, "and I do not want to see you sitting around bemoaning your fate and worrying about the sheriff."

Two days later the three men asked for another conference with Jones. They apologized to him and wanted their stock back. He agreed. All of his companies survived the panic in good shape; and also he was able to make some desirable purchases.

Jones had hardly gotten his frightened lumber associates back on the track when he had a visit from a banker associate. Jones, by invitation, had become interested in banking in 1905. In that year the Texas state banking laws came into operation, and the Union Bank and Trust Company was organized, with Charter Number 1. Jones was a substantial stockholder and a member of its board of directors.

In 1906 the Lumberman's National (later to be the Second National, and the Bank of the Southwest) was organized by S. F. Carter, a former associate of M. T. Jones in the lumber business. Carter had insisted on Jesse's taking some stock and accepting a vice-presidency in the Lumberman's. None of Jesse's borrowing had been from the two banks of which he was a director.

All during the early autumn of 1907, while Jones had been in New Hampshire, there had been speculation concerning his financial solidity; and, as soon as Carter heard of his return, he decided upon a personal visit. Carefully closing the door behind him, he said to Jesse, "They are talking about you."

"What are they saying?" Jones asked.

"They say you owe a million dollars."

Jesse laughed.

Carter did not see any cause for gaiety and said as much.

But Jesse replied, "Mr. Carter, I owe 3,000,000 dollars."

This astonished Carter, who was thinking about his bank and not about Jesse's welfare. Seeing that there was nothing he could do about it, the banker left without further comment.

Jones' explanation of this debt, which he had not felt called on to give Carter, was: "I had been picking up good investments where I could find them. This was the reason I owed this much."

Only one bank called a loan on the Jones companies in 1907; and he was afterward to learn that the panic conditions were not the cause for this.

> One of my companies owed this bank $75,000, maturing $15,000 a month [Jones wrote]. My general manager wrote to me in New England that summer that this bank wanted us to pay the $15,000 maturing in August. The same thing happened with respect to the note due in September. I, of course, wrote him to pay. By the time the October note came due, I was back in Houston, and the banker called me into his office. (I was officing in his building.) He reminded me that we had a note maturing the following day, and asked what we wanted to do about it. I told him we expected to pay it.
>
> He probably felt a little mean about having called our notes, and suggested that we renew it, which we were glad to do. Anyway, there were signs that the general situation was easing up, and our account was profitable to his bank. I later learned that he had called our line because this particular company of mine had borrowed $25,000 from another bank without telling him about. That taught me the importance of always keeping your banker informed about your business.

Since he had opened his Edgewood addition a few years before and had been selling the small houses built there, on the installment plan, he had a safe crammed with notes against the homes he had sold. They ran in amounts from 2000 to 5000 dollars, payable monthly from twenty-five to fifty dollars, over a period of years. He wrote:

> During the panic in the fall of 1907, when many people had lost confidence in banks, I was able to sell all of these real-estate mortgages. In most cases, those who bought the notes were older people, and they usually paid for them in currency which they had previously withdrawn from the banks, because of fear.
>
> Two lawyers, whose clientele included many older people, knew of my building operations and selling homes on the installment plan; and they would come to see me or call me to know if I had a mortgage against a home for, say, $3,000, maybe a little more, maybe a little less. I would reply that I had, and would give the street number of the house on which I held a mortgage, for whatever the amount might be.
>
> Usually, within a day's time, the lawyer would call me and say: "We will buy that book of notes." The notes were in monthly installments, and I had them printed in book form so that, when a note was paid, we would simply tear it out and give it to the maker. Usually, it requires lawyers a week or two to pass on a real-estate title; but, in those instances, it would require only about a day, because their clients were anxious to invest their money. This convinced me that, in the final analysis, people have confidence in real estate as a safe investment.

A year later Jones pretty well knew what his future would be. He was to be in building and banking in Houston the rest of his life, with most of his investments in real estate and buildings that he was to construct. Gradually he not only sold his sawmill interests but also his sixty-five lumber yards, all except one in Houston.

"I kept this one because I wanted Joe Didiot and some other old employees to have jobs as long as they lived," he explained. "They might not have kept their jobs if I had sold the yard."

When Jesse Jones died forty-eight years later, Joe Didiot still had that job.

7

The Lure of Building

JESSE JONES came out of the panic of 1907 the biggest young man in Houston. He had shown a financial dexterity that greatly surprised men who believed he was on a very slippery slope and would be unable to withstand any sort of a general business setback.

Having not only weathered the storm himself but having helped some other persons and business institutions through it and having come out of it better off than he went into it, he was now ready to move onto a larger stage, and his activities were to be quickly accelerated.

Jones was approaching thirty-five. Of the more than nine years he had been in Houston, seven had been in the management of the M. T. Jones interests, which had been a noteworthy achievement. His exclusive attention to his own business affairs had been a matter of less than three years.

His own lumber and building activities had been a financial success; and, while he would still be a borrower when that was profitable to him, he was also in a position to be a lender.

His reputation for sure-footedness was building up. Men who had been skeptical of his judgment now conceded that he was a practical man, who was never decoyed away from realities. He had become more active in civic affairs, worked well with other people, but evinced a deep determination to keep himself in the background. To men who knew him well and worked with him, he was friendly and congenial but seldom chummy.

If Jones had advanced in the years in the flat city on the bayou, Houston had loitered. Its skyline remained the same; it still had a sort of serene, mellow, complacent look and seemed entirely undisturbed by its slow growth. It still had its bumpy streets and poky transportation; it still retained the grace and lassitude of the old South, but it had not retained its place in Texas' population standing. Dallas had again passed it.

When Jones went to Houston, some of its citizens could remember the days when Texas was a Republic and Houston its capital. In the romantic old homes on Main Street, people talked genealogy. To be Son (or Daughter) of the Texas Republic was something. For this Jesse could not qualify, but as a native Tennessean he could have some pride in the fact that such nationalist expansionists as Sam Houston and Davy Crockett had a part in making that republic.

The failure of the T. W. House bank had eliminated one of the last substantial fortunes, dating back to the days of the Republic, and House, the city's first citizen up to now, was thereafter to take a very minor role in its affairs. He had a valuable home that, owing to the Texas homestead laws, could not be taken away from him. He had also some connection with the gas company, from which he got a little income.*

Before most of Houston was aware of Jones, he had firmly fixed in his mind that Houston's prospects were better than any other Southern city and by 1908 he was prepared to help it reach that destiny.

In 1906 W. B. Chew, president of the Commercial National Bank, in association with Dan Ripley, a steamship man; John M. Dorrance, a cotton factor; and Hyman Levy, of Levy Brothers, merchants, bought the land on which were located two old residences, the homes of Augustus C. and John K. Allen, the brothers who laid out the town of Houston in 1836. The intention of Chew and his associates was to build a much-needed hotel for Houston.

Soon thereafter Mr. Chew called Jones into his office and proposed that he take a one-fifth interest in the property at the same price they had paid for it, and assume the lead in building a hotel. Chew told Jones that he thought he and his associates were too old and probably too conservative to build the kind of hotel which the city needed.

* In 1912, when Woodrow Wilson was elected President, the onetime private banker became postmaster of Houston, the appointment having been obtained by his brother, Edward M. House, through his close association with President Wilson. Jones and T. W. House always remained warm friends.

Jones said that he would think it over. But as he did so, his old instinct to avoid partnerships asserted itself. On the other hand he knew of Houston's need for a hotel and the site was probably the best available. And so he told Chew that, while he felt honored to be invited by a group of men all successful and his seniors, he could not join them if a cash investment was required. However, if they were agreeable, he would trade them a block of residence property in a development he was promoting, and every time he built and sold a house would pay them an installment of his share in the deal.

A few days later Chew notified Jones that he and his associates would accept the proposal. Shortly afterward Jones succeeded in acquiring the remaining four fifths of their property on the same conditions. This gave him a very valuable downtown location with no mortgage against it—and—what was important to him, no partners.

While Jones was comfortably, profitably, and, he felt, permanently in the building business his interest in the construction of residences had begun to wane. Most of his adult life he had lived downtown in hotels. There had been an exception. After he closed the M. T. Jones estate he continued to look after the interests of Mrs. M. T. Jones and her children and had closed his bachelor headquarters and gone to live with the M. T. Jones family at 2908 Main Street. Jesse had a lasting affection for this delightful home and many happy memories clustered about his days there, but the pull of downtown living had always remained strong. Yet he was reluctant to build the needed hotel on the fine site he owned. He knew nothing about the hotel business and had no desire to learn.

But he went ahead and prepared plans for a 500-room hotel. He took them to Buffalo and showed them to E. M. Statler, the hotel wizard. It was the kind of hotel Jones thought Houston should have, and he tried to persuade Statler to build and operate it. Statler commended Jones upon the impressive plans but told him Houston would not support such a large hotel. Jones felt obligated to make good the original purposes of Chew and his associates. He returned to Houston and built the ten-story, 200-room Bristol on a less valuable site than the Allen tract.

Even the Bristol was an audacious undertaking in a city that was still feeling the effects of the depression which followed the 1907 panic. Its décor was something new to South Texas. It had a roof garden—the first in Texas—a center of merriment and good times. A famous chef prepared excellent food. During the day diners enjoyed a fine view of the surrounding country, and at night there was the accompaniment of soft music under the starlight.

The Bristol was completely fireproof. As a departure from standard Houston custom, there were no rocking chairs in the lobby. The fine marble used in the staircase was the talk of the town. Everything in the hotel was the best that money could buy.

The Bristol was the tallest building in town; but Jones before the end of the year 1908 was to begin two more ten-story buildings in a town which, up to then, the six-story Binz Building had been the highest. One of them signalized the beginning of the movement of petroleum companies to Houston. The Texas Company wanted to bring its general offices from Beaumont. Jones erected a building for them, and they moved in.

Marcellus E. Foster, principal owner of the struggling Houston *Chronicle*, with a circulation of only 23,061, decided he wanted a fine new building across the street from the Houston *Post*, from which he had resigned as managing editor at a small weekly wage to embark on the new journalistic venture. The first issue of the *Chronicle* had gone on the streets on the afternoon of Monday, October 14, 1901, at two cents a copy.

Foster approached Jones to provide a new building for him, and offered half-interest in the newspaper as a down payment, with twenty years to pay the remainder. Jones agreed, and the resulting Chronicle Building was one of the finest in the South.

At the end of 1908, when Jones had given the imbedded conservatism of the town a shock by his building splurge, Houston had three ten-story buildings, all by Jones; and his skyline had just begun. The construction of these buildings lifted Houston out of the dumps. Somehow the appearance of these handsome structures built by a young man whose daring was a reproach to their fearfulness awakened a pride and determination in people that had all but died during the panic. In 1908 panic was forgotten, and the city was on its way. It never stopped growing, becoming the largest city in the South.

If Jones had been able to have his way, it would have remained a city with a ten-story skyline. On his first trip to Europe he had been impressed by the gracious harmony of the buildings in the five-story skyline of Paris. That height might not be commercially feasible in Houston, but ten stories, he thought, was.

When Jones heard that the Gulf Oil Company, owned by the Mellons of Pittsburgh, planned to move its general offices from Beaumont to

Dallas, he set out to bring the company to Houston instead; and, with the cooperation of Judge F. C. Proctor, its general counsel, he was successful. Still adhering to his ten-story ideal, he built an office structure for them. Added to the Texas Company, Jones had now located two major oil companies in Houston.

Jones was now being saddled with more and more civic duties. It had become the custom to make him chairman of all sorts of committees. Once he complained, "You are working me harder than the town pump," and he got the reply, "Well, this is just another of the projects your Houston *Chronicle* has been advocating."

Actually, although Jones owned half-interest in the *Chronicle*, he had as yet paid little attention either to its management or its policies.

John T. Scott, the Houston banker, gave this explanation of why Jones was so often in the forefront of civic movements:

> Jesse was always a jump or two ahead of anybody else in Houston and if he didn't take the lead we forced it upon him. People reposed so much trust in his judgment that he could go into a meeting with men pulling in a dozen different directions and it would end up in his having them all pulling the same way.

In 1909 the principal Methodist Church in Houston was the Shearn Church, located downtown at Milam Street and Texas Avenue. Bishop Seth Ward wanted a new church in the south end of the city, to take the place of the one that was being crowded by business. He asked Jones to head a building and finance committee to make plans for it, employ the architects and contractors, and raise and borrow the necessary money.

Jones demurred on the ground that he was a Baptist. Bishop Ward took the position that this would make no difference. Jones, feeling that there was no difference in the purposes of the two denominations, accepted the responsibility and joined the Methodist Church. He employed the architects and contractors, supervised the construction of the church, raised most of the money to build it, and borrowed the rest. The new church was named St. Paul's.

When it was entirely completed, Jones went to the pastor and told him he thought he should withdraw and go back to the church of his father's faith, the Baptist. The pastor, Reverend George Sexton, replied, "You cannot withdraw until the church is paid for."

This required another twenty years. By that time there was a new bishop in charge named Sam R. Hay. He wanted St. Paul's moved still farther from the business section. The Methodists then sold their church to the Baptists, and Jones joined the building committee of the beautiful new St. Paul's Church, which did not get out of debt until 1952.

By this time there was still another Methodist bishop in Houston, Bishop A. Frank Smith, very prominent in church affairs, and a close personal friend of Jones. Jones discussed going back to the Baptist Church with Bishop Smith, who agreed but doubted if Jones would be any happier. So Jones remained a member of the Methodist Church.

In 1910 Jones suggested to Mayor Baldwin Rice and the Houston City Council that the city build an auditorium large enough to accommodate any gathering that might reasonably be expected to come to Houston. Rice, who owed his election chiefly to the support Jones and the Houston *Chronicle* had given him, enthusiastically pushed the proposal through. Then, at the request of the mayor and City Council, Jones employed architects and supervised the building of the auditorium, with a seating capacity of 4500.

In 1912 Jones was to see the end of his dream of a Houston skyline limited to ten stories. His old associate, S. F. Carter, built a sixteen-story structure. And so Jones reluctantly began preparations to build a building higher than the Carter one.

First he leased the old Rice Hotel from the William Marsh Rice estate for ninety-nine years with an option to extend it for an additional ninety-nine. Then he demolished the ancient five-story building and began the construction of an eighteen-story, 500-room modern hotel.

The Rice occupied ground that had been the location of the capitol of Texas when it was a republic. There Sam Houston, first President of Texas, received the diplomatic representatives of European nations, as well as envoys of Presidents Andrew Jackson and Martin Van Buren, from Washington. There also came to the capitol in the live-oak wilderness the naturalist Audubon, searching for rare birds, but who wrote instead of the plumage of Sam Houston, "in scarlet-velvet coat and trousers trimmed with broad, gold lace; around his neck a cravat somewhat in the style of '76, boots with red tops and silver spurs. . . . I drank a grog with him, wishing success to the new republic."

Jones himself drew the plans for the hotel; and, to be sure that the arrangements generally were what he wanted, he shipped a few carloads of lumber to a vacant plot and erected the ground floor plan to scale, and also a room plan to scale, as well as the second floor, where the ballroom and entertainment rooms were to be located.

At the entrance of the hotel Jones placed a tablet: *Site of the Capitol of the Republic of Texas, 1837-38. Commemorating days when, after her glorious struggle, Texas stood an independent nation.*

Jones took a suite on the top floor of the hotel. In a duplicate suite on the floor below he established his Aunt Nancy, with a companion to live with her; and, as long as she lived, each morning when he was in Houston, Jones stopped by to see her.

The Rice was opened with a dinner at which Governor Oscar B. Colquitt of Texas, Mayor Ben Campbell, and Houston's men of affairs, heaped praises on the hotel's owner; but Jones soon found that E. M. Statler was right: the Rice lost money for its first five years. That did not discourage him. He was building Houston, and it must have a good hotel. Afterward, when it began to pay, he added 500 more rooms, making it the largest in the South.

The hotel that at first he was reluctant to build soon became an object of Jones' unabashed pride. It was to be for more than forty years the place of Houston's biggest social and civic functions, of cotillions and debutante parties—it was an institution.

Above the ground where the capitol of the Lone Star Republic stood was about as near a capitol as the fast-rising Petroleum Republic was to know. From the first day it sheltered and was the home of the oilmen. In the rooms of the Rice were dreamed the dreams that came true in fabulous fortunes; the geology which led to great oil-field discoveries was studied; the plans of great petroleum industries were hatched.

Stories abound of the petroleum deals made within the four walls of the Rice. Sometimes the transfers were by word of mouth, and the principals did not get around to drawing the papers for months. In the elapsed time properties might undergo great increases or losses in value; but the deals stuck because words were bonds.

Although the Rice catered to persons of varied interests, Jones took pains to see that it never lost its petroleum atmosphere. In time its eighteenth floor was entirely occupied by the Petroleum Club, one of the most luxurious in the nation.

The Rice was continually getting redecorated and refurnished and modernized. When air-conditioning and escalators came along, it got them; and a television set went into every room.

In 1912, while he was building the Rice, Jones made his first contribution to the Fort Worth skyline, with the nineteen-story Fair Building and Department Store, the eighteen-story Worth Hotel, the Worth Theatre, and the twenty-story Medical Arts Building.

Insofar as Houston was concerned, Jones' interest was now centered around Main Street. That street begins on the city's north side and with a north prefix and takes a curving, southeasterly course until, with one jog and a couple of sharp turns, it reaches Buffalo Bayou. When it is carried by a viaduct across the bayou, it reverses, moves sharply southwestward and passes through the campus of Rice Institute; then, a few miles beyond, at the city limits, it plunges into a state highway to the Rio Grande Valley.

When Jones first saw Houston, its business section extended over a half-mile stretch from the bayou to Texas Avenue, and the Jones-built Rice Hotel was to mark the boundary and the bridge between the gingerbread Houston of the past and the new Houston. Other Jones buildings carried business farther south and away from the bayou.

The city's contour lines and physical conditions decreed that, businesswise, it would be a Main Street town, with the two streets parallel to Main on each side taking a modest part in whatever commercial business was to come. Jones' early firm belief was that even if it attained a population of some two or three million, Houston could go in only one direction—south. He had acquired much property in this line of growth, practically all of which was bought on long-term credit, usually with a separate corporation for each purchase and a small down payment. If the city showed any reluctance to continue in that direction, Jones was prepared to nudge it.

Some of the property he bought had little immediate value, but would have the greatest value if Houston became the city he thought it would. Jones envisioned Main Street not merely as the principal thoroughfare of the town; nor did he put any such limitations on it as the Main Street of Texas. He pictured it as the Main Street of the South and Southwest, the biggest and finest of all Main Streets.

From the beginning Jones drew or outlined the plans of his buildings, because: "I think I can plan them better for practicability and revenue than the architects." When a structure became uneconomic or fell below the standards of its location, it crumpled under the sledges of wreckers, as did the archaic old Bristol Hotel, first of the three ten-story ones he built. The two others were useful as ever when middle-aged. The Chronicle Building, still beautiful with its white glazed brick exterior, was thoroughly modernized. The Goggan Building, the first home of the Texas Company and in later years called the Bankers' Mortgage Building, was likewise modernized and in 1956 was still the home of the Bankers' Mortgage Company and Jones' own private offices.

There was never to be a Jones Building. He had a firm conviction against naming a building for himself. But he took a keen interest in christening, and often in rechristening, his structures.

The contour of the buildings changed often, but their names were likely to change oftener. Sometimes they were named for their major tenant. If the tenant needed a larger building Jones would erect it, transfer the name, and rename the old building. Sometimes the names were topical and were relabeled as time or changing circumstances outdated their appellations.

He named the Kirby Building after John Henry Kirby, because the Kirby Lumber Company occupied a large part of it; the Commerce Building because the Chamber of Commerce was a tenant. But he wrote, "Commerce is such a good name that I would have used it sometime, anyway."

The Milam Building honored the memory of Ben Milam, a patriot of the Texas revolution, who died storming the Mexican garrison in San Antonio; and the Rusk Building was named for General Thomas J. Rusk, second only to Houston as a liberator of Texas from Mexico and Houston's colleague as first United States Senator from Texas. The Mason Building commemorated an old resident who formerly owned the ground. The Electric Building was so named because it housed that utility.

It was not until 1923 that Jones ever publicly discussed his abiding passion for building and the pride in what he had accomplished for his city up to that time. This was at a dinner attended by bankers, merchants, industrialists, lawyers, physicians, clergymen, educators, and labor leaders who turned out to honor him as Houston's skyline frontiersman. By this period many of his early dreams for Houston had become realities, and in the speech he made other prophecies that were fulfilled much earlier than he expected.

> I do not feel that any unusual credit is due me because of any work I have done [he said]. I have not built in Houston without hope of financial reward. I may say, however, that the rent check is not the only compensation; indeed, it is the least that I get out of it. Money loaned and interest compounded would bring a better financial return than investments in buildings, and without the vexations and hazards. But I find no fun in lending money, and there is a great deal of fun and satisfaction in planning and building. It is when I am thus engaged that I am happiest.
>
> I have no hobbies or illusions about buildings. They must be safe for those who occupy them, and practical from the standpoint of revenue.
>
> My early experience in building was, in part, the result of the foresight of our friend, Mr. Foster. He had ambitions for his paper, and persuaded me to assist him in erecting the Chronicle Building. His good salesmanship in that instance helped me discover Houston. Once started, I continued it because I loved it. Of course, I could not have continued if Houston had not supported my building ventures.

We have seen Houston grow and develop for the past dozen years; but I wonder if we can visualize the city which is to be here a generation hence. I doubt it.

To get a picture of the Houston of the future, we should have to get a picture of the whole growing empire of the South and the Southwest.

Chicago, the miracle in growth of modern cities, has not become what it is because of any unusual natural advantages, but because it was in the lines of travel and progress by land and water. The natural growth and agriculture made necessary a midwestern clearing house; and Chicago has grown because of the growth of that vast empire of the Middle West and Northwest. The situation here is very similar.

There is now a decided movement of business and population southward. Twenty years ago, the South and Southwest were not commercially important; it was looked upon by people of the North chiefly as a land of old romance. Now it is a land of immense commercial potentialities. Capital has begun to flow in and population has begun to flow in, both seeking new opportunities. Our ship channel and the great transcontinental railway systems, meeting deep water here, make Houston the inevitable gateway through which the products of this growing southern and western empire can best reach the markets of the world.

We pride ourselves that, by the expenditure of a few million dollars of public funds, we have provided navigable waters up to our city for ocean-going vessels. We have shown the world that we have a safe and economical port. Well done thus far; but, in doing this we have only laid the foundations on which private enterprise will build, by the expenditure not of millions but of hundreds of millions.

Private industry and the common carriers, by land and water, will invest sums here compared with which our own public investment will appear infinitesimal and, before the children of today have become the representative men of tomorrow, every foot of water frontage from Main Street to the Gulf of Mexico will be in use, not because of the efforts of any man or any set of men, but because of the natural movement, growth, and progress of civilization.

I am glad to be able to do something toward building one of the great cities of America.

Each of his buildings had to be an economic unit. It was common for Jones to build, for instance, an eight-story building with foundation and framing to carry an additional ten or fifteen stories, and later add to them.

When the opportune time came to build on the unimproved piece of property he had acquired in the direction he had thought Houston would build, he did so and the new Houston took form. By the mid-twenties Jones had approximately thirty commercial structures in Houston, all of which he had built himself. There was the one to house his newspaper. There were hotels, theaters, department stores, and other mercantile establishments, banks, radio stations, a bus terminal, utilities, warehouses, a laundry, public garages; and his buildings supplied the bulk of the office space in Houston. Two of his theatres seated more than 2500 each.

Beginning with 1908, Jones built an average of one substantial building a year up to 1956 and in that year had enough projected to carry that average past 1958, the golden anniversary of his entrance into that field. His operations in that period had extended from Houston and Fort Worth to New York City.

Twice his building operations were halted, first by a world war and again by a depression and a world war. While his activities in his first foray into this field from 1908 to 1917 were to be dwarfed by those that followed, these earlier ones in the town of less than 100,000 population were the daring ones.

8

Banks, the Bayou, and the Canal

ALTHOUGH Jones was to have control of some one of the Houston banks for a period of approximately fifty years, he was at the outset firmly set against getting himself deeply involved in the banking business. His first ventures into this field he regarded as transient ones and in some cases they originated as rescue operations.

He realized it was not good to permit a Houston bank to fail, and he was quick to offer such financial aid as he could. There was another factor at the beginning of his bank stock purchases that played an important part in his making them. Houston banks were not so strong as those in New Orleans and Dallas; and to Jones, with his rapt devotion to his city, this was intolerable. Dallas was Houston's principal Texas business rival and Jones was already looking forward to the employment of a worse-than-useless bayou as the means of putting Houston in New Orleans' class as a port.

In 1905 when the Union Bank and Trust Company was organized Jones became a substantial stockholder. Two years later he found bank trouble only a few steps away. The Planters and Mechanics Bank, located next door, got into difficulties and was taken over by the Union Bank.

On the last Saturday before the Union absorbed the Planters and Mechanics, Jones sat with the president of the P. and M. prepared to provide the necessary cash from the Union to meet withdrawals. But no such help was necessary; the ailing bank was taken over by the Union after banking hours that day.

The short but tornado-like 1907 panic had seriously shaken the nation's financial structure. Houston as an adolescent city felt the shock acutely.

In 1908, the year he built his first skyscrapers, the thirty-four-year-old Jones personally came to the rescue of two other newly organized banks: one, the Central Bank and Trust Company; and the other the National City Bank.

In the case of the Central Bank and Trust Company, the deposits did not amount to a great deal, and Jones provided the cash to pay them off, and got his money back through the liquidation of its assets.

The other, the National City Bank, had been organized the previous year, with J. M. West, a former prominent lumberman, as its president. West, who had been operating a sawmill in east Texas and had sold his lumber interests for something over a million dollars the previous year, had moved to Houston. He was persuaded to accept the presidency of the bank, though he knew nothing whatever about banking.

When West found that the bank, whose deposits were not large, had run short of funds he went to Jones and asked him what he would charge for a certain amount of cash, feeling that he would have to pay Jones a price for that much money at that crucial time. He also knew that Jones could always find cash when he wanted to, and West had too much pride to go to the larger and older established banks for help. Jones weighed the situation for quite some time and finally said to West:

> I will make you a personal loan for the amount you need, if you will buy the sawmill I have in Louisiana, about which you are familiar. As you know, I acquired the sawmill through trying to help a friend, and he finally turned it over to me for the debt. I have been unable to operate it profitably. My investment in it is approximately $150,000, and I will sell it to you on credit at its cost to me, payable $5000 a month. You know how to operate a sawmill profitably in the woods, and I do not. You should be able to sell enough lumber to pay it out. I will take your personal notes for the mill and for the new money.

West replied by saying he would look at the mill the next week. Jones closed his desk to go home. "But I want the money now," West said. Jones replied, "You get the money when you buy the mill, and not otherwise." West remonstrated, but he finally said, "All right."

Jones drew the papers in long hand, and the transaction was closed about midnight, after seven or eight hours of negotiating and dickering. West left Jones' office with a bill of sale to the sawmill and Jones' check for the money he needed, leaving his own notes payable for both the sawmill and the cash.

Jones learned later that the National City Bank could not have opened the following morning without the cash he loaned West. West made money with the sawmill.

Soon after this deal the Comptroller of the Currency instructed the directors of the National City to assess its stockholders 10 per cent of their holdings to cover losses. West, tired of being a banker, then traded his stock to Jones for a parcel of real estate, and Jones took his place as president of the bank. Jones was not sure the amount asked by the comptroller would meet any contingency that might arise. He immediately called the directors together and assessed the stockholders 50 per cent instead of 10, as directed by the comptroller. This safety precaution was typical of Jones' financial philosophy.

Jones operated the bank for about a year, got it in good condition, and transferred its business to the Lumberman's National, at exactly the price he paid for it. At that time he was vice-president of both the Union Bank and Trust Company and of the Lumberman's National.

In the spring of 1908 Jones also bought controlling interest in the Merchants National Bank, and later consolidated it with the Union, which made him by far the largest stockholder in the Union. This consolidation was also made without profit or loss to him, and was on pursuance of his stout desire to see all Houston banks in good hands, and strong. Ultimately Jones became dissatisfied with the management of the Union, and when he was called to Washington in 1917 he sold his stock.

In 1907 the Bankers Trust Company was organized by J. S. Rice, president of the Union National, and a number of his associates, all prominent in the community. The Bankers Trust capital was 500,000 dollars, with some surplus. Its business was lending money on mortgages and selling the mortgages to investors with the company's guarantee. A year or two later its capital was increased another 750,000 dollars. This stock was sold at 150 dollars a share.

In 1909 Jones organized the Texas Trust Company, with a capital and surplus of a million dollars. He subscribed for a majority of the stock and took its presidency. The institution loaned money on real estate but did not sell guaranteed mortgages. Soon realizing that there was no profitable field in Houston for two mortgage-trust companies, he negotiated a merger of the Texas Trust Company and the Bankers Trust Company in 1911.

In bringing about the consolidation, Jones was trying to rid himself of the responsibilities of managing a trust company, but he soon learned that he was so deeply involved that he had to take over the consolidated company. He changed the name to Bankers Mortgage Company. It became and remained a sound and useful institution.

When the 1908 Presidential election came along, Jones cast his vote for William Jennings Bryan, partially because he was a born Democrat and partially because of Bryan's advocacy of the guarantee of bank deposits. Jones was not sure that Bryan had worked out a sound formula to implement his deposit guarantee, but his banking experience had convinced him that the Commoner was advocating a necessary reform.

A good many phases of the nation's banking structure other than deposit guarantee were interesting Jones now. He knew as everyone else did that the nation's cash was in bank deposits and that these deposits were heavily concentrated in the East. People had always emigrated westward and money had always emigrated eastward. After the 1907 panic had shaken up the nation's economic system so badly, there had been dozens of bills introduced in Congress intended to prevent a recurrence of such a disaster, but none of them appeared to Jones likely to shift the nation's economic center of gravity any farther westward.

In 1912 the National Bank of Commerce was organized, with a capital stock of 500,000 dollars and a surplus of 25,000 dollars. J. M. Logan, a national bank examiner, who promoted it, became vice-president and managing officer; Colonel O. T. Holt, former mayor of Houston, was its president.

The bank got off to a bad start, and a new vice-president soon replaced Logan. Colonel Holt died and was succeeded by Gus Street, who was a highly regarded, well-to-do man but who had no particular business interest. Stock in the bank was selling at a substantial discount.

Jones, having had so much to do with cleaning up the bank situation in Houston after the 1907 panic, bought a few shares in the National Bank of Commerce. Soon Street asked him to get a new president, saying he was not a banker. At the next board meeting R. M. Farrar, vice-president of Jones' lumber company, was elected president of the bank.

At the time Jones became interested in the bank, it was the smallest in the city, with deposits of less than a million dollars. Jones built a new building for it and helped it grow until it became one of the largest in the city.

Jones, as a rising businessman, had been convinced that the future of his city depended upon what use it could make of Buffalo Bayou and the advantage it would be able to take of expanding oil developments. Houston was a rail center and wages paid to employees of the carriers was the town's principal money crop. But neither its status as a rail center nor as a rival to Dallas and Galveston as an important cotton market gave promise of any great contribution toward swelling its population.

Buffalo Bayou, turning and twisting as if it were having a great deal of trouble in finding its parent, the Gulf of Mexico, finally made the juncture fifty miles from the city limits of Houston, through the San Jacinto River, San Jacinto Bay, and Galveston Bay. Some small boats had sailed the bayou even when Texas was a part of Mexico, but it was very light-draught navigation. As early as 1899, Jones' second year in Houston, Congress made a small appropriation toward the improvement of the waterway; but work on it had lagged.

In 1898, about the time of Jones' arrival in Houston, gas in small quantities had been found on the outskirts of the city; and, in 1904 the Humble oil field, thirty miles away, came in. These in no way interested Jones personally. When he did begin to think about petroleum, his thoughts extended beyond any benefits Houston would derive from nearby oil bonanzas. The city's location, he thought, made it the ideal refinery center, as well as the petroleum-exploration capital of Texas, Louisiana, and Oklahoma. It would be some years before he could give his attention to making Buffalo Bayou work toward the growth of Houston, but he had in 1908 induced a petroleum concern, the Texas Company, to move there.

When the census of 1910 was announced, Houston had a population of 78,800 and was in third place behind San Antonio, with 96,614 and Dallas, with 92,104. There was just one thing to do if Houston was not to lose the population race to its two rivals. It would have to dredge the channel of Buffalo Bayou and bring the sea fifty miles inland.

The federal government was proceeding on the project at a snail's pace. Houston wanted fast action. It decided to send a committee of its leading citizens to Washington, with an offer to pay one half the cost if Congress would push the project to completion. In a hearing room filled to overflowing with Houstonians, the Rivers and Harbors Committee listened in disbelief.

Here was an unheard-of thing in the United States, a community offering to share equally with the federal government in the construction of a waterway that would be longer than the Panama Canal and twice as long as the channel connecting Manchester, England, with the sea. The congressional committee promptly voted to accept the plan proposed by the Houston citizens. A few days later it decided that the system it had voted for the Houston project was so sound that it would be made the policy for the development of other waterways in the nation.

Jones called the bankers of Houston together, and each bank agreed to buy its share of the bonds necessary to finance the city's share of the cost.

With the deep-water port assured, Mayor Ben Campbell went to Jones and said:

> I have come here to offer you the most important post in the city of Houston, one which, depending on the man who fills it, in the next five years will go a long way toward shaping the future of this town. It will require a man of practicability, resourcefulness, imagination, and energy. We all think you are the man for the job. It carries great responsibility but no salary. I want you to be chairman of the Houston Harbor Board. It will have five members. You may choose or approve the other four to serve with you.

Jones expressed his appreciation of the compliment which Mayor Campbell had paid him. He thought, however, he hardly merited it. Moreover he felt that there had never been a time when his own affairs required more attention.

But Campbell was insistent and Jones accepted the arduous task. He picked and recommended as his colleagues on the board four of Houston's leading citizens, all older than himself. They were Thomas H. Ball, R. M. Farrar, C. G. Pillot, and Dan Ripley.

Ball was a former member of Congress, served on the Rivers and Harbors Committee, and was therefore familiar with ports and waterways throughout the nation. Farrar, a lumberman and banker, was a business associate of Jones. Ripley was in the steamship business, and Pillot in the grocery business. All four were prominent in the community. It was an earnest, good-tempered board, but one that left it to the chairman to do most of the work.

Jones, with his customary thoroughness, began an intensive study of water transportation in general, and necessary port facilities for Houston in particular, together with rail connections, differentials, wharves, piers, storage, towage, anchorage, tides, silting, bank stabilization, and a ships' turning basin. A man by now accustomed to delegate in private life, he assumed full responsibility in this public job and tried to familiarize himself with the facilities and necessities of a port for which the city and navigation district voted millions in bonds.

In 1914, a year after Jones assumed the chairmanship, the waterway was completed to a depth of twenty-five feet. Jones wanted the event properly noted. He believed the best way to announce it was to fire a cannon, and in order that the cannon shot be heard in as many as possible ports around the world and that shipping interests everywhere be notified, the cannon ought be fired by the President of the United States. With the assistance of his brother-in-law, Daniel E. Garrett, Representative-at-Large in Congress from Texas, President Wilson's consent was obtained. On November 10 the President left a Cabinet meeting in the White House, stepped into the Oval Room, and by remote control fired a mortar emplaced on the banks of Buffalo Bayou. It was perhaps the most significant moment in the city's history, for at last, Houston was an inland port.

Houston was fifty miles from Galveston by direct line, but actually the tortuous channel of Buffalo Bayou turns and twists for seventy-five miles before entering San Jacinto River, nine miles above Galveston Bay; and many cutoffs and easements of bends had been necessary in building the canal.

Jones and his associates on the board almost immediately began efforts for enlarging the channel. "I do not expect Houston to become the first port in the nation," he said, "but it must be among the first few. We will have a million people in this city within fifty years."

Jones, from the time he began to study the port's potentialities and Houston's strategic location with respect to the South and West, never doubted that Houston would have the million people and that industries located along the channel would furnish the livelihood for a large proportion of them.

Major General Dan C. Kingman, Army Chief of Engineers, who thought Jones implausibly optimistic about Houston's future, asked, "Just how wide and deep do you think this waterway ought to be?"

"Wide enough and deep enough for anything which floats," Jones replied.

No vessels were in sight to sail from Houston to the ports of the world on the day of this interchange between Jones and the Chief of Engineers. Less than a year later, however, Jones and his Harbor Board had induced the Southern Steamship Company to put in a line of coastwise steamers.

The company's first seagoing vessel, the 315-foot SS *Satilla*, arrived in Houston on August 22, 1915. Jones first gazed at the vessel coming around a slow bend of Buffalo Bayou as he stood on a spot near the point where, many years before, Sam Houston had ordered Deaf Smith to destroy Vince's bridge, and the furious Battle of San Jacinto which was to win the freedom of Texas, had begun. For 200 miles the *Satilla* had fought its way through a Gulf hurricane.

The generally eastward course of Buffalo Bayou is through gently sloping coastal prairie; and from a distance there is an illusion that a boat is coming overland across the smooth, flat expanse. Buffalo Bayou, to most persons, was an ugly duckling; but to Jones, watching the ship's approach from the fringing growth which lined the bayou, it was transformed into the loveliest stretch of water in the world.

In Houston, Jones and the bigwigs of the city welcomed the ship as she came up to Houston's uncompleted first wharf. From then on, the port of Houston was to have a development unparalleled in the history of waterways.

The contribution of Jesse Jones to Houston's welfare through the years was to be unique. Without him many things that came to Houston would have otherwise been impossible. Certainly, without his guidance in its early days, the port of Houston would not have achieved the results it did, faced as it was with the competition of so many ports.

Jones left the chairmanship of the Harbor Board in 1917 for war service in Washington; but, before he left, thirty-eight industries had been induced to settle in Houston solely because of the ship channel, and the port was then handling over a million tons a year. In the 1926-27 cotton season 2,232,250 bales of cotton moved through the port of Houston. In that year fifty-seven ship lines were operating out of this port.

In 1929 the United States Shipping Board, in issuing a report showing the amount of Houston's cargo-tons of imports and exports from the United Kingdom and Europe, the north and east coasts of South America, the West Indies, the Orient, Canada, and Newfoundland, said, "It will be seen from these figures that Houston's trade is well distributed. The mere recital of the facts shows the importance of the Port of Houston to world commerce."

Its contribution to world trade continued; its tonnage statistics fattened until in 1952 it had reached the rank of second port in the nation in point of tonnage. By 1953 it had risen to a peak of 44,144,305 tons. The ships of the world's major freight lines include Houston as a port of call. The channel has been further deepened and widened until in 1956 it was near the goal set for it by Jones more than forty years before; that it should accommodate anything that floats; and along the channel leading to the mighty port of Houston industry had made capital investments of more than two billion dollars. Only Jones of the original Harbor Board was to live to see the gigantic plants line the banks of the once-stagnant bayou in the heartland of the new industrial south.

The days when Jesse Jones was single-handedly conducting a private building program for Houston and making himself useful in various ways in its public business were happy and rewarding ones for him in a more personal way. The youth who had made his own way since he was fourteen was now more than financially independent.

He had insisted on shouldering responsibility for the family upon his father's death. His own self-support at that time was not only imperative but the scanty family treasury also needed bolstering. He was always to continue that intense interest in the welfare of his brother, sisters, and close relatives.

Not only had Aunt Nancy come to Houston but so had his sister Ida, who had become Mrs. Daniel E. Garrett, his sister Elizabeth, who was Mrs. John B. Farthing, and his brother John T. On one occasion Jesse had written that his family was not a clannish one, but it was a very congenial one.

With only himself of all his family remaining unmarried, he was by 1912 abundantly supplied with nephews and nieces, to all of whom he was a generous uncle. There was a pleasant irregularity in the way he did things.

Jones got his first automobile about the time Pierce-Arrows came on the market. He had an open one and a closed one. Next he had a Packard, then a Cadillac, both limousines.

His niece, Anne Garrett, named the big gray Pierce-Arrow the Gray Eagle. His first chauffeur, who was named Moffat, remained with him until he died; and Jones never got another who suited him so well. Jones said, "He was the best chauffeur in the world; and if I had told him to run over someone, he would not have hesitated."

In 1915 Jones gathered all his nieces and the daughters of N. E. Meador, a business associate, and in munificent but what he thought would be an entirely unostentatious manner, took them, four mothers and fourteen children (Farthings, Garretts, Joneses, and Meadors), to New York to see the city.

Moffat went ahead in the Gray Eagle to serve the group in New York. Once there, the big car with its Texas license plates, and with Jones and half-dozen or so of the pretty nieces, was an unusual sight on the streets of New York.

They remained until they had seen all the shows they wanted to see, including Laurette Taylor in *Peg o' My Heart*, Doris Keane in *Romance*, Barney Bernard and Alexander Carr in *Potash and Perlmutter*, Mary Pickford and Lillian Gish in *A Good Little Devil*, Wilton Lackaye in *Fine Feathers*, Chauncey Olcott in *The Isle of Dreams*, Billie Burke in *The Amazons*, Tom Wise in *The Silver Wedding*, Arnold Daly in *General John Regan*, Ethel Barrymore in *Tante*, and Frances Starr in *The Street*.

It would be difficult to name anyone who was a Jones crony, but he had many stanch friends and was a good companion. He had a knack of making friends with men of widely different personalities.

A case in point was Dr. Stockton Axson, a brother-in-law of Woodrow Wilson and professor of English literature at Rice Institute, and Dick Coon, a cattleman of the rough, old-school type, and a champion "cusser." Sam Taub, a long-time friend of Jones, told of the day Jones introduced Dr. Axson and Dick Coon in the lobby of the Rice Hotel.

"What kind of doctor are you, a horse doctor?" inquired Coon, the rough-hewn diamond.

Taken aback, the erudite Axson replied, "No, Mr. Coon, I am professor of English literature at Rice Institute."

"No offense meant," said Coon. "I never know who this so-and-so Jones introduces me to, whether he is a preacher, a gambler, or a horse thief."

Dr. Axson and Dick Coon became warm friends.

Jones had a way of seeking advice; but no one has any recollection of his ever acting in accordance with the advice he received. Jones himself told this story:

"On one occasion, when I asked J. M. Rockwell, my close business associate, what he thought about my making a property purchase, he replied, 'Why do you ask my advice? You never take it.' "

Facetiously, Jones replied, "I always do the opposite of what you advise."

But frequently he acted on unsolicited suggestions. He was once a heavy smoker, first of cigars and then cigarettes. One day when he was about forty, Walter Sterling, a son of Governor Ross Sterling of Texas, a young man about nineteen, came to see him about a matter of business for his father. When the matter was disposed of and Walter was leaving Jones' office, he said, "Mr. Jones, you are smoking too many cigarettes."

Jones had smoked two or three during the short interview and felt that the young man was right, for he had become a chain smoker. He never smoked after that day.

While in his thirties and his fortune still moderate, Jones' mind turned to the problem of directing his surplus energies and means toward enlarging opportunities for others, especially through education.

The kind of education he wanted to help these young people get had not taken shape in his mind and he had never discussed it with anyone. In somewhat imperfect outline he was thinking of a plan to help young men and women whose backgrounds were somewhat similar to his own in his youth. His mature experience had convinced him that perhaps it was more important to teach these young people how to work than how to think.

Jones' idea was firmly in his mind even if he was somewhat vague about how to do it when the Reverend John E. Brown came to Houston in 1909 to conduct a religious revival and was a guest in the home of Mrs. M. T. Jones. Brown had a sharply defined idea of the sort of school about which Jones had thought in very general terms.

His school, as Brown outlined his plan, would take no students from families of wealth or even from families in comfortable circumstances. The students would be taught a vocation as well as given complete academic and scientific courses. Each would have to work his way through the college and each student would be required to work at least three hours a day in a school shop or on its own farm.

It embodied basically what Jones envisioned, for he had never thought of a strictly vocational school.

> I am thinking of working leaders, not tradesmen [Jones told the clergyman], and I know of no section of the country which is going to have a greater need of them, for the South is on the threshold of great industrial development. I believe that everyone should have to work, and when you teach young people how to work with their hands as well as their heads and at the same time inculcate in them the true principles of life, you give them about all the training necessary for a useful and happy life.

Jones liked the idea of the school so well and had such faith in Brown that he handed him a substantial check toward founding it.

Then to the preacher, speechless at the generous and unexpected gift, Jones said, "Get some mountain boys and girls into that school. They are the best, hardiest stock and most of them will not get an education except in such an institution as you suggest."

Brown selected Siloam Springs, a pretty little town in the Arkansas Ozarks, for what was to be known as John Brown University and made plans to find his students in a distinctive area—Arkansas, a part of Missouri, Oklahoma, Louisiana, and Texas. Brown was not able to get other financial aid he had expected to get and Jones agreed to enlist the aid of some of his friends. And even if they did not assist, he himself would see that the college was built. World War I made it necessary for Brown to delay its opening until 1919.

The war also was to cause Jones to resign as chairman of the Harbor Board and postpone a number of projected buildings in Houston.

From the day when oil shot geyser-like from the Lucas well at Spindletop, except for the few early trades he made at Beaumont, Jones had firmly adhered to his resolution to have no personal dealings in petroleum. He had wanted Houston to be the petroleum capital of the nation, had induced two major companies, the Texas Company and the Gulf, to locate there, and had erected buildings to lease to them.

Early in 1917 plans were under way to form the Humble Oil and Refining Company. Here was a chance to locate a third oil company in Houston. It was being formed by men who were close friends of Jones. They wanted him to join with them. An investment would be in no way speculative. It had proven production sufficient to make it a sound project and potential enough to make it one of the giants of the industry. Jones became one of the original stockholders along with Ross Sterling, William S. Farish, R. L. Blaffer, W. W. Fondren, and others.

The company was formed in March; war came in April. A few weeks later Jones was called by President Wilson to become Director General of Military Relief in the American Red Cross.

Before leaving Houston Jones took stock of his property holdings. He realized that his absence might be a lengthy one and very expensive. So he sold his stock in the Humble Company, which was about the only property he held that could be disposed of without disrupting his main business. Had he held the Humble stock it would, with its accumulations, have yielded him many millions of dollars.

PART III

Wider Horizons

9

Washington in World War I

AS Jones entered his fortieth year three circumstances drew him into public affairs and public service. In the first place, he had reached a position in Houston and Texas where his success and capacities were a matter of quite general recognition. Hence, there was an increasing demand upon him for public services of various kinds. There was also the fact that the security of his economic position released more and more of his time from private business. Finally, his interest in politics and national affairs was quickened by the election in 1912 to the Presidency of a man and a Democrat who elicited his fervent admiration.

Jones, always interested in local and state government, had begun to take a measurable interest in national politics in 1896. He found that his conservative instincts were sharply challenging his inherited loyalty to the Democratic party. Populism was abroad in the land. In Texas a Populist, Jerome C. Kearby, seriously threatened the re-election of a conservative Democrat, Charles A. Culberson, for governor. Nationally the inflationist left wing of the party had taken command and had nominated William Jennings Bryan.

This greatly disturbed Jones, who believed that a dollar should have good muscles. He liked less and less Bryan's talk about Free Silver and ended by voting for McKinley in November. He was glad to give his vote in the state to Culberson, who was elected. By 1900 he felt that the Free Silver menace was sufficiently eclipsed to enable him to return to the party fold and to vote for Bryan. He voted for Parker in 1904. In 1908, as we have seen, he also voted for Bryan, largely because he believed in the guarantee of bank deposits.

In 1912 the candidacy of Wilson made the Democratic party for him not only a tradition but a glorious crusade. For Jones believed himself to be a liberal in the sense in which Wilson so eloquently defined that faith.

Jones contributed money and considerable effort to the preconvention Presidential contest in Texas; and that state sent the so-called "immortal forty" delegates to the Democratic national convention at Baltimore, where in the long deadlock they stood like a stone wall for Wilson through the forty-six roll calls.

Jones also worked for and contributed to the autumn Presidential campaign of Wilson. Colonel E. M. House, of Texas, Wilson's principal adviser, knew Jones well and had a very high opinion of him. He frequently spoke to Governor Wilson, William F. McCombs, and William G. McAdoo, suggesting that Jones was the type of young Southerner the Democratic party should encourage to assume leadership and to enter public service.

After the victorious Wilson campaign, McAdoo (who was made Secretary of the Treasury) offered Jones the place of First Assistant Secretary (the title of which was later changed to Under Secretary), which Jones declined. He was also offered the post of Ambassador to Argentina or to Belgium, which failed to entice him. The President-elect then raised the bid and through Colonel House offered Jones appointment as Secretary of Commerce and held it open until late in February when on Jones' declination he appointed William C. Redfield of New York.

Jones had felt that he was not ready for public service on a national scale. He took very seriously his pledge for the building of the port of Houston, and had accepted the first chairmanship of the Houston Harbor Board. Furthermore, he was at a stage in his own business life where his absence from Houston would be risky.

During the four years of the first Wilson term the President heard a good deal about Jones and his interest in public affairs generally from Dr. Stockton Axson, as well as from Colonel House.

Consequently when the United States entered World War I, Jones had a telegram from the President, asking him to attend a Red Cross meeting in Topeka, Kansas. Henry P. Davison, senior member of J. P. Morgan and Company, had accepted the chairmanship of the American Red Cross War Council and at Topeka outlined a plan to raise 100,000,000 dollars for the agency, to meet its immediate war needs.

Jones was given the responsibility of raising Houston's quota of 150,000 dollars. It seemed a large sum to Jones, for people had not yet become accustomed to giving money in such large amounts, and Houston did not have a great many well-to-do people. On the way home he decided on his strategy.

He wrote out his check for 5,000 dollars to the Red Cross and went to see Captain James A. Baker, who was his personal friend as well as his attorney. He showed the check to Baker, who was a man not known to give away money in large amounts. Baker commended Jones warmly on his generosity.

"The reason I showed it to you was that I want you to match it," Jones said.

Baker said he would make a modest contribution, but any idea of his giving such a large amount was nonsense. They argued an hour and then Baker capitulated and agreed to go with Jones anywhere he wished to get similar amounts. Jones showed Baker's check to W. T. Carter and got Carter's check for an equal donation.

He was sure of his quota from business friends and associates in amounts from $500 to $5000 before general solicitation began. He raised twice his quota and was the first fund raiser in the nation to send his report to Washington.

A few weeks later there came another telegram from President Wilson. This one was an urgent request that he come to Washington for service in the Red Cross.

Jones adjusted his affairs, gave Fred J. Heyne, his principal assistant in all his business operations, an unlimited power of attorney that enabled Heyne to do anything Jones could in Jones' name and behalf, and left for Washington.

Jones walked into the new Red Cross Building on a hot summer day in 1917 and reported to Davison. The spick-and-span white marble national headquarters on Seventeenth Street, facing the White House ellipse, had been occupied for the first time in January, three months before American entry into the war, and was formally dedicated on

May 12, 1917, a month after the declaration of war. On the same day President Wilson had appointed Davison chairman of the War Council.

Never well organized in the Spanish-American War, the American National Red Cross had been incorporated and nationalized in 1905; and now as it faced its first real test, it not only had very little organization but, until Harry Davison's hundred-million-dollar fund-raising drive, very little money.

Davison, who had worked untiringly at his job, welcomed Jones with his reputation of organizing ability, and after a short talk escorted the newcomer to a vacant desk and said, "This is the desk of the Director General of Military Relief for the American Red Cross. You will find plenty to do here."

Jones had come to his new job unacquainted with most of the men and women with whom he was to be associated. Generally, they were from big business and for the most part stanch Republicans. President Wilson regarded many of them as none too friendly to his administration but recognized their patriotism and their loyalty to him insofar as the war was concerned. Jones more and more found them largely men of his own thinking, except as to politics, with whom he could work congenially.*

Soon Jones' old friend and counselor, Judge Robert S. Lovett, joined the volunteer war workers in Washington as counselor and member of the War Industries Board. Lovett and Jones were to spend much time together.

John W. Davis, Solicitor General of the United States, was also counselor for the Red Cross. He and Jones soon became fast friends. Seven years later, when Davis was nominated for the Presidency on the Democratic ticket, he chose Jones to finance his campaign.

Cleveland Dodge, another prominent Democrat in the high brackets,

* These individuals with some of whom his contacts were to become so important in later years included John D. Ryan, the picturesque Montana copper magnate; George W. Hill, vice-president of the American Tobacco Company; Robert W. de Forest, the New York banker; Grayson M. P. Murphy, New York financier; Edward N. Hurley, of Chicago, who had originated and developed the pneumatic-tool industry; Cornelius N. Bliss, Jr., of New York; Cleveland H. Dodge, of the Phelps-Dodge Company; Harvey D. Gibson, president of the Liberty National Bank in New York, who was active President of the American Red Cross; Charles A. Coffin, first president of the General Electric Company; Dr. William C. Gorgas; Dr. Simon Flexner; Jacob H. Schiff; George W. Perkins; George F. Baker, Sr.; Henry Clay Frick; Felix M. Warburg; Nicholas Murray Butler; Alton B. Parker; Charles Evans Hughes; Eliot Wadsworth of Boston; Mrs. August Belmont; Miss Mabel Boardman, of Red Cross fame; Mrs. Herbert Hoover, later to be the First Lady of the land, but whose husband was then assuming the job of Food Administrator; and Mrs. E. H. Harriman, widow of the railroad man.

and a strong friend of President Wilson, was in and out. He and Jones became particularly good friends. Stockton Axson got leave from Rice Institute to become general secretary of the Red Cross.

But the man to whom Jones was drawn closest was Davison. They had the same kind of country-boy background, Davison in Pennsylvania and Jones in Tennessee. They shared a similar lack of college education. But each had done a very good job in self-education. When they met in the Red Cross Building, Davison had just passed his fiftieth birthday; Jones was forty-three.

In banking, which Davison had entered as a bookkeeper at Troy, Pennsylvania, before he was twenty-one, he had risen to the point where he was considered one of the top bankers of the world. He told Jones that he got his life's greatest pleasure out of the consolidations of the New York banks, which he worked out after the 1907 panic: the Morton Trust, the Fifth Avenue Trust, and the State Trust Company, to form the Guaranty Trust Company, thus strengthening the New York banking situation.

Jones, having had a similar experience in consolidating and reorganizing banks in Houston during and after the 1907 panic, found this mutual experience one more bond with the Red Cross Chairman.

Davison's team soon brought order out of the chaos they found under the roof of the marble building.

Jones' genius for organization left its permanent imprint on the structure of the mercy agency. The four principal bureaus he found in the Department of Military Relief were all entirely rebuilt and others erected, until the agency touched the American soldier at all points from enlistment to discharge.

In an incredibly short time Jones had fifty base hospitals functioning, and later set up forty-five reconstruction hospitals. The agencies under his directions recruited physicians and nurses for ambulance companies at home and abroad. The Bureau of Motor Service, which he set up to remove sick and wounded men from ships and trains to hospitals and homes, put into operation hundreds of motor corps. He organized a Bureau of Construction that erected convalescent homes, recreation centers, warehouses, and miscellaneous construction costing millions of dollars. Jones himself drew the plans for a number of these buildings. In his first year as Director General of Military Relief the Jones-directed agencies set up eighty-four canteen depots and 14,300 canteen services. They distributed mountains of sweaters, wristlets, mufflers, and socks, along with 3040 other separate and individual items. His bureaus outgrew the space allotted him in the Red Cross Building and overflowed into temporary war-constructed buildings.

Long before there was a battle casualty Jones was working on the problems of the rehabilitation of wounded and disabled men. On December 19, 1917, he was able to announce that he had accepted the offer of Jeremiah Milbank of money and quarters for the establishment in New York City of the Red Cross Institute for Crippled and Disabled Men.

As the work of the agency grew from its original conception of "succor to the wounded individual" to include "succor to the wounded nations," men worked heavy hours, doing a full day's work, then coming back in the evening. Jones worked perhaps the longest hours of any. There were meetings, too, and planning, which were carried on away from the building in the evening.

Jones, who had been described in a Washington society column dealing with the new personages brought to Washington in the war effort, as "happily unmarried," lived for a time in a house on Wyoming Avenue, with Colonel Joseph M. Hartfield, Harvey Gibson, George Murnane, and Henry Davison. Later Davison moved to Twin Oaks, the Alexander Graham Bell estate on Woodley Lane, and made it a sort of second Red Cross headquarters, especially for evening meetings. When others of the group in the Wyoming Avenue house left, some to go with Davison and others to go abroad, Jones retained the house for his own use.

The Wyoming Avenue house was fairly large with five or six bedrooms, and soon became known by his friends from Houston and elsewhere as the Jones Hotel. Jones, however, constantly forgot its limitations, and often had more guests than rooms. His housekeeping staff consisted of a cook, a housekeeper, a maid, and a Japanese butler. There was usually a state of war between the butler and the housekeeper.

During the summer of 1918 former President Taft was Jones' guest for several months. Taft was doing some war work mostly at a desk in the Jones house. The summer was very hot, and the ex-President spent most of those pre-air-conditioning days working in his nightshirt. Taft proved an able arbitrator in some of the disagreements between the Jones housekeeper and butler.

Jones had little leisure; but his next-door neighbor on Wyoming Avenue was an agreeable gentleman and a member of the United States Senate from Ohio. He and Jones became fast friends and occasionally had a golf game together, sometimes including Judge Robert S. Lovett and other co-workers. The Senator was Warren G. Harding who, three years later, became President of the United States.

Of all the men gathered under the Red Cross banner only Jones, Dodge, and Axson had easy access to the White House. Dodge was away from Washington most of the time, and Axson seemed to be a little in awe of his brother-in-law, the President. Jones, whose closeness to the wartime President continued to increase, constantly assured the President of the dedicated patriotism of Davison, as well as the other big businessmen associated with him. But these men, whose importance in the business and financial world was so great, always felt (undoubtedly with good cause) that President Wilson was, in a measure, prejudiced against them. Thus Jones' ability to get the ear of Wilson was very valuable to Davison and the Red Cross War Council.

The remarkable success Jones developed in dealing with President Wilson, whom many found to be a difficult, headstrong man, resulted in the historic speech that Wilson made in the Metropolitan Opera House in New York on May 18, 1918, after the President had marched up Fifth Avenue at the head of the Red Cross parade.

The inception of this event was in Davison's request to Jones that he persuade the President to review the parade opening the fund-raising effort. At the White House Jones had found a dejected President. Hopes of bringing Russia back into the war had all but vanished and the fate of the deposed Czar and his family was a matter of deep concern. Jones presented the request that Wilson review the parade, and further suggested to the President that in view of the world situation he make a speech in Madison Square Garden.

The President told Jones quite bluntly he would not go to New York; furthermore, he never expected to make another speech in Madison Square Garden.

Then, looking out on the White House lawn to the herd of sheep put there to graze as an example of thrift to a nation at war, the President said, "But I would like to do something for the Red Cross. Are those sheep ready to shear?"

Jones thought they were. Wilson asked how much his sheep would clip. Jones made a guess.

"Then I will have them sheared and give you the wool for Red Cross sweaters," the President volunteered.

The wool came over to the Red Cross the next day. It was weighed and divided into forty-eight packages and sent to the governors of the states to be auctioned to set off the fund-raising campaign in their states.

Jones had not accepted the President's refusal to go to New York as final. He went back to the White House, thanked the President for the wool, but added, "That was not enough; I still want you to go to New York." Again the President refused, saying with apparent annoyance, "I told you I would not go."

Without telling Davison of the President's attitude, Jones said that he thought there was a good chance he would go and that he was proceeding accordingly. Two days later Jones was waiting in the White House residence quarters when Wilson came over from the executive offices. The President greeted his visitor jovially.

"I have," said Jones, "come to talk to you further about going to New York. It seems to me that you should use the occasion to make a speech to the world, to the Allied Powers, to the Central Powers, and especially to the American troops in France. The occasion is a perfect setting for you. I think it would shorten the war."

The President reflected for a moment and then said, "I will think about it."

On Monday, May 13, Jones sent the President a note asking whom he would prefer to preside at the meeting. Wilson sent a reply by messenger in an hour saying that he would prefer Cleveland Dodge, and that if he spoke he ought not to try to do so in any auditorium larger than the Carnegie Hall or some of the larger theaters.

Jones telephoned to Dodge and asked him to arrange for a hall and prepare to preside at the meeting but to make no announcement that the President would attend.

On Friday, Jones accompanied the President and Mrs. Wilson, Dr. Grayson, and Joseph B. Murphy, chief of the Secret Service detail, to New York in a private railroad business car. The party stayed at the Waldorf-Astoria Hotel. The President intended to go to the theatre Friday night and had still made no promise about either the Saturday parade or the speech. Only Davison had been announced as a speaker at the rally.

Just before twelve o'clock on Saturday, President Wilson telephoned to Jones to come to the Presidential suite for lunch. Jones found the President reading war dispatches. The news was ominous. A half-million American soldiers were on French soil, but most of them far from battle-ready. Between the Belgian coast and the Oise River 140 German divisions of nearly 2,000,000 men were poised, ready for an attempt to break the railroad between Amiens and Clermont. Field Marshal Haig was bracing to meet the onslaught.

Lunch was brought in; the little group ate in silence. Wilson was in deep thought. Suddenly he got up from the table and said, "Jones, I want to march with you in the parade; but I will not march with those Wall Street fellows!"

Jones reminded the President of the hazards involved. He knew that most of the police had been sent to the reviewing stand to guard the President there.

"I think I will be all right," the President replied. "Do not tell the police or Secret Service that I am going to walk with you."

He went into his bedroom to put on his cut-away coat and top hat. Jones had no such articles of apparel.

At two o'clock Mrs. Wilson appeared, unescorted, at the reviewing stand, where Governor Whitman and Mayor Hylan awaited the arrival of the President. She volunteered no explanation of the President's absence.

The President, Jones, Grayson, Secretary Tumulty, and Starling (of the Secret Service) started up Fifth Avenue, with Jones wondering how he was going to manage with the President's determination not "to walk with those Wall Street fellows." But, as they approached the parade, Jones saw that a group of mounted policemen was riding in front of it. He had the chauffeur turn the car around quickly. The President and Jones got out, stepped in front of the mounted police, and headed the line down Fifth Avenue. There was no delay; it worked perfectly, exactly as though it had been planned.

New York saw the most dramatic and thrilling demonstration that had occurred since the war began. The President had marched less than fifty feet when the crowd, recognizing him, sent up the cry, "The President of the United States!"

Fifth Avenue was instantly a cloud of waving flags, streamers, hats, and handkerchiefs. The soul-stirring demonstration increased as the word sped down the parade route ahead of the President, who marched with erect carriage at the head of 70,000 persons.

That night, before an audience which jammed the Metropolitan Grand Opera House to the uppermost gallery seat, speaking without notes, Wilson lost no time in meeting the issue presented to him. Alluding to German peace feelers, that the Central Powers would make certain concessions in France and Belgium if Russia and Rumania were turned over to them, the President said:

> We are not diverted from the grim purpose of waging war by any insincere approaches upon the subject of peace. I can say with a clear conscience

that I have tested these intimations and have found them insincere. I now recognize them for what they are, an opportunity to have a free hand, particularly in the East, to carry out the purpose of conquest and exploitation. Every proposal with regard to accommodation in the West involves a reservation with regard to the East. Now, as far as I am concerned, I intend to stand by Russia as well as by France. If any man in Germany thinks we are going to sacrifice anybody for our own sake, I now tell him that he is mistaken.

A moment later the President told the nation what lay ahead of it:

"I have heard gentleman say that we must get five million men ready. Why limit it to five million? I am asking Congress that there be no limit."

Still a moment later he gave the Red Cross a slogan:

"When you give absolutely all you can spare, do not consider yourself liberal in giving. If you give with self-adulation, you are not giving at all; you are giving to yourself. If you give until it hurts, then your heart blood goes into it."

With "Give Until It Hurts" as a slogan, the Red Cross drive that was intended to raise 100,000,000 dollars actually produced 170,000,000, the largest sum that had ever been raised by private subscription for humanitarian purposes.

In November two weeks after the armistice was signed, Davison, back from an arduous trip to Europe, approached Jones about a new project. He handed him a slip of paper on which was written:

The American Red Cross has shown the way, during the war, whereby peoples may be of great help to their unfortunate fellow men in time of catastrophe. The good will and sympathy engendered by the Red Cross spirit must not be lost. While the governments are arranging a political peace, let the Red Cross societies of the world come together in a union and add weight to that spirit of reconciliation which should succeed this war.

Then Davison explained in detail his plan for "a service for peace."

"The meeting I have in mind," said Davison, "will have to be held in Europe, and I hate to go back over there so soon; but I think two such distinguished linguists as you and I should go over and sell the plan." (Neither Jones nor Davison knew any language but English.)

Jones endeavored to make an appointment for Davison to talk over the plans with President Wilson; but Wilson, preparing to leave for Paris aboard the *George Washington* on December 4, had no time to examine the proposals and asked Jones to have Davison prepare a summary of his suggestions, so that the President might study them aboard ship.

Late in December, 1918, Davison and Jones sailed on the trip that was to take them to London, Paris, Cannes, and Geneva, to organize the League of Red Cross Societies. They arrived in London on December 26. On the same raw day Woodrow Wilson left Calais, after his triumphal reception in France, and landed at Dover.

Davison, anxious to have a quick decision on his desire to disband the Red Cross War Council by March, 1919, again put his reliance upon Jones' way with Wilson to bring about the desired result.

In Washington, because of the time usually necessary to make an appointment with the President through his secretary, it had been Jones' custom to go to the White House without first making an appointment, and he had always been able to see the President.

So, in late afternoon of December 27, Jones got into a cab at Claridges and told the driver to take him to Buckingham Palace, where the President was staying during his London visit. The driver hesitated, but the taxicab starter told him to carry out Jones' order.

As Jones arrived at the gates of Buckingham Palace, outriders came out, muffled in great coats against the freezing weather. Following the outriders was a carriage in which was the scarlet-coated high sheriff of London, with some bewigged official in the seat beside him.

Jones waved a greeting to the two officials in the carriage, and they waved back. The waved greetings must have given him security clearance in the eyes of the two gate officers for they merely listened as Jones told them he was there to see President Wilson, and motioned him on.

As Jones entered the large, oblong reception hall at Buckingham Palace, he saw at the far end a big, roaring fire. It was a welcome sight, for he had not been warm since his arrival in London.

Being advised that the President and the King were out and would not be back for probably an hour, Jones sat down before the crackling wood fire, turning first one side then the other toward the welcome heat. Finally he was thoroughly warm, except for his feet. With the directness with which he met all situations, he removed his shoes and stretched his stockinged feet out to the warm fire.

The conference that the President and the King had been attending did not last as long as expected; and suddenly there was a commotion as they and their retinue entered the long entrance hall of the palace.

Jones had no time to put on his shoes. Standing up in front of the fire and looking straight ahead, he hoped he would not be noticed. But the President's party had to pass near him; and when the President saw Jones, he walked over and spoke.

If the President noticed anything amiss, he said nothing; so the embarrassed Texan told the President his reason for being there.

"Davison wants to retire as chairman of the Red Cross," he said, "and to dissolve the Red Cross War Council. He wants Dr. Farrand to succeed him as head of the organization. He would also like to talk to you about the advisability of creating a League of Red Cross Societies."

The President asked Jones which Farrand it was. He said there were three of them in the educational field. Jones did not know. He made an engagement to see the President a few days later in Paris, at which time he would have the necessary information.

The story of Jones' discomfiture was immediately put into circulation by his close personal friend, Admiral Cary Grayson, the President's physician, who was in the President's party. Needless to say, it lost nothing in the telling, but was embellished by Grayson, with white socks and rolled-up trousers.

Subsequently President Wilson followed Davison's recommendation and appointed Livingston Farrand despite the fact that he was one of the brothers who had most bitterly opposed Wilson at Princeton.

Not only did the President appoint Farrand, but Davison and Jones got Wilson's promise to insert the general idea of Red Cross Societies in the Covenant of the League of Nations. With a letter from Wilson warmly backing the plan, Davison and Jones went to Cannes and met representatives of France, Great Britain, Italy, and Japan and drew up the agreement for the Red Cross League.

Davison already had begun to suffer headaches before he and Jones completed a second organization meeting at Geneva. He had grown worse in Paris at the session that saw the League of Red Cross Societies launched on May 5, 1919. Despite this illness Davison agreed to accept the chairmanship of the Red Cross League's board of governors, but he was to be disabled for most of the three remaining years of his life. On May 6, 1922, he died as a result of an operation for brain tumor in his fifty-fourth year.

Jones was always to remember his association with Davison while Director General of Military Relief for American Red Cross, as a member of his War Council, and in helping to create the League of Red Cross Societies as among the most satisfying experiences of his life.

Back to Main Street

"JESSE JONES came back to Texas a cosmopolite," said the rival newspaper, the Houston *Post* in a laudatory editorial on his return to Houston in 1919.

No doubt his two years in Washington and abroad had given stature and maturity to Jones. He had acquired a broad circle of new friends and acquaintances in many important fields of activity. Most of these were notable leaders in national affairs. They would remain his business and political associates or cherished personal friends for the remainder of their lives. His work had been on an exalted plane, national and international. His mind had gathered ideas for business, philanthropy, and government. He had made himself a more useful citizen of the world.

But he would have vigorously rejected the characterization "cosmopolite"; nor did he think he had been a provincial when he closed his big desk and went into war service. Perhaps the thing that had happened to him was best described by Wilson himself in an article published in the *Century* magazine in 1901 entitled "When a Man Comes to Himself":

It is a very wholesome and regenerating change, which a man undergoes when he "comes to himself." . . . He comes to himself after the experience of which he alone may be aware, when he had left off being wholly preoccupied with his own powers and interests and every petty plan which centers in himself; when he has cleared his eyes to see the world as it is and his own true place and function in it. . . .

A man is the part he plays among his fellows. . . . His life is made up of the relations he bears to others, is made or marred by those relations, guided by them, judged by them, expressed in them. There is nothing else upon which he can spend his spirit, nothing else which we can see.

Jones had come back to Houston with a greater ferocity of attachment to his home city than when he left, and with an unrestrained enthusiasm for anything that would advance Houston's interests. He was determined that it should go further, and began making plans to help it grow.

The town had done very well in his absence; it was bulging with new people. But Dallas, which had been and would continue to be its rival, had bulged more. The 1920 census was to show Dallas with a population of 158,976; Houston with 138,276. The great forward movement to Houston was to come in the next ten years.

On the day he returned, Jones rode the full length of Main Street. There was no doubt now that Houston's business and commercial life would cling to Main Street like Spanish moss to the live oaks that fringed the city's outskirts. The property for which he had paid more than many competent authorities thought it was worth had increased in value even more than he anticipated. Jones had always wanted to put Houston's best foot forward for all the world to see; and Houston's best foot was Main Street.

Jones, deeply immersed in plans for new buildings, did not suspect that he would soon be the center of the bitterest civic encounter he was ever to have in Houston.

In the summer of 1920 a controversy was joined when the Houston Harbor Board undertook to buy a tract of land several miles below Houston.

Jones first heard of the contemplated purchase when R. M. Farrar, a member of the Harbor Board who had been appointed at Jones' suggestion, and who was president of the National Bank of Commerce, of which Jones owned a majority of the capital stock, quite casually mentioned that the land was to be bought.

Jones, who was sitting near Farrar's desk in the bank, was surprised and instinctively remarked, "You cannot do that."

Farrar replied coldly, "Who is going to stop us?"

"It is not a question of any one trying to stop you," Jones responded. "But you should not want to buy it; the port has no use for the land."

Besides Farrar, the members of the Harbor Board were John T. Scott, president of the First National Bank, chairman; R. S. Sterling, later to be governor; J. S. Rice, president of the Union National Bank; and William D. Cleveland, a cotton man. They were all among the more prominent citizens of the city.

Jones felt that members of the board undoubtedly believed that they were acting in the interest of the port. But he knew the value of every acre of ground along the ship channel and, in his opinion, the price was much too high; furthermore being situated several miles below the port it could not be of any use.

Farrar at a session of the Harbor Board reported his conversation with Jones in such a manner as to cause resentment against Jones, who was soon to hear that a member of the Board remarked at the meeting, "Who is Jesse to tell us what we can do?"

The port was a joint operation of the city and county, and concurrence of both the city council and county commissioners' court was necessary for any important expenditure by the Harbor Board. Also, a vote of the people was required before bonds could be issued to pay for the land.

The Board unanimously favored the purchase, as did the mayor, the city council, and the county commissioners' court; and an election was called.

Jones issued a statement opposing the purchase and giving his reasons. The Houston *Chronicle*, of which he was then only part owner, also opposed it. The Houston *Post* and Houston *Press*, the two other city newspapers, strongly recommended the purchase and viciously criticized Jones for his stand. A large citizens committee, including almost all the city's leading businessmen and bankers, was organized to promote the purchase. The Chamber of Commerce, the Real Estate Board, labor organizations, and all the city's civic clubs endorsed the proposal.

With this formidable support the proponents made it appear that the whole town was for buying the land, except the *Chronicle* and Jesse Jones. The intensity of the personal attacks on him was a new experience. Daily he saw himself labeled as a "port killer" in page advertisements that ran in both the Houston *Post* and Houston *Press*. As an answer to the charge that he was a "port killer" Jones relied on the common knowledge among Houston people of his leadership in the fight for deep water and his guidance of the affairs of the port in its infant days and that from the standpoint of investments no man in Houston had a bigger stake than he.

The final argument for the land purchase was a full-page advertisement in the Houston *Post* signed by R. S. Sterling, W. S. Farish, S. F. Carter, Sr., H. R. Cullen, Will L. Clayton, W. M. Rice, and other names equally potent in Houston. The signers accounted for about all the city's financial strength except Jones.

A landslide majority, representing 73 per cent of the voter turnout, stood with Jones and the *Chronicle* on election day.

The bitterness engendered in the fight extended into Jones' National Bank of Commerce. Soon after the election R. M. Farrar sent word to Jones to get a new president.

Next a prominent member of the board of directors of the bank called on Jones and told him that, if Farrar were allowed to leave, he and several other members of the board would resign and sell their stock. This director went so far as to say, "The people of Houston will not let you run a bank." Since the people in voting had been on his side, Jones took this as a threat from the big interests he had opposed. He replied calmly, "Such a thought had never occurred to me; and it might be a good idea to find out."

He got another president for the bank, and new directors to replace those who wanted to resign, and he took over their stock.

Jones had gone to Navasota, a nearby town, to get a new president for his bank, Ewing Norwood. After a year Norwood told Jones he did not like living in a city, and would like to go back to his own bank at Navasota.

Jones then offered the bank presidency to Judge S. A. Lindsay, of Tyler, Texas, who was, at the time, president of the Federal Farm Loan Bank in Houston. Lindsay was a very able and a very well-to-do man. After about a year Jones said to him one day, in all friendliness, "Judge I think you are too fat, too lazy, and too rich to work at this bank job."

Lindsay replied, "I agree with you, and suggest you get someone to take my place."

So Judge Lindsay moved back to his home town, where he had an excellent bank of his own.

Jones then took the presidency himself and retained it until he went to Washington in 1932, as a director of the Reconstruction Finance Corporation.*

* He was succeeded by one of his associates in the lumber business, N. E. Meador, who only lived for about a year.

The directors then promoted A. D. Simpson to the presidency. Mr. Simpson had come to the bank as a bookkeeper. He soon became one of the best-known bankers in the United States, and was made vice-president of the board.

Simpson was succeeded in the presidency by R. P. Doherty, who also started with the bank as a bookkeeper.

Jones himself remained chairman of the board as long as he lived.

When Farrar left the bank, it was the smallest in town, with deposits of only 4,689,000 dollars. Under Jones' general direction, the bank took on new growth, and became one of the largest in the city, with deposits, by 1956, of more than 300,000,000 dollars.

In 1920 Jones became chairman and president of the Bankers Trust Company, which he soon changed to the Bankers Mortgage Company.

Thus, the principal Jones corporations became the National Bank of Commerce, the Bankers Mortgage Company, the Houston *Chronicle*, and many real-estate corporations headed up by the Commerce Company, a Texas corporation. He did not add the C. and I. Life Insurance Company until years later.

Discussing financing of his building operations Jones once said:

> For each new building, I created a new corporation so that, if one building got in trouble, it would not involve any other.
>
> I built the first three in 1908, out of the proceeds of the sale of some lumber yards. When a building was completed, occupied, and showed earnings, I mortgaged it for cash to build others. You get a much better deal when you have established earnings to show the lender.
>
> Usually, business buildings which are properly planned, located, and constructed will earn themselves out, if not mortgaged for more than 60 per cent of the cost; 50 per cent is better. Fortunately, after I got well started, I just about always had enough in the till to erect a building or two.

The year 1920 was to hear wedding bells for Jesse Jones, then forty-six. On December 15 he was married to the former Mary Gibbs, daughter of Dr. and Mrs. Jasper Gibbs of Mexia, Texas. They were to have many years of companionship. Mary Jones' great interest was to stand at her husband's side; every interest he had she shared. Her greatest joys came from the charities they planned together and soon undertook.

The newly married couple went to New York City on their honeymoon; and during their stay there Jones saw the possibility of some building operations in that great city.

Jones began building in New York City in 1921. He named his principal New York company the Houston Properties Corporation.

"I came to New York to teach New Yorkers how to pronounce Houston," he once told his friend, Charles M. Schwab.*

In 1921 the National City Bank of New York was looking for a new president to succeed James A. Stillman. On the committee of the bank's directors to make the selection was Judge Robert S. Lovett, chairman

* One of the oldest streets in the business section of downtown New York is Houston Street, but it is pronounced "Howston." General Sam Houston and the city named for him had the "Hews-ton" pronunciation.

of the board of the Union Pacific Railroad, having succeeded E. H. Harriman at the latter's death.

Lovett went to Jones, explained the situation, and said that his committee would be glad to recommend him for the place. Jones declined. "You have known me since I was a very young man," he said to Judge Lovett, "and this suggestion is the greatest compliment I have ever had paid me. I have been a stockholder in a number of banks in Houston, and an inactive vice-president of two of our national banks at the same time, as well as a director and the largest stockholder in another. But I have never had a desk in one. Frankly, I would not like the personal limitations necessary in operating a bank."

An additional reason played a part in this decision. He and Mrs. Jones had learned that they would not like to live in New York by the simple experiment of spending six months in one of the Jones cooperative apartments on Fifth Avenue. They were happy to return to Houston.*

Later he built a twenty-four-story office building at 200 Madison Avenue; a sixteen-story hotel, the Mayfair House, on Park Avenue at Sixty-Fifth Street; a forty-seven-story office-and-store building on Fortieth Street between Fifth Avenue and Madison Avenue; a twenty-story apartment building at Fifty-Seventh Street and First Avenue; and a doctors' office building and hospital at 40 East Sixty-First Street.

Except for the cooperatives and the hospital, he continued his ownership of the New York properties. He had quickly sold all the residences he built in Houston, and all the cooperatives he put up in New York were built for sale and he had no trouble in disposing of them. But he was just as reluctant to sign a deed to a piece of business property in New York as he had been in Houston and Fort Worth.

In 1927, after he had been married seven years, Jones gave thought to building a home for himself. He gave no consideration to any of Houston's good residential areas. He was a Main Street man for both business and living purposes. He still had the site of one of his first lumber yards in Houston. On that site he built another hotel, the sixteen-story Lamar, named after Mirabeau Buonaparte Lamar, second President of the Republic of Texas.

* So, too, was Lilly, their cook and maid. Lilly had a mind of her own. The wages of the Jones servants were paid at his office. Not long after returning to Houston, Mrs. Jones learned from the office that Lilly's salary had been raised. She took it up with Lilly and asked her, "How come?" Lilly replied, "Mrs. Jones, I didn't want to bother you so I just went to Mr. Heyne at the office and had him raise my wages."

There was no great need for a hotel of the character of the Lamar at the time I built it [Jones wrote], but I wanted my home downtown, and needed a good place to build it. The top of the sixteen-story hotel was an ideal location for our home. We traveled considerably, and, when we left the city there was never any problem of caretakers.

Jones' old friend, Charles Gates Dawes, once Vice-President of the United States, said, "Jesse Jones is, at heart, as much of an empire builder as James J. Hill or Cecil Rhodes were; but he likes to have his empire where he can see most of it most of the time."

The seventeenth-story windows of the Jones home which faced in all directions, literally made this possible.

If Jones had been asked for a description of this home, which embodied so much of the unusual in design and decoration, his answer would have sounded very much like a classified advertisement in the *Chronicle:* "Living room, drawing room, dining room, three bedrooms with baths, entrance hall, kitchen, servants' quarters."

Jones' lack of awareness of the details of his surroundings was entirely in character. He demanded no ostentation anywhere; but he did want comfort and convenience.

All of these requirements were met by Mrs. Jones in the quiet elegance of their apartment home. Its beauty and richness were never at the expense of comfort. Jones was accustomed to draw the plans for all his buildings and had accounted for a great deal of architecture. He did draw the plan for the forty-by-forty wood-paneled drawing room, with the high ceilings of knotty pine, done in Georgian style, with its huge, wood-burning fireplace of Italian marble.

The rest of it reflected the understanding of design and gift for decoration of Mary Jones; the thirty-by-forty living room, with doorway of lacy wrought-iron gates, the light and sunny dining room, the bed-sitting rooms, the guest rooms.

It was Mary Jones, too, who through the years was to gather the wall coverings, the rugs, and the furnishings. Some of it Early American, other in antique Chinese, English, French, and Italian, it all blended in a way to give an atmosphere of quiet restfulness.

In the Lamar, Jones was able to indulge his desire to have his family as neighbors. He built an apartment for his aunt, Mrs. M. T. Jones, who was to outlive her husband by thirty years. She closed the big Jones home at 2908 Main Street and resided at the Lamar the rest of her life. His brother, John T. Jones, lived there until his death; and his widow remained there the rest of her years. His widowed sister, Mrs. Daniel E. Garrett, also resided there.

Aunt Nancy Hurt died before the Lamar was built. After her home burned she lived in the suite at the Rice, where she could see busy downtown Houston and enjoy a daily visit from her devoted nephew, who, when away, never forgot to write. When Aunt Nancy was stricken with her last illness in 1925, Jones was in New York. He hurried to Houston and found her in a coma and she gave no sign of recognizing him, but Jones sat by her bedside holding her tiny hand in his big one until she peacefully passed away.

Jones had reason to marvel at the farsightedness of J. K. and A. C. Allen, the brothers who laid out the village of Houston through the wild woods and prairie in 1837. Its streets were wide, and its square blocks 250 feet each way; and there were no alleys. The blocks fitted so well into building customs at the middle of the twentieth century that Jones could erect, on the one block which had been the site of his lumber yard, not only the Lamar Hotel but the McKinney Hotel, two large theaters, and a twenty-two-story C. and I. Life Insurance Building.

When Jones changed his original plan and built the Rice on its historic site, he had left the residence tract of the Allen's, Houston's second most historic site, for later improvement.

Here in 1928 he built a thirty-four-story building. He took great care in drawing the plans and prepared four or five designs of the top of the building before he reached a final decision on its architecture. The tall building seemed to symbolize Jones and reflect his character. Many Houstonians felt that here surely would be the one that would be named the Jesse H. Jones Building, but he had no such intention.

It was named the Gulf Building and the oil company for which he had erected a ten-story structure when it came to Houston in 1914 moved in as the chief tenant. The old Gulf Building became the Rusk Building. With his ten-story-skyline-for-Houston dream long since shattered he had made the new Gulf Building the tallest and most outstanding in Texas.*

The lower floors of the Gulf Building housed Jones' National Bank of Commerce. It, too, was of his own designing, seventy-five feet wide and 125 feet long, with a ceiling height of forty-three feet, and without a column. Its walls were of colored marble.

A quarter of a century afterward, when he had seen all of the bank-

* The Gulf Building was the tallest in Texas from 1928 until 1954 when Fred Florence, a friend of Jones, needed a new home for the Republic National Bank in Dallas. Florence erected a forty-story bank and office building.

ing edifices in this country and Europe, he still believed it the most perfect banking quarters ever erected in any country. The cathedral-like room made an ideal setting for the bank's own choir, which gave recitals for a week each Christmas.

In 1956 Jones still owned or controlled the half-hundred buildings he had erected in Houston, except one that he sold in 1951. This maintenance of personal ownership and control was possible because of the extraordinary competence of the people he had gathered into his organization. In discussing this in 1956 he said:

> F. J. Heyne, the operating head of all my investments, has been with me forty-nine years. Ben Talbot, auditor and assistant to Mr. Heyne, has been in the organization forty years. R. P. Doherty, president of the National Bank of Commerce; and A. D. Simpson, vice-chairman of the bank, have been with me forty and thirty-nine years respectively. Many others have grown old with me. Only two or three have retired; and none has ever been discharged, or none ever quit.
>
> Generally, the men in charge for me in Houston, Fort Worth, Dallas, and New York City are the men who started with me when the various enterprises came into being. I have seldom gone outside of the business family to augment my staff, believing that the way to build a better business is to have the men grow with it and select their own personnel, making the enterprises their responsibility more than my own.
>
> The men I have put into the management of the businesses were conservatives. I was the one to take the chances, to make the mistakes. I do not remember ever having had a sharp word with anyone in the employ of any of the enterprises. Because the people in charge had the responsibility, with authority, I seldom offered suggestions; but, if I had any, they were offered to the head of the business. I, of course, did the expanding or starting new businesses.

On the subject of partners and employees, he wrote:

> Believing that few people think alike on all subjects, I decided early as a general policy to have no partners or major stockholders in my various enterprises except, of course, in the banks. I tried to take good care of the people whom I entrusted with our various operations.
>
> It has always been my view that a business is as responsible to the people who operate it as those who operate it are responsible to the business. It has been my experience that, if a business has confidence in those it chooses to operate it, and loyalty to their efforts, that feeling becomes mutual.

On another occasion Jones wrote, "Building a business is of no consequence unless we build men and women along with it."

A. D. Simpson, who went to the National Bank of Commerce as a 120-dollar-a-month bookkeeper in 1918 and went through promotions until he had been its president, then vice-chairman of the board, said,

"I think the thing which impressed me most about Mr. Jones was his tremendous loyalty to the people who work for and with him. That, I think was his dominant trait."

There was overwhelming evidence that, with Jones, loyalty to his employees and associates outweighed everything else. He began to show that interest in his personnel in his early business life. He sought to learn about the families of his employees. If there was distress in a family he quietly tried to find what he could do about it.

To these employees no courtesy was too small to neglect, no service too big or troublesome to perform. Few people knew the time he took to call on the sick in the families of his associates and employees.

A woman who had been in his employ for many years thought his outstanding characteristic was "his ability to bring out the best in people, encouraging in them a sense of personal worth, and inspiring them to their best efforts; his wonderful sense of humor and tolerance of the frailties of people, including his own."

In 1925 in preparation for an insurance and pension system for his employees in all enterprises, Jones brought into his growing empire Milton Backlund, an insurance expert. The system started modestly—too modestly to suit Jones. He wanted to give every one of his employees an insurance policy free of charge. Many of them were beyond the age or for other reasons could not get life insurance. Sometimes these were the persons who needed protection most.

To accomplish the purpose a group policy was written to cover all the employees of the Jones interests, the premiums to be paid by the company for which the employee was working.

It was soon obvious that the expense would not be justified by confining its operation to Jones employees, so Jones organized the Commercial and Industrial Life Insurance Company to write life insurance generally. It was put in a twenty-two-story Jones building, renamed the C. and I. Life Building. The company was so successful that it was soon in a very strong financial condition, with a ratio of surplus to its liabilities many times the average.

In the pension system that he inaugurated, retirement was *optional* at sixty-five.

From the time Jones acquired half-ownership of the Houston *Chronicle*, in 1908, M. E. Foster (who had begun publication of the newspaper seven years earlier) had continued as editor and publisher and directed its policies, except as to politics, where he and Jones would consult.

In 1922 the Ku Klux Klan had a big membership in Houston and was active in politics. The *Chronicle* was strongly anti-Klan. Foster contrived to get reports of secret Klan meetings. These he published under the by-line "Kash Kay Kale," giving the names of some of the members. As a result the lives of both Foster and Jones were threatened.

The race for the United States Senate was hotly contested that year. Senator Charles A. Culberson, whom Jones supported, was too ill to leave Washington and was eliminated from the runoff. The final contest was between James E. Ferguson, who had been governor of Texas (removed from that office after conviction by a court of impeachment), and Earle B. Mayfield, a member of the Texas Railroad Commission.

Mayfield was backed up by the Klan in the nominating runoff; and Foster wanted to support Ferguson in a front-page column which he wrote daily under the name of "MEFO," a coinage from his initials and the second letter of his surname. Jones vetoed support of either Ferguson or Mayfield.

Relations between Jones and Foster remained amicable. Jones now had a strong liking for his newspaper but expected that Foster's lifetime would be given to managing it. Early in 1926, while Mr. and Mrs. Jones were in New York for a long stay in connection with Jones' building activities there, Foster called on Jones to discuss candidates in the state races in Texas that year and other matters with respect to the *Chronicle*.

Sensing that there was a growing resentment at having to discuss *Chronicle* matters with him, Jones asked Foster, "What will you take for your interest in the paper?"

Foster replied, "What will you give me?"

Wanting to be liberal with Foster if I bought him out [Jones related later], since he had created the paper and originally owned most of the stock, and had made a success of it, I thought for a while before answering and finally asked him how much he owed.

He replied, "On real estate and everything, about 200,000 dollars."

I then said to him that I would give him 300,000 dollars in cash, having in mind that this would pay his debts and give him 100,000 dollars spending money. In addition, I would give him a note for 500,000 secured by a mortgage on the Chronicle Building, the note to be payable (interest and principal) at the rate of 35,000 dollars a year for thirty-five years, which I figured was about his expectancy. I would also pay him 20,000 dollars a year as editor of the paper and 6000 dollars a year to continue writing the daily front-page column, "MEFO," on the condition that either of us could cancel the editorship and/or the MEFO-column contracts on six months notice, and that, if I canceled both the column and the editorship, I would give him an additional 6000 dollars a year for life.

I considered the offer substantially more than the *Chronicle* was worth at the time. No sooner had I finished stating my proposition than he said: "I will take it," and the transaction was completed accordingly.

Subsequently Foster retired from the *Chronicle* and became editor of the Houston *Press*.

After his return from world war service in 1919 Jones had so built his organization that there was always a man ready to step into a place when needed. An exception was the Houston *Chronicle*.

C. B. Gillespie, who succeeded Foster, died shortly afterward. No one had been trained for editor. Jones made his attorney, W. O. Huggins, editor. Huggins did not live long; and George W. Cottingham, trained on the newspaper, succeeded him. When Cottingham died, Emmet Walter, another *Chronicle*-trained man, was his successor.

J. H. Butler, vice-president and general manager of the *Chronicle*, a fifty-year man with that newspaper, began by selling it on the streets. Later he was its office boy. G. L. Mims, vice-president and treasurer, was nearing fifty years with the *Chronicle* in 1956.

Jones' policies were well known; and he gave few directions to his editors. Occasionally he would try his hand at an editorial and for a while, in 1945 and 1946, he devoted considerable time to editorial writing on international affairs.

Once, when George W. Cottingham was editor, Jones submitted the outline for an editorial. Cottingham puckishly returned the outline with a memorandum that it was not consistent with the editorial policy of the paper. He heard no more about it.

On another occasion, when in Europe, Jones sent some opinions on European matters to Emmet Walter, his editor, with the memorandum: "You can use this, correct it, distort it any way you like, or chuck it in the wastebasket."

Walter thought it was a fine reportorial job and printed it without use of his editorial pencil.

In assuming full control of the *Chronicle* in 1926, Jones had said in a signed editorial:

> I regard the publication of a newspaper as a distinct public trust, and one not to be treated lightly or abused for selfish purposes or to gratify selfish whims. A great daily newspaper can remain a power for good only so long as it is uninfluenced by unworthy motives, and unbought by the desire for gain.
>
> A newspaper which can be neither bought nor bullied is the greatest asset of a city or state. Naturally, a newspaper makes mistakes in judgment, as it does in type; but, so long as errors are honestly made, they are not serious when general results are considered.

The success or failure of a particular issue is of little consequence compared with the all-important principle of a fearless and honest newspaper. This I intend the *Chronicle* shall always be, a newspaper for all the people, democratic in fact and in principle, standing for the greatest good to the greatest number, championing and defending what it believes to be right, and condemning and opposing what it believes to be wrong.

Such have always been the policies of the *Chronicle* and to such it is now rededicated.

On July 7, 1926, a convalescing Franklin D. Roosevelt wrote to him from Marion, Massachusetts:

"Will you let me tell you of my pleasure at the announcement of your purchase of the Houston *Chronicle*. It is delightful to know that you will direct its policies in the future; and it is a paper which has more than a local hearing."

Jones replied:

"It is really a fine newspaper, and successful on its own. It has had many fights about men and measures, losing some and winning some; but getting stronger all the time."

11

The Illness of Woodrow Wilson

AS Woodrow Wilson approached the end of his historic tour in support of the League of Nations, he fell ill at Pueblo, Colorado, on September 25, 1919. His physician, Rear Admiral Cary T. Grayson, ordered the cancellation of further engagements and an immediate return to Washington. Shortly after his arrival at the White House, the President on October 2 suffered a thrombosis that paralyzed his left side, and from that moment he was a physically broken man. He did not appear at a public occasion again until he rode to the Capitol to witness the inauguration of his successor, Warren G. Harding.

After he returned that day to his house on S Street he was, except for Saturday visits to Keith's Theatre, a secluded invalid. Grayson and Mrs. Wilson were his most intimate confidants and contacts with the world outside.

Some time after the inauguration of Harding, Jesse Jones went to the White House and asked to see the President. George B. Christian, the President's secretary, knowing of the cordial relations of war days, escorted the Texan to Harding's office immediately.

Jones came to the point at once. He expressed his warm admiration for Wilson and described the indispensable role that Admiral Grayson was playing in the care of the sick man.

"As an officer of the navy," he said, "Cary Grayson is subject to change of assignment. I want to ask you that under no circumstances you allow him to be transferred from Washington during Wilson's lifetime."

Harding arose, extended a generous hand, and assured his visitor that "as long as I am President and the need of Grayson by Woodrow Wilson exists, the Admiral will stay on assignment in Washington."

Two years after Jones' meeting with a hearty and apparently robust Harding, Wilson made one of his rare public appearances. He rode down Pennsylvania Avenue in the funeral procession of his successor as President. There was never so moving a bit of proof of what the Presidency demands of the men who hold that office.

President Harding's intention to keep Grayson in Washington was well known, and President Coolidge carried out the promise during the six months that Wilson lived after Harding's death.

In the years that Wilson remained in seclusion in the S Street house, he saw occasionally and often heard from such old friends as Cleveland Dodge, Hugh Wallace, Charles Crane, Norman Davis, Cyrus McCormick, and Jones, all of them now in private life; and from John Sharp Williams, Claude Swanson, Carter Glass, and Joseph T. Robinson, still in the Senate. But the face-to-face meetings with them in which Wilson formerly took such delight were no longer possible.

Jones' devotion to the President had increased with the years. He had stood a few feet from Woodrow Wilson when he delivered his New Freedom inaugural address on the cold, blustery March 4 in 1913. With every piece of that New Freedom domestic program Jones was in hearty agreement, and later had given the same sort of support to Wilson's foreign relations policy.

Not only had Wilson evinced the greatest affection for Jones, but his regard for Jones' ability had constantly grown. This had been shown when the first airplane production program was being arranged. Both the President and Secretary of War Baker thought Jones was the man for the job.

Jones realized the importance of the program, but he had no experience in manufacturing and he thought that his Red Cross assignment was the one in which he could render the greatest service. This opinion was reinforced by Harry Davison and Cleveland Dodge. Dodge went to the White House to tell the President that he and Davison were in agreement that Jones' organizing ability could ill be spared by the Red Cross.

Later, when Russia fell out of the war, President Wilson considered sending a delegation to Russia in an effort to get them back. He wanted Jones to head the delegation. This assignment Jones would not have been able to decline; but subsequent developments convinced Wilson of the hopelessness of success and he abandoned the idea. Some of the details of this episode appear in a letter written some years later by Dr. Stockton Axson:

> In the summer of 1918, as the Kerensky government struggled to keep in power against the Bolshevik bid for control, President Wilson said to me at the White House: "I am going to send a Commission to Russia in an effort to bring that country back into association with the Allies and put her soldiers back on the eastern front against the Central Powers; and I am going to make Jesse Jones head of the Commission."

Axson told Wilson he thought that, if anyone could succeed on such a mission, the practical-minded Jones would have a better chance than a diplomat or a military man.

"It seemed as if Mr. Jones was about to receive orders from the President to lead a perilous adventure," Dr. Axson wrote.

In Paris after Davison and Jones had put the organization of the League of Red Cross Societies under way, President Wilson employed Jones on a highly confidential assignment in connection with the Peace Conference.

Jones saw Wilson for the last time as President at the Palace of Prince Murat, which had been assigned to the President of the United States during the Peace Conference. Jones was leaving for the United States and Wilson expected to go home within a few days. Jones knew the conditions under which Wilson had worked, believed that the treaty then in its final draft was a good one and that only Wilson, with the towering strength he then had in Europe, could have obtained it.

Wilson had been weakened by a brief but severe illness in Paris. This gave some apprehension to Jones when Wilson told him of his intention to stump the country in support of the League of Nations. So while Jones realized the moving effect on opposition Senators by such an appeal to the people he felt the risk to the President's health was very great. This opinion he expressed somewhat indirectly in a letter he addressed to the President after he returned to Houston.

> In making your speaking trip through the country [he wrote], I believe you should go as far as your strength will permit, and let as many people as

At left: Jones, as Director General of Military Relief, American Red Cross in World War I. *Below:* Jones (at far left) marching with President Wilson (center) at the head of 100,000 Red Cross workers in historic New York parade, May 18, 1918.

Above: Royal A. Ferris, Dallas banker, gave Jones his financial start and remained his lifelong friend. *Below:* Woodrow Wilson influenced Jones' political philosophy and encouraged his interest in public service.

Above: The Red Cross War Council of 1918. *Left to right:* Cornelius N. Bliss, George Case, Elliott Wadsworth, Henry P. Davison (chairman), George Scott, and Jones. *Below:* Jones, in four months' time, built this Convention Hall (seating 25,000) to house the 1928 Democratic National Convention, held in Houston.

Jones, at the time of the Democratic National Convention at Houston, was placed in nomination for President of the United States *(Cecil Thomson Studios photo)*.

Mr. and Mrs. Jesse H. Jones in 1930.

Above: Jones, with his close friend Charles M. Schwab, chairman of the American Iron and Steel Institute.
Below: Mr. and Mrs. Jones with Mr. and Mrs. Harvey Firestone in Miami, Florida.

This portrait of Jones was commissioned by the Texas Legislature, and now hangs in the State Capitol in Austin.

Mrs. Jesse H. Jones (*Harris & Ewing*).

possible see you, and talk to as many people as possible. I believe that this trip will do a great deal to settle the unrest in the country; but as much as I believe that, I hope you will not undertake such a program as to overtax yourself. The world is going to need you as much during the next few years as in those just passed.

Jones' belief in Wilson's personal appeal through the West was considerably influenced by his conversations with Charles G. Dawes, the Chicago banker, who was a close friend of Henry P. Davison. Dawes had been a brigadier general on the staff of General Pershing and had served as Purchasing Agent for the AEF. At the time of his talks with Jones, Dawes was in Europe serving as a member of a liquidation commission to dispose of surplus war supplies. Serving with Dawes was Judge Edwin B. Parker of Houston, a close friend of Jones. Dawes, like Jones, favored our participation in a League of Nations.

"This peace conference," Dawes had written from Europe, "has probably done the very best it was possible to do in the environment in which it acted."

In an interview paralleling this statement Dawes said:

"I look forward to an ultimate rally of American public opinion behind it, as embodying the hopes of a better future for ourselves and the world."

Wilson, writing from the White House to Jones a week after his return from Europe, made no reference to the suggestion of warning that he should not overtax himself. He thanked Jones warmly, complimented him for his public service, and expressed the hope that he might see him soon.

It was eighteen months later, however, before they met again, and a year before their correspondence was resumed. Those were months of trial and tragedy for the President.

Meanwhile the Democratic party gathered itself for what most everyone regarded as a hopeless effort to win another Presidential election. Jones supported through his newspaper and contributed financially to the Cox-Roosevelt campaign.

After the landslide election of Harding, Jones began to discuss with a few close friends the idea of rehabilitating the defeated party in support of the Wilson policies. On December 4, 1920, he wrote to Wilson:

I do not believe that the overwhelming Republican vote meant in any sense a repudiation of the League of Nations. I am firmly of the opinion that the people of this country want the League of Nations; but the thing dearest to the great majority of the people is their pocketbook, and they thought the Republicans would, in some way, manage to reduce taxes, and possibly to bring about a return of the prosperity to which all had become accustomed and liked. . . . What I hope most is that you are not permitting this apparent change in sentiment to depress you. . . . Your life has been a fight for democracy and my greatest desire and ambition has been to be of some slight service to you; I shall be proud of the privilege to respond to any suggestion or call from you in the years to come.

Wilson's reply was a reaffirmation of his belief in his cause and his appreciation of the loyalty of Jones.

Jones the builder and organizer now turned to aid in the reorganization of the badly shattered Democratic party, advanced practical ideas and much-needed money. He felt that the off-year election was not too soon for beginning that job. The elections were surprisingly favorable to the Democrats. The Republican majority in the House was cut from 170 to 20. Seven new Democratic senators, replacing Republicans, brought the Senate majority down to ten. A Democratic senator was elected in Michigan for the first time in seventy years.

The Democrats also won in seventeen of the twenty-nine gubernatorial contests. Governor Alfred E. Smith, who went down in the 1920 landslide, rewon the New York governorship by 400,000. Even in Massachusetts, Wilson's old enemy, Henry Cabot Lodge, barely scraped by in a race against a political unknown.

Jones, engaged for the moment in business in New York, wrote to Wilson after the election a letter of cheer and congratulation, followed with a telegram on Armistice Day. Wilson replied with a friendly, cheerful note.

The next year, in May, citizens of Houston gave a testimonial dinner to Jones, and Wilson sent a congratulatory message. In his acknowledgment to this Jones expressed the hope that he might see the former President some time during the following July or August, when he and Mrs. Jones planned to be in Washington.

Wilson replied, saying that he and Mrs. Wilson would be most happy to see them.

In July when Jones called on Wilson at the S Street home he found his fighting spirit unchanged, but his physical condition was a great shock to his visitor. Wilson's vitality was perceptibly ebbing, and his eyesight had failed so much that he was able only to scan illustrated magazines. He depended upon Mrs. Wilson to read to him.

He greeted Jones in his bedroom, which he also used as a sitting room, in bathrobe and slippers. When he rose to greet Jones he leaned heavily on a cane. In addition to the paralysis he now had to contend with a return of neuritis in a very painful form.

Another concern entered the practical mind of Jones. Wilson, in common with many other Presidents, had left the White House with little means of support, and the United States had made no provision to meet this need. After he left the Wilson home he learned from Grayson that the former President's financial situation was becoming precarious. The house and its furnishings had taken almost all of the combined resources of Mr. and Mrs. Wilson. The funds necessary to maintain the house and essential employees had become a great burden.

Before this visit to Washington, Jones had hoped that Wilson might be able to do some writing and perhaps make a speech or two before the next election. Wilson told him that he had done only a short article for the *Atlantic Monthly* which was to appear in August. For this he received only the nominal sum of 300 dollars, although had he so chosen he might have sold it for much more to a less distinguished magazine.

The law partnership that Wilson had formed with his old friend and Secretary of State, Bainbridge Colby, yielded him nothing. The old Wilson conscience barred the acceptance of most of the cases offered the firm.

From Washington, Jones went to New York and called on Cleveland Dodge, who had been Wilson's classmate at Princeton and his lifelong friend. He told Dodge of his great concern about the state of Wilson's health and finances and that he felt it imperative that some way should be found by which friends might offer some material assistance. This both men knew would be no easy task, considering the proud and scrupulous nature with which they would have to deal.

They agreed to give serious thought to ways and means. Later both were moved profoundly by the reports of the pathetic picture of Wilson at the funeral of President Harding on August 8. Soon after, Dodge and Jones agreed upon the gift that they would offer to Wilson. It would have to be modest, they realized, or Wilson would refuse to accept it. They made many drafts of the letter that would carry the offer. Finally, on October 2, 1923, Jones wrote as follows to the former President:

My Dear Friend:

I have been visiting some this summer at his office with Mr. Cleveland H. Dodge and, both being friends of yours (his friendship of much longer standing but, I hope, no more sincere than mine), have talked a great deal about the great and useful life you have lived, and how little, in comparison, the rest of us contributed to the world welfare.

You have devoted your entire life unstintedly and unselfishly to education and statesmanship and to politics, uninfluenced by or unafraid of the power of gold or greed. No man has done as much. You have been fighting a great battle, and have won a victory of which the world will be increasingly conscious.

Because of these things, and the innumerable reasons which we might, with time, set down, and because we want to, we have taken the liberty of forming a very close personal trust as a slight reward and as a slight token of our love and admiration of you. It is not our intention or desire that there be any publicity or public record regarding it; and, unless advised to the contrary, payments will be sent to you at your Washington address quarterly, by Mr. Dodge. It is his opinion, however, that Mr. Cyrus McCormick, also a lifelong friend of yours, will want the privilege of joining; and he expects to speak to him about it when the occasion arises.

I enclose a letter formally setting out our purposes.

With assurances of my great esteem.

Very sincerely yours,
Jesse H. Jones.

Enclosed was the letter, only nine lines long, which Dodge and Jones had drafted and redrafted:

Honorable Woodrow Wilson
Washington, D.C.
Dear Friend:

We have created a trust which will provide an income to you, throughout the remainder of your life, of $10,000 a year; and, though we are prompted by our love and admiration of you, the trust is in fact intended as a slight material reward for your great service to the world. While being cognizant that, in taking this privilege of friendship, we are honoring ourselves, we are nevertheless unwilling that you deny it to us, because it is indeed a very great privilege and pleasure.

Yours sincerely,
Cleveland H. Dodge
Jesse H. Jones.

On October 4, 1923, the former President replied:

My Dear Friend:

I must admit that I am quite overwhelmed by the wonderful kindness and generosity of which the letter signed by you and Dodge informs me. I cannot for a moment consider myself worthy of such friendship or of such benefits. I can only hope that they will inspire me for the services which lie ahead of us in the redemption of the country from the ignoble position into which it has been drawn by ignorant and unprincipled partisans.

I will not attempt to express my gratitude to you and those with whom you are associated in an ideal act of confidence and friendship. I know of no words which would be adequate; but let me say at least that I am deeply proud that such men should think me worthy of such benefits.

Mrs. Wilson joins me in messages of warm friendship to Mrs. Jones and you; and I beg to subscribe myself.

Affectionately,
Woodrow Wilson

Wilson began to show distinct improvement by later October, 1923. He made his first radio speech on November 10. His subject was "The Significance of Armistice Day."

On Armistice Day morning telegrams poured in, congratulating him; and the executives of radio sent him word that he had addressed the largest audience ever to hear an address over the nation's new medium. Dozens of baskets of flowers arrived at the S Street home.

On Armistice Day a great crowd had gathered in S Street. Senator Carter Glass of Virginia addressed them. Then the former President, in a silk hat and leaning heavily on his cane, was assisted to the door of the Wilson home by the faithful servant, Isaac Scott, and made a short, characteristically Wilson, fighting speech.

On January 4, 1924, Wilson wrote to Jones:

My Dear Friend:

The check which I have just received from Cleve Dodge again makes me vividly conscious of the extraordinary privilege I enjoy in having such friends as you and he and the others of the little group who have so generously and so thoughtfully relieved Mrs. Wilson and me of the pecuniary anxieties. He also writes me that you have joined with the others in the gift of the beautiful car which I received on my birthday.

There are no adequate words in which I can express my feeling in this matter. I can only trust that, as the years go by, I may have many opportunities of making you conscious of my deep affection, trust and gratitude.

Mrs. Wilson joins with me in the hope that Mrs. Jones and you may find the New Year a time of peculiar happiness and contentment.

Please do not fail to let me have a glimpse of you whenever it is possible for you to come this way.

With most affectionate regard.

Gratefully yours,
Woodrow Wilson

On January 9 Jones replied:

My Dear Friend:

Permit me to acknowledge your letter of the 4th instant, and to assure you that I have never done anything which gives me the enjoyment and satisfaction I get and shall always have from my participation in the "Woodrow Wilson Personal Trust." It is a rare privilege you have given me and the other three gentlemen with whom I have honor to be associated in this matter; and I am perfectly sure that neither of us will ever again have an opportunity to do a thing which will afford us as much pleasure, or which we will take as much pride in doing.

In dedicating your life to teaching and political leadership, without thought of your own welfare, you have rendered a service to mankind impossible to measure; and I am proud beyond expression of having so large a share of your friendship. I value the distinction, and wish you many years of health, happiness, and usefulness. Mrs. Jones joins in these felicitations, which extend to and include Mrs. Wilson.

Your friend,
Jesse H. Jones.

On December 28 these friends had observed Wilson's birthday by the gift of a new automobile to replace the old White House car that the Wilsons had purchased when he left office. But his birthday drive in this car was destined to be his last. The final days of December and most of January were cold and raw. On January 29 Wilson suffered a relapse and it was evident to Grayson that the end was near. For four days the patient was in a coma and on Sunday morning, February 3, the people gathered before the S Street house heard the news that the former President was dead.

Jones and Mrs. Jones attended the funeral, the former as a pallbearer. He did not know until six months later that one of the last letters Wilson had dictated was to Jones and the others who had participated in the trust fund. Mrs. Wilson wrote on June 21:

My dear Mr. Jones:

I am enclosing to you one of the last things Woodrow dictated; and, as you see, his signature shows how weak and unsteady he was. It was dictated two weeks to the day before his death, but signed the following day.

He wanted a duplicate of this sent to Mr. Dodge, Mr. McCormick, and Mr. Thomas D. Jones. I know it will be a very precious message to you; and may I add my own gratitude for what you did for him, and for continuance of the "special fund" to complete the year ending July, 1924.

I wrote to Mr. Dodge that I feel that, after the last check which he sent to me on April 1, the new state of things should begin, when I must order my life on simpler lines. But he writes me that he had already adjusted things to cover the first year, and he wishes it to obtain.

I must repeat that through Woodrow's own message of January 20 runs my own sense of deep gratitude, and the assurance, which comforts me, of your unchanging friendship.

Edith Bolling Wilson

The letter, with the unsteady signature of Woodrow Wilson read:

To Cleveland H. Dodge, Jesse H. Jones, Thomas D. Jones, and Cyrus H. McCormick:

To this group of uncomparable friends, I owe a debt of inexpressible gratitude for having lifted Mrs. Wilson and me out of the mists of pecuniary anxiety, and placed us on the firm ground of ease and confidence. More than that, they have blessed me with the knowledge that I have won the affection and loyalty of the most ideal body of friends which ever gave a man reason to believe himself worthwhile. I can offer them in return only deep affection, but I do offer that by the heart full. They have afforded me the most powerful reasons for continuing to try to be what they, in their generosity, believed me to be.

Cyrus H. McCormick and Thomas D. Jones, both of Chicago, who had joined with Cleveland Dodge and Jesse Jones in the trust, were both, like Dodge, in Wilson's class which graduated at Princeton in 1879, when Jones was a five-year-old boy on a Tennessee farm.

12

A Democrat Serves His Party

JESSE JONES and John Nance Garner were delegates from Texas to the Democratic National Convention which met in Madison Square Garden in New York City on June 24, 1924. Both were ardent Wilsonites anxious to see Wilson principles again ascendant in government. Both were convinced that the scandals that had broken out in the Harding regime gave the Democratic nominee a real chance of election. Garner was by this time regarded as a foremost party leader because of his expert management of the small minority in the House in fiscal legislation after the Harding victory. He had made a notable fight against Treasury Secretary Mellon's tax policies and the Fordney-McCumber Tariff Bill.

The Texas delegation had been instructed to support William Gibbs McAdoo, who was regarded as the leading candidate for the nomination at the time. Governor Alfred E. Smith, however, was formidable opposition, and because of his tremendous victory in New York in 1922 he had attracted great national attention. Garner and Jones both regarded the possibility of McAdoo's or Smith's attainment of the two-thirds majority, necessary at that time, with serious doubt.

These doubts were soon confirmed, for on the first ballot McAdoo received only 431 votes, which was 301 short. Smith had 241. Senator Oscar W. Underwood of Alabama, Governor Albert C. Ritchie of Maryland, and fifteen other favorite sons shared the remaining 424 votes.

Jones and others sensed the bitter and inflexible antagonism between the Smith and McAdoo forces and anticipated a deadlock. After surveying the scene, they decided that John W. Davis of West Virginia, whom Jones had known well during war days in Washington, offered the best chance of bringing the warring factions together on a compromise candidate. Davis had been Solicitor General of the United States and later Ambassador to the Court of St. James. Jones had been greatly attracted by the brilliant capacity of Davis as a lawyer, and their wartime acquaintance developed into a warm friendship. At the beginning Davis had little strength as a candidate, with only thirty-one votes, sixteen of them from his own state. Jones' exploration of the situation convinced him that neither the McAdoo nor the Smith forces were in any mood to discuss a compromise.

On the seventh day of the seventeen-day convention, Garner rose from his seat as the ninth ballot was tabulated and said to Jones, "Hell's bells! This convention won't nominate a candidate in a hundred ballots. It has already signed the party's death warrant for November. I'm going home."

Jones, equally pessimistic, replied, "I'm going farther than that. I'm going to Europe."

Garner went to the McAlpin Hotel, packed his suitcase, and returned to Uvalde. His offhand remark, which was merely an expression of the barren outlook, proved to be accurate. It required 103 ballots to choose a candidate and by that time the candidate, John W. Davis, labored under the handicap of a party hopelessly divided.

Jones remained until the convention adjourned, and two days later he and Mrs. Jones sent their baggage to the *Leviathan*, scheduled to sail for Europe. Before they left the hotel, however, Jones received a telephone call from Clem Shaver, whom Davis had selected as National Chairman. Shaver asked Jones to become his director of finance and raise the money for the campaign.

Jones explained that he was ready to sail, but Davis, who came to the telephone, would not take a refusal.

"I'm not a politician, and I know nothing about financing a campaign," said Jones.

"Well," Davis answered, "I am running for President, and I know nothing about that either. Suppose you cancel your trip and learn how to finance a campaign while I learn how to run for President. I am sure you can rely on B. M. Baruch for a contribution of at least 200,000 dollars to get started, and probably as much from Tom Chadbourne."

Jones tried to prevail upon his friend, W. L. Clayton, the cotton merchant, to accept the responsibility for financing the campaign. He took Clayton to see Davis at his Locust Valley home. Clayton, however, joined with Davis in insisting that Jones take the post.

"I think the bleakness of the outlook determined Jesse to take it," Davis said. "He never could turn down a tough job where he considered his country's or his party's interest involved. We parted with the complete understanding that we would both do our best with the jobs at hand."

Jones sent to the *Leviathan* for the luggage. Some of the bags and trunks were already aboard and could not be located; so they made the trip to Europe. Jones spent the next few days organizing his offices in the old Murray Hill Hotel and getting outfitted with enough clothes to do him until the liner returned.

A few days later he moved to larger headquarters in the Belmont Hotel, and undertook the money-raising for a campaign that was doomed from the first by the bitter fight in the convention, and doubly doomed by the third-party La Follette-Wheeler ticket.

"I soon found that both Davis and I were right about our estimates of our capacities in the roles in which we found ourselves," Jones wrote with wry humor in after years. But, while both knew the odds against them, neither admitted it. Jones wrote: "Davis made an impressive campaign, as though he fully expected to win. There were no better public speakers than John W. Davis, and his speeches were models of oratory and argument."

The party leaders who came to Jones' sixteenth-story office in the Belmont were mostly in the pits of pessimism. The nomination of Charles W. Bryan as Davis' Vice-Presidential running mate was highly unpopular in the East. The defection of Democratic Senator Burton K. Wheeler, to be La Follette's ticket mate, hurt in the West.

Franklin D. Roosevelt, who sat in a wheelchair behind a desk a few doors down the hall from Jones, seemed optimistic at first; but he had not sufficiently recovered from his long illness for any sustained effort, and soon appeared less and less at headquarters.

Smith had offered his full support; but McAdoo, sulking, sailed with

Mrs. McAdoo for Europe. Then Baruch, whom Davis had assured Jones would be a liberal contributor, also sailed for Europe.

Clem Shaver, of West Virginia, who promoted the Davis preconvention efforts and, as chairman of the Democratic National Committee, was manager of the Democratic Presidential campaign, was not highly rated by men of substantial means. But Jones thought Shaver had undoubted political talents that would have shown more brightly in a less hopeless campaign.

Such old party warhorses as former Vice-President Thomas Riley Marshall, Tom Taggart of Indiana, Thomas J. Spellacy of Connecticut, George White of Ohio, Key Pittman of Nevada, and Dan Roper of South Carolina, took desks in headquarters, for such aid as they could render.

There was help, too, from Tom Chadbourne; from Alton B. Parker, the 1904 Presidential candidate; Bainbridge Colby; Norman Davis; Lindley M. Garrison; George Gordon Battle; James A. O'Gorman; John Godfrey Saxe; Martin Vogel; Judge Samuel Seabury; Samuel Untermyer; and Colonel Joseph M. Hartfield. But Davis' candidacy had difficulty in getting off the ground.

McAdoo returned from Europe in early autumn. Jones had been led to believe that he would now heartily support Davis. A press conference was arranged at the Vanderbilt Hotel. The grudging statement by McAdoo was of no help whatever.

Baruch also returned from Europe and invited Jones to luncheon at Baruch's home. There were, in all, a dozen persons at the table.

> Baruch was very critical of Davis' campaign and, in fact, everything done by the committee [a memorandum written by Jones said]. Finally becoming tired of the criticism, I excused myself before the luncheon was over, on the pretense that I had an engagement.
>
> Later, Baruch sent for Clem Shaver, Chairman of the Democratic National Committee. Shaver told me of the invitation, and asked for suggestions. I said to Shaver: "Don't ask him for money." Shaver came back with a check for $12,500. A little later, Baruch sent for Shaver again, and again I counseled him not to ask for money. He came back with another check for $12,500, which was the limit of Baruch's contribution.

On October 1 Jones wrote a letter to Baruch, reminding him of the desperate need of funds for the Davis campaign and severely criticized Baruch's failure to contribute more liberally. Baruch replied that he was amazed and hurt at Jones' letter. The exchange of letters brought to an end the friendship that had existed between the two men. It was never more than partially restored.

Jones, hiding his inner apprehensions under an outward appearance of complete confidence in his party's fortunes, went about the job of collecting such funds as he could:

"I raised money with difficulty; for there was a general feeling that we were in a losing fight, that the Democratic party had assured the election of Calvin Coolidge by its bad convention behavior."

Mostly, the contributors had been the old faithful of the Wilson Administration, such as Chadbourne and Thomas Fortune Ryan. Jones and Ryan, with 50,000 dollars each, had been the biggest donors. James W. Gerard, the National Committee's Treasurer, abandoned all hope in October and made no effort to aid in gathering funds, except to make a substantial contribution of his own.

Two weeks before the election Jones asked the money-spenders of the campaign for an estimate of what each would need to pay his bills, and got commitments from friends of the party sufficient to cover the amount. But the division heads had not given him an accurate accounting and the committee wound up 300,000 dollars in debt. Jones made the rounds again and got commitments sufficient to cover the deficit.

Jones, however, decided against the immediate collection of the commitments. He believed it unfair to ask a few faithful party friends to pay the deficit. Moreover, he believed that both the McAdoo and the Smith factions would attempt to get control of the National Committee, and for either to do so at this stage would not benefit the party. If the committee was deeply in debt, he reasoned, neither side would try to gain control. Jones, with the consent of the committee, borrowed 300,000 dollars from the New York Trust Company on very agreeable terms.

Election nights in the national headquarters of defeated parties are always somber occasions. That of 1924 was merely the middle one of three doleful ones for the Democrats in the 1920's. Perhaps a smile or two could have been forced, had the party faithful gathered for the obsequies been able to read a description written by Paul L. Wakefield, a young newspaperman with a gift for unusual words, who had been one of Jones' executive assistants.

> The somber-faced politicos [wrote Wakefield], on that fateful 1924 election night, walked softly on the plush red carpeting of the old Belmont Hotel, in an atmosphere of dephlogistication which would have wilted a Texas cactus.

The gathering place was Jones' office. Franklin D. Roosevelt was the first arrival. At eleven o'clock, Roosevelt said, "On the basis of returns we have already received, I believe the party is defeated. But there are men in this room tonight who will live to see the Democratic party in power again."

Roosevelt was wheeled from the room. Jones and a few others still listened to the radio returns. Davis got the electoral vote of only the eleven Confederate states plus Oklahoma, a total of 136; LaFollette the thirteen of Wisconsin; and Coolidge the 382 of the other thirty-five states. In popular votes Coolidge had 15,725,016, to Davis' 8,385,586.

Jones' method of handling the committee finances between 1924 and 1928 met with the wholehearted approval of the members of the National Committee. However, in the early summer of 1926, he received a telegram from the New York *World*, of which Herbert Bayard Swope was editor, asking for information about the committee's finances and the pledges held by Jones. Swope was in the Smith faction and a close friend of Baruch. It was evident to Jones that the *World's* inquiry was the forerunner of another Smith try for the Presidency. Although Jones thought that Smith would probably be the 1928 nominee, he felt that to give the information to the *World* at that time would be helpful to a faction and not to the party, and declined to furnish it.

Shortly after the *World* telegram, Franklin D. Roosevelt wrote to Jones from Marion, Massachusetts, under the date of July 7, 1926.*

> I heard in a roundabout way the other day that you had given out some sort of statement about Democratic finances, in which you took me to task for something. What it was I do not know, as I have seen nothing printed in the New York papers. Whatever it was you said, I feel certain that you will appreciate that I never criticized you personally; nor have I ever given out any statement. Nor would I do so; for I am utterly opposed to any public divisions among individual Democrats at a time like this, when people of the same political faith should work together. I have never, even in private conversations with Democrats, gone beyond what I have told you myself; i.e., I have been opposed, in principle, to the collection of Democratic funds, either for campaign purposes or to pay off deficits, from contributions from a mere handful of very rich or moderately rich gentlemen, and, as you know, I think other means should at least be tried. The other means may not succeed; but I believe that, in principle, they are more sound.
>
> In spite of all this, I think you are to be congratulated most heartily, as I am told you have actually succeeded in raising the full amount of the debt of the National Committee so that, from now on, we can start with a clean sheet.

Jones replied to Roosevelt's letter on July 14, 1926:

* Letter in Jones' file.

As for my statement appearing in the *New York World* . . . I am certainly not finding any fault whatever with you, my good friend. As a matter of fact, I regard you as one of the best assets of our party. I unreservedly say this whenever I am discussing our party affairs . . . and it is my sincere wish, and has been right along, that your health would so improve that you could take a more active part in our national politics.

I can see no possible harm to come from patriotic Democrats giving substantial sums to pay for stale water long since gone over the dam, and I cannot see any advantage to come from a widespread campaign to pay the deficit of 1924. People are usually willing to give money for a live issue; but few are willing to contribute where there is no hope of reward, or possibility of the enjoyment of success to the enterprise contributed to.

We should all go to the next convention prepared to nominate the strongest man available at that time; and I think you know that I have no narrow views in that respect.

Jones' reply apparently satisfied Roosevelt. There was no public and little private discussion of the party debt and two years later Jones called for payment of the pledges given him and received money enough to discharge all the party's financial obligations.

By 1925 the matter of helping young men and women to get an education had become one of Jones' most absorbing interests. When he made the first contribution to John Brown University he was a bachelor. Now he was married and Mary Jones was as enthusiastic about the education of young men and young women as was her husband.

Although he had taken care that no fuss was made of it, his large contributions to that purpose were well known. In 1925 he was given the first of more than a dozen honorary degrees he was later to receive from colleges and universities all over the United States and one in Canada.

This honorary Doctor of Laws that came to him from Southwestern University, the pioneer Methodist school at Georgetown, Texas, was because "of your distinguished service to the nation and the State of Texas in the world of business and politics, and because of your great interest in humanity."

Up to now Jones' speaking to groups or audiences had been impromptu remarks before business or civic gatherings in Houston. The longest of these had kept him on his feet five minutes at a dinner honoring him in Houston in 1923.

The Georgetown occasion was noteworthy in that the commencement address he prepared and delivered there was Jones' first formal public address. In it he gave the students what had been one of the cardinal principles of his life.

> Positiveness is necessary to succeed [he said]. You will never succeed by "don'ts and can'ts." It is sometimes taught that one of the most essential elements of success is the ability to say "No." But I want to tell you from the fullness of my practical experience, of far greater importance is the ability to say "Yes" and back it up. The "No" sayer and the "Don't" sayer never get very far. It takes vision, faith and courage, to say "Yes." By saying "No," you forego the possibility of gain, whatever the proposition may be. You may save yourself trouble and losses, but there can be no profit if you say "No."
>
> The fellow who is able to analyze everything and tell you why it should not be done never gets any real practice in doing. It is the affirmative one, the positive man and the one who tries again and again after each failure, who gets practice enough to succeed. It is necessary to say and act "Yes" more times than you say "No," and at the right times. I would not say there is no place in our life and language for "Don't," but I do say the word "can't" should be abolished. Too many timid people stumble over it. There is a way to everything worth doing, if we can find it.

The address attracted rather wide attention, much to Jones' surprise. Chief Justice William Howard Taft, who had lived with Jones at his Washington residence part of a war summer, wrote to him, "You laid down a doctrine of life which will do these youngsters good."

13

A Convention Comes to Houston

IN 1926, the year when Jones came into full possession of the Houston *Chronicle* and was at his busiest period of building, his home state called upon him for another public service.

In the early 1920's leading citizens of the state began to discuss some sort of a fitting celebration of the one hundredth anniversary of hard-won independence from Mexico, which would come in 1936. A centennial governing board of ten members was designated. For two years the board had meetings and discussed plans but made little progress.

Finally in 1926, with the Centennial still ten years away, Jones was induced to assume the post of Director General. This placed upon him the responsibility of planning and promoting the celebration.

His suggestions to the committee involved a suitable recognition not only of the historic events that marked the progress of the state to independence status as a nation and to membership in the Federal Union but of the part played in a century of Texas history by the various natural divisions. For due to its vast size and diversity it was recognized at the time it was annexed that it might ultimately be divided into five states.

There would have to be a central exposition where could be exhibits and historical presentations showing the results of 100 years of progress, and only Dallas which had fine permanent buildings used for its annual state fair, could be considered for that. Fort Worth, too, would have to have its part in the celebration.

It would be to Dallas and Fort Worth that the crowds would come during the celebration year. But after the celebration was over in these two cities he wanted every section of the state, perhaps every one of the 254 counties, to have a monument, memorial, or marker, Jones told the committee.

The Alamo, where Travis, Bowie, Bonham, and Crockett and their men had died, stood restored and sturdy and needed nothing more than a memorial shaft on its plaza. A suitable memorial was needed at Goliad where after their surrender Colonel J. W. Fannin and his 300 men were massacred at the order of the Mexican commander and president, Santa Anna.

Jones especially stressed the proper marking of San Jacinto battlefield, twenty miles from Houston. San Jacinto, he told the committee, had been responsible, wholly or in part, for ten states and one third of the area of the United States and the expansion of the nation westward to the Pacific. "There could be no United States, as we know it without San Jacinto," said Jones.

In the busy years that followed, Jones made speeches in various Texas cities and great interest was generated throughout the state. The plan he had outlined to the committee was carried out in detail. While Jones was steadily working on the many aspects of the event he contrived a quite unexpected coup for the state.

On January 12, 1928, the Democratic National Committee assembled in Washington to select the city in which that year's national convention would be held. Jones as finance director of the committee attended. Clem Shaver, still chairman, appointed Arthur G. Mullen of Nebraska, Bruce Kremer of Montana, and Jones as a subcommittee to receive and analyze the money offers and available facilities of the competing cities. They met in the parlor of Jones' suite in the Mayflower Hotel.

Jones was especially interested in the offers of money because he had resolutely set out to clear the party of debt before the next campaign. He realized that if the committee could get a sufficiently large contribution from the city selected that this money might, along with the pledges he held, wipe out the debt and provide something to start the next campaign. A few weeks prior to the meeting Jones solicited offers from a number of cities, including Cleveland, Detroit, Chicago, and San Francisco. He had not thought the committee would consider going so far south as Houston in the hot summer months and had not given his home town an opportunity to consider making a bid. Cleveland offered 100,000 dollars; Detroit, 125,000 dollars; and Chicago, 130,000 dollars.

Isadore B. Dockweiler, National Committeeman from California, had been charged with the responsibility of getting the convention for San Francisco. He was prepared to bid high for it. He made a private agreement with Shaver to make his bid after all the others.

As Jones with the other two members listened to the various bids before the three-man subcommittee, his loyalty to Houston asserted itself. To get the convention would be a distinct civic honor for it. Even if he failed the offer would get his home city some notice. So he asked his two fellow subcommittee members to excuse him and he went into his bedroom. There he dictated a letter to his secretary, Bill Costello. The letter, addressed to the National Committee, was a specific bid for the convention to be held in Houston. He pinned to this letter his personal check for 200,000 dollars and rejoined Mullen and Kremer. They were amused at Jones' bid and invited Dockweiler, the last and highest bidder, to present his offer.

Dockweiler on behalf of San Francisco presented certified checks to the subcommittee amounting to 250,000 dollars.

After the Mullen-Jones-Kremer subcommittee reported to the full committee, meeting downstairs in the Mayflower, representatives of the various cities made their pleas. This is always an occasion for florid oratory. Climate, hotel space, amusements, and the great good heart of a city are presented in exaggerated terms. But usually the matter is determined according to the private calculations of the national committee members present and the size of the check offered with the bid.

Jones knew that Dockweiler's speech would be in fulsome tradition of such an occasion and also that he had the highest bid. Jones, with the largest offer except Dockweiler's, was next-to-the-last speaker.

As Jones arose to present the invitation of his beloved Houston, the entire membership of the National Committee rose to its feet cheering. This applause expressed their admiration for the valiant, devoted services of Jones to the party in years past. No one had gone down in his pocket so often to meet the impoverished party's necessities. He had for the last four years carried the burden of the committee's finances. The idea of choosing Houston as the convention city, however, was new to them.

Jones clearly realized now what a national convention would mean for Houston. It would draw thousands of visitors. Moreover the proceedings of the two conventions of the major parties in 1924 had been the first that were carried by radio, and now, four years later, the growth of that medium would enable many millions to follow the proceedings and, with the commentary, to hear plenty about the city in which it was being held. Millions would also read it in newspapers and see it in the news films. Jones concluded that Houston would be repaid many times over for what it would spend as a host.

Dockweiler was soon convinced that the Houston threat might be a serious one and tossed in what he believed to be his winning card.

"How many people did the gentleman from Texas say his convention hall would seat?" he asked.

This gave Jones the chance he needed to make a breath-taking addition to his bid.

"I said 5000," he replied, "but if you give us the convention we will build one to seat 25,000."

After Jones' appeal half a dozen committee members left the meeting and followed Jones into an adjoining room.

Thomas J. Spellacy, a popular Connecticut leader, asked Jones, "Do you really want this convention?"

Jones assured him that he did.

"Then I am going to vote for Houston," replied Spellacy.

"So will I," said Frank Hague of New Jersey.

Spellacy and Hague were Smith men and this broke the ranks. It had been expected the Smith forces would be solidly for San Francisco.

On the first ballot Houston received thirty votes, San Francisco twenty-five, with the others scattered. On the fifth ballot Houston won with fifty-four votes to San Francisco's forty-eight.

Houston was completely taken by surprise when the news arrived there that Jesse Jones had made a winning bid for the convention. Telephone calls to Jones, including one from Mayor Oscar Holcombe, asked for the extent of the city's obligations. Jones told the mayor:

"Two hundred thousand dollars in money and an auditorium to seat 25,000 people."

By the time Jones' train reached Texas on February 1, the state had become aware of the honor that had come to Houston, and there were friendly greetings for Jones at every stop. At Houston a temporary platform was erected at the railway station and a crowd of 50,000 assembled to greet him. A happy parade through the streets of the city followed, with Jones the hero of the occasion.

A few days later 600 persons gathered in a banquet hall for one of the testimonial dinners that Houston had given Jones over the years. Dr. Stockton Axson, brother-in-law of Woodrow Wilson, sounded the keynote:

> I say tonight that Jesse H. Jones had passed all local boundaries; he is now a great national figure. I know that his principles are those of Woodrow Wilson; and, were Wilson alive today, I believe I am safe in saying that he would favor Mr. Jones, of all men, to be President of the United States.

Dallas and Fort Worth, taking the winning of the party's convention to be a triumph for all Texas, gave him similar dinners and again his qualifications for the Presidency were stressed.

Jones discouraged all such talk. He was certain Smith would be nominated with nothing more than token opposition. To promote the utmost harmony and to assure Smith's supporters that they were to have friendly hosts in Houston, Jones selected Tom Ahearn, a member of a prominent New York political family, as one of his chief assistants in planning and holding the convention.

Despite his negative attitude toward any honor for himself the State Democratic Convention at Beaumont instructed for Jones for President.

Jones had devoted most of his time to details of the convention hall to seat 25,000 people. The hall of perfect proportions, equipped with all necessary facilities, was completed between February and mid-June. Jones also had a new office building just being completed at the time. He housed the convention offices in it, and as had been his custom in naming buildings in honor of tenants, he named this one the Democratic Building.

Always a far cry from a summer resort, Houston was steaming hot when the first delegates began arriving on June 23. It was hotter still when 25,000 people crowded into the new convention hall for the convention's opening session on June 26; and it was no cooler on any of the other three days of the convention.

Houston deserved great credit for the way it cared for its visitors. Hotel accommodations, ample for normal times, were inadequate for the great crowds which descended upon the city. Many of its citizens made rooms available to the visiting delegates, most of them without charge. Some spent the nights in Galveston.

Alfred E. Smith was nominated for President on the convention's first ballot. Jones, placed before the convention by former Congressman

Thomas H. Ball, received the forty votes of Texas, and three from Alabama. Votes were cast for Cordell Hull of Tennessee, James A. Reed of Missouri, Atlee Pomerene of Ohio, Gilbert M. Hitchcock of Nebraska, Walter F. George of Georgia, Evans Woollen of Indiana, and Pat Harrison of Mississippi.

After Smith's nomination the convention adjourned until the next day to await the preference of Governor Smith for a Vice-Presidential running mate.

That night Judge George W. Olvany, leader of Tammany Hall, of the New York delegation, sent his friend (and Jones' friend) Colonel Joseph M. Hartfield, to ask Jones if he would accept the nomination for Vice-President. Jones declined.

The next day Senator Joseph T. Robinson of Arkansas, the Democratic leader in the Senate, was nominated for the Vice-Presidency. The Smith forces had wanted a Southern man on the ticket.

In comparison with other Democratic conventions, the one at Houston furnished little that was notable. Its nominating speeches were unusually drab.

Franklin D. Roosevelt, no longer on crutches but supporting himself by a cane and holding the arm of an ever-present companion, was again the Smith nominator, but his effort lacked the fire of his "Happy Warrior" speech in Madison Square Garden four years before. The tariff plank in the party's platform was a strange one for the Democrats. It was a concession to John J. Raskob and other Eastern industrialists. The Prohibition plank was a straddle; and the foreign-policy section a deep disappointment to Jones and other members of the old Wilson following.

The convention adjourned in an air of defeatism.

The delegates, while most of them entertained no personal prejudice on religious grounds, knew well what a fatal toll would be taken among voters throughout the country on that point. They knew also that the intense prejudice of voters in the Midwest and the South against Tammany would be another handicap. As the event proved, these misgivings were well grounded.

In the 734 votes cast for Governor Smith out of the convention's total 1100, he had received from the South only one of Alabama's twenty-four, seventeen of Arkansas' eighteen, Louisiana's solid twenty, four and two-thirds of North Carolina's twenty-four, and six of Virginia's twenty-four. The bulk of the South's votes were divided among others; and the successful candidate had received no votes from Florida, Georgia, Mississippi, South Carolina, Tennessee, and Texas.

When the convention was over, Jones from the money in the party's coffers paid all committee debts and convention expenses. In addition, he handed over to Herbert H. Lehman, his successor as Director of Finance of the Democratic National Committee, 151,000 dollars in cash and several unpaid pledges, with which to start the new campaign.

This was probably the first time in the history of politics that the finances of a defeated party were in such sound condition. Lehman, however, apparently took it as a matter of course and expressed no appreciation.*

It is doubtful if the Democrats could have won in 1928 with any candidate. Calvin Coolidge, as President, had suited the mood of the country.

Except for rumblings in the West and South because of low farm prices, and the beginning of the textile-industry sag in New England, the nation seemed contented with the state of economic affairs. The states with the big electoral votes were prosperous. It was an era of great urban growth and building; and the cities, which customarily had been a reservoir of Democratic strength in the vital states the party had to carry to win, were in no mood for a change.

Moreover, Herbert Hoover, whom the Republicans had named as their standard-bearer at Kansas City, had a definite appeal to Democrats. He had made his greatest record as Food Administrator in the Wilson Administration. The New York *World*, the political Bible for a large segment of the Democratic party, had urged Hoover as the 1920 Democratic Presidential nominee; moreover a number of Democratic figures, including Franklin D. Roosevelt, had advocated Hoover as the 1920 nominee. With his popularity Hoover would in any case cut into the South which, at that time, still regarded him as more of a Democrat than a Republican.

Immediate events after the adjournment of the convention had not improved the situation. Raskob's appointment as Chairman of the Democratic National Committee was not popular. James J. Hoey, George R. Van Namee, and others of the intimate Smith group of managers, concentrated on New York and the East and neglected the South and West.

Jones notified the Smith managers that he stood ready to do anything

* Lehman was later governor of and United States Senator from New York.

possible for the ticket, and sent in a contribution of 25,000 dollars to the party funds.

Two weeks after the convention Jones called Senator Robinson in Arkansas and asked the Vice-Presidential candidate what his plans for the campaign were, and if there was anything he could do to be helpful.

Robinson replied that he had not heard from Governor Smith or any of his people in New York since the adjournment of the Houston convention, which indicated that Smith and his advisers, like many New Yorkers before and since, were hopelessly unaware of conditions and sentiments over the nation.

Jones immediately arranged for a special railway car from Houston to New York City, which would stop at Robinson's home in Little Rock to pick up the Vice-Presidential candidate. Jones sent a telegram to Governor Smith at Albany saying that Robinson and he were en route East and that he had asked the railroad company to stop the train at Albany for a short visit with the governor.

Governor Smith met the train at Albany with a band and a delegation. There was a thirty-minute stop, and the visit helped the Democratic cause.

Later, on August 22, Mr. and Mrs. Jones went to Albany when Governor Smith received formal notice of his nomination and delivered his acceptance speech.

Jones spent much time at Democratic headquarters in New York during the remainder of the campaign; but it was obvious to him that the Democratic chances grew less day by day. The religious issue was cutting deep in the South.

> During the campaign, Governor Smith came to me one afternoon in New York headquarters just before starting on a tour through some of the border Southern states [Jones wrote]. He wanted to know if I had any advice.
>
> I hesitated for a moment and it must have come to the Governor's mind that I was thinking of the religious issue, because tears came into his eyes and he said: "I have wondered if I did not make a mistake in accepting the nomination."

From headquarters in New York, Jones, in his effort to help the ticket, kept in close touch with the Southern states, particularly with Texas. By late September the rapid deterioration of the Democratic chances there were easily discernible.

While Smith's landslide defeat in November was no surprise to Jones, he did not expect such states as Texas, Virginia, Florida, Tennessee, and North Carolina to vote Republican.

Since he had become actively interested in national politics, his party had won two victories and now had suffered three straight defeats. Death and retirement through the years had decimated the old Wilson following in the councils of the Democratic party.

Jones went back to Houston convinced that his party was due for a long period of wandering in the political wilderness. He little thought that a call for what was to be his longest period of public service would come from a Republican President, and that panic and Depression would so soon alter the political climate.

PART IV

The Battle For The Banks

14

The Depression Comes to Houston

THE summer of 1929 saw Jesse Jones at the peak of his business activities. He was rounding out the building program he had undertaken in New York City; he was well on the way to dominating the skyline of Fort Worth; and from the observation tower of the thirty-four-story Gulf Building in Houston, he would look out at more skyscrapers than any other man had ever owned in an American city.

Jones was fifty-five now. In none of his businesses did he have a partner; nor was there even a major stockholder in one of them except himself. It had been thirty-one years since he came to Houston, and he had been unusually active in all those years. No man had ever been more closely tied up with the growth of a city. He was, by common consent, "Mr. Houston." He was the best-known private citizen of Texas.

His newspaper was prosperous, his hotels successful but not big money-makers, and his bank was growing. But most of the increasing Jones fortune was, of course, in buildings.

To inquiries why he preferred building to other activities, he sometimes jocularly replied, "Any dumb person can put up a building; all you have to do is to find a piece of properly located land, put a building on it, and rent it."

More seriously, he said to a group of students who came to his office, "In substantial part, I have made what I have in real estate and buildings. I built to the reasonable limit of my resources, and looked to the income and increased values for profits. I had faith in the future, and it has been justified."

Jones sometimes put up office buildings by stages, as economic conditions appeared to justify it.

Starting with an adequate foundation, the eight-story Democratic Building which he was just completing, in which he had his offices for holding the Democratic National Convention in 1928, wound up as the twenty-two-story C. and I. Life Insurance Company Building.

The Commerce Building began with eight stories in 1929, and became a twenty-two-story building. This was the only building he ever sold. It cost him about 5,000,000 dollars and he sold it for 11,000,000 —too cheap, he often said.

The financial plans of his buildings always assumed that their operating income would amortize the mortgage.

If he seemed to some more conservative men to be too venturesome in buying real estate, there appears always to have been ample caution. He simply took a longer and wider view than most of his contemporaries in Houston in those days.

Jones confessed himself to be astounded at the fact that he acquired and operated so many hotels, despite the fact that, at the beginning, he had an antipathy for the business.

He would explain how he built the Bristol in Houston to carry out a moral obligation made to four older men, to build a needed hotel in Houston; then how, after failing to get E. M. Statler to build a better hotel in Houston, he put up the Rice because he was ashamed of the fact that the city did not have a first-class hotel. His shamefacedness in this respect had made it necessary to pay the deficit for the five years the Rice ran at a loss. But, when the Rice was a sedate forty-year-old, he was proud that it was as modern as any hotel in the country, and a place of dignity and prestige.

He had originally intended to build an office building on the site later occupied by the Lamar Hotel; but he primarily wanted a home, and a home needed a hotel, not an office building, under it.

"He wanted to be downtown so he could be near his buildings," Mrs.

Jones once said. "He has great sentiment about all of them. Every time he passes one, he pats and pets it."

The Worth in Fort Worth preserved, in modern physical layout and equipment, one of the most honored hotel names and meeting places in the gateway to the cattleland of west and northwest Texas. As was the case also with the Rice, he never let the Worth get old. Some form of rejuvenation was continually going on.

In 1929 Jones came into possession of another Houston hotel. Some promoters started construction of the sixteen-story building at Rusk and Fannin Streets; but the bonding company that was financing the building failed while it was under construction. Jones took it over, completed it, and named it the Texas State Hotel, still sentimental over his adopted state.

In 1929, when Jones was spending considerable time in New York because of his large building operations, he was persuaded to build the Mayfair House at Park Avenue and Sixty-Fifth Street. It was located almost directly across Sixty-Fifth from the adjoining town houses of Franklin D. Roosevelt and his mother. Mr. and Mrs. Jones maintained an apartment in this hotel, which continued to be reserved for their exclusive use, although they were to spend very little time in it.

The Mayfair took its name from the fashionable Mayfair in London and quickly became and remained more residential than transient. Debonair Mayor James J. Walker took one look at it and rented an apartment. He was a Jones tenant for some years.

The McKinney in Houston was the last-built of the Jones hotels and, like the Rice, the Lamar, and the Worth, it kept alive an honored Texas name.

The federal census of 1930 disclosed that Houston had passed both Dallas and San Antonio, to become the first city in Texas. While its 292,352 left it far short of New Orleans in the race for the South's largest city, its rise in rank had been phenomenal.

When Jones went to Houston in 1898, it stood seventy-second among the nation's cities; now, in 1930, it was twenty-fourth. "In my lifetime I expect to see it one of the first dozen," Jones said.

That order was a large one, even for fast-growing Houston, since in the forty years since 1890, only one new city, Los Angeles, had entered the select company of the first fifteen; and, while there had been shifts in the positions of these cities themselves, they had excluded all newcomers except Los Angeles. Houston itself was to be, in 1950, the second city in sixty years to break into this circle. The ten years between

1920 and 1930 were years of great growth for the port of Houston, which Jones had undoubtedly more to do with bringing into existence than anyone else.

Houston recognized that. His home city had never been reticent about giving Jones full praise. Of the Main Street of which Jones had always been so proud the magazine *Houston* said in an editorial:

Our city officials would confer a much deserved honor that would be appreciated not only by a great host of Mr. Jones' personal friends, but by the citizens of Houston as a whole, if the name of the city's principal thoroughfare was changed to Jones Avenue. This would indicate to the world the vital role Mr. Jones has played in the development of Houston. It would be a graceful and impressive gesture demonstrating the affection and esteem with which Mr. Jones is held in the hearts of his fellow townsmen.

Fort Worth gave him a dinner—an annual affair for the man who has contributed the most for Fort Worth in a year. For the assorted buildings he had constructed and without which Fort Worth's skyline at that time would have been a meager one, he was adopted as a citizen of the city and his name enrolled in a book of golden deeds. Amon G. Carter, its best-known citizen, said on that occasion, "Jesse H. Jones has done more for Fort Worth in the last two years than has been accomplished in the fifteen years before."

Suddenly, in the midst of a period in which the fortunes of Houston as well as those of its distinguished citizen seemed so assured and the future so bright, the Depression broke there as well as everywhere else in the Western world.

In 1931, as the Depression deepened, two of Houston's seven banks fought for their lives. Jones was well aware of their situation and was certain that the repercussions that would follow a Houston bank failure would affect a large part of the South and Southwest—if, indeed, its terrifying effects could be confined to that geographical area. He remained in Houston all summer, during the travail of the two financial institutions, in order to be able to do what he could to relieve the situation, if and when the blow fell.

One of the banks was the Houston National, of which R. S. Sterling, then governor of Texas, was principal owner. Sterling had been a successful oilman and one of the founders of the Humble Oil Company, but had become extended in his personal operations, and this had affected his bank.

The other bank that found itself in trouble was the Public National Bank and Trust Company, controlled by W. L. Moody, III, and Odie

R. Seagraves. Moody and Seagraves owned gas fields and had built a number of pipelines and were extending their operations in many directions when the Depression hit them hard.

On Friday, October 23, 1931, it was obvious to Jones that these two banks could not last longer than the next day, Saturday. On Sunday morning, sitting alone at his home, Jones called the heads of all the other banks in the city, asking them to meet him in his office on the thirty-third floor of the Gulf Building at two o'clock that afternoon; and he added that it was important, and not to tell anyone where they were going.

Jones' office high above the city's streets was the one place such a meeting could be held without attracting notice. By two o'clock on Sunday afternoon the head of every bank in Houston, and many of the directors, had crowded into the big office.

Jones, speaking calmly but with conviction, told the grave-faced men about the situation. He offered no solution. His first job was to get them all thoroughly alive to the fact that there would be two closed national banks in Houston the next morning, and that others would necessarily follow unless something drastic was done.

When the meeting had progressed to the point where everyone was aware of the gravity of the situation, Jones broke in with the first concrete proposal.

"Suppose," he said, "before we start out saving these two banks, we find out how sound ours are."

Each representative of a bank insisted that his would have no trouble. Jones knew that they were over-optimistic. He knew that by all accepted standards Houston banks except the two under consideration were sound and could probably weather any kind of storm. But the Depression was already two years old. Under such conditions if the two banks went down the effect on the public was certain to shake depositor confidence and lead to heavy withdrawals and hoarding. He knew also that few banks anywhere could pay all depositors, should all depositors demand their money.

Speeches were made, arguments presented. Finally, about seven o'clock, Jones ordered sandwiches and coffee sent over from the Rice Hotel. The meeting lasted all night. In the meantime committees of bank lending officers were examining all of the remaining banks in the city, as well as the two which were in trouble, to get a true picture of the entire situation.

Occasionally a haggard, heavy-lidded, tired man would want to go home, and Jones would say to him, "Go ahead if you want to; but it is our responsibility, and we must see it through. We have set ourselves up as leaders; if we cannot lead, we ought to abdicate."

No one left.

The meeting adjourned at five o'clock on Monday morning, after Jones had been instructed to keep the two failing banks open on Monday, for the joint account of the remaining banks.

At five o'clock on Monday afternoon they met again. A deadlock quickly ensued. S. M. McAshan, president of the South Texas National Bank, had taken the position, from the beginning, that the failing banks had not been properly managed, and deserved to fail. R. M. Farrar, who had been president of Jones' bank but was now president of the Union National, took the same position. Jones felt that, even if their opinion of the management of the two banks was true, it was impractical and dangerous to refuse aid at such a time.

At midnight on Monday the lending officers who had been examining all the other banks reported their finding. They said the two troubled banks could be saved for about 1,250,000 dollars.

That was no insignificant sum in those days, and McAshan and Farrar were adamant.

In his sawmill days Jones had learned a very simple fact: In a log jam, extricate one or two logs, and the whole mass will move. McAshan, president of one of the hesitant banks, was the strong man against him. At three o'clock on Tuesday morning Jones got Captain James A. Baker, chairman of the board of the South Texas National Bank, on the telephone. Captain Baker was at Bassrocks, Maine.

Jones explained the situation, and Captain Baker asked to speak to McAshan. Baker instructed McAshan to go along as Jones suggested, and to put up their share of money. That left only Farrar dissenting. But, as his support slipped away from him, Farrar capitulated.

The meeting continued in session until the entire 1,250,000 dollars was raised. This was done by assessing each of the remaining banks approximately in proportion to their deposits. In the meantime Jones had called into the conference the heads of the two utilities companies, the Houston Lighting and Power Company and the Gas Company. The Gas Company contributed 150,000 dollars and the Light Company 100,000 dollars.

Jones also telephoned E. D. Nims, president of the Southwestern Bell Telephone Company at St. Louis, owners of the Houston Telephone Company, and explained to him the situation. Mr. Nims promptly said,

"Put us down for 50,000 dollars." Anderson-Clayton Company, cotton merchants, contributed 25,000 dollars.

Joseph F. Meyer, a well-known and well-to-do merchant and capitalist, bought control of the Houston National from Governor Sterling at a reasonable figure and assumed the presidency of the bank. Jones believed that Meyer's standing in the community would bring public confidence to the bank, and it did. Using the 1,250,000 dollars that had been raised, the committee took all the doubtful assets out of the Houston National.

The question then was: Who would take over the permanently disabled Public National Bank? None of the larger banks would consider doing so.

Jones finally said, "The National Bank of Commerce is the smallest bank in town; but, if no one else will take the Public National, we will. But I will add my personal check for 100,000 dollars to the 1,250,000 dollars already raised, to any other bank which will take it."

None would; and the result was that Jones' National Bank of Commerce took over the Public National and assumed its deposits and liabilities.

It was six o'clock in the morning when adjournment came. Jones had asked the Houston *Post-Dispatch*, the morning newspaper, to hold up publication to the last minute, saying that he would have an important statement to make.

That statement by Jones for publication was that the National Bank of Commerce had taken over the business of the Public National; that it had bought its assets and assumed its liabilities, deposits, and otherwise; and that customers of the Public National would be welcome at the National Bank of Commerce, where they would find most of the officers of the Public National. The consolidation worked out smoothly and there was no disturbance.

The announcement also stated that the Joseph F. Meyer interests had bought control of the Houston National Bank from Governor Sterling; that Mr. Joseph F. Meyer, Jr., vice-president of the Houston National, would continue in its management and announce his plans later. The Meyer family was known to be rich and conservative.

> Jesse Jones went through a terrific struggle to save the banks of his beloved City of Houston [wrote Frank Andrews, the noted attorney, who participated in the meeting]. After the all-night vigils, conferences, plans, counterplans, and objections, he emerged triumphant. His plans were adopted and carried out without a single bank failure in this great city.

Of the fifty or seventy-five men who participated in these conferences, everyone will tell you that it was the financial genius and the unyielding struggle for success, the driving power which would not be stayed, and the unselfish personal sacrifices of Jesse H. Jones which carried the program through and left the city's banks unscathed; and no depositor lost a cent or was denied his cash on demand and for the amount of his deposit. That program saved many scores of small banks in the Houston territory which deposited with the Houston banks and were dependent upon them for the payment of their depositors.

The Houston National prospered after the deal; and Jones' National Bank of Commerce continued to grow, and soon became one of the largest in the city. Moreover, by carefully handling and conserving the slow assets of the Public National for several years, the National Bank of Commerce suffered no loss from the liquidation of the Public National Bank.

There were no more bank troubles in Houston, even in 1932 and 1933, when thousands of banks all over the country failed. Furthermore, there was no Reconstruction Finance Corporation when the Houston situation arose; no government officials were called in. Houston had taken care of its own troubles, under the leadership of Jones.

In 1931 Jones also acquired another newspaper, the Houston *Post-Dispatch*. The *Post-Dispatch* was a merger of two newspapers: the Houston *Post*, a fifty-year-old morning newspaper; and the Houston *Dispatch*, founded in 1923 and shortly afterward taken over by R. S. Sterling. After buying the *Dispatch*, Sterling, then at the zenith of his spectacular oil and political careers, bought the *Post* and combined the two as the *Post-Dispatch*.

Sterling built the twenty-two-story Post-Dispatch Building for his newspaper. Associated with him in the management of the paper were W. P. Hobby, former governor of Texas, and R. L. Dudley. Neither Hobby nor Dudley was a stockholder in the organization.

Sterling's 1931 financial reverses, which lost for him control of the Houston National Bank and other properties, also cost him the *Post-Dispatch*. It was purchased by Jones in the name of J. E. Josey, chairman of the board of the National Standard Life Insurance Company, J. E. Josey being a brother of Robert A. Josey, a close personal friend of Jones. The newspaper's earlier name of the Houston *Post* was resumed in 1932.

The *Post* was a moderately successful newspaper. But Jones owned the highly profitable Houston *Chronicle*. Opposed to newspaper monopoly, Jones felt that Houston would be better off if the *Post* was under separate ownership. Accordingly, he sold the *Post*, including the KPRC radio station, to W. P. Hobby, on such easy terms as to enable the ex-governor to pay for it out of the earnings of the paper and the radio station.

Hard on the heels of the successful bolstering of the tottering Houston banks, Jones was called back into public service again, on a nation-wide scale, for a task that was destined to last for thirteen years.

15

Jones Joins the RFC

ON January 6, 1932, while at breakfast in his apartment at the Mayfair in New York, Jones noted in the morning newspaper that the Democratic National Committee would meet in Washington two days later to select a city for the next national convention. Since he had no reason to stay in New York, and since the National Committee four years before had granted his desire that the convention of that year be held in Houston, Jones decided to pay the committee a courtesy call. On his arrival in Washington he attended the meeting at which the National Committee selected Chicago for the convention and, after visiting with old friends on the committee, proceeded to the Capitol.

First he went to the office of John Nance Garner who, only the month before, had been elected Speaker of the House of Representatives. Although Garner and Jones were the two Texas citizens best known to the nation in 1932, and had marched to eminence with matching steps, they were only slightly acquainted with each other. In 1898, when Jones assumed management of the M. T. Jones Lumber Company, Garner won a seat in the Texas legislature. Four years later, when Jones was entering the lumber business on his own account, Garner was elected to Congress. During the years Jones was in Washington during World War I, he met Garner occasionally. Also, they were fellow delegates at the Democratic National Convention of 1924. But their first really serious discussion took place on that January day in 1932.

Garner explained that he found himself in the difficult spot of serving as Speaker of a Democratic House while, at the other end of Pennsylvania Avenue, a Republican Administration held the reins. The Senate was nominally Republican by a single vote, but neither party actually controlled it.

Neither President Hoover nor Speaker Garner was in a strong position; but, politically, Garner's was presently the stronger. The President was facing a critical national election, with the terrible handicap of a great economic depression on his hands. In addition, he had lost the support of many of the Republicans in Congress. Garner had only a thin Democratic majority, but it was rather well united behind him, and he could depend on some Republican assistance.

At the very heart of the Depression's problems was a shaky credit situation which threatened all sectors of the national economy, and basic to the rescue of that credit structure was the banking system. President Hoover's first step in an effort to meet the situation had been to call together a group of bankers in 1931 for a conference, out of which was created a National Credit Corporation, with 500,000,000 dollars in funds voluntarily contributed by the stronger banks for loans to weaker ones on their frozen securities. This, however, failed to stem the panic; and in December the President recommended to Congress the creation of a federal corporation with a capital of 500,000,000 dollars and authority to borrow three billion more from the Treasury and from private sources. These federal funds were to be thrown to the rescue of weak points in the private economy.

When Jones visited Washington in January, Garner had decided that federal help was essential; but his canny and experienced mind recoiled from the idea of a huge government institution that might become a pipeline to the Treasury for partisan favors to many who might be chiselers, imposters, and to hopelessly mired businesses. Garner turned to Jones for advice, since he entertained a great respect for the Houston businessman's sagacity in financial affairs.

Jones said the country undoubtedly needed some such help as had been recommended by the President. Garner then asked Jones for suggestions for members of the board of the proposed corporation, because Hoover, as an assurance that the government lending institution would be bipartisan and nonpartisan, had promised that Garner might name one of the directors and Joseph T. Robinson, Senate Democratic leader, another.

Jones suggested the names of Edward N. Hurley, of Chicago, a prominent World War I administrator, and Nathan Adams, a Dallas banker.

Jones entertained strong feelings against the domination of banking by the Eastern seaboard, and made the comment, as he suggested the names, that: "If such a government agency is to be created, the directors should realize that most of the country lies west of the Hudson River, and none of it east of the Atlantic Ocean." His comment was immediately prompted by the defaulted foreign loans made during the twenties by the great New York banking houses.

Jones then called on his old friend of World War days, Senator Carter Glass of Virginia. Although a Republican from South Dakota, Peter Norbeck, was chairman of the Senate Banking and Currency Committee, and Senator Duncan U. Fletcher, of Florida, was the ranking Democratic member. Glass actually dominated the group in the hearings on the Hoover proposal for a Reconstruction Finance Corporation. Glass also asked for suggestions for directors, and Jones offered the same names as he had submitted to Garner. Jones concluded his Washington stay with calls on Senators Robinson, Pat Harrison, and Cordell Hull.

During the following week the RFC Bill was passed by overwhelming majorities in both houses, and on January 22 the President signed it. The bill provided that, of the seven directors, the Secretary of the Treasury, the Governor of the Federal Reserve Board, and the Farm Loan Commissioner should serve *ex-officio*. For the remaining Republican place the President selected former Vice-President Charles G. Dawes, who was then Ambassador to Great Britain. None of the Democratic members had been announced. Both Garner and Glass disregarded the names submitted by Jones, and ignored his statement to them that he did not want to be considered. Both made a single recommendation: Jesse H. Jones. Robinson suggested Harvey C. Couch of Arkansas.

The names had been sent to the President in confidence, and Jones in New York was unaware that his name had gone in. His account of what happened is this:

> From the National Committee meeting in Washington on January 8, I had gone to New York. Two weeks later, my secretary, William C. Costello, reminded me that Bascom N. Timmons, Washington correspondent for my paper, the *Houston Chronicle*, was to be inaugurated President of the National Press Club that evening. Mr. Costello thought I should attend, and I did. The next morning, Sunday, I had a telephone call from President Hoover, asking if he could send my name to the Senate as a director of the new RFC. I replied to the President that I would be glad to be of any

assistance I could. I had a glimpse of him the evening before, at the National Press Club meeting honoring Timmons. I had known Mr. Hoover slightly during World War I, when he was Food Administrator, and I was Director General of Military Relief of the American Red Cross.

While in New York during these two weeks in January, 1932, I had learned that conditions throughout the country were much more serious than I had thought. I felt it my duty to do anything I could in the general interest, regardless of my personal affairs. I had an impression, however, that the RFC directors would employ executives to operate the Corporation, and that the principal job of the Board would be to outline policies and supervise the operation, and that it would not be a full-time job. I had not read the law.

Had I known it would be a full-time job, I doubt if I would have thought it possible to accept the appointment, although each of my business enterprises was under competent management. As it turned out, I went to work two days later with General Dawes, the only other appointive director on the job.*

On Monday, January 26, President Hoover sent to the Senate the names of Dawes, Jones, Harvey C. Couch of Arkansas, and Wilson McCarthy of Utah, who, with the *ex-officio* members, completed the seven-man board of the colossal new government corporation.

Jones telephoned to Mrs. Jones in Houston: "Pack your trunk and come on up. I am stuck with a steady, 365-day-a-year job."

"She protested vigorously," Jones said years later, "and wanted me to resign and come home. I finally persuaded her to come to Washington for a while. She came and soon became reconciled. However, she returned to Houston later, closed the home, had a good cry with the two old Negro servants, and came back to Washington."

For the next thirteen years they lived in Washington hotels and were able to get back to Houston only occasionally for Christmas.

Without waiting for the United States Senate to confirm their nominations, or for Couch and McCarthy, the two other full-time directors to arrive in Washington, Jones and Dawes tackled the job of doing something about the nation's acute economic plight. They had no office space.

"Maybe," said Dawes, "Uncle Andy Mellon will lend us a room." Mellon, after serving as Secretary of the Treasury under three Presidents, was preparing to go to London to succeed Dawes as Ambassador to the Court of St. James.

On their way to Mellon's office Dawes suggested that they drop in at the office of the Comptroller of the Currency. Dawes himself had the

* Jesse H. Jones, *Fifty Billion Dollars* (New York, Macmillan, 1951), p. 514.

distinction of being the youngest man ever to have held that post. In 1897, at the age of thirty-two, he had been appointed by President McKinley, and served five years.

They found that the Comptroller was in California keeping an eye on a proxy fight between A. P. Giannini and Elisha Walker for control of the big Bank of America. Dawes suggested to the secretary in the reception room that he and Jones occupy the Comptroller's private office until other arrangements could be made. This was agreed to.

Prominently displayed on the wall of the borrowed room was a portrait painted by Dorn, a Swedish artist, of a youthful mustached Dawes. When that portrait was painted, Dawes was engaged in rescuing banks that had suffered in the depression of 1893 and the perilous years which followed.

There was scant time for reminiscence; and, with Dawes occupying the desk he left three decades before to become a famous banker, Purchasing Agent for the AEF during the First World War, first Director of the Budget in 1921, then Vice-President of the United States, and with Jones occupying another desk moved in for the purpose, the life of the Reconstruction Finance Corporation began.

"I think," Jones said to Dawes, "whoever wins that Bank of America proxy fight will be our first customer."

Dawes agreed that was probable, and suggested that, as their first act, "we find out something about this corporate animal." They spent their first two hours reading the law and going over statements by President Hoover as to its purpose, and some of the debate in Congress while the RFC measure was under consideration.

When President Hoover made his bold and imaginative proposal to bring the still-powerful credit of the United States to the support of individual institutions, he had visualized that it would be used chiefly by smaller banks and financial institutions and by the railroads and that its general effect would be to stop deflation in agriculture and industry. The big industries and big banks, he said in a statement, "are amply able to take care of themselves." *

As Jones and Dawes now considered the gravity of the job before them, and the means provided by Congress to accomplish it, they were convinced that President Hoover had been too optimistic in saying that the big banks and industries would not need assistance. In this they were correct.

* The Hoover account of the creation of the RFC is fully covered in *The Memoirs of Herbert Hoover:* Volume III, *The Great Depression,* Chapters 9 and 10.

A few days later all the directors of the RFC gathered around a table in the old Department of Commerce Building at Pennsylvania Avenue and Nineteenth Street. In addition to Dawes, Jones, Couch, and McCarthy, the appointive members, there were Ogden Mills as Secretary of the Treasury, Eugene Meyer, Governor of the Federal Reserve Board, and Paul Bestor, Farm Loan Commissioner.

Jones' prediction had come true. A. P. Giannini had won the proxy fight and gained control of the Bank of America, which he was to see the biggest bank in the world; and, as RFC officially began business, Giannini waited outside the directors' room to tell the new lending agency that his bank needed a lot of money to meet withdrawals.

As the six-foot-four-inch Giannini was admitted to tell of the plight of the nation's biggest banking chain, two quiet, shy-appearing, but smooth-talking men, their once-reddish hair now graying, stood in the cold, windy corridor of the old building, and were to be received next. They were Oris Manton Van Sweringen, fifty-three years old, and his brother, Mantis J., two years younger. On that day the Van Sweringens controlled a three-billion-dollar network of railroad lines aggregating 28,031 miles, the greatest mileage of any railroad system in the United States; and they were deep in trouble.

The RFC voted to put plasma into the blood stream of the Giannini banking empire, and then began consideration of the Van Sweringen application. The war against the Depression was under way.

Jones held up immediate action on the Van Sweringen Missouri Pacific loan, arguing that it was not in the spirit of the law establishing the RFC. General Dawes, as president of the board, proposed that the loan be authorized, with Jones recorded as voting "No." Jones, looking further ahead than Dawes, did not want the RFC Board to get started making loans on a divided basis, and suggested that action be deferred until the next day. He added that, if he could not convert others to his point of view, he would not vote against it. His efforts failed, so the loan was voted; but, as a concession to his views, the amount was reduced.

The RFC took over two floors of the old Department of Commerce Building, but its business grew so fast that the entire building was occupied. The offices remained there until the Lafayette Building was erected and occupied by the corporation in 1940.

The major contribution of Meyer, who became RFC Chairman, in those early weeks was the recruiting of a staff, in part from the old War Finance Corporation of World War I, and in part from selections made from the regional Federal Reserve Banks. Through the Federal Reserve organization, it was possible to obtain, for advisory purposes in granting loans, the advisory boards of the regional banks which, in the aggregate, consisted of 363 leading bankers, farmers, and industrialists; and also to obtain invaluable help in setting up the RFC's thirty-three field agencies.

When the meetings of the RFC Board began, Jones knew only Dawes, who was elected the RFC's first president. Secretary of the Treasury Mills was a man of strong convictions and, since his point of view was strongly colored by his residence in New York, he often disagreed with Jones. Meyer, and occasionally Bestor, shared Mills' views. Jones and McCarthy were essentially Westerners, and often found Dawes on their side. Couch was as likely to be on one side as the other.

Such differences were never on partisan lines. Mills and Meyer were inclined to ignore the three Democratic members with respect to loans to railroads and other large institutions; but the division here was on an East-versus-West basis. Indeed, Meyer and Mills showed a tendency to set policy and make commitments without consulting any of the other five men on the board. Jones soon forced a genuine showdown on some of the larger loans and on the appointment of a general counsel. There were also some clashes between Meyer and McCarthy over cattle and sheep loans. McCarthy was experienced in stockmen's problems, and the board sided with him.

> All those clashes [Jones wrote later] were necessary to establish a proper relationship among the directors. The ultimate result was that there was no more bickering with respect to the granting of loans. If any director thought a loan should not be made, it simply was not made; and almost the contrary was true. There was a proper division of the classes of loans for which an individual director had the principal responsibility.

It is unnecessary to guess what might have happened with this somewhat oddly assorted group because in July new legislation by Congress removed Meyer and Bestor from the board. Even before this, Dawes had resigned, on June 15, because of momentous events in Chicago. The Dawes resignation was dramatic. He went to the board room and abruptly told his fellow directors that he was going home to save the Central Republic National Bank and Trust Company, popularly known as the "Dawes Bank." He gave no further explanation and immediately left to board a Chicago train.

Dawes had established this institution in 1902, after his retirement as Comptroller of the Currency. The bank grew and prospered; but, after the beginning of World War I, public office took more and more of Dawes' time and attention.

When Dawes returned to Chicago on this occasion, he startled the members of the board of his bank by demanding that he be elected as chairman. He told them that the bank was, in his opinion, perfectly solvent, and that he proposed to labor with them in the interest of the many depositors who had come to the bank because of his connection with it.

Dawes' actual personal financial interest in the institution was only fifty-two shares, with a market value on that day of 2444 dollars. The firm of Dawes Brothers, Inc., of which he was the largest stockholder, however, held several hundred thousand dollars in shares as an investment.

Ten days after the Dawes resignation from the RFC, Jones arrived in Chicago with two missions in mind. The one, political, was to help with the campaign of Garner for the Presidential nomination at the convention soon to be held; the other, a deep interest, as a member of the RFC Board, to see the Chicago banking situation with his own eyes.

That situation was not good. Within a few tempestuous days twenty-five suburban banks had closed their doors; a chain of seven more failed to open a day or two later; and, finally, eight of the smaller banks in the Loop folded. However, despite these repercussions, Jones was told that the five major banks in the city, including the Dawes institution, could survive.

Jones wondered if this optimism could be justified. On his way to his hotel, he passed crowds collected before the big banks. He soon learned that a run of great intensity was going on and that, at the seventy-year-old First National, the president, Melvin A. Traylor, had climbed to a marble pedestal in the savings department and eloquently assured the panic-stricken depositors that the bank was solvent and that their money was safe.

The day following the arrival of Jones in Chicago was Sunday. There was a mood of tenseness in two quarters which had little direct contact with the activities usually associated with the Sabbath. In and around the hotels swarmed an array of Democratic politicians and newspapermen, intensely concerned with the rumors and reports concerning the contest going on for the Presidential nomination to be made in the week just beginning. Nor was there any holiday spirit in the offices of the great banks where weary, nervous men were seeking to devise means of keeping their businesses alive. Jones, almost alone in the city, was a major figure in both the political and financial situations.

Dawes had called a meeting, in his office, of the executives of his own bank and the heads of the other big Chicago institutions. He announced that, overnight, he had decided that the Central Republic would not open its doors on Monday morning. Traylor, who was present, then said he would like to summon a larger meeting for noon that day. Then Traylor sought Jones at his hotel. This is Jones' memorandum on this conference and the meeting that followed:

> Mr. Traylor came to my hotel room and asked me to go with him to a meeting of bankers. He did not tell me the purpose of the meeting or where it was being held; but his mien indicated it was serious and important. We got to the Central Republic just before twelve o'clock. Thirty or forty of the leading bankers, bank directors, and other men prominent in the business and financial life of Chicago sat around. An atmosphere of graveness pervaded the room.
>
> Immediately on the arrival of Traylor and me, the meeting began. General Dawes was the coolest man present, and he dominated the gathering just as I had seen him dominate other important ones. He was concise and convincing. He said that most of the others there knew the situation in minute detail, and he would give a brief resume for my information.
>
> In six days, Loop bankers had paid out more than 100 million dollars in currency over the counter. Additional millions had disappeared through the clearinghouse. In a voice which was a blend of force and gentleness, he explained how he had weighed all elements in the situation and now wished to inform the other banks in Chicago, and me as a government official, that he did not intend to open his bank the following morning. There was no doubt in his mind, he said, that the bank was solvent, but it was perfectly evident what would happen. The bank's cash would continue to disappear through the clearinghouse and by over-the-counter withdrawal by frightened depositors until the bank would eventually have to close anyway.
>
> Such a situation would throw the brunt of the trouble on friendly, trusting depositors, who would have to wait for their money until the bank was liquidated.
>
> General Dawes made it clear that he was not asking assistance, but wished to fulfill an obligation he felt he owed to the other banks so that, knowing his decision, they could use such means as they saw fit to meet their own requirements. It must have been apparent to all of those present, as it certainly was to me, that a continuation of the bank runs and clearinghouse withdrawals would force all banks in the Chicago area to close, if not most banks in the country, for the simple reason that, however solvent a bank may be, its assets cannot all be in cash. It must make loans to pay expenses and dividends.

When Dawes finished, Traylor said, "If General Dawes closes his bank, all other Chicago banks will have great trouble keeping open, if indeed they can."

Dawes interrupted to say that he believed that the time might be near when all banks would have to cease operation until curative banking legislation could be enacted.*

Traylor and others at the meeting beseeched Jones to call President Hoover and enlist his help to keep the Dawes bank open. Jones replied that he was inclined to believe that a Chicago catastrophe might become national; but he lacked, at the moment, the firsthand information to advise the President. He would, he said, be glad to call him after he had a chance to examine the facts in more detail.

This he immediately set himself to do; and, after he was satisfied that his facts justified it, he called President Hoover and said, in effect:

> I have made a horseback appraisal of the Central Republic Bank which, for the purposes which must be quickly served, is about as useful as would be a detailed analysis of the bank's assets supported by credit information. I think it too hazardous, from the national standpoint, to allow the Dawes bank to close; and I am willing to accept responsibility for making the loan, in cooperation with the local RFC agency and its Advisory Committee. There cannot be any great loss to the Government in the liquidation of the bank if we make the loan and it comes to liquidation.

President Hoover answered that he would immediately call Secretary Mills and other advisers, and lay the matter before them. A few hours later the President called Jones and told him to make the best trade he could, but that he had better save the bank.

In the interval Jones kept working with the Chicago committee and examining the Central Republic situation. Then Wilson McCarthy, another Democratic director of the RFC, arrived in the city for the Democratic National Convention. He joined Jones and readily concurred in the necessity of saving the situation.

Rules and regulations governing loans by the RFC required that all loans should be fully and adequately secured, and so certified by the RFC agency in the Reserve district in which the borrower was situated. Each agency had an advisory committee, usually composed of bankers, businessmen, and, where practical, a farmer or two.

So, in the case of the Dawes loan, the Chicago agency of the RFC and its Advisory Committee would have to recommend the loan as being fully and adequately secured.

* In later years Jones himself was to believe that it might have been better then and there to close all banks, pending the passage of some effective deposit-guarantee law. The bank holiday did actually come nine months later, after inestimable damage and losses had been sustained.

News of the Chicago crisis had spread to New York, and New York bankers began telephoning to Chicago and Washington. The New York situation itself was too sensitive to withstand a major Chicago bank failure.

Jones had originally proposed that it would require a loan of 95,000,000 dollars to save the bank, and that the RFC would take 90,000,000 dollars of it, if the other Chicago banks would take the other 5,000,000. The banks had complained that 5,000,000 was too much for them; so, about three o'clock on Monday morning, Jones and McCarthy felt that they were probably crowding the other banks too hard, and decided to accept a 3,000,000-dollar participation by the Chicago banks, which was agreed upon.

Just before daylight all details of the Dawes loan were arranged; and on Monday and Tuesday the RFC put 40,000,000 into the bank's vaults as a first installment.

In that all-day and all-night session Jones considered two Chicago bankers to be outstanding. They were Melvin Traylor, president of the First National Bank, and Herman Waldeck, vice-president of the Continental Commercial Bank. They seemed to have a clear understanding of the situation and of values.

Two days later Melvin Traylor was placed in nomination for President of the United States by the Illinois delegation.

While the Dawes loan was finally paid in full, with interest equal to about 2 per cent, the public received an unfavorable impression of the transaction that was never fully eradicated. But Jones, a stanch Democrat, upon whose considered and informed advice the loan was made, said, "As it looked to me then, the country could not stand the shock of the closing of a big Reserve-city bank. From the Government's standpoint, it was a sound and constructive loan, probably the most constructive of any loan the RFC made."

A situation that necessitated this large loan in Chicago and storm warnings from Cleveland and Detroit pointed to the need of new protective bank legislation.

16

Changing Crews in a Hurricane

THE story of the desperate, almost mortal illness of the American banking system in the eight months which elapsed between the nomination of Franklin D. Roosevelt at Chicago on July 1, 1932, and his inauguration in March of the next year offers a profoundly important reminder of the most serious defect in our constitutional system; tenure in office is inflexible.

Literally, come hell or high water, war or depression, elections are held at stated times; and, because of the nature of this political strait-jacket and the basic nature of man, partisan advantage is elevated over the national interest. Against this Procrustean arrangement, the British contrivance offers a bright contrast; for, had the British faced a situation such as confronted the United States in 1932, they probably would have formed either a coalition cabinet or, as in 1931, gone to the country with a national ticket composed of leaders of both parties.

A considerable body of testimony has accumulated during the years since, from persons whose opinions are worthy of respect, that the natural turning point of the Depression arrived in midsummer of 1932; and, except for the intrusion of politics and the paralysis of an Administration facing defeat, steps could have been taken through which the banking system might have rapidly returned to normal at the end of the year, and the economy of the nation could have had a tremendous lift.

Indeed, the RFC by June, 1932, turned the tide of bank misfortune. Before the creation of that institution in January, bank failures had amounted to 200,000,000 dollars a month while, in the months which followed, the amount fell to 10,000,000.

There are Republican and there are Democratic versions as to why the steps were not taken. President Hoover felt that politically-minded Democratic members of Congress were out to embarrass him to the utmost. In his memoirs * Hoover offers some commendation for the cooperation of Senate Democratic Leader Joseph T. Robinson, and says that Speaker John Nance Garner "was a man of real statesmanship when he took off his political pistols." But he concludes that these pistols were working in those last weeks of the session of Congress in 1932. For Henry Rainey, then Democratic House Leader, Hoover allowed himself free rein.

Garner, on the other hand, in 1932 pointed out his record of cooperation and added, "When such issues as now confront the country are up, it is no time for partisan politics. But cooperation does not mean that one party to it shall claim the right to have everything it asks enacted into law, to the exclusion of what the other party deems necessary for the public welfare."

Garner was also irked by speeches of Cabinet members taking full credit for legislation that would not have passed except for Democratic support. He thought the President should have rebuked the Cabinet members, and that he might have told the country that there could be no partisanship where the country's welfare was at stake.† Garner also believed that, had Mr. Hoover been as active in cooperating before the election as he was between December, 1932, and March following, the country would have been spared much of its troubles.

It was obvious in the spring of 1932 that amendments to the RFC were necessary, and the President made a series of recommendations. Prior to this Jones, through a mutual friend, had sent word to the President that Congress should increase the borrowing authority of the RFC to seven billion dollars and "turn it loose," which meant the removal

* *The Memoirs of Herbert Hoover*, Vol. III, pp. 101 *et seq.*

† Garner's views of incidents during this period can be found in Bascom Timmons' biography, *Garner of Texas* (Harper & Brothers, New York. 1948), pp. 131-151.

of restrictions preventing a bold and constructive effort to stop the panic. Jones never knew whether this message was delivered.

At any rate, Hoover recommended that certain conditions imposed on the RFC in the January legislation be relaxed. He felt that, in seeking loans, the security that banks were able to offer was depressed below its true worth, and the RFC should make allowance for that. He renewed his recommendation that the RFC have authority to make loans to industry for the improvement of plants, to make certain types of loans to stimulate the export of agricultural commodities, to lend to public agencies for reproductive public works, and to help the closed banks, through loans, to distribute the cash value of their assets.

Congress now, in midsummer, followed Hoover's advice in passing the one billion eight hundred million dollars for reproductive public works, 300,000,000 for loans to states for relief, and authorized the RFC to create the Agricultural Production Banks.

Congress did not go along with the proposal to ease restrictions on loans, to give authority to make loans to industry for plant expansion or allow loans to closed banks on their assets. The borrowing power increase was far less than the seven billion dollars Jones thought was necessary.

Hoover also thought that the provision backed by Garner, for publicity of loans, led to runs on many banks. Garner insisted that the people were entitled to know to whom public funds were lent. He summed up his position: "If the truth scares people, let it come. Let the people know all about everything the government does."

Jones thought it was undoubtedly true that the fact that the RFC loans were made public influenced some bankers against applying for help. He attributed this attitude on the part of the banks as "probably a combination of fear and pride." He wrote:

> Some bankers whose banks failed in 1932 and 1933 felt that they could have weathered the storm if it had not been made public that they were getting help from the RFC. It is doubtful if any of them were right. . . . It was quite some time before bankers became reconciled to the fact that it was better to admit the truth and take RFC help than to continue trying to put up a bold front which was not justified by the circumstances.*

The Rainey Bill, passed by Congress on July 16, 1932, and signed by the President five days later, made other far-reaching changes. Of great importance was the fact that Eugene Meyer, the RFC chairman, and Paul Bestor, another *ex-officio* member, were legislated off its Board.

* *Fifty Billion Dollars*, p. 82.

Thereafter, all directors except Secretary of the Treasury Mills were to devote their full time to RFC's affairs.

The President had appointed and the Senate confirmed Gardner Cowles, Sr., a newspaper publisher from Des Moines, to succeed to the vacancy caused by the Dawes resignation. This was the last of the Hoover RFC appointments on which the Senate acted; nor was any other Republican ever to exercise the leadership Dawes had in the early days of the RFC.

Deeply disturbed by the adverse publicity he had received concerning the Dawes loan, Hoover decided to emphasize the nonpartisan character of the RFC by selecting a Democrat for chairman and giving that party four of the seven directorships. He offered the chairmanship to Newton D. Baker, who had been Secretary of War in World War I. Baker declined.

There is no doubt that Jones felt that, since the new chairman was to be a Democrat, he would be eminently suitable. After Baker declined, Jones called on Secretary Mills and asked if they (meaning Hoover and Mills) did not know who to make chairman. Mills replied, "Yes, we know—and we are going to appoint him—the biggest Democrat in the country, former Senator Atlee Pomerene of Ohio."

That Mills failed to take the broad hint that he recommend the appointment of Jones was not surprising, since Jones had crossed swords with the aggressive Treasury Secretary on several occasions at board meetings.

Along with Pomerene, the President had appointed Charles A. Miller, a banker from Utica, New York, thus filling the places vacated by Meyer and Bestor. Miller became RFC president. It was unfortunate that Jones was not appointed instead of Pomerene. Although he was a distinguished lawyer and an outstanding Senator, Pomerene knew little about the practical side of business and banking.

The Senate was not in session when Pomerene and Miller were appointed; and, when the lame-duck session of Congress met in December after Roosevelt's election, the Senate failed to act upon their confirmation.

There was, moreover, little chance that Pomerene would ever be confirmed, since Roosevelt carried over from Wilson days a special grudge against him. Pomerene, like Newton Baker and other senior members of the Wilson Administration, entertained no feeling of respect toward Roosevelt, the youthful Assistant Navy Secretary; or was Pomerene's opinion of him enhanced during Roosevelt's tenure as governor of New

York. He thought Roosevelt "a very shallow fellow who does not think, but has some very expensive 'happy' impulses."

Thus the RFC, with a chairman and president who were not sure of their tenure, was compelled to limp along for several months. But, in the four months from July until the election, the bank situation improved. Reopenings exceeded failures. In this period the skill and forcefulness of Jones brought leadership for which official status was lacking.

In the long, agonizing period from mid-1930 to the inauguration in March, 1933, there were at least two men in Washington who believed profoundly that the Depression might be gotten under control more easily if the federal banking laws were thoroughly revised. The one was President Hoover, and the other was Senator Carter Glass. In many respects their ideas were identical. When Jones came to the RFC, he became the third who joined in the efforts for reform. However, his absorption on the day-to-day business of the RFC prevented his active support. In their efforts Hoover and Glass met immeasurable discouragements.

Hoover began his labor for banking reform in his message of December, 1930. In the following January, Glass began writing the bill that was to bear his name. Hoover, in December, 1931, recommended a number of the Glass provisions and, in addition, legislation to separate promotion affiliates from commercial banks.

Glass reported his bill in January, 1932, but it was soon returned to the Senate Banking and Currency Committee. Then there ensued months of delay. Nothing definite happened in the Senate during the rest of the year.

Jones had long nourished the conviction that a major factor in banking reform should be federal deposit insurance. He found that Speaker Garner agreed with him. Garner told Jones that, in his opinion, Hoover and Glass were ignoring the most important ingredient in banking reform, and one without which the banks would never fully regain depositor confidence.

Shortly after this conversation between Jones and Garner, the Speaker urged Chairman Henry B. Steagall, of the House Banking and Currency Committee, to make a study of the subject and see what could be done toward preparing and passing legislation on the subject. In April, 1932, Steagall went to Garner's office and said to the Speaker, "This fellow Hoover is going to wake up someday and come in here with a message recommending the guarantee of bank deposits; and, as sure as he does, he'll be re-elected."

"You are right as rain, Henry," answered Garner, "so get to work in a hurry. Report out a bill, and we will shove it through."

Steagall prepared the bill and piloted it through his committee; and, a month later, on May 25, it passed the House after a brief debate. Garner hoped it would be merged with the Glass Bill in the Senate and passed. But, when Congress adjourned until after election, no action had been taken on either the Steagall bank deposit bill or the Glass banking reform bill.

When, after the election, conditions grew worse, Garner and Robinson met with the President and Secretary Mills at the White House. They all agreed that it was of the utmost importance that the Glass Bill should be passed without delay.

Instead of a deposit guarantee, the bill provided for a lending corporation to speed up payments to depositors in closed banks. It also contained many other far-reaching reforms.

After the meeting Garner, Robinson, and other Democratic leaders met with President-Elect Roosevelt in New York and discussed the plan. On leaving the Roosevelt home, where the meeting took place, Garner and Robinson told newspapermen that there had been an agreement on certain reforms that paralleled their agreement with Hoover. At that time Roosevelt indicated no disapproval.

But a few days later Roosevelt changed his position and told Garner he could not go along. Garner, deeply embarrassed, went to Hoover and said, "For the first time in my life, I find myself unable to carry out an agreement. Governor Roosevelt is opposed to what we have planned; and it is a waste of time, in the present situation in Congress, to attempt any legislation to which he will not assent."

Hoover agreed that nothing could be done in Congress without the sympathetic cooperation of the President-Elect; and this left the defeated Administration and the RFC to do what could be done to meet the gathering storm.

Glass got his bill to the floor; and ultimately, in January, 1933, after bitter attacks upon Glass by Senators Huey Long and Elmer Thomas, the Senate passed it. But it was well understood by now that the Congress would complete no legislation not sanctioned by the man who soon would hold the mighty power and patronage of the Presidency.

In the months between election and the inauguration, Roosevelt rejected all appeals for cooperation, and Hoover and the Congress were frozen in hopeless inaction so far as remedial legislation was concerned. Consequently the banking system of the nation was rapidly disintegrating.

This storm had been brewing for a long time. During the ten-year period before 1931, there were 9277 bank closings in the United States, an average of more than three for every banking day. Of these failures, 5642 occurred before the panic caused by the stock-market crash of October, 1929. These banks were relatively small and mostly confined to the farm areas, which were depressed for years before the pinch hit industry. After the crash middle-sized banks began to fall; and later there were multimillion-dollar institutions.

The RFC had grappled with the bank problem from the day in February, when it opened up shop and found A. P. Giannini, of the great California Bank of America, one of its first customers. But the period of greatest strain was after the election and before the Roosevelt inauguration. The gloom deepened as Christmas approached. There were bank runs in the Midwest. In the East, Pennsylvania banks were in trouble. The President-Elect's stubborn refusal to join the movement for relief was a disheartening milestone in the downward drift.

When January came, things grew worse. Cleveland, St. Louis, Little Rock, Memphis, Chattanooga, and Mobile hoisted danger signals. In early February there were simultaneous bank disturbances in Baltimore on the east coast, San Francisco on the west, and New Orleans in the South. Kansas City and Nashville furnished bad tidings. But the most dramatic of all was the situation in Detroit, urgent news of which came to the RFC as early as February 9.

In the great motor center in Michigan the tragic antagonisms of strong personalities, coupled with political paralysis, brought distress and near-ruin to tens of thousands.

The ailing Detroit banks first presented themselves as patients to the RFC in the soggy heat of the Fourth of July week end in 1932. Officials of the Union Guardian Trust Company and the Guardian National Bank of Commerce told the RFC that the Detroit situation was of great gravity.

The directors of the RFC learned from them that, while no city had enjoyed such prosperity in the booming twenties, it had suffered more than any other as the Depression took hold. In the years of boom tens of thousands of workers were drawn to Detroit, and the banks there had financed homes for them. One institution, the People's Wayne County Bank, held 50,000 mortgages on those homes, with a total paper value of 150,000,000 dollars. When the great automobile companies slowed down their operations in the winters of 1931 and 1932, the occupants of those houses left the city in droves, for the most part seeking cheaper living in the bland climate and friendly atmosphere of the South. Thousands of defaults were the bitter harvest of the overextended banks.

The Guardian group of banks was in trouble as early as 1930. These banks, twenty-one in all, were known as Ford institutions, since Henry and Edsel Ford were heavily interested in them and had lent them 9,500,000 dollars to produce a temporary mitigation of their troubles. But by 1932 the Fords' cash position itself had receded; and so, after the July conference with the Guardian people in Washington, the RFC authorized a six-month loan of 8,733,000 dollars to the Union Guardian to tide things over until the Fords worked out a plan of rehabilitation.

Such a plan failed to appear, and the entire Detroit situation slid downhill. In the state of Michigan there were 195 urban and rural bank failures between January 1, 1931, and January 25, 1933.

An epochal struggle to keep the Detroit banks open followed. In those weeks from early January to the final closing of all Michigan banks in February, there was displayed by some of the most powerful citizens of Detroit a tragic lack of civic spirit.

A major responsibility for that condition must be attributed to two men, Henry Ford and James Couzens, once a Ford partner and, at the time of the crisis, senior United States Senator from Michigan.

Early in February the Guardian group applied to the RFC for a loan of 50,000,000 dollars. Jones, by that time recognized as a strong director of the corporation, felt that before such a loan was made full information should be obtained concerning the possibility of securing enough cooperation among the Detroit people themselves to make such a loan unnecessary. So the RFC sent John K. McKee, its chief bank examiner, to Detroit. McKee's report was deeply disturbing. He said that not only were the banks in trouble, but there was danger of riots among the city's unemployed; and that the city government itself was in a virtually bankrupt condition. McKee told the board that there was insufficient security in the Guardian vaults to cover a 50,000,000-dollar loan.

Since the loan requested by the Guardian banks could not legally be made, Hoover, Secretary of the Treasury Mills, Atlee Pomerene, RFC Chairman, and Under Secretary Ballantine proposed a pool plan, in which the most important figures would be Ford and Couzens. The latter was a man of large wealth. He had sold out his Ford interests in 1919 for more than 23,000,000 dollars, after a violent disagreement with the automobile pioneer. Hoover undertook to get the cooperation of the two in working out the pool plan. The result was a series of distressing rebuffs and an exhibition, by Ford and Couzens, of childish petulance and callous disregard of the interests of their city and nation.

Hoover began by asking for the help of Couzens, which was flatly refused. Then he called Ford, who agreed to subordinate his loan of 9,000,000 dollars to the Guardian if an RFC loan were made. General Motors and Chrysler agreed to put a million each into the bank.

Then the President asked Couzens to add a million of his personal funds. Again the Senator angrily refused and threatened to denounce the RFC directors for a violation of their oaths if they made any such loan. Hoover concluded the interview with the comment, "If 800,000 small depositors in my home town could be saved by lending 3 per cent of my fortune, I certainly would do it."

Ignoring Chairman Pomerene and the Republican members of the RFC, Couzens went to Jones' office several times after he had visited the White House.

Jones had met Couzens frequently after he came to Washington, and knew of him as a liberal Republican Senator but, in close negotiations with him, found Ford's old partner to be a bitter, ruthless, and vindictive man.

Jones' argument to Couzens paralleled, for the most part, that of Hoover's. The basic fact was, Jones told the Senator, that Detroit, more than any other city, boiled with trouble that might quickly inundate the well-being of the nation, and there was little time to be squandered if it was to be averted.

Jones' patience and restraint paid off at least to the extent that he was able to induce Couzens to call Ford from Jones' office. It was their most extended conversation since the ruckus that led to Couzens' retirement from the Ford Motor Company. Jones was at a third telephone in the hookup. The two old partners were polite with one another but promised nothing. To Jones, Couzens said he was not in favor of trying to save any banks that were not sound and solvent.

On February 10 President Hoover dispatched Treasury Under Secretary Ballantine and Commerce Secretary Roy D. Chapin to Detroit. Since Chapin had been a Detroit industrialist before joining the Hoover Administration, it was thought he might be especially helpful.

On the following day Walter P. Chrysler and Alfred P. Sloan, Jr., came to the White House for a conference with the President, Secretary Mills, and President Miller of the RFC. Chrysler and Sloan renewed the offer to advance a million each, while the President and the members of his Administration who were present agreed that the RFC should furnish direct relief to Detroit to meet its payrolls for teachers, firemen, police, and other employees of the city. Meanwhile Ford withdrew his earlier offer to subordinate his loan of 9,000,000 dollars.

On the day following this meeting at the White House, several Chicago and New York bankers, alarmed lest a debacle in Detroit engulf the nation, arrived in Detroit. This group with a number of Detroit bankers and industrialists, including Walter Chrysler, met to consider what might be done. Ford refused to attend but asked a business associate to keep him in touch with developments.

During this meeting the news arrived that Couzens had stated for publication in Washington that it was his opinion that the weak banks over the nation should be allowed to die, and that a moratorium should be effected, out of which only the strong institutions would emerge with whole skins. Ford's associate at the meeting telephoned the substance of this to Ford, who remarked that "For once in his life Jim Couzens is right." The meeting adjourned. It had been only a death-bed watch.

The next day Ford saw Chapin and Ballantine. He offered no hope that he might provide aid for the Guardian group, then added that, if those banks closed and thus tied up his 32,000,000 dollars in deposits, he intended to draw out the 20,000,000 dollars he had deposited in the First Wayne National Bank.

Then Chapin and Ballantine played their last card. They said that, if Ford carried out that threat, both the Guardian and the First Wayne banks would go down; then only a miracle could avert a nation-wide panic.

Ford's reply is famous. The exact wording was reconstructed by Chapin and Ballantine after they left the fruitless conference. It was this:

"All right, then, let us have it that way; let the crash come. Everything will go down the chute. But I feel young; I can build up again."

As Chapin and Ballantine left, Wilson W. Mills, president of the First Wayne National Bank, arrived to keep a luncheon engagement with Ford. Only on the Saturday before, Wilson Mills had learned of the Union Guardian's request for another loan from the RFC. He had immediately telephoned to President Hoover, to Senator Couzens, and to Jones and Ogden Mills at the RFC that the First Wayne National, too, would have to have a loan. He asked Couzens not to oppose it, but the Senator ranted over the telephone that he was "not going to have the United States government lend money to bail out Henry Ford." In his conversation with Jones, Mills said that, if the Union Guardian collapsed, the First Wayne National also would fail, unless he could "placate" Ford and get him to agree to leave his 20,000,000-dollar deposits there.

Mills' mission on Monday was in furtherance of his plan to placate Ford. But Mills got from Ford the same kind of animosity toward Couzens that Couzens had expressed to him about Ford. When he asked Ford to subordinate his loan, Ford responded:

"No, no! There is no reason why I should. There is no reason why the government should make me the goat. There isn't any reason why I should tie up several millions to keep Senator Couzens from shouting from the housetops; and there isn't any reason why I, the largest individual taxpayer in the country, should bail the government out of its loans to banks."

The animosity of Ford toward Couzens and Couzens toward Ford had banished all hope for the Union Guardian. Its directors decided it could not open the next day. Mills had not completely given up hope of keeping the First Wayne National open. He telephoned to the RFC in Washington that he would open the bank Tuesday morning, provided they could get a loan of 100,000,000 dollars from the RFC. To the RFC it was plain that such a loan would merely postpone the inevitable and favor a few depositors who would quickly withdraw their money.

That night Governor William A. Comstock drove from Lansing to Detroit, canvassed the situation, and was convinced that no Michigan bank could keep open in the face of the closing of the First Wayne National and the Guardian. The Michigan governor with his legal counsel, drew up a proclamation for an eight-day bank holiday, which would have carried it past Washington's birthday. Actually, no Michigan bank again opened until the end of the national holiday proclaimed by President Roosevelt when he assumed office. The First Wayne National and the Guardian group had closed their doors forever.

The effect of the Detroit catastrophe was quickly felt over the entire nation. All the news after that was bad news. On February 24 Governor Albert C. Ritchie proclaimed a bank holiday in Maryland, in the face of runs on big Baltimore banks. Legislatures in Ohio, Pennsylvania, and Delaware passed laws empowering banking authorities to limit withdrawals.

Late in February, President Hoover belatedly came out for a guarantee of bank deposits. The plan, which he had worked out with Secretary of the Treasury Ogden Mills, provided a federal guarantee of each individual depositor's account, up to the value of the assets of the bank. It was actually a 100 per cent guarantee, the President insisted; for it was self-evident that there were 100 per cent of assets in most of the banks, a claim that subsequently was vindicated. But where, for instance, there was only 85 per cent of assets, the deposits would be guaranteed to that amount, and the other held in abeyance until new capital could be brought in through reorganization.

The President got only a part of the Federal Reserve Board to back his plan; nor could he get congressional support in the face of Roosevelt's opposition.

Hoover, in an effort to prevent hoarding, now turned to Section 5 of the Enemy Trading Act, which gave the President emergency power to limit the use of coin and currency to necessary purposes. The law had never been repealed; yet there was the possibility that the courts would say the peace treaty with Germany made it inoperative. But the situation was so desperate that Hoover was willing to invoke it to keep the banks open, provided the man soon to be President would give his support to the use of the executive order. Again Roosevelt refused.

On March 1, with some of their strongest banks staggering, Oklahoma, Alabama, and Louisiana declared banking holidays. The paralysis spread. On March 2 holidays were proclaimed in Texas, Washington, Oregon, Idaho, Nevada, and Arizona.

On March 3 Franklin D. Roosevelt arrived in Washington for his inauguration, when the bank crisis was at its height. Speaker Garner, who was to become Vice-President the next day, accompanied by Senator Augustine Lonergan, of Connecticut, called on the President-Elect at the Mayflower to make another appeal. Garner held hope that, if Roosevelt would not agree to the broad-scoped Glass Bill, he might at least agree to deposit guarantee.

"We passed the Steagall Deposit-Insurance Law in the House nine or ten months ago," Garner said to Roosevelt, "and it is still in the Senate Committee. Hoover is now for some sort of guarantee. If you will support it, we can get together on a bill and have it the law of the land when you take office."

Again Roosevelt refused his consent. "It won't work, Jack," he said. "The weak banks will pull down the strong."

Garner replied, "They are about all down now anyway, the weak and the strong. You will have to come to a deposit guarantee eventually, Cap'n."

Wisconsin, Georgia, Missouri, and New Mexico declared bank holidays a few hours after Garner and Lonergan called on Roosevelt. State moratoriums were declared in New York and Illinois between midnight and dawn on March 4. When Franklin D. Roosevelt stood up to take the oath as President of the United States at noon on Saturday, March 4, every bank in the United States was closed. In every case it had been by state, not federal action.

When Hoover relinquished the burden of the Presidency and, weary and depressed at the turn of events, departed Washington on March 4, there was left behind at least one Democrat whose services in his Administration had evoked something akin to affection and respect.

Jones had been in a position, in those thirteen months, where he could see and fully appreciate the ordeal through which the President had passed. The disaster was not of his making; the remedies he had sought to apply were sound, but the inexorable play of politics had balked his efforts to give them effect. In later years Jones was to write of his impressions of the President who had appointed him:

> As a minority member of the Board during 1932, I did everything I could to uphold the policies of the Administration and make the RFC perform the service for which it had been created.
>
> Mr. Hoover was a very unhappy man most of his four years as President. He saw distress gradually creeping up from every segment of our society. The tide was so strong that he could not stop it. No one could have. Conditions were so bad that they had to run their course.

17

Reconstructing the Banking System

THERE was a saying in Washington at the end of the first Roosevelt term that "Roosevelt closed the banks, but Jones opened them and kept them open."

A recital of the events that followed that gray day when the new President took office fairly well proves this to be true.

As a new Administration came to the forefront and an old one receded, Jones stood out as a logical link between the two. But his importance in those days rested upon something much more substantial than the mere coincidence that he was a Democrat who had served under a Republican president. He was possessed of the wisdom, convictions, experience, and, above all, the aggressive force that always moves some men, regardless of formal titles or legal authority, to the decisive spots in a crisis.

On March 4 only three of the original RFC directors were still in office. They were Jones, Couch, and McCarthy; and by their own testimony, the latter two regarded Jones as the natural leader. There was no chairman and no president, because Pomerene and Miller automatically passed out of the picture after the inauguration, because they had not been confirmed by the Senate.

Over the week end, which began on Saturday, March 4, plans were hastily prepared to impose, by edict of the federal government, a general, nation-wide bank holiday. This was officially done by an executive order, under the legal authority of the old Trading with the Enemy Act of World War I. By proclamation this order took effect on Monday, March 6.

This invocation of a law of doubtful validity was exactly the basis of the authority that Hoover had sought to use to keep the banks open.

In the unprecedented conditions that faced Jones and others, there was little time to consider whether the banks might have been kept open. They were, by state authority, temporarily closed; and the immediate problem was to see how, in the time borrowed by Roosevelt's action, preparations could be made to open them with safety.

In the confusion that attended the closing, in which a jumble of conflicting suggestions were tossed into the conferences attended by officials of the outgoing Administration, the incoming Administration, members of the two houses of Congress, and distracted bankers who had come to Washington, Jones calmly held to his conviction that three fairly simple steps were essential. These were (1) more capital for the banks; (2) a federal deposit guarantee; and (3) conservators for shaky institutions.

Jones clearly remembered how profoundly he had been impressed by a remark by Melvin A. Traylor at the time of the Dawes crisis in June in Chicago:

"What the banks need is not loans, but more capital," Traylor had said to Jones. Almost every case of bank trouble that Jones had examined in the months that followed confirmed him in the belief that Traylor was right.

Many years had passed since, as a rising young businessman, Jones began borrowing money from banks and, in doing so, spent many hours on the nature and functions of credit and the part played by banks in economic life. It is clear that by 1907 he had decided that banking security should rest upon the widest possible distribution of risk. A government guarantee of deposits seemed to be the logical answer.

In 1908 William Jennings Bryan advocated a federal guarantee law, and Jones found himself in hearty agreement on that point with the candidate of his party.

Jones had believed that, to be successful, a big government-supervised and, at least in its early stages, government-backed corporation, with sufficient income to handle all banks on a sort of actuarial basis, would be necessary. But after Bryan's 1908 defeat eight states (Texas, Oklahoma, Kansas, Nebraska, North and South Dakota, Mississippi, and Washington) tried out state bank-deposit guarantee laws.

The general argument for the guaranty plan began with the premises that "property can be insured, and bank deposits are property."

Jones was not surprised that the plan on a state basis was unsuccessful. Generally speaking, the big banks were national banks. It was the smaller banks that were hit by the farm depression and caved in. In 1927 the Texas State Bank-Guaranty Law was repealed.

Jones' conviction that a federal deposit guarantee was necessary had been deepened by the knowledge he gained at the RFC, of the great increase in hoarding as, during the critical days of 1932 and early 1933, the public lost its confidence in the stability of even the strongest banks.

By mid-February, 1933, there were six billion five hundred million dollars in circulation which did not show in bank deposits. The greater part of this was hidden away.

Jones perfected the idea of bank conservators as temporary custodians of troubled banks. A conservator was really a receiver, although its connotation was less displeasing. A bank placed under a conservator was permitted to place its new deposits in a category permitting their free use by the customer. A depositor who had funds in the bank at the time it fell on evil days could get the portion of his money the conservator thought the bank could safely pay him. A bank under a conservator could keep its doors open and work out of its trouble, whereas a bank in receivership would have to shut down.

All during February, while President Hoover tried one strategem after another to keep the banks open, Jones worked on plans for legislation he thought necessary for a permanent solution of the problem. With Roosevelt's mind made up against insurance of deposits, Jones made many drafts of proposed legislation that would move the RFC out of its status of a lending agency only, and permit it to buy preferred stock in banks as a means of increasing their capitalization. In the drafting of new legislation Jones was assisted principally by Stanley Reed, RFC chief counsel and later Associate Justice of the United States Supreme Court; and James B. Alley, RFC counsel in charge of bank reorganization. Secretary of the Treasury Mills, Under Secretary Ballantine, and Acting Comptroller of the Currency Francis G. Awalt had offered suggestions.

In final form both the preferred-stock amendment to the RFC law and the provision for conservators in the Banking Act were prepared by Walter Wyatt, general counsel for the Federal Reserve Board.

So urgent was the need for banking legislation that Congress took it on faith. Not a single copy of the bill was in the hands of Senators or Representatives when Speaker Rainey in the House and Vice-President Garner in the Senate gaveled it through. The RFC Amendment was pushed through on the same day as the banking legislation.

Many agencies would take part in the opening of the banks. The office of the Comptroller of the Currency was principally interested in national banks; the Federal Reserve Board was concerned with its member banks. The RFC and the Treasury had responsibility for both state and national banks. The top agency in the gigantic task would be the RFC, which had the money for bank loans or additional capitalization; and, by now, Jones, though yet not named chairman, *was* the RFC.

On Tuesday, March 13, began the big job of opening, in three short days, all of the remaining banks that could safely be allowed to resume normal business. On that day Jones told the Chairman of the Senate and House Committees on Banking and Currency that Congress had provided only two of the three tools that were essential to the rebuilding of the broken banking structure. The first was provision for conservators, who would be necessary only in the period of transition; the second was permission for the RFC to purchase nonassessable preferred stock in national banks, and capital notes or debentures in banks chartered by the states. Nearly all banks, he thought, would be able to retire this stock in from five to ten years.

The remaining requirement was a bank-deposit guaranty law. Only this, Jones told them, could restore the confidence of small and middle-sized depositors. But more than three months were to pass before such a law became a reality.

The institutions authorized to resume business during the three days after the holiday were the so-called "A" banks. The first day, March 13, was set for banks in Federal Reserve cities. On that day Detroit was fairly stunned by the news that the Guardian groups and the First Wayne were to remain closed. Conservators were named for them, however, along with seven other large banks in other cities. The conservators were allowed to carry on certain services through the banks.

The next day was the turn for the 250 cities having recognized clearinghouse services. There were disappointments there, too.

On the fifteenth came the most numbing shock of all. This was the day for the little fellows in towns and cities with 50,000 population or less. In some communities this was doomsday. A great many of the banks in those towns and cities were not permitted to open; and in some instances sizable communities were without banking facilities for months.

Altogether, in the three days, 4510 national banks, with deposits of more than sixteen billion dollars, had opened; but 1400 national banks were kept closed. These had deposits of two billion dollars.

There can be no doubt that, in those feverish three days, there were errors of judgment. Some banks were kept closed that should have been opened, and some were opened that should have been kept closed. This was not strange, because assets are dependent for their value upon subjective as well as objective factors; and those who made the decisions were only mortal men, whose days were measured by only twenty-four hours.

The men upon whom the solemn responsibility of making those decisions rested were the new Secretary of the Treasury, Will Woodin; the hold-over Under Secretary, Arthur Ballantine; the acting Comptroller of the Currency, Francis G. Awalt; the banking departments of the forty-eight states; and the board members and officials of the RFC. Ogden Mills, the outgoing Secretary of the Treasury, remained a few days to help his successor. While 12,817 national and state banks were in operation by mid-April, it was the considered opinion of Jones that at least 4000 of them needed new capital. It became the RFC's first order of business to see that they had what they needed, or to close them again.

In that task Jones and a devoted and dedicated staff were to spend months, working evenings and Sundays following long weekdays at their desks. Even clerks and stenographers, with that depth of loyalty that distinguished the RFC from other government agencies, volunteered their services for after-hours work. It was not an ordinary government agency at all, these employees would tell you proudly. THEY were the corporation; and they were. It was a team pulling together.

Jones worked longer hours than any of them and took the responsibility in doubtful situations. Seemingly, most of the top officials of all the banks in the nation, strong or frail, knocked upon his doors in the spring and early summer of 1933 to tell him of their problems, or problems in their communities.

Several times in this period Jones left his office, packed his bag, and made a trip. The first was to Detroit. The big First Wayne, with its deposits of 373,000,000 dollars, and the Guardian Bank, with 108,000,000, had been shut tight.

Jones found Detroit a city where large employers were bringing their payrolls in armored trucks from other cities. One large one had opened

At left: Jones at the time of his appointment as chairman of the RFC. *Below:* First RFC Board under Jones. *Left to right; seated:* John J. Blaine, Carroll B. Merriam, Secretary of the Treasury William H. Woodin, and Jones. *Standing:* Frederic H. Taber, Wilson McCarthy, and Harvey C. Couch.

At left: Jones, with Governor James V. Allred of Texas and Senator Alben W. Barkley, on the occasion of the unveiling of the Jones portrait in the Texas State Capitol. *Below:* Vice-President and Mrs. Garner, Mrs. Jones, Jesse Jones, and Mrs. Woodrow Wilson, in Washington.

Above: Jones, with Vice-President Garner and his wife, and Will Rogers, at a dinner given by Garner (*Wide World Photos*).
Below: Jones referees a mock Dempsey-Tunney fight. It's the right Tunney—but the Dempsey is Representative Jack Dempsey of New Mexico (*Harris & Ewing*).

At left: Salmon fishing in Oregon with Fred Fisher of Detroit. Jones caught the fish. *Below:* Jones lunched frequently with William Green, president of the American Federation of Labor.

Above: President Roosevelt and Jones arriving at a Jackson Day dinner in Washington.
Below: Roosevelt and Jones at the opening of the Texas Centennial in 1936.

Above: Jones, with Andrew Jackson Houston, last living son of General Sam Houston, laying the cornerstone of the San Jacinto Monument, 1937. *At left:* Jones, with Attorney General Frank Murphy and FBI Director J. Edgar Hoover, in front of the completed San Jacinto Monument.

Above: Jones greeting Roosevelt, as Postmaster General Farley, Secretary of Commerce Daniel C. Roper, and Secretary of State Cordell Hull look on *(Acme photo)*. *Below:* Jones, with Vice-President Garner, Postmaster James A. Farley, and Senator Carter Glass, at a luncheon in honor of Glass *(Harris & Ewing)*.

Above: Senator Harry S. Truman shows Garner and Jones pistols used by the outlaw Jesse James. *Below:* Jones chats with Howard Hughes and French Ambassador René St. Quentin *(Harris & Ewing)*.

its own private bank for the convenience of its employees. Some of the others imported payroll money in suitcases. Several hundred thousand small depositors, in addition to the big ones, were being denied the use of their money.

A group of bankers and industrialists were assembled to hear what Jones had to say, and what they heard was stern but sound advice. He told them it was essential to provide some good, strong banks in the city, not only because they were needed for the city's business, but because it would contribute confidence for the entire country. It was hardly necessary to remind them that the debacle in Detroit, which was popularly attributable to the feud between Henry Ford and Senator Couzens, had shaken the entire nation and greatly contributed to the panic elsewhere. In short, the eyes of the nation would be on Detroit for a long time.

"But first of all," Jones said, "we should see that the hundreds of thousands of these small depositors should be able to get their money in full, and as they want it."

Jones reviewed briefly the efforts which had been made to keep the Detroit banks going, and said, "We are going to have to have new thinking and new attitudes, not only here but throughout the nation, if we are to get out of trouble. I came here not for the last rites of the old banks, but with hopes for the christening of new ones."

Jones added that, since he could be in Detroit only a short time, it would be necessary to select someone to take leadership in the program he had in mind. He pointed to a man in the far corner of the room, whose name he did not know, and said to him, "I think you are the Moses to lead us out of the wilderness."

The man whom Jones addressed was Edward Douglas Stair, publisher of the Detroit *Free Press*. He was also chairman of the Detroit Bankers Company, which was the holding company for the First Wayne National group of banks; and a director of the Wabash Railroad. Moreover, at seventy-four, he was the senior member of the group present, and a man of capacity and of high standing in Michigan.

Publisher Stair promptly accepted the assignment. Thereafter, Jones was to write Stair's name high on the scroll of unselfish men whose vivid concern for the welfare of his home city and whose intelligent leadership accelerated its revival.

Under the plan worked out by Jones and Stair's committee, with the wholehearted cooperation of all Detroit interests, deposit accounts up to 300 dollars in the First Wayne National group were paid in full.

There were 600,000 of these. In the Union Guardian all accounts up to 1000 dollars were paid in full. There were 116,000 of these. This immediately relieved the tension in Detroit and throughout Michigan. The RFC advanced 190,000,000 dollars to the conservators and receivers of the two banks for this purpose.

In the end the RFC collected its loan in full, with interest; and every depositor in a Detroit bank received his money in full. The stockholders themselves received a substantial refund of the assessments made against them to help pay the depositors.

After he left Detroit, Jones quickly started negotiations for two new banks: one to be backed by General Motors and the other by Ford.

A day or two later John T. Smith, chief counsel for General Motors, and Donaldson Brown, chairman of its finance committee, went to Jones' office in Washington and agreed to a plan whereby General Motors would go 50-50 in capitalizing a new bank. General Motors took 12,500,000 in common stock, and the RFC 12,500,000 of preferred stock.

The bank was opened March 31, 1933, less than three weeks after the bank holiday ended. Here, too, the RFC got its 12,500,000 dollars back with interest. General Motors, which organized the bank for the sole purpose of getting a bank started for Detroit, sold its stock to the public after the success of the bank was assured.

Here was a bank whose career Jones followed with special interest. As the plan for its opening was completed in March, 1933, Jones suggested that it be called the National Bank of Detroit. Brown and Smith agreed that the name was appropriate.

"Now you have suggested a good name; choose us a good president," Brown said.

Jones selected Walter S. McLucas, then chairman of the Commerce Trust Company of Kansas City. Soon Charles T. Fisher, Jr., joined the bank as vice-president, and some years later Jones suggested to McLucas that he take the chairmanship and make Fisher president.

In the first seven months of its life, deposits of the National Bank of Detroit increased from 29,000,000 to 163,000,000 dollars, and its accounts increased from 4386 to 90,000. On March 31, 1954, when the bank celebrated its twenty-first birthday, Fisher, still its president, sent its statement to Jones. The deposits had climbed to a total of $1,674,175,288.51.

The Manufacturers National Bank, backed by Henry and Edsel Ford, opened in August, 1933. Edsel Ford, who was to control the bank until his death, declined to accept RFC participation in the capital structure.

This bank's deposits increased from 36,000,000 at the beginning to 578,755,000 dollars in 1954.

Jones bypassed Senator Couzens in the Detroit negotiations. The RFC, with its new legislation, was equipped to handle the situation and get Detroit's banks started. Moreover, Couzens' influence had begun to wane in Michigan with the failure of its banks, which many people believed Couzens could have averted. But, with Senator Arthur H. Vandenberg, Couzens' junior colleague, Jones kept in the closest touch.

Upon his return from Detroit, Jones told Vandenberg:

"We are going to get you some new banks. I am not certain what they are going to do about getting depositors, unless you give the man who wants to open an account some assurance that he will get his money back. When we start the banks, they will be in safe hands; but it may not be easy to convince the depositing public that they are."

Vandenberg replied, "I've got an idea I will show you."

A few days later the junior Michigan Senator gave Jones a copy of a proposed deposit-insurance plan.

"Give us some legislation like that, and the people will put their money in the banks instead of stuffing it in their socks," Jones told him. "A man ought to be able to insure his bank deposits against loss, just as he can insure his home against fire loss. In time, accounts should be insured up to 10,000 dollars. But start with 2500 dollars immediately. That will care for most depositors."

Jones told Vice-President Garner of the Vandenberg conversation, but thought of it no more for some time. He had another trip to make. This time he was going to see J. P. Morgan.

The only New York City bank that shut its doors during the holiday, never to be reopened, was the Harriman National Bank and Trust Company on Fifth Avenue. It was not a large bank, and it had deposits of only about 11,000,000 dollars. Jones thought that, if Morgan would take the lead in getting the Harriman bank's depositors paid in full, it would have an encouraging effect not only in New York City but throughout the country, particularly since almost all the banks of the country carry some of their reserve balances in New York City banks.

In March, 1933, at the time of Jones' visit, Mr. Morgan was regarded as the leading banker of the world. In the period between 1919 and 1933 the underwriting of J. P. Morgan & Company and its allied syndicates had run into billions of dollars. Jones felt that with J. P. Morgan & Company leading the list for a small amount he would have little difficulty getting the other banks to do the job with little if any ultimate loss.

Jones opened the conversation with Morgan, at his office at 23 Wall Street, by telling him that he had come to talk about means of paying the depositors of the Harriman National Bank. He said that, with what the RFC could do, it would not take more than 1,500,000 or 2,000,000 dollars additional to pay the depositors in full; and that he would like Morgan to head the list by writing his check for a substantial amount, and by helping to raise the balance of the money necessary to do the job from the New York banks.

Morgan's reply was substantially as follows: "I have no responsibility to the depositors of the Harriman National Bank. Moreover, it is not my business to tell the other bankers of New York City (or to tell anyone, for that matter) what to do."

"It is probably not my business, Mr. Morgan," Jones replied, "to tell *you* what to do. However, it is *my* business and my responsibility to save depositors where possible, in New York City as well as elsewhere in the United States. It is not a political or a sentimental job; it's business. The small amount of money it will take to pay depositors in full, in the only New York City bank that failed to weather the storm, would be a good investment for the banks of New York."

A partner of the Morgan firm, a friend of Jones, joined the conversation and said that there was no moral obligation on their part to help the Harriman depositors. To that Jones replied:

"The Clearinghouse banks of New York City ran a full-page advertisement in a New York newspaper a few days before the Harriman Bank failed, emphasizing that no depositor in any bank which was a member of the New York Clearinghouse had ever lost a penny of his deposits. The Harriman Bank was a member of the Clearinghouse when that advertisement appeared. What was the purpose of the advertisement? Was it to induce depositors to leave their money in failing banks, and lose it?"

There was no reply to the question; but Morgan declined to take any interest in the matter, so no effort was then made to save the Harriman Bank and it did not open. The depositors received $83.29 out of every 100 dollars, a loss of less than 2,000,000 dollars in all.

On May 19, 1933, the Senate, in addition to its heavy calendar of emergency legislation, was sitting as a court of impeachment in the trial of Harold Louderback, a judge of the United States District Court of the Northern District of California.

Vice-President John Nance Garner, who was presiding over the court, left his chair on the dais and walked down to the seat of Senator Vandenberg on the Republican side. The Vandenberg amendment would accomplish about what Garner had expected to accomplish in the Steagall bill which he pushed through the House in 1932.

"Arthur," Garner inquired, "how fast can you get on your feet?"

"As quick as any man in the Senate, I think," Vandenberg replied.

"You'll have to do a damn sight better than that," said Garner. "You have to be *faster* than anyone. Where's that deposit-insurance amendment of yours?"

"It's never been out of my pocket," said Vandenberg.

"Well, I am going to suspend this court in a few minutes and go into session of the Senate, and recognize Carter Glass to bring up some more banking legislation. I want you to get on your feet and get your amendment out of your pocket, and I think we will get it in the bill," Garner said.

Vandenberg said he would be alert.

"All right," continued Garner. "I am going to look for you. My best eye is the one I use on the Republican side of the chamber; and besides, with fifty-nine Democrats and thirty-seven Republicans, there is less congestion on your side, and you are big enough for me to see."

In a few minutes the court suspended and the Senate began considering the Glass-Steagall Banking Bill. Garner again went to Vandenberg's seat.

"I was just talking to Carter Glass," the Vice-President said. "Next to me, he is the most cantankerous man in the world; but he is in good humor now, and I don't think he will fight your amendment too hard."

With Garner sitting in the seat next to him, Vandenberg offered his amendment to insure immediately bank deposits up to 2500 dollars. It was overwhelmingly adopted.

When the bill reached conference between Senate and House, President Roosevelt sent a note to the conference asking that they reject the Vandenberg amendment in toto. The conference refused the demand of the President.

The new banking law creating the Federal Deposit Insurance Corporation was signed by President Roosevelt on June 16, despite his objection to the Vandenberg amendment.

Jones regarded it as a real landmark in legislation. He had the thing he wanted most of all to restore the banking system. Ironically, President Roosevelt despite his last-ditch opposition, in later years claimed credit for the legislation.

Jones had secured the three tools he needed to rehabilitate the banking system, as he had won all his victories in the past, by being in just the right position with the right equipment when the greatest need appeared. That is how it had progressed over all those years since the son of William Hasque Jones moved out into the great adventure of life. If he had put his personal prescription for success into words, he might have improved Lincoln's "I'll study and get ready, and maybe the time will come." Jones believed there were no "maybe's" about it; for the man with capacity, the time is bound to come. The only problem is to recognize the right moment.

That is why his elevation to the chairmanship of the RFC was inevitable and natural. He had been the *de-facto* chairman for a long time before the formalities were complied with.

His next problem in getting the RFC set for the tasks ahead was to bring within his control and to limit publicity on loans. He knew bankers just as he knew the lines of his palm; and, knowing them, he realized that their fear of publicity would deter a great many from getting the help that was needed not only for their institutions but in the general public interest.

But to alter the policy determined by Democratic leaders, including his friend Garner, would take some doing; for Jones himself was a recognized Democrat, and he was facing years of service in an overwhelmingly Democratic regime. His course was a masterpiece of common sense. While he believed that full disclosure of loans and applications for loans and other assistance would serve a bad purpose in many cases, he was nevertheless convinced that a policy of arbitrary and complete secrecy had come to have less and less to justify itself.

Looking back, he felt that the public had gotten a distorted version of the Dawes loan, the largest made in the first year of the RFC's life; and that, if a true account of what happened in that case had been made at the time, the loan would have had public approval. Instead, the RFC was criticized for making the loan.

So, on assuming the chairmanship, he immediately instituted press conferences, usually holding them twice a week. They were among the best attended in the capital, since Jones was known around Washington by now as a virtuoso in the art of salty expressions and conversation, and the sessions were good entertainment. Moreover, there were few among the several hundred special newspaper correspondents who had no "situations" in their communities where it was known that the RFC was helping or being asked to help.

At his first press conference Jones told the gathering of newspaper men and women and representatives of the radio chains:

I am reversing the policy with respect to publicity which has heretofore existed in the RFC, but I am in no way criticizing that policy. I am going to handle it in the way I think it should be handled at this stage of the game. Most of you come here representing newspapers, and are interested in particular cities or regions which are the primary circulation areas of your newspapers. In some of them, important applications are under study, and loans are being made every day.

In some cases, the granting of loans means that a great many people will be kept at work or put to work. A denial of the loans could mean the reverse. We in the RFC are interested in helping every section where help is needed; and so are you men and women. I am going to be frank with you about specific situations; and there will be many of them. Sometimes, I will tell you I do not think it wise to print them, and will rely on you not to. This is my request for your cooperation for the good of the country. Your judicious choice of what to print and what not to print, and how to write what you do print, can be very important.

Soon a case where publicity of a bank's trouble helped instead of hurt was cited by Chairman Jones. It was that of the Merrill Trust Company of Bangor, Maine.

So widespread would have been the effect of the bank's failure that Governor Louis J. Brann, of Maine, accompanied a dozen of the bank's directors to Washington. Jones thought the bank needed 4,000,000 and promised a loan of 2,000,000 if it would raise 2,000,000.

When Jones refused to budge from his position that the RFC would make no loan without a matching amount, the bank directors went home, put advertisements in the newspapers, and took time on the radio and frankly told the public the bank's predicament.

As a result 5000 people made contributions to the bank's capital. Instead of the 2,000,000 dollars Jones had asked them to raise, they got 3,000,000 dollars from the people in the community. The RFC put 2,000,000 dollars in preferred stock. Not a cent was lost by anyone. The campaign of candor had saved a desperate situation.

18

Converting the Saved

THE behavior of a great many bankers, in the months after the storm had passed and they were enjoying business as usual, prompted a friend of Jones to quote the old lines:

> The devil was sick; the devil a saint would be.
> The devil got well; the devil a saint was he.

Those on the ground at the time will testify that the most badly perplexed participants in the banking crisis were the bankers themselves. Men like Jones and Woodin and others in the government kept their heads and threw the immense credit of the federal government to the rescue. But later Jones found that a task greater and more exasperating than saving the banks was the conversion of the bankers to a program designed to place firm foundations under their institutions.

In approaching this task, Jones, the sympathetic physician in the crisis, became the stern schoolmaster in the convalescence.

In an address before the American Society of Newspaper Editors in Washington on April 28, 1933, he frankly sought the help of the editors toward dispelling the fears of bankers to accept the RFC's offer to buy preferred stock in order to build up the capital structure of the banks. Some bankers, who had not had time to decide who were the conservatives and who were the radicals in the Administration, feared that the

New Deal was reaching out for control of the nation's banking structure. Jones attempted to banish any such ideas.

"As I see it," he said to the editors, "there is no reason why even sound banks should not avail themselves of the privilege of issuing preferred stock and selling it to the RFC in order to provide great strength and liquidity, and to put themselves in a better position, not only to make loans to their customers but to others as well. There can be no return to normal conditions without actual, available bank credit for all legitimate purposes."

But from March through July only three large banks, one each in Minnesota, Michigan, and Maryland, and a small bank in each Texas and Utah had sold preferred stock to the RFC.

On August 1 Jones took to the radio to spur the lagging preferred-stock campaign, outlining his plan for a partnership between the government and the banks. Parts of the address were repeated before cameras and shown in motion picture theaters throughout the country. He urged banks to extend credit for all sound business purposes.

Jones' speech was an earnest, reasoned plea for cooperation by the banks to get business going again. In it, he asserted that the Glass-Steagall Act, providing authorization to the RFC to buy preferred stock in banks together with deposit insurance, was "the greatest forward step in banking legislation since the passage of the Federal Reserve Act."

When Jones' radio plea seemed to fail to convince the bankers, he asked the American Bankers Association to give him a place on the program at its annual convention to be held in Chicago. They complied and scheduled his address for September 5.

Jones prepared this Chicago speech carefully; but, as he sat listening to the address of Francis H. Sisson, president of the association and vice-president of the Guaranty Trust Company of New York, a strong and liquid bank (and a man with no patience with any bank, large or small, which was in a weakened position), Jones decided that his own prepared remarks were too mild.

Sisson, in part of his speech, seemed to be directly replying to the Jones radio address. He implied that the government was carrying on propaganda bringing pressure upon the banks to adopt ultra-liberal lending policies. Sisson also attacked the Glass-Steagall Act as "so basically unsound as ultimately to force its own repeal." The most questionable feature of the new law, Sisson said, was the guaranty or insurance of bank deposits.

Jones listened with growing indignation. When he arose to deliver his own comments, the bankers heard him in silence. Some seethed with resentment, especially at the barb he interjected:

> Be smart for once. Take the government in partnership with you in providing credit which the country is sadly in need of. I do not mean loose credit or unsound credit, but credit which can be made on a safe basis if the banks will really try to do it.
>
> It is easy to say "no"; and, if that is the program and we want the government to do our banking, O.K. The office boy can say "no," and the note teller can collect the notes if they are good. What is to become of our high-priced banking talent?

There was no applause.

Eugene Black, governor of the Federal Reserve Board, followed Jones. By implication he apologized for much of Jones' speech. He did not, he said, see eye to eye with the RFC chairman on many things. He, too, had opposed deposit insurance and had much doubt about other features of the new banking legislation.

That night the Reserve City Bankers gave their convention-week party, which was an established part of the annual bankers' session. Then Eugene Black (father of Eugene R. Black, who later was to be president of the International Bank for Reconstruction and Development), made another enthusiastically received speech. When Black finished, Jones was called upon but declined. The crowd insisted, and he finally arose.

"I made one speech today, and you did not like it," he said. "Now, I suppose, I ought to say something to redeem myself in your eyes. What I say here is being said at a private dinner, and is 'entirely off the record'; and, if there are any newspapermen here, they will so treat it. . . .

"Half the banks represented in this room are insolvent; and those of you representing these banks know it better than anyone else."

Jones sat down, again amid dead silence; but immediately after the meeting adjourned, bankers surrounded him, wanting to know what they should do. The brutal truth, brutally told, had brought them to their senses.

Jones returned to Washington with the feeling that this trip had been successful and that his preferred-stock campaign might well be put over before January 1, when the deposit-insurance law became effective. He felt also that, if the campaign proved to be effective, he would be able to forestall a movement under way among the left-wing elements of the New Deal to take the government deeply into the lending field.

Unknown to the bankers, he had been fighting this battle in their behalf.

His Chicago speech brought a deluge of applications from small banks. On some days as many as 100 applications were processed. The RFC found it necessary to borrow junior bank officers from all over the nation to help its overworked personnel.

One day in mid-October, Jones had a call from the White House, asking him to come over at once. When he arrived at the President's office, he found Eugene Black, Lewis Douglas, director of the Budget, and Henry Bruere, president of the Bowery Savings Bank in New York. Bruere was a long-time friend of Roosevelt's.

The President told Jones that his three visitors were deeply troubled about the banking situation, especially in view of the fact that deposit insurance was scheduled to go into effect January 1; and that, at the rate the RFC was going, a great many banks could not qualify for this insurance, which would cause another bank debacle.

The President asked each of them to speak and give their reasons for apprehension.

Black and Douglas vigorously criticized the way Jones was handling the job. Bruere had little to say, but seemed deeply concerned over the outlook. Before the second speaker had finished, Jones realized that he was on trial and that the President was the trial judge. Jones was convinced that what they really wanted was to set up a new agency to do the job.

After they had finished, Jones said, "These men don't know what they are talking about. They tell you that it will take 600,000,000 dollars to make the questionable banks qualify for deposit insurance. They know less about it than I had given them credit for. I tell you it will take one billion two hundred million dollars to do the job, double the amount they think. The RFC can and will do the job, in the required time. Furthermore, these men all put together could never do it."

Roosevelt reached for a cigarette, fitted it into a holder, lit it, and said, "Boys, I am going to back Jess. He has never failed me yet. Henry, you and Lew and Jess get together and work out a plan."

Jones' plan was already in operation, but he agreed to meet Bruere and Douglas at breakfast the following morning.

After Douglas and Bruere had left, Jones went back into Roosevelt's office.

"I would like for you to make me a promise," Jones said to Roosevelt.

"What is it?" the President inquired.

"Promise me that you will forget that there is a bank in the United States; and I promise you there will be no more bank trouble."

Jones met Douglas and Bruere at breakfast. They had worked late at night and had drawn up a program of five or six pages suggesting procedure. Jones read through the first page, which was one of generalities. He halted on the second page when he came to a proposal for an organization with a New York banker at its head.

"There is no use going any further, gentlemen," he said. "The RFC is doing this job, and we will not invite any New York banker to head any committee or tell us what to do and how to do it. I might add that, every so often, some would-be savior of the country, who is envious of the RFC, tries to 'horn in' and get some part of it to play with." That ended the conversation.

For two months Jones had been making a vigorous effort to get the New York banks to take some preferred stock and capital-notes money, in the belief that, if the big, strong banks joined the program, other banks throughout the country would follow their leadership.

In October, Harvey D. Gibson, president of the Manufacturers Trust Company of New York and Jones' associate in the Red Cross during World War I, came to Washington with Thomas L. Chadbourne, attorney for the bank. They sought an appointment with Jones; but, since they were afraid to be seen at the RFC, the meeting was held at their hotel. Gibson said the bank needed 25,000,000 dollars badly. Jones agreed and added that they should provide him with the capital notes of the bank in return. Capital notes would, of course, be preferred to the capital stock of the bank.

Shortly after that incident Jones made another trip to New York and met a group of bankers. He found the atmosphere somewhat less frigid than before. Some of them agreed that, after all, there might be something to the idea that they ought to lead the way in securing more capital, even though they were well fixed without it. They recognized their obligation to set an example to other less fortunate banks in other parts of the country. After a second meeting with more bankers, it was suggested that a meeting be arranged between the President and a committee of three from their number.

Jones arranged the meeting with the President, suggesting to him at the same time that the bankers should be told that the problem with which they were concerned was their own responsibility and that they should determine for themselves what they should do.

Jones escorted the committee to the White House. It was composed of James H. Perkins, chairman of the National City Bank; William C. Potter, head of the Guaranty Trust Company; and Percy Johnson, president of the Chemical Bank and Trust Company. Jones knew that neither the Guaranty Trust nor the Chemical Bank needed any new capital, but he thought the National City could well afford to join the program.

Mr. Johnson spoke first. He asked what the government wanted the banks to do. Roosevelt, following Jones' advice, answered that it was a banking matter and that they should do what they thought best. Immediately Mr. Perkins, president of the National City Bank, said, "Mr. President, to be perfectly frank, I would like very much to have 50,000,000 dollars new capital in our bank."

Soon after this a number of other New York banks fell in line. Winthrop Aldrich, president of the Chase National, issued 50,000,000 dollars in preferred stock, sold 46,000,000 to the RFC and 4,000,000 to the bank's common stockholders.

This meant that the two largest banks in the nation, the Chase and the National City, had set the example. Eleven New York State banks sold 44,000,000 dollars in capital notes to the RFC; and soon after applications from all over the nation poured in.

There were plenty that were in need, because Jones had estimated that, of the 14,000 banks then operating, at least 5000 needed additional capital.

By early December the RFC had been able to make safe 3000 of these banks, but there remained 2000 in very bad shape. These Jones separated and analyzed, showing how much new capital was necessary in each of them. He wanted more time to get stockholders and committees to put in additional capital. The needed time would extend beyond January 1, when federal-deposit insurance was to go into effect.

The policy followed by the RFC was to put capital into all banks whose assets appeared to equal 90 per cent of their total deposits, upon the theory that recovery and earnings would soon make the preferred stock a sound investment.

In December, two weeks before the deposit insurance law was to become effective, Jones consulted with the Senate Banking and Currency Committee about what he intended to do about the 2000 banks. He did not want formal action by the committee but felt that they should be advised of his intentions. The committee was perfectly willing to have Jones act as he saw fit. It was a grave responsibility, however, and his action was stretching the law to the utmost.

The law creating the Federal Deposit Insurance Corporation contained a clause providing that no bank could be insured unless the Secretary of the Treasury certified on January 1, 1934, that the bank was solvent.

So, on December 28, Jones went to the Treasury and told Secretary Morgenthau that there were still 2000 insolvent banks open and accepting deposits; and, while more than 12,000 were sound, it would create a panic in the country if those 2000 banks were closed on the second day of January, because they could not qualify for federal-deposit insurance.

"I have a plan to avert this catastrophe," Jones said. "We probably opened 5000 banks in March which were not solvent.

"The RFC has made 3000 of them solvent, and we can do the same job for the other 2000; but it will, in all likelihood, take six months to do it.

"Here is a list of these 2000 banks, showing exactly how much new capital each of them requires. You certify that the banks are solvent, and I will give you a guarantee from the RFC to make them solvent in six months. Here is my 'guaranty' "; and he handed it to the Secretary.

Morgenthau was frightened but had no recourse other than to agree. "I had purposely not told him earlier, because I knew it would frighten him," Jones said later.

The Jones plan worked out successfully. By the end of the prescribed six months all of the 2000 banks had adequate capital, and all were opened with their deposits insured on January 1. This meant that the officers and directors of those banks had raised, in all, 180,000,000 dollars in private subscriptions, and the RFC put up whatever more was needed to provide adequate capital. Most important, this method enabled the people of the communities concerned to know that the banks belonged to them and not to the RFC.

When the American Bankers Association met in Washington on October 24, 1934, Jones was again the speaker. Francis M. Law, president of the First National Bank of Houston, was now the association's president. Every seat in the huge auditorium was filled when Law said:

"The statement is frequently made that the banking structure of the nation is stronger than ever before. Whenever we hear this said, we think instinctively of the man who, more than any other, has made that possible. He is a citizen of my home town; he is Jesse H. Jones, chairman of the Reconstruction Finance Corporation."

Far back in the audience, a banker with a fog-horn voice shouted, "Hurrah for Uncle Jesse!"

The big crowd rose to its feet, cheering.

Jones made no allusion to his previous address other than to say:

"We are better acquainted now and, I hope, have a somewhat better understanding. I shall try to be less blunt than I appeared to be in Chicago. Perhaps it is just as well that I spoke frankly, inasmuch as we had a big job to do, and many of us were unwilling to admit the facts."

In this 1934 speech Jones emphasized the necessity of long-term credit to business and industry, assistance to railroads, and the re-establishment of a nation-wide market for sound real-estate mortgages. He brought cheers and laughter from his audience when he said, "Most banks are now living off their slow loans."

Jones knew as he spoke now, and his audience knew, that, while the banks still had their problems, insolvency was not one of them.

Years later the reckoning showed that the RFC had invested $1,171,411,111.56 in the capital structure of 6105 banks. This was within 28,000,000 dollars of the amount Jones had estimated when he went to the White House Conference in 1933 with Douglas, Black, and Bruere.

In 1956, twenty-three years after the first purchase of preferred stock by the RFC, that stock in all but two banks had been retired or transferred to other purchasers. The amount still held by the RFC at that time was only 4,900,000 dollars.

PART V

From Depression To War

Rescue of the Railroads

JONES, who had entertained a deep fascination for railroads ever since his boyhood in Tennessee, realized from the beginning of his service in the RFC that the banks might be put in order in a year or two. But the railroads, he knew, presented a knottier problem, which would require much more time. He therefore made the railroads his main concern, next to the banks, from the beginning. Eventually, on behalf of the RFC, he assumed personal charge of practically all of the corporation's negotiations in the railroad field.

The Van Sweringens, who were the first to come to the RFC for help, were relatively new in railroading. They were, until 1916, interested almost solely in real estate. They had developed a large area southeast of Cleveland; and, in order to provide access from this development to the heart of the city, they were compelled to promote the construction of a suburban rapid-transit line.

That led them to the acquisition of the broken-down Nickel Plate from the New York Central. After their purchase of that 523-mile line, their ambitions led them to add other railroads to their holdings; and, for a while it looked as if another great railroad mastadon was rising out of the rust, dust, and debts of what they controlled, and all on borrowed money.

In the daring but tenuous financial transactions that accompanied their growth as railroad magnates, the Vans developed somewhat close relations with the Morgan bank and with other interests connected with the New York Central. The climax of their financial operations was the addition of the immense Missouri Pacific to their network. This came too close to the Depression for comfort; and it was to get help in this deal that they betook themselves to Washington to see the managers of the new RFC.

Secretary Mills strongly urged that the RFC lend 14,700,000 dollars to the Van Sweringens' Missouri Pacific. Half of the loan was to pay off indebtedness to Morgan. Jones dissented, asking, "Are we voting oats for the iron horse or bailing out the Morgan bank?"

Despite Jones' objections a loan in a somewhat smaller amount was authorized.

After this, considerable aid was given to railroads in the early months of the RFC, but not anywhere near what was provided for banks.

Jones was no stranger in the railroad business. He had been a director of one of the major Texas railroads for a number of years.* Those years were a period of vast highway building, rapid increase in private automobile use, and the start of public buses and trucking. This meant serious competition. Hence, the troubles of the railroads were not born in the Depression. The economic convulsion of 1929 had, of course, immeasurably intensified their problems.

Other factors had also contributed to the deterioration of the railroads. In general, their management had proven itself unable to meet the new competition with aggressive and progressive improvements designed to attract customers. Will Rogers made the remark that the only change in a Pullman sleeper in a generation was the addition, in their washrooms, of a slot for the disposal of safety-razor blades.

After the railroads had been given back to their owners following the brief and not too happy government operation during World War I, there had been passed the Transportation Act of 1921. In this the government, which had frowned at consolidations in the days of Theodore

* Just prior to the advent of the Van Sweringens into railroading, Thomas Cochran, a senior member of J. P. Morgan & Company and a personal friend of Jones, asked him if he would like to go into the railroad business. The Morgan firm, Cochran told Jones, would be glad to finance him. Jones expressed appreciation of the confidence and friendship indicated by the suggestion but said he was not interested. Soon thereafter the Morgan firm was financing the Van Sweringens.

Roosevelt, completely reversed itself and not only legalized mergers but encouraged them. But, since the unions were against any cutting of mileage that would throw workers out of their jobs, there were very few moves made to cut out unprofitable lines.

Nevertheless, during the 1920's, piping prosperity and inflation gave the railroads a fresh but false sense of security.

But by 1932 they were in deep trouble again. In the first nine months of that year Class I railroads, to the number of 122, were unable to earn their fixed charges. Even the strongest of them had a difficult time. Stock of the New York Central fell from a high of $256.50 a share in 1929 to a low of $8.75 a share in 1932. In the same period the Pennsylvania Railroad's common stock fell from $110 a share to $6.50; Missouri Pacific from $101.37 a share to $1.50; St. Louis-San Francisco from $133.75 a share to $5.75; Baltimore & Ohio from $145.12 a share to $3.12.

Railroad bonds, which had also shrunk to a fraction of their former value, were among the chief investment holdings of life-insurance companies, savings banks, and educational and religious-endowment funds.

While banks presented a great number of local and, to a degree, isolated problems, the over-all railroad problem was a continental tribulation. In 1929 the railroads employed 1,671,000 persons, the largest of any industry at that time. In 1933, when Jones took over, on behalf of the RFC, the troubles of railroads, only 971,000 were still on the pay rolls of the carriers; the other 700,000 had been laid off. There was no money to pay them. Of those still employed, many were subject to frequent layoffs.

Practically every application to the RFC for a railroad loan told the same story. For the period between 1929 and 1932 railroad expenditures had equaled and, in many cases, exceeded their revenues. As the deflationary grasp tightened on them, revenues lagged still further. From 1929 to 1933 freight revenues on the nation's Class I railroads had fallen from 4,825,622,121 dollars to 2,492,679,146 dollars and passenger revenues from 873,564,246 dollars to 329,341,830 dollars.

Many railroads were unable to pay their taxes. In hundreds of counties of the various states this was a major item; for railroads were often the biggest taxpayers. Consequently, local improvements were suspended, and the salary payment to schoolteachers and county employees stopped.

Railroads throughout the country had been the best buyers of a wide variety of manufactured products.

When the purchases of Class I roads descended from 853,721,000 dollars in 1929 to 103,947,000 dollars in 1933, the factories supplying the carriers curtailed employment and in some instances shut down entirely. Maintenance of way and of equipment had been cut to the bone. Tired old locomotives, in such disrepair that many of them barely held together, wheezed along, pulling equipment just as dilapidated. Much of the roads' rolling stock lay rusting on side tracks, for lack of money for repairs.

Applications for abandonment of trackage clogged the calendar of the Interstate Commerce Commission. Few were granted. A feeble bank could close its door and pull down its window shades; the trains had to be kept moving.

There was another great difference also between the banks and the railroads. The banks had fought hard to maintain solvency; while many railroads, unable in the worsening situation to find enough money to pay wages and for fuel, supplies, interest, and taxes, were actually glad to go into receivership. Under the shelter of a federal court—or perhaps it might be called entrenchment behind a receivership—there would be no fixed charges to keep them awake at night. A third of the nation's 250,000-mile network of railroads was in receivership; and perhaps another third would have been, but for the RFC.

Only a little later than the Van Sweringens, there came to Jones' office such railroad chieftains as Daniel Willard of the Baltimore and Ohio, Harold Vanderbilt and F. E. Williamson of the New York Central, Hale Holden and Paul Shoup of the Southern Pacific, John J. Pelley of the New Haven, Fairfax Harrison and Ernest Norris of the Southern, L. W. Baldwin of the Missouri Pacific, James M. Kurn of the Frisco, Ralph Budd of the Burlington, and E. S. French of the Boston and Maine.

Some of their lines were already in receivership but needed money for repairs and improvements. The New York Central needed equipment. The Baltimore and Ohio avoided bankruptcy or receivership only through the continued attention and help of the RFC, including one or two amendments to the Bankruptcy Act that Jones was able to get through Congress.

Not all of the loans that were to go to the eighty-nine railroads, representing two thirds of the nation's trackage, were made on the railroad's own initiative. Some of the ultimate billion dollars in loans to railroads was initiated by Jones himself. In practically all such cases he was motivated by a desire to relieve unemployment.

As Jones fought to help the railroads, he often found himself in conflict with the railroads' bankers. In many cases it was the bankers who had given orders to railroad management to lay off men, close down repair shops, and otherwise curtail expenditures. This influence emanated from such banking houses as J. P. Morgan; Speyer and Company; J. and W. Seligman and Company; Kuhn, Loeb and Company; as well as a number of commercial banks such as the Chase National, New York Trust Company, National City Bank of New York, and the Continental Illinois Bank and Trust Company of Chicago.

Jones had not realized it but soon learned that the railroad-banking houses did not lend their own money but usually set up the loans for sales to investors. They nevertheless frequently dominated the roads' management.

Jones tilted with the railroad bankers over a number of railroad loans. During the first year's operations he opposed a loan of 90,000,000 dollars to the Pennsylvania Railroad for electrification of the road, double track, New York to Washington. Afterward he wrote:

> I opposed the Pennsylvania loan because I thought the railroads' bankers should lend the money. I did not know at the time that most railroad bankers were, in fact, only note brokers. I was in error in opposing the loan, because it would have meant the expenditure of this large sum for materials and labor at a time when it would have been very helpful.

One requirement of the law under which the railroad loans could be made was that "The Interstate Commerce Commission shall, in connection with approval thereof, also certify that such railroad, on the basis of present and prospective earnings, may reasonably be expected to meet its fixed charges, without a reduction thereof through judicial reorganization."

During most of the period when Jones was making railroad loans, the ICC Division, having jurisdiction of such certification, was composed of Commissioners Claude R. Porter, Charles D. Mahaffie, and B. H. Meyer, whom Jones found to be very cooperative.

In the loan to the Southern Pacific, made in May, 1933, Jones first imposed the widely discussed limitation of salaries to be paid by borrowers from the RFC. Among the conditions of the loan, Jones required that salaries of 100,000 dollars a year or more should be reduced to 50,000 dollars, and those of less than 100,000 dollars be cut in proportion.

Hale Holden, chairman of the Southern Pacific, had received a salary of 150,000 dollars, the largest of any railroad executive in the country.

Paul Shoup, vice-chairman, was drawing 100,000 dollars; and Angus D. McDonald, president, 85,000 dollars. These officials made no protest at the action that cut Holden's salary to 60,000 dollars, Shoup's to 50,000 dollars, and McDonald's to 42,500 dollars since, above all, they were anxious to keep their road out of receivership.

The Southern Pacific loan was also noteworthy in that it marked the beginning of an effort by Jones to induce executives of borrowing lines to live on the road. Holden, Shoup, and McDonald all lived in New York, and the nearest their road came to New York was New Orleans or Houston.

Jones dealt straight from the shoulder in his first talk with Holden and Shoup:

"You live too far from your tracks. The place for a man to run a railroad is on the line. If I were a railroad executive, I would live near my rails, and ring door bells to get acquainted with the shippers and traveling public in my territory."

Subsequently, President McDonald came to Washington to see Jones, to tell him that he was moving his headquarters from New York to San Francisco, and would operate the railroad from there, and that Holden and Shoup were resigning, and their places would not be filled.

While resident management was not a condition of the Southern Pacific loan, it was made a requisite of the M-K-T that its president spend at least half his time on the railroad. Matthew S. Sloan, its president, lived in New York.

"You ought to live in St. Louis or Dallas," Jones told Sloan.

Later Sloan's successor as president did live in Dallas, and the chairman of the road in St. Louis.

Jones pointed out that many railroads were forced to discharge employees and cut down maintenance because the bankers were unable to sell their securities; yet interest rates and underwriting fees imposed on the roads by some of the bankers took no corresponding cut.

Problems connected with interest rates and underwriting fees were highly dramatized in the case of the refunding of the maturing 107,000,000-dollar Great Northern 7 per cent bond issue.

The Great Northern was one of the soundest and most important roads in the country. It had never had a losing year or failed to meet any obligation. The bond rate on the 107,000,000 dollars not only bore a high 7 per cent interest but the road sold the bonds to the bankers at ninety cents on the dollar.

Shortly before the bond issue would be due, W. P. Kenney, president of the Great Northern, went to see Jones to see if the RFC would help him if he failed to make a satisfactory deal with the bankers.

Jones was anxious for bankers to make the loan, but agreed to take 50,000,000 dollars at 4.5 per cent, if the bankers would take the other half at the same rate and terms. The bankers refused. Jones then offered to lend the entire 100,000,000 dollars for ten years at 4 per cent on the condition that Kenney would try to sell the bonds on the line of the railroad. He had by now come to the conclusion that a 4 per cent interest rate was justified, as he believed it was to the benefit of the country that the roads be able to get their money without paying exorbitant rates.

Kenney put the employees of his road, all along the line, to work selling the road's bonds to its customers, neighbors, and friends, and they sold every bond of the 100,000,000-dollar issue; the RFC did not have to take any of them. This saved the railroad many millions of dollars.

Similarly, the New York Central and other railroads were enabled to get money from private sources, by offers from the RFC to advance money if it could not be obtained elsewhere at reasonable rates. No road fought harder than the New York Central to stay out of bankruptcy during the Depression. The RFC participated to the extent of about 80 per cent of the 43,468,000 dollars, government money, advanced to it.

The rest came from the Public Works Administration. At the same time the Central was borrowing heavily from banks.

In 1935, when the New York Central owed 90,000,000 dollars to its bankers and to the RFC, Harold S. Vanderbilt, of its Executive Committee, and F. E. Williamson, its president, went to see Jones in an effort to have a due note of 15,600,000 dollars to the RFC extended. The railroad's bankers, at the same time, were holding its notes of 63,000,000 dollars payable on demand.

Jones asked the railroad to undertake new financing to remove the large demand debt, saying that it constituted a hazard to general railroad financing. The railroad's bankers disagreed and offered an alternative plan that all the Central's loans be placed on a demand basis. The bankers wrote a letter to the RFC, severely criticizing Jones for "agitating" publicly for the refunding. Jones then wrote a letter to Vanderbilt of which the following is an excerpt:

> I appreciate that some bankers and corporate officials do not like publicity; but railroads are required by law to make public their entire activity, as is also the RFC. Yours is one of our prominent railroad systems, and the

condition of its finances is of interest to the public. One very good way to avoid further publicity of this character would be to put your finances in order.

Jones' firm position did not impair his deep affection for Vanderbilt and his friendly relations with the railroad's bankers. When he reduced the Central's interest rate to 4 per cent, provided the banks would charge no more on their loans, the banks acquiesced; and a year later the demand debt was refunded for a longer term and at more favorable rates.*

One of the most discussed of the RFC conditions was the one providing that it might name some of the directors of a borrowing railroad's board. Usually the provision was for two or three RFC-selected directors.

Sometimes the right was exercised, and sometimes it was not. It was not, for instance, in the case of the Colorado and Southern, under the supervision of Ralph Budd, whom Jones regarded as "one of the most competent managers in the history of the railroad industry." On the other hand, he did exercise this power in the case of the 88,000,000-dollar Baltimore and Ohio loan, with the Erie, and in other instances.

In dealing with the Rock Island, Jones felt that a change of management was called for; and he brought in John D. Farrington as the railroad's chief operating officer in 1936.

Jones also insisted upon the selection of Wilson McCarthy as president of the Denver and Salt Lake. Here the RFC had a heavy stake. It had made a loan of 3,850,000 dollars for the Dotsero cutoff, which, with the Moffat tunnel, had probed a corridor through the Rockies and shortened the rail distance between Denver and Salt Lake City by 175 miles, and connected the Denver and Salt Lake with the Denver and Rio Grande Western. The RFC had loaned the D. & R. G. the money to buy control of the Denver and Salt Lake. McCarthy reluctantly quit his law practice to take the job.

McCarthy made an outstanding record in the management of the properties. He brought in as an assistant A. E. Perlman, another RFC man, who attracted so much attention that later he became president of the New York Central.

When the Chesapeake and Ohio, which controlled the Erie, declined to help that line, and let it fall into bankruptcy, the RFC, to protect its

* In his book, *Fifty Billion Dollars*, published in 1951, Jones gave a graphic account of some of his railroad negotiations. Intricate though the financial edifice of most of the railroads was, and firm the stand he took to assure compliance with plans which would assure the payment of the loans to the government, these dealings were usually carried out with high good feelings between him and the railroads.

loan of upward of 30,000,000 dollars, put three directors on the Erie Board. Jones also insisted on three directors on the Chicago and Eastern Illinois. In reply to criticisms of this insistence upon naming directors of borrowing lines, Jones wrote to Vice-President Garner on November 6, 1934:

> I am making it clear to the roads which need to come to the Government for help that we must have a look-in on the management. Probably a fair criticism of railroad executives would be that they are always reluctant to allow any sort of government interference. That is perfectly all right as long as they do not have to come to the Government for money. But, if the Government must be the banker, it should exact intelligent and efficient management. Some are accepting it gracefully, others less so.

Perhaps no railroad, not even the B & O, took more of Jones' time than the 1400-mile M & St. L. Minneapolis and St. Louis was its official name; but at the RFC it came to be known as "Misery and Still Limping." The road was in its eightieth year in 1933, and during most of that period it had been in receivership. It had slid into bankruptcy for the last time in 1923.

Back in 1853 its projectors had hoped that it would extend from St. Louis to the Pacific coast. But it got only as far as the Missouri River. Neither was its eastward goal of St. Louis reached. The last tie and rail were in the shade of a big distillery at Peoria, Illinois. Thus, it ended up being a north-and-south line in a territory where most of the traffic flowed east and west. It tried to hide its ignominy and frustration by calling itself the "Peoria Gateway" line.

All sorts of solutions for its grief were studied, including a plan to have seven railroads parcel it out among themselves.

Finally Jones made a suggestion that he thought the road had better try to get along without a loan: "You are already in receivership. Let the management ring a few doorbells and try to drum up some more business."

Its president (and receiver from 1935 to 1945), Lucian C. Sprague, whom Jones had placed in that position, followed religiously the advice that Jones gave to so many railroad officials: "Live on the line, know your territory, and keep abreast of the time in improvements."

Sprague had started out as a call boy at seven dollars per week, had come up through the ranks and was, in 1935, vice-president and general manager of a Utah short-line railroad.

Jones heard that Sprague would take the job and, after looking into his record, ordered him put in charge.

Sprague was a master salesman and administrator. He contrived ways of proving to shippers that there could be economies in using his railroad while he gave them service that held their business.

In 1943 the line ended its twenty years of receivership. Its new directorate was made up largely of its major shippers. Its roadbed and rolling stock were among the best in the nation. In 1953, when Sprague left the line, it owed nothing to anyone and had no bonded debt or preferred stock.

The Southern railroad's president, Fairfax Harrison, first came to the RFC for help in February of 1932, a few days after that agency began business. While only sixty-three years old, Harrison seemed so weary and harried that Jones thought he must be at least eighty. He had just cause to be worried because, in 1931, the directors of the road had paid three quarterly dividends at the same rate the road had been paying before the Depression, and four dividends on their noncumulative preferred stock. This was in the face of the fact that the road had lost money equivalent to $6.87 per share of its common stock.

After that exhibition of outrageous improvidence the road's credit entirely disappeared. The 7,500,000 dollars which the RFC let it have in February was soon exhausted, and three more loans were made that year.

One day in 1936, when the Southern's debt to the RFC had reached 31,405,000 dollars, John J. Pelley, president of the American Association of Railroads, asked Jones to have lunch with him and Harrison in Pelley's apartment. During the lunch Harrison said, "Mr. Jones, I had too much pride to go to your office to tell you what I must tell you. I am going to have to put my road in receivership and under the protection of the court, to try to work out a plan to save it."

Jones did not want to see any more railroads in receivership. Ninety-eight were already in receivership or bankruptcy.

"I think the collateral we already have is sufficient to justfy another rather substantial loan to the Southern," Jones said, "and I think it would be better to try to avert receivership."

The road did not go into receivership.

After Harrison died, in 1938, Ernest E. Norris succeeded him. The following year Norris told Jones that he intended to pay every cent of the road's indebtedness.

In the spring of 1938 Jones secured legislation permitting the RFC to make loans on equipment-trust obligations without permission from the ICC.

Jones' first caller after the legislation became effective was Norris.

"Jesse, what you told Congress about the need of this kind of legislation sounded like you were talking about the Southern, although I know you had all the railroads in mind. The Southern hasn't bought a freight car in eight years. You are the only man in the country who possibly would consider a loan to me, and I already owe you 30,000,000.

"More than half the car-making plants are shut down. The only people who can get a job with them are the guards for their gates. The Southern needs new freight cars badly, maybe 8000 or 9000 of them. That would give a lot of employment to carbuilders."

"All right," Jones said, "we will lend you the money and take equipment-trust certificates in payment. We will charge you 4 per cent."

The whole conversation lasted less than fifteen minutes, but it launched the RFC on a program of buying equipment trusts. It later bought many million dollars' worth of them, including 107,000,000 dollars taken over from the Public Works Administration. The RFC sold every equipment trust it held from any railroad at a profit.

Thus, the railroads were able to get thousands of new freight cars, locomotives, and streamlined passenger trains, and otherwise increase their traffic-carrying capacity. Neither Jones nor any railroad foresaw the immense, almost providential value of this equipment in the coming world war, when the government became the great volume user of transportation.

Through his organization Jones came to know more about the financial structures of all the railroads in the country than probably any other man ever did. He watched their large maturities and would sometimes advise them to seek loans in advance of the date they would need the money.

An instance of this was in the case of the Illinois Central, a fine railroad system largely controlled by the Union Pacific. Jones sent for the road's president, L. A. Downs, and suggested that he make application for a loan to meet the maturity, and helped him get ICC certification that the road was not in need of reorganization. Thus the line was saved from bankruptcy.

Jones was proud of the fact that the Illinois Central showed its appreciation by becoming one of the first railroads to use diesel engines for the purpose of operating high-speed passenger trains. The Green Diamond, first of these trains, cut the running time between Chicago and St. Louis to less than five hours. After the train had been christened by the fourteen-year-old Jones granddaughter, Audrey Louise Jones, on

May 18, 1936, she, with Mr. and Mrs. Jones, W. Averell Harriman, chairman of the line, Downs, the president, and Charles F. Kettering, who developed the engine, made the run from Chicago to St. Louis.

The most discussed of all the railroad loans made by the RFC in Jones' thirteen years as a government lender was that to the Baltimore and Ohio. Its application for a loan of 55,000,000 dollars was made in March, 1932, and caused some of the directors to gasp.

"You could buy half of Arkansas for that amount," Harvey C. Couch said to Charles G. Dawes. The very size of the B & O's immediate money needs was a startling warning of the critical condition of the nation's railroads; for this had been one of the country's oldest and best companies. The RFC directors were unanimous that this oldest of the big trunk lines must not be allowed to slide into bankruptcy. Daniel Willard, its president, who began as a railroad brakeman and was one of the most popular railroad men in the nation, was making a gallant fight to keep the road solvent.

The B & O loan from the RFC at one time amounted to 88,000,000 dollars but both the RFC and the ICC felt that it was well collaterized. The B & O also faced maturities to private lenders within a few years of 185,000,000 dollars. Congress passed the Chandler Act, which permitted a rearrangement of the debt structure of a corporation beset by the problems then faced by the B & O. The lowering of the fixed charges kept the road going, and when Willard died in 1942 at the age of eighty-one he knew his ten-year fight to keep the road out of bankruptcy had been won. The last 65,000,000 dollars of the B & O loan was sold in 1954 to an investment house and to the railroad itself. The interest paid on it had established a profit to the government.

Throughout his service to the government Jones had steadfastly held to the position that railroads should, if possible, be kept out of legal bankruptcy and reinvigorated. Often he manifested more faith in the companies than did their management. When he left the government nearly every railroad had reduced its long-term indebtedness and modernized its operations, and a half-million men had been added to their payrolls. They had also made large expenditures in expansion. Their condition was better than it had been since the turn of the century.

The loans had been colossal, amounting to more than one billion two hundred fifty million dollars. It was said that a person might ride 219,000 consecutive miles without leaving rails on which Jones had made a loan.

In 1956, two years after Congress had ordered the liquidation of the

RFC and transferred its assets to the Treasury Department, all but four railroads, all of them small ones, had paid up. These owed 9,100,000 dollars, most of which would eventually be collected. If all of this should become a loss, it had been made up many times over in interest on the big loans.

20

The Many-sided RFC

JONES had early recognized that unsound banks, the dilemma of the railroads, and sulking prices of farm products were the trinity of economic culprits plaguing the country and standing in the path of its recovery. Banks and railroads were giving him quite enough problems. He had expected no part in the agriculture program.

Suddenly, on October 17, 1933, the Commodity Credit Corporation burst upon the Washington scene. It was the first of the RFC's special-purpose children, conceived to bolster the precarious instability of particular industries. CCC was incorporated, like all its later sisters, under the laws of Delaware, and domiciled with RFC. With its birth Jones was in the farm-commodity loan business.

President Franklin D. Roosevelt was deeply worried over the farm situation in that autumn of 1933. So were men wiser in the field of the national economy than he. There had been the plowing under of every third row of cotton as a panacea for Dixie's despair; the experiment of the killing of the 6,000,000 little pigs as a solution of the corn-and-hog problem of the Midwest, and the various other dubious Henry Wallace stratagems. But there was still the painful fact that the price of farm commodities was at a disastrously low level.

The prospect was especially wan for cotton, the South's principal money crop. There was a tremendous hang-over of the unmarketed yield of other years; and the forecasts were for a bumper new crop.

One day, when pickers were just entering the fields of the Southland in full force, Oscar Johnston, a big Mississippi planter, regarded as one of the nation's leading authorities on cotton, went to the White House to tell the President that ruin faced him and all the growers.

"We'll see what Jones can do about it," Roosevelt said. He called Jones and asked him to come to the White House.

Jones had not taken his chair in the President's office before Roosevelt said, "Jess, Oscar says cotton is selling at nine cents a pound, and may go lower if we don't do something to support the market. Cotton ought to be worth ten cents."

"All right," Jones said, "we will make it worth ten cents."

"How can you do it, and how soon?" Roosevelt asked.

"We will offer to lend ten cents a pound anywhere in the cotton-growing section," Jones replied.

"Yes, but the law says you can lend only on 'full and adequate' security."

"Certainly; I know that. I also know that cotton is worth ten cents a pound; and, if all our loans are as well secured as loans on cotton will be at ten cents, we'll be mighty lucky."

"Who decides what 'full and adequate' is?" Roosevelt asked.

"Our board," Jones replied. "Our loans to banks and railroads have always been made on what we regard as full and adequate security, and I think we will get our money back. I think cotton is worth more than ten cents a pound, even though it is selling at nine; and there will be no loss to the government."

Jones returned to his office, called in Stanley Reed, his general counsel, and together they studied the problem. Reed agreed that the ten-cent cotton loans could be made.

"If we lend on cotton, we are going to have to lend on corn, wheat, potatoes, tobacco, peanuts, butter, and a lot of other things. So we had just as well prepare," Jones said.

Thus the Commodity Credit Corporation was set up, and in the six years of its life under RFC it made loans to farmers that topped the government's help to railroads, and was second only to the amount dispensed to banks and other financial institutions. Years afterward Jones was to say:

> I feel that the Commodity Credit Corporation, as much as and maybe more than any government agency, saved the country from disaster. The

money it advanced enabled the farmers to market their crops in an orderly manner. We raised the price of farm products. We took some losses; but there were more gains than losses, and we came out ahead on the books.

The Commodity Credit Corporation brought to Jones an association which was no contribution to his happiness. President Roosevelt felt that the Secretary of Agriculture should be included on the CCC Board of Directors. Theoretically, of course, this was perfectly sound practice; and so, at the President's request, Jones made Henry Wallace a member of the board of directors of CCC, along with several RFC men, Jones continuing to dictate its management and policies. Jones' opinion of Wallace at the time was low; it never ascended.

Jones, as was his custom, provided a device to keep RFC loans on cotton as few as possible. He had believed as proved to be the case, that the offer to lend ten cents a pound, with no recourse on the borrower, would quickly establish the value of that commodity. It was arranged that the farmer who wished to borrow on his crop could go to the most convenient bank or warehouse and there pledge his cotton as security for a Commodity Credit loan at 4 per cent interest.

A lending bank could present the farmer's note to the nearest RFC agency and get its face value in cash plus 4 per cent interest. As an incentive to the bank to carry the note, there was the provision that the originating country bank could keep 3 per cent and send the remaining 1 per cent to Commodity Credit, which stood ready to take over the note at any time.

An enormous crop of 13,100,000 bales was picked in the autumn of 1933. However, Jones' plan of guaranteed private-bank loans at ten cents a pound resulted in only 103,000,000 dollars' worth of cotton being pledged for these CCC loans. But in later years the management of the cotton loans came to require great skill.

The Jones cotton-loan plan worked so well in its first year that President Roosevelt, with his usual cavalier approach to serious economic problems, ordered an increase to twelve cents a pound on the 1934 crop. This 20 per cent increase in the loan resulted in 1,198,000 separate loans to farmers on approximately 4,500,000 bales; and in the spring of 1935 producers were sending their cotton to twelve-cent loan warehouses instead of to the market.

Jones thought the twelve-cent pegging price went too far, and protested against it. An adroit plan was finally formulated by Jones, under which any farmer might claim the cotton that he had warehoused with the government, for the average price of ten "spot" cotton markets on the previous day, less twenty-five points, or $1.25 per bale. This offer would be carried out whether or not the price at which the farmer took his cotton out of the loan would pay his note; and there would be no further recourse on the farmer. The move resulted in 2,000,000 bales of government cotton coming into market in 120 days, on a rising market.

As the program continued, Commodity Credit had almost unlimited discretion in handling its cotton for three years. But, by the time the enormous 19,000,000-bale 1937 crop came in, Congress had amended the Agricultural Adjustment Act to make it mandatory that loans be made on cotton, wheat, and corn whenever the three commodities reached a price fixed by the Secretary of Agriculture.

The result might have been foreseen. Soon Commodity Credit had on hand 11,000,000 bales of cotton, with a market value of 90,000,000 dollars less than the loans. The Jones plan had combined resourcefulness, imagination, and sound judgment. President Roosevelt, under Wallace's influence, had substituted economic charlatanism.

Cotton had taken all the money that CCC had in its till by the time wheat and corn farmers began clamoring for loans in 1938. Congress was not in session and Roosevelt was not in Washington. Jones was in a difficult spot. He could not secure enabling legislation to make wheat and corn loans until Congress came back in January. So he asked Stanley Reed, his general counsel, if he could have RFC buy 150,000,000 dollars in cotton-farmers' notes from the CCC to give the latter agency money to lend on corn and wheat.

Counsel Reed reported back to Jones that he could not do it. Jones wanted to know why. Reed replied, "There is no provision in the law for it."

Jones then wanted to know what would be the penalty if he took the action without authority from Congress. "Can they hang me if I do it?" he asked.

"No," Reed replied.

"How long is the jail term?" Jones pursued.

"There is none," Reed informed him.

"What can they do to me?"

"They can fire you," Reed said.

"Is that all?" Jones asked. Reed assured him that it was.

"Well, the ox is in the ditch, and it's up to us to get him out," Jones said. "I will have RFC buy from Commodity Credit Corporation 150,000,000 dollars' worth of farmers' notes secured by cotton. This will give us the money to lend on corn and wheat." The RFC had ample borrowing authority.

When Congress came back into session in January, 1939, Jones went before the Senate Banking and Currency Committee, asking for a billion-dollar increase in borrowing authority for loans on cotton, corn, and wheat, and perhaps some other farm products. He told the committee what he had had to do to be able to make loans on corn and wheat the previous year.

Robert A. Taft, who had been elected to the Senate for the first time the previous fall, had been made a member of the Banking and Currency Committee. He questioned Jones rather critically about the method used to get money for the corn and wheat loans. Finally he said, "Mr. Jones, you have violated the law."

"No, Senator, I have not violated the law," Jones replied. "I have construed the law and administered it according to my best judgment under the circumstances; and if you think the increases I have asked should not be voted, vote against them. What I did was what I felt sure the Congress would have authorized me to do had it been in session. I felt that it was my responsibility to meet the situation, and did, always having something to go home to when my services are no longer required."

That ended the matter. Taft joined in voting for the billion dollars Jones asked.

From cotton, corn, and wheat the Commodity Credit loans quickly extended to butter, tobacco, turpentine, pecans, peanuts, prunes, potatoes, hops, wool, mohair, and raisin grapes.

The RFC or its subsidiaries made millions of loans on farms and farm equipment. A fifth of these were for less than 250 dollars each; but there were big ones too. The largest went to the King Ranch in Texas, the largest ranch in the world, which borrowed 2,000,000 dollars, put up the entire ranch as security, and paid the loan within a year.

Along with his loans to railroads, banks, and agriculture, Jones sponsored many other activities to offset the heavy and continuous blows that the Depression was striking. He told the Washington *Star* Forum, "An incredibly large part of the world's working capital has been lost. This applies to agriculture, business, and industry of all kinds." Or, as he said later in an address at Richmond, Virginia:

> The offices of the RFC were like a huge hospital behind the battle lines, with the maimed and wounded coming in from every battle front; strong men beaten down to the point of despair; institutions of long standing going on the rocks; and credit literally dried up. The days and nights were not long enough to see and wait upon those who came for assistance. Such days we would like to forget, but never can.

The plight of real-estate mortgages claimed his early and vigorous attention. In the surging era of building in the 1920's there had been enormous activity in this field; and, when the Depression hit, private sources held thirty-five billion dollars in mortgages on urban property alone. In New York City there were more than two billion dollars in guaranteed mortgages and mortgage certificates in the hands of the public. Disaster quickly smote the real estate mortgage market. In Chicago alone two to two and a half billion real-estate bonds were soon in default.

Jones went before the Senate Banking and Currency Committee in 1934 to ask authority to buy preferred stock in mortgage companies. Congress granted it but, in a nation deep in pessimism, no one could be found to take stock in such enterprises. So he created the RFC Mortgage Company, then the Federal National Mortgage Association. Through the RFC Mortgage Company's activities, thousands of apartment houses, hotels, office buildings, stores, warehouses, and factories were brought out of receivership and reorganized in the interest of the bondholders and equity holders, and without loss of the new money put into them.

A concomitant of the frozen-mortgage situation was the wrecking of some of the nation's biggest surety and casualty companies. The distressed companies not only had issued bonds and policies of a face value of many billions but had guaranteed other billions in real estate bonds. Bright chapters were written by the RFC in the rescue of such companies in New York, Chicago, Baltimore, and elsewhere. New capital was supplied and in some cases new corporations were created and some new faces supplied; many losses to investors were averted and on the total operation the RFC came out ahead.

In the assets pledged to the RFC by one of the failed investment companies was a lien of 1,700,000 dollars in the Ringling Brothers-Barnum & Bailey Circus. Even the circus note yielded a profit to the RFC.

Jones' role as consultant to the nation at large in financial matters was illustrated no better anywhere than in the self-liquidating loans the RFC made to states and municipalities in order that they might construct needed public works, thus giving employment to the jobless. He never seemed too busy, even in his monumental task of rehabilitating banks and railroads, to see a delegation that wanted RFC help and his advice on a public-works project.

From New York to San Francisco, and from the Canadian border to the Gulf of Mexico, are projects that graphically mark Jones' activities along these lines.

There is a vehicular bridge at Puget Sound; across the Mississippi at New Orleans is another bridge. There are a New Orleans airport and dormitories for Louisiana State University at Baton Rouge. There is a vehicular tunnel under the Mobile River in Alabama.

In New York a bridge above and a tunnel beneath the East River; a bridge across the Hudson; a tunnel under New York Bay from lower Manhattan; the improvement of Jones Beach in New York; all stand as landmarks of the self-liquidating program.

In Pennsylvania there is the 160-mile toll highway from Pittsburgh to Harrisburg, on which the RFC loaned the Pennsylvania Turnpike 35,000,000 dollars. This not only proved profitable but was the start of a toll highway that was to extend from New York to Chicago.

An outstanding one was the 244-mile aqueduct that carries water from the Colorado River to Los Angeles, San Diego, and two dozen smaller communities. When F. E. Weymouth, of Los Angeles, took the application for the 208,000,000-dollar loan to Jones, he asked, "As a hard-boiled realist, what do you think of the project?"

It had been the great dream of Weymouth. It would immediately furnish a water supply for 3,000,000, which might eventually rise to 10,000,000 people. If carried out it would be the largest water-supply system in the world.

Jones scanned the application with a practiced eye, asked a few questions, handed the papers back to Weymouth, and said, "Build it. When prosperous conditions are restored, it will cost you two or three times what it will cost you now."

The project gave work directly to 35,000. It used 70,000 carloads of material, equipment, and supplies brought from all parts of the nation, resulting in the employment of additional thousands.

Jones' prophecy of future greater cost was borne out. The RFC sold the 208,000,000 dollars in bonds of the Metropolitan Water District of Southern California at a profit of 12,000,000 dollars, after voluntarily reducing the interest rate, resulting in a saving of many millions to the borrowing district.

On August 11, 1939, more than 700 Angelenos, business and civic leaders, greeted Jones at a "Jesse Jones luncheon," given by the city's chamber of commerce, to celebrate the completion of the aqueduct. In presenting to Jones a huge vase sent from the Metropolitan Water District W. P. Whitsett, chairman of its board of directors, said, "For the past ten years the foremost problem in America has been to find useful employment for millions of our citizens who were victims of economic chaos unprecedented in history.

"Our honor guest today, as chairman of the Reconstruction Finance Corporation, has made possible honest creative work for hundreds of thousands of men on constructive, self-liquidating projects which will stand as monuments to his wisdom and ability in the administration of public funds."

The vase which Whitsett handed to Jones bore this inscription:

Honorable Jesse H. Jones,
great administrator and practical statesman,
whose lasting service, nation-wide and to California,
is gratefully appreciated.
Presented by Board of Directors of
Metropolitan Water District of Southern California,
August 11, 1939. Los Angeles, California.

There were other projects almost as spectacular as the aqueduct; there were hundreds of other pay-for-itself improvements in cities and villages, in many cases being loans of only a few thousand dollars.

Finding money for the schoolteachers in Chicago was another task for Jones. There were 19,000 of them, and for fifteen months they had been without pay. Representative Adolph J. Sabath went to the RFC for assistance. There was nothing it could do under existing statutes; but Jones told him a law could be passed.

Sabath had difficulty in drawing a bill. The predicament of the unpaid teachers so appealed to Jones' sympathy that he went to Chicago and spent two days helping the Board of Education work out ways to get funds.

He discovered that the Chicago school system, which owed its teachers millions of dollars, owned an entire block in the downtown Loop district bounded by State, Madison, Dearborn, and Monroe Streets. Jones suggested that Sabath draw his bill to provide that the RFC could loan money where the security was the property of the school system but not used for school purposes, which made it impossible for any other schools except Chicago to qualify. The bill went through, and Jones sent a check to pay the long-overdue salaries.

Jones had been chairman of the RFC for more than a year when, in June, 1934, Congress, at his request, amended the law permitting it to make loans to business and industry.

In the next four years it made 9000 loans aggregating almost 500,-

000,000 dollars. Most of the money went to little businessmen rather than to big corporations. More than a third of the loans were for 5000 dollars or less; well over half were for 10,000 dollars or less. Loans for 50,000 or more amounted to only 17 per cent of the whole.

Jones gave an inordinate amount of his time to these small-business loans. He knew little people and little businesses, and their trials and struggles. In a colloquy with Miss Jessie Summers, a Congresswoman from Illinois, he said. "Do you know how many businessmen there are who do not fail? It is a very small number. I am for the fellow who fails and gets up and tries again."

Originally the law required that loans be "fully and adequately secured." It was in the interest of small business that Jones asked Congress to amend the law to read "so secured as reasonably to assure its repayment." Because of this liberalization the loans to small business showed the greatest percentage loss to the government of any of its peacetime loans, about 10 per cent. But Jones felt that the number of people these loans put to work or kept at work justified the loss.

Business loans had the effect of saving many businesses, including a national department-store chain with stores in a dozen of the nation's largest cities. The telegraph companies were not getting along well financially. He got Congress to allow Western Union to take over Postal Telegraph, to which RFC had loaned 12,600,000 dollars, and so effect a consolidation of the two companies.

He also loaned the money for the first underground parking space in the United States, under Union Square in San Francisco.

A business loan of boldly pioneering nature, important to the United States and especially to the South, was for the construction of a newsprint mill at Lufkin, Texas, to make newsprint from yellow pine.

Rural Electrification got its big leap forward in a quick meeting between Senator George W. Norris of Nebraska and Jones. Norris' plan called for the spending of between 500,000,000 and one billion dollars to take electricity to the farms through cooperatives. He took the plan to the White House. Jones was on the President's visiting list just before Norris.

Marvin McIntyre, the President's appointment secretary, came in to announce that Norris had arrived.

"Jess," said Roosevelt, "George Norris is coming to see me about some grandiose rural-electrification scheme. It's too far up in the milky way of finance for me to comprehend. I am going to talk to him about some other things; then I want you to see about his cooperatives." Norris came in.

"George," Roosevelt greeted the Senator, "I want you and Jess to go into the Cabinet Room and see if you can make a deal."

"Oh, Mr. President," Norris responded, "I don't think Jones and I could get together in the rest of our lifetime."

"Why?" asked Roosevelt.

"Well, he's a banker; he wants too much interest and too much security," Norris replied.

Roosevelt suggested they make a try of it anyway.

"How much do you think it will take?" Jones asked Norris when they were in the Cabinet Room.

"To carry electricity to the farms of the country will probably take a billion dollars," Norris answered.

"How fast can it be spent?" countered Jones.

"That's anybody's guess; but I would say at the rate of 40,000,000 dollars a year," Norris estimated. "But your interest is too high; the farmers should not have to pay more than 3 or 4 per cent."

Jones asked how 3 per cent would be, and Norris thought that was about right.

"Then," Jones said, "the RFC will lend up to 40,000,000 dollars a year for the next ten years, at 3 per cent interest, secured by notes of local rural electrification organizations such as cooperatives, with a 20 per cent margin to the RFC. That means we will lend 80 per cent of the face value of the farmers' note to the local agencies."

A little groggy because he had worked out his whole dream in a ten-minute conference, Norris went back to the President's office with the RFC chairman and said: "Mr. President, Jones and I are in agreement. He must have been raised on a farm."

Twenty years later Jones looked up the record of the Rural Electrification Administration. He found that its delinquencies had represented less than 1 per cent of the amount due. In 1935, 11 per cent of American farms had electricity; in 1955 the percentage was 95.

In the Export-Import Bank, which became an RFC subsidiary in 1934, Jones was to pursue a policy similar to that which he had followed on domestic loans. He expected his loans to be paid back, and attempted to get proper security.

One foreign loan that Jones made seemed to be running counter to Administration policy. It was 16,000,000 dollars to the Franco government shortly after the end of the Spanish Civil War. The purpose of that loan was to enable Spain to buy surplus American cotton. It was promptly paid.

Poland's record on a loan to buy cotton was almost as good. Even after Stalin and Hitler divided between them the homeland of Kosciuszko, Pulaski, and Paderewski, the payments were kept up by the Polish government-in-exile, through funds that had been kept in the United States.

Although Jones had a preference for private rather than government loans, he had a painstaking study made of the export-credit agencies of all countries; and there were important government loans in South America, Europe, and the Far East.

The government of Chiang Kai-shek in China wanted to borrow 25,000,000 dollars, and promised to pay it back by the shipment of tung oil. Jones made the loan but thought it doubtful that the Chinese could get the oil to the ships, so critical was its internal condition—plus the fact that many of its ports were occupied by the Japanese. But Chiang's government got the tung oil to the United States on time, despite these many obstacles. Later another loan was made, and China was again as good as its word and paid off in tin and tungsten its entire pledge, although the Japanese by now had nearly all of its ports. The Chinese loans brought necessary increments to the great war stockpiles that Jones built up.

Jones was especially interested in loans to Central and South America. The Export-Import Bank that he headed made loans looking toward the placing of orders in the United States for big electrical projects in Brazil, Chile, and Colombia. To Chile, Brazil, and Paraguay went loans which were used for the purchase in this country of railroad equipment and road-building machinery. Venezuela was aided in getting first-class meat-packing plants.

In one instance the Minister of Finance in Argentina, called Jones by long-distance telephone and wanted to borrow 50,000,000 dollars for six months.

Jones asked how he expected to pay it, was satisfied, and told him he could have the money, and to let him know in what New York bank he would like to have it deposited. The obligation was promptly paid at its maturity.

To Brazil went loans to develop the rich Itabira iron ore; to rebuild and modernize the rusty Victoria Minas Railroad in order to bring this ore to ports; for the construction of a modern steel mill by Companhia Siderurgica Nacional at Volta Redonda; to enable Lloyd Brasileiro, a steamship line, to purchase the American ships that proved so useful in the commerce between the United States and Brazil in World War II.

In the Brazilian negotiations Jones dealt principally with Ambassador Carlos Martins and with Oswaldo Aranha, the Brazilian Minister of Foreign Affairs. Both Jones and Martins were excellent bridge players; and some of the aid to Brazil, which also proved very helpful to the United States, was made over the bridge table at the Brazilian Embassy.

21

The Jones Pattern of Management

IF the pages of this book fail to convey the stature and lineaments of the most extraordinary public administrator of his time, perhaps of all time, the blame must rest with the author, not the subject. For while his methods conformed to none of the stereotyped patterns of administration his results were amazingly successful. Comparison with notable administrators of the past cannot be conclusive, not only because of the unique methods that Jones followed, but because of the fact that administrators like Alexander Hamilton, in the Treasury of the infant republic, or Elihu Root, reorganizing the War Department at the turn of the century, were dealing with the affairs of a much smaller country.

Comparison with contemporary administrators in other fields are likewise inconclusive. Commanding generals or heads of great civil departments have had advantage of long-established and well-tried formulas and methods of management. Jones in the RFC was compelled to create his own formulas and precedents from day to day in a field that had no traditions. The tasks assumed were massive beyond comprehension, and the results stand unmarred by legitimate criticism.

In the field of money-lending Jones was most often compared with the elder J. Pierpont Morgan who died in 1913 when Jones was thirty-nine years old. But the conditions that faced Jones differed in many ways from those prevailing in private banking, and the amounts handled by Jones in a very few years were far in excess of the Morgan operation over decades.

Some idea of the administrative burden carried by Jones can be had by considering some of the common varieties of administrative operations, most of them relatively uncomplicated and capable of fixed standards of conduct.

There is the task of directing a private business in which many interests, including labor, customers, and stockholder-owners, must be balanced, and in the course of which the vagaries of a prying government, a fickle public opinion, and mysterious economic tides have to be encountered. Some of these were not among the worries of Jones, but at the same time they are capable of rational calculation.

Then there is the pattern of management of the professional civil servant in Britain and the British Commonwealth. He may steer his course fairly detached from political currents and party vicissitudes. He also has the advantage of long traditions that have channeled grooves of conduct through which he can move with little exercise of initiative, imagination, or innovation.

There is the old Prussian type, arbitrary, autocratic, respected, and feared. He, too, operated within limited horizons and with ample blueprints from the mill of experience.

There are also the rules and plans, highly theoretical, of American professors and pundits who write about a science of administration, and who have over a period of forty years given us a considerable literature on their subject.

The complexity of Jones' task, which he seemed to perform with such ease, can be properly appreciated only by listing some of the cross-currents with which he had to deal, and which none of the foregoing types of administrators or plans of administration were compelled to include in their calculations.

Foremost among the annoyances with which Jones had to cope were the innumerable jealousies, ambitions, and feuds that can plague any administration but which in the Roosevelt years were especially violent. Jones managed to maintain peaceful and cooperative relations with all of Roosevelt's strange and ill-assorted top administrators except, as we shall see. Henry Wallace, Secretary of Agriculture and Vice-President, and Harold Ickes, Secretary of the Interior, and Public Works Administrator.

There were the many real and alleged White House intimates without official status, but who were for one reason or another eagerly seeking some sort of official favors. There were also the many members of the Roosevelt family with axes to grind. Jones dealt with such diversionary factors as they came, mostly with success but always with tact and skill.

Swarming in Washington in those days was a host of chiselers and other unsavory gentry who would have, if they could, made their way into the rich resources presided over by Jones. Never until the departure of Jones from Washington was this type to gain favor with the RFC.

There were also the special problems that Jones faced in dealing with Congress and with the members of Congress individually. These relations demanded a great deal of Jones' time and attention.

A major complication in managing the vast affairs of the RFC was the inevitable confusion attending the multipurposes of a government business. A private business has as its objective the making of a profit and incidentally of providing service for the public and fair treatment for its employees. A government business is not being run for the purpose of making money, no matter how well it may be managed. The spirit of the times demands of government two other objectives: service to citizens and institutions and the public welfare. Since ours is a political government, there is an element of politics that may or may not be wholly harmless and legitimate according to the standards of the times. Jones repeatedly made it clear that the RFC was a nonpolitical operation, which meant that it was not to be used to serve any party or personal advantage. And the record shows that he not only meant what he said but fulfilled his assertion to the letter.

In the administration of the great affairs of the RFC, Jones was compelled to navigate his craft in a sea whipped by political winds that blew in all directions at all times, all during the Roosevelt Administration. Because of this Jones' canny political instinct was indispensable. Only those who understand politics can avoid its perils.

In the Roosevelt years the government's concern with what was called the public welfare was stressed far beyond anything that had happened in the past. And in thrusting the hand of government into private affairs there was a great deal of politics. Jones was genuinely concerned with promoting the well-being of every citizen, but he was also concerned with conserving the interests of every citizen as a taxpayer.

It was such elements in the administrative task bestowed upon Jones that made it unique in the history of government. It was his success in the job which is the measure of his greatness as an administrator; for the time and the complexities of the task required unique qualities, and Jones proved that he had them.

After the initial rescue operations had somehow been carried out, with improvisation the order of the day, and with Jones almost single-handedly bearing the burden of making decisions, Jones' pattern of management began to emerge. A review of the first few years made it clear that the very looseness of the legal structure of the RFC, and its freedom from bureaucratic restraints, had made it possible to accomplish its ends. In operating it, Jones had, in fact, ignored almost every condition that academic and bureaucratic treatises on administration have prescribed.

There was never a clear differentiation between policy and administration. Board members themselves generally did their own investigation and made their decisions on the basis of what they personally found out. But from beginning to end Jones freely mingled policy and administration. This was possible, of course, because, drawing upon long business experience and plenty of innate political skill, he had clear ideas of what policy should be. The point was that he never bothered to freeze the rules and principles by which he, the board, and his subordinates (to whom he always referred as "associates," never as "subordinates") were expected to follow.

After the advent of the Roosevelt Administration and the critical months that followed, it seemed to be assumed by the public that the RFC and Jesse Jones were one and the same being, with Jones in complete dominance. Officially, the corporation was under the direction of its board, which until 1938 consisted of seven members. In that year, on the recommendation of Jones, Congress reduced the number to five, which it remained thereafter. Directors were appointed for terms of two years all of which expired at the same time. When that time came, Jones would remind the President and suggest his own ticket. When there were differences of opinion because of patronage considerations, they were ironed out and Jones' recommendations were in the end followed although, at times, tardily.*

Jones himself solemnly maintained that he was only one member of a board of directors, and there was always a majority of the board recorded in favor of any action taken; but Carroll B. Merriam, a Re-

* See Chapter 23, p. 267.

publican member of the board for eight years, said, "When Mr. Jones favored something, it never occurred to any of us to oppose it."

Emil Schram, who succeeded Jones as chairman of the RFC when Jones became Federal Loan Administrator, gave this reason for the clear fact that Jones' influence was dominant after the first few months of the life of the RFC:

> In the most critical part of the depression, the RFC required a prophet, a man who could forecast what would be the result of a specific action. Mr. Jones had an uncanny way of knowing how a loan would not only help a business, but how that help would benefit a community and benefit to that community fit into the national recovery. His nature and experience ripened him for the decisions and conclusions he had to make. But he never forced an action on his fellow directors. There were high-class men on the RFC Board of Directors who would not have hesitated to say so if they had disagreed with him. None of us had his experience, his training, his outlook, and unerring judgment. We were proud to follow his leadership.

Wilson McCarthy said, "Soon after the RFC was organized, we found that the old maxim that ability sits at the head of the table was doubly true at RFC; for at the head of the table sat Jesse H. Jones. The major contributing influence to the greatness of the agency was the work and character of Mr. Jones."

Jones was always generous in according credit and praise to his fellow board members after the early period. This is reflected in his account of the informal but correct manner in which business was dispatched:

> After the first year, the demands upon the RFC became so heavy that it was necessary to allocate certain types of loans and investments to individual directors [Jones wrote]. As was generally known, I concerned myself chiefly with railroads and with bank loans, giving a great deal of time to purchase of preferred stock in banks, or their capital notes and debentures. I had general supervision over the RFC, and counseled with other directors in reference to their problems.
>
> While the Board, in its consideration of the various applications for loans, necessarily had to be guided by the judgment of the individual director and his examiners who were in charge of the case in question, every loan or investment, with one or two exceptions, had the unanimous approval of the Board.
>
> Shortly after I became Chairman, I suggested to our Board that we amend our bylaws so as to give any three directors, regardless of their politics, authority to make loans. Within the Board, we had an executive committee composed of three directors, selected without regard to political affiliations. In practice, the committee was interchangeable from day to day, and without formality. Any three members of the Board could constitute themselves an executive committee and make commitments. Then, when the Board was in

session, which usually was daily, what an executive committee had done would be reported and confirmed, or become board action. This procedure enabled us to act faster. While a little unorthodox, it worked. I can truthfully say that politics never influenced any action of our Board from the time I became Chairman; and I never saw any sign of such influence, even before that.

We went on the principle that, if any director could give a valid reason why a loan should not be made, generally it was not authorized.

Once in a while, a director might be recorded as not voting, or even as dissenting; but always because of the apparent insufficiency of the security offered. Usually, we acted unanimously. There were, during the first six months of the Corporation's work, some clashes and differences of opinion at Board meetings; but, when Mr. Meyer was no longer with us, we had complete harmony.

Thus the Jones pattern of board management provided at once expedition and dispatch, with strength and continuity over the long years beginning with 1933.

During those years H. G. Wells came to the United States to witness the renowned New Deal experiment. In the course of his visit he spent several hours in Jones' office. Here is his report:

I sat back on a comfortable sofa and watched one of the most extraordinary men (perhaps the most extraordinary) I have ever seen perform his functions through a bustling day. He was entirely uninhibited. He offered to allow me to examine the papers and documents on the business in hand. There is no snap of authority in the man's mien. He has great fidelity to his associates and subordinates, and places much reliance in them. He seems at once to be working leisurely and running at top speed solving the problems which crowd in in engulfing abundance.

Fancy the presiding official of the Old Lady of Threadneedle Street (the Bank of England) carrying on affairs in such fashion.

Hardly in history has one man had his country's resources so much at his command; and hardly in history have resources had such acumen at their command.

Roosevelt, who never cherished the prominence or power of a subordinate who might be a potential rival, once said admiringly, "Jesse Jones is the only man in Washington who can say 'yes' or 'no' intelligently twenty-four hours a day." * This indeed was praise; for the President was notorious for his lack of ability to say "no" without an escape clause.

Jones' capacity for personal and decisive action amazed Bruce Barton, who wrote at the time:

* Message of Franklin D. Roosevelt to Houston dinner honoring Jones on October 20, 1933.

I recall one meeting with Mr. Jones. It was an appointment in his hotel room in New York. He came in, took off his coat, kicked off his shoes, lay down on the bed, picked up the telephone, and proceeded to make rapid decisions on a half-dozen big RFC situations in widely separated areas across the country.

But Jones' informality when Barton saw him was not standard procedure with him. After the rush of emergency work of the first years was over, he provided himself with new and commodious quarters.

For seven years the RFC conducted the biggest banking business in the world in the leased obsolete old former Department of Commerce Building at Pennsylvania Avenue and Nineteenth Street. Then Jones picked up his organization and all of its subsidiary corporations and moved, bag and baggage, to a new building across Lafayette Park from the White House.

Jones financed the handsome, twelve-story building in the typical Jones manner. Other government agencies were functioning in cramped quarters for which they paid exorbitant rents. Jones found a firm that could erect a satisfactory building. He lent them the money and took an option to buy the building at cost or to lease it at a reasonable rate. He first exercised the option to lease, then the one to buy it.

The structure seemed large when the RFC moved in; but two years later, when in the war effort the number of RFC employees reached the peak of 12,000 men and women, it was crammed, and the RFC was also occupying parts of five additional buildings. Fifteen years after Jones pioneered that method of obtaining quarters for the RFC, the method used to build the Lafayette Building was adopted by Congress, in a law specifying the procedure to be followed in building new post offices and federal buildings throughout the nation.

Jones had designed the building; and, for himself, he took a 1000-foot-square office on its top floor. Around the big room, which was paneled in knotty pine, were half a dozen other offices or conference rooms, most of them with doors opening into Jones' office. Into these private rooms the Jones office staff distributed his callers as required by the size of the group. An individual went into an office, a delegation into a conference room. From these either they could be ushered into Jones' office or Jones would leave his desk and join a waiting group. Thus he was able to keep a half-dozen important conferences going at once. Jones never appeared hurried at any of the meetings; and each of his visitors was often unaware that he was only one of a half-dozen individuals or groups with whom Jones was dealing, all at the same time.

But for all his seeming unhurriedness in such meetings Jones had a way of keeping them short. Usually he had made up his mind, one way or another, before long-winded group spokesmen were half through their arguments. He used various methods to shorten such presentations. A favorite one was to halt the spokesman for the would-be borrower, ask to see a balance sheet, glance at it, then give his decision on whether to make a loan, and the terms on which it would be made if it were.

One room was so set up that it could be used for dining. Jones lunched there almost every day, and seldom alone. The guest or guests might be an old journalistic friend, other Cabinet officers of agency heads, an ambassador, a Senator or Representative, a member of the Supreme Court, or some of his RFC staff. Usually business was talked at this luncheon.

That much-abused and, in Washington, much-exploited official function called public relations was never strictly formalized in the Jones scheme of management; but its substance was never neglected. Jones was his own public-relations counsel, and no one ever did the job more effectively. His earlier years in Washington had taught him the innumerable pitfalls that threaten the unsophisticated public official there, the caprices and preferences and habits of Washington representatives of the press, and the vital necessity of building a favorable public opinion concerning such a new activity as that of the RFC. Moreover, in his years in Houston, Jones had learned the highways and byways of opinion; and he knew the newspaper business from all angles through his own *Chronicle*.

His never-humdrum press conferences were valuable both to him and to the news men and women. Jones knew more news writers than anyone in public life; he saw them when they came on special news matters, or was available by telephone. His acquaintance was large and, in many cases, intimate with the chiefs of news bureaus and older news correspondents.

He was a special favorite of the Gridiron Club, a limited-membership newspaper dining organization, which has a length-of-residence requirement that practically assures that its membership will be none but veteran Washington newspapermen. Once that club at a dinner departed from a half-century of custom and gave him, a nonmember, a speaking part in one of its skits.

There was another organization of newspapermen, the duties of whose members chiefly were news coverage of the White House. It called itself a school of expression; and its mythical campus was the White House lawn, and took the name of J. Russell Young, the dean of its writers. It had mock annual graduating ceremonies at which diplomas were given to public figures. Jones, as its first graduate and tallest member, always walked at the head of the daisy-chain parade. His ability to drop his heavy responsibilities long enough to engage in such horseplay did no injury to the personal esteem most Washington news writers had for him.

In his operations Jones sometimes would invite newspapermen or magazine writers to watch the corporation at work. They might be invited to a meeting of the board of directors. He would receive borrowers in their presence, let the writers hear every phase of the discussion. Sometimes he would let the writers stay for an entire day if they wished. He not only let them hear the conversations with the borrowers; if he had a conversation over the telephone, he would tell his visitors who the call was from and what was said on the other end of the line.

Like most businessmen, his public utterances during his earlier years were few and informal. From the time he made his first real public speech before a college graduating class in 1925, until he was appointed to the RFC, he made only a few more. But under the stress of the years after 1932 he became an effective speaker. Writing a speech, however, was an arduous task, a task that, unfortunately, most high officials soon consign entirely to ghostly assistants.

Jones used the suggestions of many people, but ultimately he laboriously worked out his own scripts. Sometimes he would ask someone to give him some ideas on paper, and sometimes he would have them prepare a full-length speech. These he never regarded as more than the raw material for his own version of what he wanted to say.

An examination of the speeches delivered by Jones in the long and critical years in Washington shows that, despite the informal manner in which they were delivered, they were carefully prepared. Jones would never settle for a word other than one that conveyed precisely what he wanted to say. This care was well rewarded; for, while his utterances were properly regarded as those of a major policymaker in the government, there is no evidence that during all that time Jones was guilty of one of those blunders that are the bane of every government.

He thought no speech ought to be over thirty minutes long, and tried to keep his own down to fifteen minutes. Jones' letters were likewise distinguished by brevity and precision. There are few letters in the files of that period which are more than three paragraphs in length. He once remarked that "if you cannot say it in one page, you cannot say it in nine."

The message embodied in almost every utterance by Jones in those years was the responsibility resting upon the RFC to justify itself as a sound and economical operation. He well knew that, if he yielded to the philosophy so prevalent in New Deal agencies at the time, the resources of which he was custodian might well be dissipated at the expense of the total safety and stability of the nation.

Jones never made this point more clear than in 1940, when he was subjected to questioning concerning the Finnish loan by the Senate Committee on Banking and Currency:

"I do not feel that the administrator of this law under which we operate has any right to lend money which he does not expect to get back."

He said before the American Bankers Association convention in 1935, "Congress gave our directors rather broad power in making loans; but we have never forgotten that it is the taxpayers' money we are lending. We have tried to be prudent as well as helpful."

"The RFC has shown that the government can function successfully in business," he told a group of Southern California financial leaders in a speech in Los Angeles.

He did not, to be sure, believe that just any government agency could do a good job in business; but he was sure the RFC could.

It would perhaps be an exaggeration to say that Jones regarded his institution as solely a business one; for mingled with the objectives he had in mind was the national welfare, which transcended merely lending and in every case getting the money back. But it was always the national welfare that he kept in mind, and not the smaller welfares that sought help at his hands. The RFC's affairs were always conducted in such a manner that, if a loss had to be risked in the promotion of the national welfare, there was always a prospective profit from a sound loan to offset the possible loss.

Most businessmen who come to Washington to assume a big administrative post bitterly resent or bear with much suffering the fact that they are not free, in government, to conduct affairs with the expedition and single-handed authority to which they were accustomed in private business. They discover that they must contend not only with the overlapping authorities among executive departments, with bureaucratic intrigues and jealousies, with the political atmosphere that surrounds the White House, but with the inexorable demands of 435 Representatives and ninety-six Senators. This collective fourth dimension in public administration usually proves the major problem with which they have to deal; and in many cases it is the reason why so many men successful in private business have failed so miserably in government.

If Jones felt this extra series of problems to be onerous or frustrating, he never admitted it in public; for he had not only a shrewd comprehension of politics but a temperament equal to the strains imposed by its infinite demands.

He was also possessed of a masterful understanding of the virtues and frailties of all sorts and conditions of human beings. Indeed, his business acumen was so great that the purely business side of his job was only an incidental in the performance of which he found excellent assistants. He devoted himself to his relations with the White House, with his colleagues in the executive departments, and with Congress with a hearty zest.

Jones' Relations with the White House

FOR twelve of his thirteen years in office Jones was associated with a President whose vagaries of administration and personnel management will be the theme of historical comment for generations. As time went on, Jones grew to know what everyone ultimately learned in dealing with Roosevelt. He learned that the man with whom he was to be associated for a dozen years was possessed of an infinitely subtle nature, in which all sorts of strange motives were veiled in almost perennial good humor.

He learned that what Roosevelt said was not always what Roosevelt meant; that, when the President told of an event or conversation, he often embellished his story to give it point or color. He also learned that the Chief Executive's mind was essentially that of a man gambling with great and seldom calculated risks; that a subordinate might be given an assignment and, a day later, another subordinate might be given an assignment that would most certainly result in conflict and confusion; and that this man who towered in his day and generation was capable of infinitely frivolous and petty affairs.

That this relationship ultimately resulted in a tragically grotesque end is not strange. It is a wonder that it did not happen earlier, a marvel partially explained by the real and urgent need of Roosevelt for at least one first-rate administrator in his official family; in part by the skill with which Jones managed his relations with the White House; but in greater part by Jones' strength with Congress.

The relations between Jones and the President provide the material for an extraordinary study, not only in contrasts and conflicts, but in mutual interdependence. Their tasks were complementary, and their success in achieving them demanded cooperation. But in background, experience, personal philosophy, methods of work, and ideals the two were wholly unlike.

Roosevelt came of a distinguished line; from the beginning he had all that wealth and genteel tradition could give. Jones was born not in poverty but in an atmosphere of hard work on the land. Roosevelt passed through long-established and notable institutions of learning; Jones' formal schooling was brief and primitive. The President was from the North; Jones was Southern by birth and sympathies. Jones was trained through hard experience in business and trade, large and small; Roosevelt was, at most, a detached observer and beneficiary of large enterprises. Jones loved and was profoundly devoted to the associates of his past; Roosevelt always seemed to be at odds with a majority of those who shared his environment and early life. Jones thought in terms of specifics, Roosevelt in vague generalities.

The approach of the two men to political problems and methods was in no way similar. Roosevelt was an extrovert, although his purposes were often complex and devious; Jones was taciturn and short of words. Roosevelt compelled himself to share the simple convivialities that went with politics; Jones found such recreations natural and shared them with enjoyment. Jones was at ease with the leaders of the business world; Roosevelt, from beginning to end, found them strange and difficult.

Ultimately these great differences prevailed and further official and personal relations were foreclosed. But for many years they contrived to work together in what was sometimes a strained but was generally an efficient harmony.

There was another potential but important barrier to any deep friendship between the two men. Jones had been a member of what might be called the senior group around Woodrow Wilson. He was a contemporary of, although somewhat younger than, Newton D. Baker, Secretary of War; W. G. McAdoo, Secretary of the Treasury; and Carter Glass, also Secretary of the Treasury for a time. Ultimately Jones became with Cleveland Dodge and Cary Grayson one of a loyal trio who stood with Wilson to the end of his life.

Roosevelt on the other hand had been a junior not only in age but in official status. As an assistant Cabinet officer he had no opportunity to enter the circles of Wilson intimates. He was not highly regarded by some of the older group, notably Baker and Glass. Some others of the senior members, perhaps without realizing it, had hurt the Assistant Navy Secretary's ego by what he felt was unjustified condescension. As President, while it became politically necessary to get on with them, Roosevelt's close alignment was with those who were of another political generation and, as it proved, of another ideological faith.

The future President and the future government banker had first become acquainted in World War I. But it was not until the Davis Presidential campaign in 1924 that Roosevelt and Jones came to know one another better than the slight acquaintance of war years. Jones, as Director of Finance of the Democratic National Committee, was in charge of raising funds for that campaign. Roosevelt, just recovering from his polio attack, occupied a desk near that of Jones in the New York Biltmore headquarters of the party.

They were on a "Frank" and "Jesse" basis at that time; but, in an interchange of letters between them just prior to the 1928 Democratic National Convention, they reverted to a "mister" basis in writing to one another. These letters had to do with the 1924 campaign deficit that Jones was engaged in liquidating. In one letter Roosevelt addressed him as "Senator" Jones, a title he had jokingly conferred during the 1924 campaign.

When Roosevelt, in 1928, came to Houston to place Governor Alfred E. Smith in nomination for the presidency a second time, they were again "Frank" and "Jesse." That is the way it was with Roosevelt for the remainder of his life; but Roosevelt soon acquired the title of governor, and Jones, no such inveterate first-name caller as Roosevelt, used this title and, later, that of "Mr. President."

Jones was a member of the Texas delegation to the 1932 convention, and thus was pledged to John Nance Garner for the nomination. But since the switch of that group and of the California delegation gave the nomination to Roosevelt, Jones was, in Roosevelt's mind, free of the "stigma" of having opposed him to the end.

Jones had no active part in the campaign in 1932 since he was a busy member of the board of the RFC at that time. But during that autumn he visited Roosevelt in Albany to ask him not to attack the RFC and to explain the wholly nonpolitical character of its loans. A memorandum by Jones tells of this:

I was told that Governor Roosevelt intended to condemn the RFC as a Republican grab bag. So I took with me to Albany a list of all applications for loans covering a period of weeks, and showed him that, instead of the Corporation being reproached for loans it was making, it could be more appropriately upbraided for not making loans. I knew we were not doing enough. I went over them page by page with him, and he told me he would make no criticisms.

A second memorandum read:

Another time, I was told he intended to charge the RFC with making large loans to railroads at the instance of railroad bankers. I went to see him at Hyde Park, and discussed the situation with him fully and to his satisfaction; and, as far as I know, he made no criticism of the RFC in public or private during his campaign.

Jones saw the President-Elect several times between election and inauguration, but with one exception these were chance meetings. That exception was on the day after Zangara attempted to assassinate the President-Elect in Miami, fatally wounding Mayor Anton J. Cermak, of Chicago, instead.

Roosevelt asked Jones, who was in Florida, to join his special train on the way back to New York. Cordell Hull, whom Roosevelt had selected as his Secretary of State, was the other guest on this ride. On this occasion Roosevelt told Jones he wished him to be chairman of the RFC.

The law provides that the RFC directors should choose their own chairman. Jones, however, felt that the chairman should be someone agreeable to the President. Some days after the inauguration, thinking it possible that the President might have changed his mind and wished someone else to be chairman, Jones telephoned to Raymond Moley at the White House and asked him to remind the President that the RFC was without a chairman.

Moley telephoned back and said that the President desired that Jones go ahead as acting chairman. This Jones declined to do, and the Democratic members continued to take turns at presiding. In the rotation each served for a day.

A little later Jones met Postmaster General Farley in the lobby of the Mayflower, where they both lived. Jones explained the situation to Farley. He told Farley the RFC ought to have a permanent chairman.

Within an hour of the talk with Farley, Secretary of the Treasury Woodin telephoned to Jones to say that the President thought Jones was already chairman. The following day Woodin, who was an *ex-officio* member of the RFC board of directors but, busy in getting acquainted with his new Cabinet office, had been unable to attend directors' meetings, came to a meeting and nominated Jones to the chairmanship. He was unanimously elected.

The necessities of the bank crisis required daily conferences between Jones and the President. In the period when the RFC was carrying on the gold-purchase program, Jones went to Roosevelt's bedroom every morning at eight-thirty, and there was fixed the price of gold for that day. Their meetings later were, of course, not so often, but it is probable that over the years Jones saw Roosevelt more frequently than any other member of the Cabinet.

> I never considered that I was working for him, but with him for the country, just as I felt that the fine organization at the RFC was working with me, not for me. In reappointing me to the RFC in 1934, 1936, and 1938, he asked me each time if I wanted the same Board of Directors, or had any suggestions about other members [Jones wrote].

If Roosevelt had a stand-offish attitude in respect to interference in any government agency, it was toward the RFC. It was not in reality an executive agency, being more of the nature of a partnership between the Executive and Congress. The directors were nominated by the President and confirmed by the Senate, but since the RFC was a corporation it is doubtful if the President could have legally removed them.

If Roosevelt did not seem to regard Jones as a subordinate of the President, neither did Congress. There came the period after the rejection of the President's plan to enlarge the Supreme Court in 1937, when Congress passed no Roosevelt-sponsored legislation and sought to retrieve for itself some of the power it had given him. In this period of distrust of the Executive, Congress gave more power than ever to Jones. It was this fact, more than any other, that caused him to be referred to as "a fourth branch of government."

Jones made every effort to keep both the President and Congress advised as to what the RFC was doing. But he seldom informed either the Chief Executive or Congress in advance of these actions.

Insofar as Congress was concerned, it had given him the law; and that law, and the circumstances in each case, would govern. Only rarely did even an individual member of Congress criticize what the RFC was doing.

In the case of the President, Jones did whatever he could to advance the Administration's recovery program; but he believed that it was the responsibility of himself and his fellow directors of the bipartisan agency to find the individual solutions that would assist the economic lift.

Jones remembered, and his records show, only a few suggestions for individual loans made by the President; and all these were denied. In one case, however, that of David Stern and the Philadelphia *Record,* Jones did arrange for the loan from banks.

It was Jones' fixed policy that, for perfectly adequate reasons, loans would not be made to four highly respectable institutions. They were newspapers, churches, automobile-manufacturing concerns, and the petroleum industry in general.

Jones, as a newspaper publisher, had been insistent on the ban on newspaper loans. He thought most newspapers that needed money could make arrangements with private banks. If the RFC made them loans, the government would be accused of attempting to dictate their editorial policies. Church loans, once started, would be endless. Loans to the motor and oil industry, under the situations then obtaining, would have been highly speculative.

At President Roosevelt's request, Jones looked into Stern's situation. Jones regarded the 1,000,000-dollar loan as a good one for a bank. Although Stern's newspaper was a zealous New Deal-Roosevelt supporter, Jones called a stanch Republican and president of a bank that had never needed RFC assistance. When he explained the situation to Joseph Wayne, Jr., president of the Philadelphia National Bank, Wayne said he would see that the loan was made, which he promptly did, setting it up through the Camden Trust Company and other participants. The loan was paid on schedule by Stern.

Roosevelt had been even more insistent that a loan be made to the Chattanooga *News.* George Fort Milton, the publisher of the Tennessee newspaper, was also a strong New Deal supporter. But the prospects of repayment of the loan were far less promising than in the case of Stern's newspaper, and Jones could not recommend it to a banker. The established policy was against loans to newspapers, he reminded the President.

"What the devil, Jess!" Roosevelt exclaimed when Jones told him he could not make the Chattanooga loan. "They are good friends of ours, and we ought to help them."

Another instance where Jones refused a request urgently made by Roosevelt, he described this way:

> It had to do with a friend of his from the days when Mr. Roosevelt was Assistant Secretary of the Navy, who wanted to buy an island off the coast of South America. This former naval officer represented that there was sul-

phur in the bed of an old volcano on the island and that the island had a large number of cattle on it. The President wanted the RFC to make this old friend a loan of approximately 2,000,000 dollars.

Because of the scarcity of sulphur, I had the project investigated, and found that there was no sulphur there, and that the cattle were not worth a dollar when their quality and the expense in getting them out was taken into account. Obviously, it was a loan the Corporation should not have made, and did not.

Most of the time Roosevelt seemed to have a genuine affection for Jones. On a number of occasions the President would cruise down the Potomac with only Mr. and Mrs. Jones as his guests. Sometimes Jones sat in poker games with the President at the White House, but Jones regarded him as a poor poker player.

Sometimes he invited Jones to Hyde Park or Warm Springs. Roosevelt often twitted Jones about being "the richest man in the Administration." When the March of Dimes campaign was inaugurated in 1939, Roosevelt insisted that Jones go to New York Avenue and Fourteenth Street in Washington, head a line of people that was two blocks long, and put in the first dime.

On occasion he would tell Jones, "Your conservatism is a good thing for us in this Administration." Several times before finally appointing Jones Secretary of Commerce, he had said, "Jesse, I want you in the Cabinet."

The first vacancy to occur was that of Secretary of the Treasury Woodin, who retired on account of ill health. Woodin had told Jones he wanted him to be his successor. But Roosevelt did not offer the post to the RFC chairman.

Then there came feelers about whether he would like to move into the vacated Cabinet portfolio upon the death of Secretary of War Dern in 1936.*

Shortly thereafter Roosevelt again informed Jones that he wanted him in the Cabinet. To this Jones replied that he appreciated the compliment but thought that whatever knowledge he had acquired in life suited him much more for the place he occupied than any other within the President's appointive power.

In May, 1939, when Secretary of Navy Claude A. Swanson was ill, the President asked Jones to find a trusteeship for Swanson that would afford him a living. "Then, Jesse, I want you to come into the Cabinet as Secretary of the Navy."

* Roosevelt never personally offered this place to Jones. But he sent Stephen T. Early, one of his secretaries, and Harry L. Hopkins to inquire if he would be interested in the post. Jones replied that he was not.

Jones regarded Swanson, who, before entering the Cabinet, had been a United States Senator from Virginia, as an able man, and told the President he was sure a suitable place could be found for him.

"But I don't know a battleship from a canoe; and I do not, under any conceivable circumstances, want to be Secretary of the Navy," Jones told the President.

Swanson died two months later, and the President appointed Charles Edison, of New Jersey, son of Thomas A. Edison, the inventor, to the post.

These offers to appoint Jones to a Cabinet post coincided with the efforts of New Dealers to find a way to remove Jones and thus to open the vast resources of the RFC to the policy of "spend and elect." Jones himself felt that the President, despite his flattering offers, had been influenced by these people, for he knew quite well that the President was lending a willing ear to the detractors.

But even if the President did not regard Jones as a "subordinate," Mrs. Roosevelt certainly did. Several years after Roosevelt's death she wrote in her syndicated column, "Jones worked for my husband for thirteen years."

Jones, in the meetings he had with Mrs. Roosevelt, came to regard her as a sort of Assistant President, rather than as the President's wife in the tradition of Mrs. Grover Cleveland, the two Mrs. Wilsons, and Mrs. Calvin Coolidge.

Jones' first visit to the White House to discuss a matter with Mrs. Roosevelt came early in her husband's first term. She had invited the RFC chairman to meet with her and a builder who proposed to acquire property, and construct some large apartment buildings on the lower East Side of New York.

Jones thought the idea a good one; but the man had no participating capital of his own, even if the RFC had had the authority to make such a loan, which it did not at that time. Later, when Jones got Congress to give him the authority and found a builder with a better bankroll than the one Mrs. Roosevelt introduced to him, Jones made a loan for Knickerbocker Village.

Knickerbocker Village was dedicated at a ceremony in which former Governor Alfred E. Smith, who had spent his boyhood in that vicinity, was the principal speaker. Jones, who attended, suggested to Smith that he use his still-great influence in Albany for legislation to permit the redevelopment of the area.

There were several hundred acres of old buildings that Jones thought ideal for modern apartments, parks, and community conveniences, within easy walking distance of the financial district. He told Smith that such a project would not only modernize the area but would pay itself out in twenty-five years. Smith apparently was not interested in promoting the plan, and nothing came of it.

Jones felt that Mrs. Roosevelt thought he could make any sort of loan he wished, and held it against him that he did not aid her "projects." He was surprised, therefore, when James A. Farley told him that Mrs. Roosevelt had argued with her husband that Jones, instead of Wallace, should be his 1940 running mate.

One of the RFC's principal pests was the shadowy G. Hall Roosevelt, brother of Mrs. Roosevelt and cousin of the President. G. Hall all too frequently appeared at the RFC to argue in behalf of some loan in which he was interested. At times he would be an extremely voluble and vociferous advocate. It was his habit to telephone, saying that the call was being made from the White House and that he would be right over. As the White House was less than three blocks away he would arrive quickly and depart far less expeditiously.

The RFC knowingly made no loans at G. Hall Roosevelt's behest; but it did make two or three small ones in which it later appeared that he had an interest. One of them was for creek-bed gold-panning in Alaska. A day after the loan had been authorized, Tommy Corcoran arrived posthaste from the White House, with a message to Jones. The President, no admirer of his brother-in-law and cousin, wanted the loan made. His reason, Corcoran said, was "to get G. Hall as far from the White House as possible."

There was the case of Basil O'Connor, Roosevelt's old law partner. The RFC had put 10,000,000 dollars into the distressed Globe and Rutgers Insurance Company, and was its chief creditor. O'Connor's firm, O'Connor and Farber, rendered a bill for 200,000 dollars for its part in the reorganization. There were eight law firms, whose total attorney's fees amounted to 619,500 dollars; the O'Connor bill was the largest.

Jones regarded this as exorbitant and flatly refused to approve a reorganization which paid any such fees. Jones went to the White House. He knew that no one was closer to the President than O'Connor, whom the President later was to appoint president of the American Red Cross, and also trustee of the Warm Springs Foundation. Jones told the President he had no intention of paying the fee. He soon learned, from the President's attitude, that he wanted O'Connor to have a substantial sum. The President suggested that maybe O'Connor would reduce it to

150,000 dollars. Jones said no to this too. Later, despite Jones' opposition, O'Connor got a court in New York to allow him 135,000 dollars.

Nothing so reveals the shrewd understanding of human nature as Jones' estimate of the President and his method of dealing with him. His relations were not on the order of those of Hopkins or Morgenthau, or even the belligerent and worrying Ickes. It early became apparent to Jones that the best means of the necessary contact with the White House was through the immediate secretarial staff around the President. But even there, Jones found, as a good many others did, that there were differences in influence.

Stephen Early and Marguerite Le Hand were his most trusted friends. He also enjoyed the respect and friendship of two career men whom he knew in the Wilson days, Rudolph Forster and Maurice C. Latta. But Jones never regarded Marvin McIntyre and Louis Howe as especially friendly.

Jones' own account of his relations with Roosevelt indicates that he learned something that very few of those who served in Washington in those years were able to comprehend. It served him well. Many others, who were less acute in their appraisal of the Roosevelt mind, failed to understand that it was safer to let the President do most of the talking.

Jones noted that Roosevelt "had a great habit of talking to one caller about the subject matter of his immediate preceding interview." He also realized that, if the person who had seen Roosevelt previously had disagreed with him on a matter of policy, the next interview would be plentifully interspersed with comments not wholly complimentary to the absent one. If the second caller was anxious to make a good impression, he agreed with the Presidential version and estimate.

Jones followed a policy of neither agreeing nor disagreeing with such talk. He realized that anything he said in agreement with Roosevelt's criticism of other members of the Administration or of Congress would be used by the President to strengthen his own estimate, and that the Jones estimate would, thus repeated, get back to the person involved.

Jones also realized that, if he disagreed forcibly, Roosevelt would probably pass on to the next caller his own depreciation of Jones' judgment. Hence he kept his own counsel and tried to bring back the conversation to the practical problem at issue.

Also, in the few cases in which the President made perfectly impractical or impossible requests, it would do little good to argue. The Roosevelt mind was not logical; it was wholly political. The talk he offered in support of a proposal would often be intended to prejudice or flatter the hearer, rather than to specify with any exactness the reasons why his view should prevail. In such circumstances Jones simply listened and failed to carry out the request. He said of such instances:

> When the President asked me to do something which we could not do or should not do—and you could count the number of times he made such requests on the fingers of one's hands—we just did not do it. There was no other way to get along with him; and I wanted to get along with him. We never had a serious argument; never a cross word passed between us, although we sometimes saw things differently.

Since the authority of the of the RFC ranged over the entire field of economic life, it was essential for Jones to maintain relations with many in the Administration. With a great majority of these, his relations were wholly cordial; with a few others, as the years passed, stresses and strains developed.

During the summer of 1933, as the nation attempted to fight its way back to economic health, a group of ten men was in charge of the most critical phases of the effort.

Jones, a hold-over from the Hoover Administration, as chairman of the Reconstruction Finance Corporation, had the only one of the agencies that was in full motion. Roosevelt, after the election of 1932, had intended to abolish the RFC and distribute its functions among other New Deal alphabetical creations. The fact that RFC was organized and ready to handle the crisis of the banks, railroads, and industry, and could assume the tasks without loss of time, and with the greatest possible efficiency, obviated any thought the President-Elect had along that line.

Jones was the senior member of this group, which also embraced Harry L. Hopkins, of Relief; General Hugh Johnson, NRA; Lewis W. Douglas, Director of the Budget; George N. Peek, Administrator of Agriculture Adjustment; Henry Morgenthau, Jr., Governor of the Federal Farm Credit Administration; Joseph B. Eastman, Federal Coordinator of Transportation; Robert Fechner, Director of the Civilian Conservation Corps; Dr. Arthur E. Morgan, chairman of the Tennessee Valley Authority; and later, Frank C. Walker, Coordinator and Executive Secretary of the Executive Council.

Of the ten men charged with the business of carrying into effect the Roosevelt Administration's relief and recovery, Douglas departed before the end of a year. Except for Jones, Morgenthau, and Hopkins, the others disappeared from the scene one by one or sank back into places of little general influence.

Not only had the men who came to Washington in that spring and summer of 1933 to reconstruct the tower of American prosperity faded from the scene; but the alphabetical agencies that had germinated had, in some instances toppled, in others changed their names.

Jones, as a businessman and a banker, represented a philosophy that a considerable number of influential people in the executive departments regarded as outworn, reactionary, and, as they put it, "antisocial." Gradually, in the period from 1933 to 1939, Roosevelt was won over to the cult of spending for spending and for politics' sake.

In these circles in the Administration that regarded the depression and the emergency powers available to combat it as a golden opportunity to extend the powers of government deeper and deeper into the nation's economy and into the private affairs and responsibilities of the people, Jones was regarded as an obstacle that, however respected, was a barrier to their plans. It was irksome to those who were intent upon making America over to realize that the agency headed by Jones, an agency created by Hoover, though so revamped by Jones as to bear little resemblance to the RFC as it had been, under Eugene Meyer or Atlee Pomerene, was more popular than any of the newer creations.

Jones also bore what to them was the mark of Cain; he was a banker. They could not believe that a money-lender could be a respected member of their happy community. They abhorred such statements as this, which Jones incorporated in a speech:

"We are going to get back to normal economic and social existence. Business is going to be carried on in a normal way; and people are going to have enough work to provide them with a livelihood."

Jones would not admit that the economy of the nation was antiquated. To him it was a superb and ultra-modern productive plant, which had merely been stalled.

Jones was sure that, had he been enticed into the Cabinet as Secretary of War following the death of Secretary Dern, or to replace Secretary of Navy Swanson the RFC would have fallen as a rich prize to the spenders, conceding that the Senate would have confirmed the nomination of his successor.

It was not easy for Jones to live in the practice of his philosophy, for, as time went on, the President lent a more and more willing ear to the planners and spenders.

The leader in the movement to have Jones curbed or replaced was

Harold L. Ickes; and Ickes furnished left-wing newspaper columnists material in furtherance of the campaign against Jones.

Jones, despite his cordial dislike for the suspicious, meddlesome Ickes, never had an angry personal argument with him, although he wrote later, "There may have been times when I felt like swatting him in the jaw."

With the mysticism of Wallace it hardly needs saying that the matter-of-fact Jones had nothing in common. Ultimately this resulted in hostilities; but in the years before the war Jones succeeded in carrying on, with no serious upset, such official relations as were essential between the RFC and the Department of Agriculture.

Jones clearly recognized that there were few in the government who were attracted by Treasury Secretary Morgenthau, but got on well with him. This was true also of Harry L. Hopkins, whom Jones regarded as the most thoroughly convinced New Dealer in the Roosevelt entourage.

Hopkins, however, was always so honest and outspoken in his dealing with Jones that the great lender conceived a real affection for the master spender. In a memorandum Jones wrote:

> Hopkins' job was to spend money—get it in circulation—and without a great deal of regard of how it was spent. He did not encourage dishonesty or anything like that, but he wanted to get government money moving around to help in recovery. He was companionable, good natured, always wanting to be helpful.

Of his Cabinet colleagues Jones' most affectionate relations were with Secretary of State Hull, Secretary of War Stimson, and Attorney General Jackson. Like Jones these three Cabinet officers knew how to play a waiting game when a Roosevelt suggestion to them for an action seemed patently unwise.

23

The House of Jesse

THE famous reply of the Abbé Sieyes when asked what he did during the French Revolution has some application to the achievement of Jones during the stress and strains of the second Roosevelt term. That answer, "I survived," implied no mean mark in history. Jones, however—during a period when Roosevelt's official family was torn by conflicts and the President's relations with a Congress dominated by his own party were something of a cold war—not only held but consolidated his power.

Roosevelt was elected on a very conservative platform; his speeches in the 1932 campaign were by no means revolutionary; and he was by conviction in those early years a believer in an economical government. But after his popularity had risen to great heights in the elections of 1934 and 1936 he moved under the powerful influence of certain advisers and of his concepts of political expediency fairly far to the left. During this shift of Presidential policy Jones' conservative outlook earned him the increased enmity of some of his radical colleagues. It is very doubtful whether he could have survived until war demands made him indispensable except for two things. He had made the RFC into an amazingly efficient, influential, and indispensable organization, and he enjoyed the full confidence of Congress.

Jones' success in dealing with Congress was no mere matter of personal popularity, although no other member of the Administration was so well liked on "the Hill." It was to a large degree well-won respect for the RFC as an institution. Its value and its importance in the government found definition in a saying current in Washington in those years: "There are four branches of government; legislative, executive, judicial, and the House of Jesse."

This organization and the shadow of Congress behind it was always a warning that even a President vested with more power than any of his predecessors in peacetime must tread lightly in his relations with the chairman of the RFC.

The RFC, moreover, differed fundamentally from the other alphabetical agencies that appeared in Washington during the first Roosevelt term. They were mostly creatures of executive orders. They looked to the President, their creator, for orders, and in many cases they were contemptuous of Congress and of its members individually. As a great majority of the top members of the Administration were becoming more and more dependent upon the President, Jones proceeded with carefully chosen steps to make the RFC a dependable favorite of Congress. Even the more astute New Dealers were not aware how thoroughly he was doing this. Roosevelt sensed it, and since in the last analysis he needed what only Congress could grant, he found himself obliged to give Jones more or less freedom of action.

This institution to which Congress so lavishly granted power and money was manned by a body of officers bound together by mutual confidence and inspired by confidence in the wisdom of their chief.

The Depression had so disrupted the private economic system that it was possible for him to shop for high-grade executives in a distressed market. He could get men to come to Washington in those early days and to work for relatively small salaries who in normal times could have commanded compensation several times what the government could offer. This is proved by the sort of positions in the world of private business that were taken by the graduates of Jones' RFC. These capable people, once established in the RFC, were inspired by Jones to give all that they had.

An excellent qualified witness of the leadership of Jones and the regard in which he was held by his associates was Stanley F. Reed, for more than two years general counsel of the RFC, and who in 1938 became an Associate Justice of the Supreme Court. The author is indebted to him for the following appraisal:

> To those of us who have been long in Washington—and long is fifteen or twenty years—experience with the agencies and departments of govern-

ment gives an acquaintance with their personalities. They are methodical or discorded, on their toes or sluggish, ambitious or satisfied, and often their qualities change under the leadership of their chief. Even more than in ordinary business groups, the abilities of the head of those agencies give color to the activities of the helpers. So it was at the RFC under the chairmanship of Mr. Jones.

His astounding capacity for work called forth a matching energy for his associates and the staff. With his eye single to perform a service to the stricken economy, selfish aims among the personnel for his personal gain or aggrandizement were practically unknown. His pride in the work of the Corporation was contagious. Men worked with self-respect and the consciousness of worthwhile achievement. The result was an honest, effective unit, respected by the Executive and Congress as an agency devoted to the public welfare.

The members of the organization were loyal to their Chairman because he was loyal to them. In the early thirties many businesses, well handled internally, collapsed from external stresses beyond the power of management to withstand. Competent five-figure executives were drawn to the RFC, a relief agency, at low-figure salaries. Mr. Jones encouraged these able and ambitious men who sought to re-enter into private business. Corporations ransacked the RFC to secure executives for high responsibility. Instead of seeking to keep these men in the RFC, a temporary agency, Mr. Jones helped them and the Nation through aiding them to make their experience available in the build-up of the reviving activities. There was a pool for replacements.

In the RFC suggestions toward the solution of difficulties that arose in its administration were encouraged. Staff efforts were recognized, contributions of ideas received and weighed without regard to the position of the giver. Any plans that offered promise of economy, increased efficiency or improvement of economic conditions were welcomed. Mr. Jones thus made everyone a responsible associate in the pressing job of the restoration of normal production, distribution and consumption. His loyalty generated a like loyalty to the Board and its Chairman. This close-knit relationship was a major factor in the efficient service of the RFC in the re-establishment of a stable economy.

Jones, as Justice Reed says, commanded the loyalty and affection of his associates because he gave them his own loyalty and concern. There were not less than forty men on the roster in whom Jones placed his highest confidence; but he would never have indicated any such limitation in number. After his retirement he wrote:

During my thirteen years of association with the RFC, no finer set of men was ever brought together, in government or in a private organization, than those we gathered there. I could name an endless list, all equally helpful and loyal.

Of all these associates, Henry A. Mulligan, treasurer of the corporation, probably came nearest to being Jones' chief aide. Of him, Jones once said, "I was first attracted to Harry through admiration of his ability to answer any question with respect to the fiscal affairs of the RFC which I ever asked him. He was one of the best bookkeepers I ever had anything to do with; but he was much more than that. A civil-service man with practically no experience in business, he was nevertheless one of the best administrators I have ever known."

During nearly all of Jones' time at the RFC, Mulligan was its Treasurer and in charge of its books and accounts. He always carried a memorandum of the current RFC operations with him when Jones would call him to the office, or when he went with Jones to the Capitol.

"Harry Mulligan ended his long government career as a Director of the RFC," Jones wrote of him; "but I am sure he still kept an eye on the books."

Sam H. Husbands had been cashier of a small country bank in South Carolina. The bank failed. The unemployed cashier came to the RFC in its early days at 200-dollar-a-month salary. He was to become successively chief of its Examining Division, president of the Federal National Mortgage Association, wartime president of the Defense Plant Corporation, and finally an RFC director. Able, good-natured, and a noted raconteur, Husbands quickly became a valuable member of the Jones "Cabinet."

Some months after Jones left the RFC, L. M. Giannini, head of the Bank of America, San Francisco, the largest bank in the world, called him by telephone and asked him to employ Husbands to go out there and take the presidency of Trans-America Corporation. Jones did, fixing Husbands' starting salary at 50,000 dollars a year, with a 5000-dollar-per-year increase until it reached 75,000 dollars.

Sam's salary as a director at the RFC was 10,000 dollars per year. He made a great success as president of Trans-America, but resigned after Giannini's death and died shortly afterward.

There was Emil Schram, a Mississippi River Bottom farmer, whom Jones brought to the RFC to handle drainage and irrigation loans. Later Schram became a director and finally chairman of the RFC board. Upon leaving the RFC board, he became president of the New York Stock Exchange, upon the recommendation of Jones. When the time for his retirement came, he went back to the farm, this time in Indiana, but with a substantial life pension from the stock exchange. He undoubtedly rendered the Stock Exchange a great service; he was in no sense a "yes" man.

John W. Snyder, who began work for a bank as a country lad in Arkansas, after six years as manager of the St. Louis RFC agency, was made an assistant to the directors in Washington; then became executive chairman and director of the Defense Plant Corporation. By appointment of President Truman, he was first Federal Loan Administrator, then Director of the Office of War Mobilization and Reconversion, then Secretary of the Treasury.

William C. Costello occupied a special place in the Jones' management. He had been with Jones in private life and continued with him as his confidential secretary. Soon the work got so heavy that Jones made Costello his adminstrative assistant and delegated to him a great deal of authority to act in his stead. Costello even had authority to sign the chairman's name to certain types of letters, which he did so perfectly that Jones could not deny the signature.

Stanley Reed's line of successors as general counsel included James B. Alley and Claude Hamilton, who left to join New York law firms; John B. Goodloe, who became an executive of the Coca-Cola Company and James L. Dougherty. Dougherty, a government career man, whom Jones considered not only a competent lawyer but an excellent administrator, was with the RFC during its entire existence.

There was a stout rule at the RFC that none of its high-ranking employees could take a salaried place with a borrower without Jones' permission. Only one man violated that rule and in his case the results were unfortunate.

Jones gave the executives and lawyers of the RFC and its various subsidiaries great latitude. He might give them a succinct suggestion on what to do or how not to do something; then they were on their own. If there were any errors in judgment, he took the responsibility; if any of them made a mistake, Jones never exhumed it to them.

The scores of laws and amendments passed by Congress comprised the basic directives under which the House of Jesse operated. But it was never necessary for Jones to exercise over a tenth of the powers that he had been given. He always wanted plenty of reserve authority to meet the unexpected.

In the thirteen years Jones was at RFC, approximately fifty billion dollars were committed, and there was never a breath of scandal.

Of the men who helped him make this record Jones said, "I have no words which could adequately express the affection and confidence I have felt for these men at RFC."

With this team at his command Jones was able to approach Congress with complete confidence in what he could do with the powers he asked for.

"We at the RFC are learning as we go along," Jones said to the Senate Banking and Currency Committee during one of his earliest appearances before it. "When we learn of a new and better way to help the nation's recovery, we will come here and discuss it with you."

The "we" who always went to Capitol Hill to discuss the affairs of the RFC was Jesse Jones; and here, too, was a method vastly different from the customary procedure. Other agency heads went before congressional committees, flanked by subordinates with bulging brief cases. Jones went alone to the committee room, unless, on occasion, Harry Mulligan went along. Jones carried in his head the facts he wished to talk about. He disdained chairs reserved for witnesses before congressional committees, but often planted his 210 pounds of weight on a witness table and talked informally and with unvarnished frankness to its members. Sometimes he would take the vacant seat of an absent Senator or Representative in the midst of the other committee members.

After almost every Jones visit to a congressional committee, the limitations on the RFC lessened, until finally its powers were so terrifying that Vice-President Garner said to him, "Jesse, Congress has given you powers which no man ought to have; and I know of no one but you who could get them."

But Garner told a group of Senators, "I myself would have voted to give Jesse every one of the powers which Congress has given him. He is 99 per cent businessman and competent administrator, and 1 per cent politician. A 100 per cent businessman would be an abject failure in the place he occupies; and more than 1 per cent of politics would be intolerable there."

There were those who might differ with the Vice-President about the ratio of business and politics in the Jones character, but somehow the proportion seemed to be exactly what was needed.

Ultimately Congress, at the behest of Jones, enacted dozens of amendments to the original RFC Act. Never when Jones really got down to his final request did Congress refuse to grant it.

Such revisions would have been essential in determining the authority of any agency that represented such an entirely novel service of government.

In the case of the RFC, however, this need was accentuated by the fact that, in battling the Depression and later, in assisting the war effort, it was required to meet conditions that might change from month to month and even from day to day.

Jones' appearances before Senate and House committees were always a delight to members. He testified in a soft-spoken, mild drawl and made his points tersely and pungently. His humor was tart and earthy. He was impressive with facts and figures, often mixing them with bits of cracker-barrel philosophy. Members of Congress found this engaging because it was so different from the ethereal language, double-talk, and cocky behavior of so many New Dealers with whom they had to deal.

In most of those early years there was an immense Democratic majority in Congress, but Jones, percentagewise, had as many Republican as Democratic friends. He had let them know in speech and in action that he was administering the RFC without partisanship. His strength therefore came from both parties.

On one occasion when Jones was before the House Committee on Banking, soon after Director Taber of Massachusetts had been replaced on the board of the RFC, a Republican Representative from the Bay State, Charles F. Gifford, asked Jones pointedly, "Now that Taber is gone who will represent Massachusetts?"

"I will," Jones replied.

"That," said Gifford, "will be perfectly all right with me."

Later in a House debate Gifford said, "The name of Jesse Jones is synonymous with RFC, and I believe in both, thoroughly."

Sometimes Jones got his legislation without a committee appearance. He made it a practice to have lunch on the Hill once a week. Sometimes the luncheons would be in Vice-President Garner's office, sometimes in the office of Edward Halsey or Leslie Biffle, who were successive Secretaries of the Senate, and, after Sam Rayburn became Speaker, sometimes in his dining room. At these luncheons there would always be several members of one or both Houses; and here he could explain needed legislation. Sometimes Jones would tip a companionable cup with a smaller group in Garner's office just off the Senate Chamber.

"I guess," said Garner, "it's *our* office. Jones uses it as much as I do."

Jones was a familiar figure in the hall of Congress during all of his service in Washington. It is probable that he appeared before the Banking and Currency Committees of the two houses more often than any other government official before or since his time.

In the House the committee was large. The thirty members sat on a raised platform, something like the Supreme Court. In testifying Jones would usually stand in order to speak more directly to individual members, making statements, answering questions, and explaining the purposes of the legislation sought.

In the Senate the committee was smaller and the members sat at a table. But as a witness could not face more than half of the members, Jones designed and ordered to be built an octagonal table. He presented it to the committee. This enabled him to see and be seen by every member.

Increasingly, lines of trade, business, and industry found need of a shoulder to lean on; and Jones was always furnishing the shoulder. Often, when a special purpose was to be served, Jones would get congressional sanction for a special-purpose corporation under the wing of the RFC. This profusion of corporate offspring in time was to make the RFC resemble the Old Lady in the Shoe, except, as John H. Crider wrote in the New York *Times*, "The Old Lady didn't know what to do with all her children; but Uncle Jesse certainly does."

Typical of the expression of confidence in Jones constantly made in Congress were those that came from the Republican side of the aisle in the House of Representatives in the debate over the extension of the life of the RFC in 1937. Speaking in behalf of the measure, Representative Jesse P. Wolcott (Republican, of Michigan) said:

There has not been any politics, as far as I know in the Reconstruction Finance Corporation up to the present time. Publicly, I want to commend the Chairman, Jesse Jones, and the rest of the Board, for doing one of the best jobs any of us have ever seen done under like conditions. We have sworn at them at times, and we have blasphemed the Board because they have not made loans which we asked them to make; but, in the quiet of our offices and our homes, we felt safe in the fact that the Board of the Reconstruction Finance Corporation had established and were maintaining safe and sound policies.

Another Republican member, Representative Robert Luce, of Massachusetts, ranking minority member of the House Banking and Currency Committee, opened his statement with the declaration:

It is idle to repeat what everybody knows, that this has been the most successful agency used to meet the depression. Its record is clean; its performance has been marvelous. No other attempt to meet the crisis has matched it in importance, value, or integrity. Everything in it we should commend.

I would vote for the continuance of the RFC so long as the Corporation is headed by Jesse Jones, who has been the outstanding man of the Administration in his efficiency, for his prudence and for his usefulness.

Senator Alben W. Barkley, of Kentucky (later Vice-President of the United States), in unveiling a portrait of Jones in the State Capitol of Texas, at Austin, said:

I believe it can truthfully be stated that the Reconstruction Finance Corporation has been the outstanding governmental agency which built a new foundation under the industrial, financial, and economic life of the nation.

It is always dangerous to say that any man is or ever was indispensable; but I have no hesitation in saying that, in the hour of need, no man in America could have brought greater experience, greater devotion, greater loyalty, greater unselfishness, greater vision or determination to the administration of this great trust than Jesse H. Jones.

Before he came to Washington to serve with the RFC, Jones had frequently contributed to the campaign funds of both Democratic and Republican candidates for United States senators and representatives in Congress. He continued to do so both while with the RFC and afterward.

Once he contributed to the funds of two senatorial candidates who were opposing one another. In explanation he said, "Both are good men; both ought to have sufficent funds to get their cases before the people. Then the people can decide."

On occasion Jones' prestige in Congress was very helpful to Roosevelt. Shortly after the outbreak of war in 1939 the President announced that he hoped to create a two-billion-dollar cartel for trading with Central and South America.

The announcement immediately aroused the opposition of Senator William E. Borah. In statements in the press and fulgurant Senate speeches the Lion of Idaho roared his opposition to the proposal.

In the face of Borah's opposition Roosevelt decided to abandon the project although, he told Jones, the idea was one near his heart, which he believed would be of great assistance to this country, should we be drawn into war. Jones suggested that he go before Congress and ask for 500,000,000 dollars for additional loans by the Export-Import Bank in South American countries. If the loans were properly made and were useful, Jones believed, Congress would always give him more if needed.

"Go ahead and see what you can do; but I think that, in the present mood of Congress, you will fail," Roosevelt said.

Jones had a bill drawn for the half-billion dollars, and got it introduced in both Houses of Congress. Its stated purpose was to help stabilize the economy of nations of the Western Hemisphere. Borah promptly attacked the proposed legislation.

Jones went to Borah's office. He took with him a statement showing what had happened to every loan by the Export-Import Bank in any country. There was not a delinquent or past-due item.

"We once had a herd of reindeer as security for a loan in Alaska, and the loan was paid. We have no notion of playing Santa Claus in any climate," he told Borah. "But we would like to be in a position to forge some firmer friendships in South America, in case of war."

"Who will make the loans?" Borah asked.

"I will," Jones replied.

"Not the State Department?" Borah persisted.

"No," Jones said. "I will not make loans in Central and South America without talking to the State Department about them; but I will be judge of the credit and the purpose of the loan, not the State Department. I have in mind loans to the countries down there for road construction or other improvements which would be helpful to the people."

"Well," said Borah, "I have not heard of any great mistakes which you have made since you became head of the RFC; and, on your assurance that you will make the loans, I will favor giving you the money."

With Borah's support in the Senate, the bill passed there and, with House concurrence, became law.

Three of the directors of the RFC under Jones' chairmanship came from the Senate. They were John J. Blaine of Wisconsin, Charles B. Henderson of Nevada, and Hubert Stephens of Mississippi.

Jones was agreeably surprised at the ability and the devotion to duty of Blaine who, while in the Senate, had the reputation of being a radical and a man of not too sound judgment. There was a great deal of bank repair to be done in Wisconsin, and Jones did Blaine the honor of sending him to his home state to work out the situation. He fell ill and died the day the job was done, but he had done the job well.

In the early part of 1935 there were two vacancies on the RFC board, one Republican and one Democratic. Jones asked Roosevelt to appoint Charles T. Fisher, Jr., of Detroit, to the Republican vacancy.

Fisher had been the first manager of the Detroit agency of the RFC, and Jones considered him very capable. Roosevelt did not act upon Jones' request for several months.

"The President never seemed to think the RFC needed any directors, and was not interested in filling our vacancies until situations arose in which he was being pressed in a patronage case," Jones said.

Ultimately there occurred a vacancy in the Atlanta Federal Reserve District. Pat Harrison of Mississippi and other Senators from that section had proposed two of three candidates and were bothering the President about it. Roosevelt asked Jones to go to the Capitol and get these Senators to agree on a man.

When he left the White House to go to the Capitol, William Green,

President of the American Federation of Labor, long a personal friend of Jones, was also just leaving after a conference with the President. He got into Jones' automobile and rode to the Capitol. Green opened the conversation by saying:

"The President said to me that you wanted him to appoint one of the Fisher boys, of Detroit, on the RFC Board, and that he was not inclined to do it, because of the affiliation of the Fishers with General Motors."

Jones then asked Green to write a letter recommending the appointment of Fisher. Green did so promptly upon returning to his office, and sent it to Jones.

The next day Jones saw the President and told him that the Senators from the South would agree on Hubert Stephens to fill the Democratic vacancy. Roosevelt asked Jones how he would like to have Stephens on the RFC board. Jones said it was agreeable to him.

Stephens had just been defeated for re-election by Theodore Bilbo and, before Jones had gone to see the Southern Senators, Roosevelt had cautioned him to be sure that he saw Bilbo first.

Jones had done this, and Bilbo had told him, "I told the people of Mississippi in our campaign that one of the first things I would do when I got to Washington would be to get Hubert a job."

Jones then handed the President the letter which Green had written, recommending Fisher. Roosevelt told him to stop by the desk of Rudolph Forster, the executive secretary, and ask him to prepare nominations for Stephens and Fisher, and he would send both names to the Senate for confirmation.

At the close of his service as RFC director, Fisher returned to Detroit and became president of the National Bank of Detroit, the bank that Jones and General Motors had created in 1933.

Henderson, the former Nevada Senator, served twelve years on the RFC board, six of them as chairman.

On one occasion Franklin D. Roosevelt said of Jones, "The importance of his achievements will be more fully understood as time passes."

That prophetic note could apply to the RFC also. As time goes by and it moves further back in the perspective of history, it is certain that future generations of historians will find it still of absorbing interest. It was born in the Republican Administration of Herbert Hoover and died twenty-one years later in the Republican Administration of Dwight Eisenhower. Its unique character is largely due to the unprecedented circumstances that gave it birth and attended its growth, and to the character of the men who managed it.

Honors, Promotions, and Politics

DESPITE the heavy burden imposed by Jones' ministrations to a convalescent economic system, he was able to take time out for a number of civic activities. One of these was his service to the Centennial of the Texas Republic.

Jones had begun this service when he became its director general in 1926, a full ten years before the 1936 celebration was scheduled to begin. He found that a constitutional amendment would be necessary before the state could extend financial assistance to the observance. This amendment carried in a state-wide election. When Jones became a director of the RFC in 1932, the state still had not made an appropriation, nor had Dallas provided the necessary funds for the central exposition. This exposition Jones had planned should depict the calvacade of progress in the hundred years since the tragedy of the Alamo and the victory at San Jacinto.

But later in 1932, with an appropriation of 3,000,000 dollars by the Texas legislature assured and with Dallas ready to spend 10,000,000 dollars and provide the fifty permanent buildings of the Texas State Fair for exhibits, Jones retired as director general of the Centennial, and the legislature in recognition of his services provided that his portrait should be painted and placed in the state capitol at Austin. The unveiling of this portrait in 1935 was signalized by a ceremony at which there were laudatory addresses by the governor of Texas, by Senator Alben W. Barkley on behalf of the federal government, and by others.

The federal government made an appropriation and authorized a United States Commission for the Texas Centennial, headed by Vice-President Garner. In appearances before this commission, the Texas legislature and other federal and state agencies, Jones asked for all the permanent memorials he had planned, including the 1,000,000 dollars necessary to provide for the 570-foot-tall shaft and museum at San Jacinto Battleground. Jones himself drew the plans for this monument—the shaft surmounted by the star at the top indicating the Lone Star State, comparable in height to the Washington monument, and resting on a two-story and basement base of 200 feet square comparable to the Lincoln Memorial.

In front of the Alamo in San Antonio was erected a heroic memorial; a memorial stadium, museum, and shaft were placed at Goliad, and thirty-seven other spots of historic state or national interest were marked; buildings and forts restored. In every one of the state's 254 counties was erected a marker indicating the date of its creation and the source of its name.

Jones induced President Roosevelt to open the Centennial celebration with speeches at San Jacinto, at the Alamo, at Dallas and at Fort Worth, and accompanied the President on the trip. At Dallas the President after his Centennial address unveiled a statue of General Robert E. Lee, and Jones delivered the principal speech at the latter ceremony.

An hour afterward Jones was involved in an airplane crash-landing that almost cost him his life. He had left for Houston with former Texas Governor and Mrs. William P. Hobby and one of his secretaries. Ten minutes after the plane took off a fire broke out in the cockpit. Despite the fact that the plane was 7000 feet in the air when the fire was discovered, Ed Hefley, the pilot, was able to endure the flames and bring the craft to the ground in a dive almost straight down, and in spite of its speed the plane hit the ground right side up.

None of the four passengers was seriously hurt, but both Hefley and the copilot Eugene Schacher were badly burned. At first it was thought Schacher was less seriously burned than Hefley. He had been able to climb out of the plane on landing. After all were out but Hefley, Jones climbed back into the plane and dragged Hefley from the cockpit a few seconds before the plane was completely destroyed.

Minus his coat and hat, which had been burned in the plane, and his shirt bloody Jones had refused to be examined until both Hefley and Schacher had been cared for. He left the hospital with assurance that both men, although badly burned, would recover.

Arthur Brisbane, in his column "Today" wrote:

> Jesse Jones, head of the RFC, is what a man from Texas should be, tall, wide, hearty and strong; not easily frightened. Dashing toward the earth at two hundred and seventy miles an hour in a blazing airplane, with the odds at least 100 to 1 in favor of death, he remained calm, and when the plane struck the ground with terrific force, Mr. Jones proceeded to help the badly burned pilot out of the blazing compartment.

The early favorable report on the pilots was not borne out. Schacher died the morning following the crash and Hefley recovered but only after a year in the hospital.

The death of Schacher deeply affected Jones. He wrote for the Houston *Chronicle* this tribute:

To Eugene Schacher:

I thought you would live, you had such determination, such courage, such endurance and self-control under the most terrifying circumstances and such great physical pain. You stuck to your post in a veritable furnace, with the white heat literally burning your clothes off your body. You did this notwithstanding Pilot Ed Hefley begged you to leave the pit to him.

When the door of the pilot room blew open, and the flames were reaching into the cabin, you came out and closed the door, going back into the furnace.

Again the door blew open, so terrific was the speed, and again you came out, this time a human torch, and went back into the fiery pit. But when it seemed the fight was winning, and the plane might be landed, you came back and warned your passengers that the landing would be rough.

You unlocked the door so that all could escape from the burning plane when the landing was made. You did this when your hands were burned to the bone. You could hardly hold the key.

Your whole thought was for your passengers, and then, when Hefley did not follow us out, you were the first to go back for him and drag him from the burning cockpit.

Your fortitude under the greatest imaginable suffering was an inspiration and a lesson. You never lost your smile during the terrible hours that followed for you. Such courage, such fortitude, such endurance, it has never been my privilege to witness.

You are up There, looking down upon your family and two lovely children, one but three weeks old, your soul as white as the clouds through which it soars, and I pray God for the knowledge to understand for what purpose He saved my life by sacrificing yours.

Jones set up a trust fund for Mrs. Schacher and her two small children to run for sixteen years, to assure their education and the maintenance of the widow. Later, when Mrs. Schacher's son had grown up and indicated a desire to take up the occupation of his father, Jones provided a course of instruction for him. At that time he also set up a lifetime annuity for Mrs. Schacher.

In October, 1936, Jones returned to Dallas for an occasion that proved to be much happier. It was to attend as guest of honor "Jesse Jones Day" at the Exposition and to receive the heart-warming greeting of fellow Texans.

The Exposition attracted attention far beyond expectations, and it was decided to keep it going for another year as the "Great Texas and Pan-American Exposition." Thirteen million visitors were counted during the two years. There was also a well-attended frontier exposition during that period offered by Dallas' friendly rival, Fort Worth.

Jones' grateful fellow Texans acclaimed him as the man who brought their state the two events that attracted the widest attention their state had ever received to then—the Democratic National Convention of 1928 and the Centennial of the Texas Republic in 1936-37.

On April 24, 1937, Jones laid the cornerstone of San Jacinto Monument and made the principal address. A year later it was the highest man-made memorial in the world, fifteen feet taller than the Washington Monument, nearly 100 feet taller than the Great Pyramid at Gizeh, Egypt.

For many years there had been a warm friendship marked by mutual admiration between Jones and Will Rogers. The death of Rogers in an airplane crash at Point Barrow, Alaska, in 1937, inspired Jones to initiate the creation of a Will Rogers Commission to perpetuate the memory of the wit-philosopher.

Jones drew up the papers necessary for the commission to be incorporated in the District of Columbia. Jones brought into the organization some of Rogers' friends including Vice-President Garner, former President Herbert Hoover, former Democratic Presidential candidates James M. Cox, John W. Davis, and Alfred E. Smith; Henry Ford, Captain Eddie Rickenbacker, Amon G. Carter, Charles G. Dawes, Owen D. Young, and Fred Stone, the actor, among others.

The campaign for funds resulted in the contribution of the million-dollar Will Rogers Memorial Hospital at Saranac, New York, and cash contributions of 1,396,598 dollars. Part of these funds went to the up-keep of the Saranac hospital and trust funds were created in the state universities of Oklahoma, California, and Texas for the education of young men and women afflicted with physical disabilities.

Jones went to Paris and made suggestions for the notable statues by Jo Davidson that stand in Statuary Hall at the Capitol in Washington and at the Will Rogers Memorial at Claremore, Oklahoma. In the principal speech at the dedication of the Will Rogers Museum at Claremore on November 4, 1938, Jones called Rogers "the best beloved man of his day."

In Washington, Jones found time for only a few of the many things to which a man of his eminence is invited and often finds it difficult to escape attending. He liked unorganized and spontaneous things rather than organized ones. To get him away from his office and ready for social events took constant prodding from Mrs. Jones.

He played bridge frequently all during his stay in Washington and, on rare occasions, sat in a poker game. Many years before, he had given up golfing, at which he was proficient, because of a back injury.

He seemed to enjoy stag dinners in Washington. He was a member of the Alfalfa Club, a fun-making dinner organization, and never missed its annual winter dinner and seldom failed to appear at its summer out-door gatherings.

Mr. and Mrs. Jones gave some large dinners. Their reception on the occasion of his sixty-third birthday was one of the largest ever held in the national capital. On this occasion Mrs. Woodrow Wilson stood in the receiving line with Mr. and Mrs. Jones.

The Jones birthday party, which came just before the war clouds gathered over Europe, brought out the diplomatic corps in force with such diverse personalities as the Ambassador of Germany, Herr Hans Luther, an intimate friend of Jones, and Alexander Troyanovsky, whom Jones once described as the "only honorable Ambassador the Soviet ever sent to Washington and perhaps the only honorable official it ever had."

Jones belonged to many clubs in Texas, New York, and Washington and seldom visited any of them. He attended some of the charivaris of the Jefferson Island Club, near Washington, which was made up of Democratic officials.

Next to John Nance Garner, Jones' closest friend in Washington was Senator Carter Glass of Virginia and next to Glass was Cordell Hull. In political philosophy Jones was close kin to Garner and Glass. He had an affectionate regard for Hull but considered him somewhat theoretical and visionary on a number of public policies. A warm friendship with Senator Robert A. Taft began shortly after Taft came to Washington and continued until Taft's death.

In 1939 President Roosevelt, using the authority given him by Congress in the first reorganization plan, appointed Jones as administrator of the newly created Federal Loan Agency. As Federal Loan Administrator, Jones retained general supervision of the RFC. There was also put into his hands over-all direction of the Federal Housing Administration, Home Owners Loan Corporation, and the Export-Import Bank.

The fact that the creation of the new agency and Jones' appointment to head it was made without prior consultation with Jones caused wide speculation that as Jones would no longer have a vote on the RFC Board the White House action was intended to separate him from direction of that important lending agency.

Jones declined to accept the place as Federal Loan Administrator unless he was permitted to retain the direction of the RFC. He had always insisted that the RFC remain in existence no longer than was necessary, and he had been responsible for the fact that the life of the corporation had been extended only for limited periods. The life of the corporation was usually authorized for two years, and Jones was reappointed to the office of chairman four times, each time for a two-year period.

By an executive order in October, 1937, Roosevelt had stopped RFC lending. This had been done by the President without conferring with Jones, who although he was the foremost advocate of the government getting out of the lending field as soon as possible, knew that 1937 was not the time, for the 1937-38 recession was in the making. Roosevelt had then been compelled to rescind his action in December, two months later.

After his appointment as Federal Loan Administrator was announced, Jones went to the White House and proposed that Emil Schram be made chairman of the RFC. This was done. He then suggested that the vacancy on the board created by his appointment be filled by the appointment of Sam Husbands. Schram also went to the White House to urge this appointment on the President.

Roosevelt did not want to appoint Husbands, and sought to win Schram to his point of view, saying, "I want the RFC to have an Emil Schram board and not a Jesse Jones board." Schram, however, was not easily beguiled. He was thoroughly in sympathy with the policies of Jones and intended that they should be continued. He insisted upon

Husbands, and the President capitulated. The influence of Jones in the RFC continued undiminished.

The exchange of letters between Jones and the President on this occasion was most cordial. The President wrote:

Dear Jesse:

I have received and accepted your resignation as a member of the Board of the Reconstruction Finance Corporation—but I do so only because of your undertaking the work of Federal Loan Administrator.

The Reconstruction Finance Corporation under your Chairmanship has made an amazing record of financial efficiency while at the same time assisting many banks, corporations and individuals to continue solvent and to do their part in giving employment and keeping the wheels of industry turning.

Your statement that the Reconstruction Finance Corporation "has sound assets sufficient to pay all of its debts and return to the Treasury the entire capital stock invested in it, with something in addition," reminds me that in 1933, 1934 and 1936 a few people in the Executive Branch of the Government, more people in the Congress of the United States, and many individuals and newspapers in civil life were announcing to the Nation that the Reconstruction Finance Corporation was broke and that the Government would not get back more than fifty cents on the dollar.

These people were in some cases honest in their belief, but in many cases were making these ghoulish statements with the hope that their own type of partisanship would thereby be served. In either case their action did little to encourage the "confidence" they were so loudly talking about. In either case their gloomy predictions proved false.

I call this matter of history to your attention because it is illustrative of the difficulty which public servants find in carrying out their duties.

You, the fellow members of your Board, and all of us who have some confidence in the good sense of the American people, and confidence in the ability of honest Government to cope with difficult situations, which have not been solved by wholly private efforts, have a right to some measure of pride in the Reconstruction Finance Corporation.

Very sincerely yours,
Franklin D. Roosevelt

There had been persistent comment beginning in 1936 that Jones might well be the logical man for the Presidential nomination in 1940. This was based upon the assumption that the two-term principle would prevail and that Roosevelt would retire. Jones pointed out that it was not likely that the party would go to Texas for its nominee but that, if so, it should be Garner.

Garner on the other hand said he would like to see Jones considered instead of himself. He said:

Jesse Jones I put at the top of all administrative officials during my time in Washington. More than any one I know in public life he rises above red tape. Yet he does things according to law. He has a head full of sense and the confidence of the country. As a Presidential candidate I think he would hold the party strength and poll more independent votes than any other man we could nominate.

At the Democratic victory dinner held in Washington in the spring of 1937 Jones was greeted with a strong demonstration from the diners.

In Oklahoma a Jones boom was launched by R. T. Stuart, John Harden, George D. Key, and John Doolin, all prominent in politics in that state. Stuart made a statement saying, "Roosevelt will take care of the common people in his second term. Then we are going to put the greatest financier in America, Jesse Jones, in as President to carry on and balance the budget."

Jones continued to discourage all efforts in his behalf and predicted that his name would never be placed before the 1940 convention as a Presidential candidate. Editorial support for him continued to come from newspapers over the country, however.

As the 1940 convention drew nearer and polls showed Garner leading for the Presidential nomination in the event of retirement of Roosevelt, Jones gave his wholehearted support to the efforts being made in behalf of his fellow Texan.

The Democratic National Convention approached and still there was no word whether the President would stand for a third term. The opinion grew that Roosevelt wanted another nomination. Roosevelt's intentions were the subject of many of the Sunday visits between Garner and Jones in the Garner hotel suite. Both opposed a third term, Garner to the degree that he said, "If Roosevelt runs I will oppose his nomination in every way I can. The arguments against a third term for any man are unanswerable. I would be against a third term on principle even if I approved every act of Roosevelt's two terms."

Jones while he disliked the idea of the third term as a matter of principle said there were conditions under which he would support Roosevelt. If the Republicans at Philadelphia nominated Taft he would be inclined to support him. If on the other hand the nomination went to Willkie he would be for Roosevelt. He regarded Willkie as "irresponsible and probably would turn into a bigger spender than Roosevelt."

Garner in the end stood for the Presidential nomination although he told friends he did not "want and am sure I could not be chosen as against Roosevelt. The law of political self-preservation will keep many men who are opposed to a third term from speaking out. I am going to do all I can to stop it."

Jones took no part in the early 1940 political activities other than to communicate with his friends in Texas and ask them to be certain that the Texas delegation was instructed for Garner. Representative Sam Rayburn, on the other hand, was convinced that Roosevelt would be renominated and he had seen to it that although the Texas delegation was instructed for Garner it had on it about as many Roosevelt as Garner adherents.

On Saturday before leaving for Chicago to attend the national convention to which the Waco state convention had named him a delegate-at-large, Jones received a call from President Roosevelt asking that he and Mrs. Jones accompany him on a yacht cruise down the Potomac. Only the President, Mr. and Mrs. Jones, and Miss Marguerite Le Hand were aboard the yacht.

> I thought perhaps the President wanted to discuss the Chicago convention [Jones wrote], but if he did he would have to initiate the discussion. From his attitude no one would have known that such a thing as a convention which might nominate him for a precedent-making third consecutive nomination was to open three days later. We fished and visited together and he was never more cordial, but he never once mentioned politics.

With Roosevelt nominated for a third term Rayburn entered the race for the Vice-Presidency and called a caucus of the Texas delegation at two o'clock in the morning to ask for its backing of his aspirations. The last-ditch Garner delegates surprised at the suddenly called caucus put Jones in nomination against him. The proceedings of the early-morning gathering of the Texas delegates ended in futility.

Rayburn undisputedly had a majority of those present, but many absent delegates had no notice of the meeting, which finally adjourned until eleven o'clock to await an indication from the Presidential nominee as to his choice of a ticket mate.

"Early in the day," wrote William Allen White, "it was certain that the majority of the convention delegates wanted Jones as Roosevelt's running mate." Jones was told by Harry Hopkins in mid-morning that Roosevelt had selected Wallace.

Hopkins said to Jones, "He would have liked for you to run with him, but he feels your health is not good enough for a campaign such as you would have to make."

Jones thought Hopkins' statement that Roosevelt had wanted him was incredible and there was never any evidence to substantiate it. As for the health consideration, the only illness he had after he came to

Washington in 1932 had been the one during a visit to Wyoming and from this he had entirely recovered.

At about the same time Hopkins was telling Jones of the Roosevelt choice of Wallace, Roosevelt had called James A. Farley, who had opposed the third term, to tell him of the Wallace choice. Farley had argued to the President that Wallace was a bad choice and urged Jones instead. Roosevelt without countering the arguments of Farley for Jones, nevertheless insisted it had to be Wallace.

Jones went from the talk with Hopkins to a meeting of a few of his friends in the Texas delegation. He told them what he had learned and asked that he receive no further consideration at the hands of the Texas delegation. He intended to support Roosevelt for re-election, he told them; the selection of Willkie by the Republicans and his feelings about Willkie's qualifications had settled any doubt about that. If what Hopkins told him was true he still would not support Wallace in the balloting that day. But if Wallace was merely Roosevelt's favorite and the convention was to have a free hand, he would want first word from Roosevelt that he would be welcome on the ticket and second would want to have an agreement with Roosevelt on who his successor as Federal Loan Administrator would be.

A few minutes later when the proposal was made in the caucus of the Texas delegation that its vote for Vice-President be divided half and half between Jones and Rayburn, Jones told his fellow Texans that he understood that the President had expressed his desire for Wallace. He did not wish under these circumstances to have the support of the caucus. It was the first information that Rayburn and most of those attending the meeting had concerning the Wallace choice. With Jones taking himself out, the caucus by a divided standing vote instructed for Rayburn.

Jones returned to the Blackstone Hotel and in the lobby passed Farley, who told him he intended to place him in nomination for the Vice-Presidency. As Farley had never mentioned it to him before Jones thought he was saying it in a jesting mood.

Shortly afterward Elliott Roosevelt came to Jones' room and expressed great indignation over the Wallace choice.

"Farley is going to place you in nomination, and I am going to second it," said the President's son, who was a delegate from Texas.

Jones replied that Roosevelt had expressed his choice of Wallace and that he would not allow his name to be considered. He gave the same answer to representatives of various state delegations who called.

A few hours later Elliott Roosevelt again went to Jones' hotel suite and insisted that Farley would nominate Jones and Elliott would second it. Jones reiterated he did not want his name considered and immediately sent a statement to the press to that effect.*

After Rayburn heard of Roosevelt's choice of Wallace, he withdrew and announced that he would second the nomination of Wallace from the convention rostrum and ask the Texas delegation to swing to the Secretary of Agriculture. With only Speaker William B. Bankhead as an avowed candidate against Wallace, Jones threw his support to Bankhead and took an overwhelming majority of the Texas delegation with him.

But this did not end it. Jones went to the convention hall at night with Mrs. Jones and Mrs. Woodrow Wilson, who had been their guest all during the convention. From the Maryland delegation Howard Bruce arose and placed him in nomination. Jones immediately went to the platform to address the convention, thanked Bruce, but requested that no delegate vote for him. Under the unit rule the entire vote of Texas was cast for Bankhead.

Wallace won the nomination from a reluctant convention. But instead of the acclamation nomination Roosevelt wanted for him, he got only 627 out of 1100 votes.

Six weeks after the adjournment of the Democratic National Convention, President Roosevelt summoned Jones to the White House and offered him the post of Secretary of Commerce. Jones had no desire to be Secretary of Commerce because of the President's general attitude toward business.

The offer to the Commerce post came as Mr. and Mrs. Jones were

* James A. Farley in *Collier's* magazine told of his telephone conversation with Roosevelt on Thursday morning and also gave the following interesting account of the protest of Mrs. Roosevelt and Elliott against the Wallace designation:

> Elliott Roosevelt came into my room to say he thought it would be a great mistake to nominate Wallace. I told him I was for Jones. He met this with, "If you nominate Jesse I will second it." I told him that this was all right with me and that we would talk it over with his mother when she arrived in Chicago.
>
> I drove out to meet Mrs. Roosevelt at the airport. She was accompanied by Franklin, Jr. When we discussed the Vice-Presidency she and Franklin, Jr., agreed that it was a mistake to nominate Wallace.
>
> At the hotel Mrs. Roosevelt put in a call to the White House.
>
> "Franklin," she plunged to the point, "I've been talking with Jim Farley and I agree with him, Henry Wallace won't do. I know, Franklin, but Jesse Jones would bolster the ticket, win it business support and get the party contributions."
>
> Finally the President asked that I be put on the phone. "I've given my word to Wallace, Jim," he told me. "What do you do when you give your word?"
>
> "I keep it," I answered quickly. Perhaps too quickly and too sharply.

leaving for Detroit for a cruise around the Great Lakes with Mr. and Mrs. Fred Fisher. From the Fisher yacht, the *Nakhoda,* Jones on 30 August wrote to Vice-President Garner at Uvalde.

> Friday, just before leaving Washington, the President asked me to become Secretary of Commerce, and to continue to act as Federal Loan Administrator. This will require a joint resolution which the Congress may or may not be willing to pass. I could probably carry on the new work with very little additional effort, as it is all in the line of business.
>
> I feel that I should continue the supervision particularly of the RFC, since much of its authority has been given to it by Congress upon my advice and testimony, and in the belief that I would look after it. I feel this responsibility keenly and would not like to be taken away from it—for any cause.

In his talk with Jones the President had pointed out that if he held the two jobs he would receive only one salary. This made little difference to Jones who had already been in Washington eight years and had never cashed a salary check.*

Promptly upon Jones' acceptance Roosevelt asked Congress for enabling legislation. It was unprecedented. In an editorial opposing such a departure the New York *Times* said, "Mr. Jones has shown great ability in his present position. He could be expected to show just as great ability as Secretary of Commerce. But to have him occupy both posts at once seems inadvisable in itself and bad precedent."

But Congress had no such misgivings. It prepared a joint resolution with Jones' name written into it so it could be made applicable only to him and then lapse. The resolution made it lawful for him to hold the offices of Secretary of Commerce and Federal Loan Administrator at the same time and to execute all the duties of both. In the Senate Robert A. Taft of Ohio arose to say:

> I do not wish to object to the resolution since I have the highest respect for Mr. Jones and think he is one of the ablest men in the public service. I merely wish to call attention to the fact that Mr. Jones already has more power than any other man in the government with the single exception of the President.
>
> He has unlimited power to lend money to anyone, to any industry in the United States, or to refuse to lend. We gave him unlimited power to lend money to any government plant which manufactures any form of supplies or any other kind of material which has the remotest relation to war. I do not

* He had been required to take the checks but allowed them to accumulate. Neither had Jones accepted the use of a government automobile but had furnished his own. Subsequently as Secretary of Commerce he was the only Cabinet member who never made use of a government automobile and during World War II used his own small car instead of a limousine.

think that with the exception of the President of the United States any man in the United States ever enjoyed so much power.

I have no great objection to giving Mr. Jones the additional power to act as Secretary of Commerce, but I think it is an extraordinary precedent justified only by the character of the man, and which I hope may not be repeated.

In an unusual Congressional compliment both Senate and House of Representatives passed the legislation without a dissenting vote. He soon had the additional duties of membership on the National Emergency Council, the Board of Economic Warfare, the War Production Board, and the Economic Stabilization Board.

When Jones came back from Alabama after attending the funeral of Speaker William B. Bankhead, whose Vice-Presidential aspiration Jones had espoused despite Roosevelt's dictum that Wallace be nominated, the President had arranged that he be sworn in as Secretary of Commerce in the Chief Executive's office.

Roosevelt had seen to it that considerable ado be made of the Jones entry into the Cabinet. The Wallace nomination had been resented by millions of Democrats, there were also scars left from Roosevelt's action two months earlier in vacating the two Cabinet offices having to do with defense and filling them with two Republicans, Henry L. Stimson as Secretary of War, and Frank Knox as Secretary of the Navy. Also, Farley, who had opposed the third term, had left the Cabinet at the end of August. But most important of all, the Willkie Presidential candidacy seemed to be popular with the country.

Jones took the oath from Associate Justice Stanley Reed of the Supreme Court standing in front of Roosevelt's desk with Mrs. Jones and the new Cabinet officer's sister, Mrs. Daniel E. Garrett, and numerous Jones relatives and staff members. And Roosevelt said as the brief ceremony concluded, "I'm giving you a lot more work to do now, Jesse."

Jones' jobs now added up to thirty-two.

In the two positions of Secretary of Commerce and Federal Loan Administrator he headed such bureaus and agencies as:

The Reconstruction Finance Corporation, the RFC Mortgage Company, the Disaster Loan Corporation, the Federal National Mortgage Association, the Export-Import Bank of Washington, the Federal Savings and Loan Insurance Corporation, the Federal Home Owners Loan Corporation, the Federal Housing Administration, the Census Bureau, the Bureau of Foreign and Domestic Commerce, the Bureau of Standards, the Civil Aeronautics Board, the Inland Waterways Corporation, the Patent Office, the Bureau of Marine Inspection and Navigation, the

Coast and Geodetic Survey, the Electric Home and Farm Authority, and such new-born defense agencies as the Rubber Reserve Company, the Metals Reserve Company, the Defense Supplies Corporation, and the Defense Plant Corporation.

He was a member of the Federal Advisory Board for Vocational Education, a member of the Foreign Trade-Zones Board, head of the Business Advisory Council, head of Textile Foundation, Inc., a member of the National Defense Council, a member of the National Archives Council, a member of the Foreign Services Building Commission, and a member of the Establishment of the Smithsonian Institution. Not only was Jones the most powerful public figure outside of the President, he antedated all high officials in public service, being the only Hoover Administration man held over.

There were, too, the responsibilities on the boards of such schools as Tuskegee in Alabama, and George Peabody College at Nashville, and his own charities. Each day he took from thirty minutes to an hour in a telephone hookup to Texas to talk to the managers of his bank, his newspaper, and his numerous other enterprises.

Jones held his first press conference in the big, comfortable furnished conference room in the Department of Commerce Building, much more sumptuous than his offices. He had acquired the offices that were built into the Department of Commerce Building for which plans were drawn when Herbert Hoover was Secretary. He made few appearances in this office thereafter, continuing at his busy desk in the RFC Building three blocks away.

When Jones went into the Cabinet he took a seat at a table he had designed, had built, and presented to the President. It was the second such table he had patterned and presented to the government, the other going to the Senate Banking and Currency Committee.

The seating arrangement at the President's Cabinet table had been unchanged since the Washington Administration. The President sitting at the head of the table saw only part of his Cabinet well. So Jones had the new table built and sent to the White House. The table proved very practical and remained in use at the White House in succeeding administrations.

Jones made one speech in the 1940 campaign, a radio address pointed at businessmen. He spoke from Washington. The critical state of world affairs made politics seem remote and irrelevant.

PART VI

The Sinews Of War

25

Mobilizing Metals and Other Materials

AS tragedy fell upon Britain and France in those fateful spring days of 1940, Washington fully awakened to the practical problems of rearmament. The essential elements of military strength, not only for us but for our friends abroad, required raw materials and still more raw materials. The extraordinary capacity of the RFC to adapt itself to the financing of domestic needs now revealed itself as capable of adaptation to the needs of war preparation. But to accomplish maximum results new legislation was necessary.

Drafts of such amendments to the RFC law emerged from daily conferences between Jones and the Advisory Commission of the Council of National Defense. These were introduced in the House and Senate on May 30.

They were designed to authorize the RFC to create and organize a corporation or corporations to purchase strategic and critical materials and also to acquire land and finance the building or expansion of plants for the manufacture of necessary equipment and supplies. In this activity the RFC could act by itself or cooperate with private industry.

The sweeping nature of the proposals prompted Senator Robert A.

Taft, then in his second year in the Senate, to comment upon the extraordinary powers that Congress seemed willing to bestow upon Jones. He said to Senator Carter Glass, "Jesse Jones under this bill could lend a hundred million dollars to a borrower for a hundred years at any rate of interest he chose."

"Yes, he could but he won't," Glass replied.

The legislation went through the two Houses quickly and the President added his signature on June 25.

That was the dark day on which France signed peace terms with Hitler and Mussolini. Nazi guns were shelling English Channel ports, and an invasion seemed imminent. With Paris, which had fallen a week before, Hitler was in possession of nine European capitals—Vienna, Prague, Warsaw, Luxembourg, Copenhagen, Oslo, Brussels, and Amsterdam.

Busy days for Jones followed the granting of his new authority. There were conferences with the President, with Secretaries Stimson and Knox, and with William S. Knudsen, who had just arrived in Washington to supervise industrial production for the National Defense Advisory Commission. After three days of preparation Jones brought into being two gigantic new agencies—the Metals Reserve Company and the Rubber Reserve Company. The colossal job of accumulating stockpiles of tin, rubber, and other materials was under way.

Just as Roosevelt had found the RFC an agency organized and ready to combat the Depression, now it was the only one ready to build plants, shipyards and pipelines, to buy and sell equipment and material, to pay subsidies where necessary to obtain the basic materials of war. Requests for action quickly came pouring in on it from the War, Navy, and State Departments, the Maritime Commission, and the Advisory Commission of the Council of National Defense.

To conduct these operations so vital first to the national defense and then the prosecution of war, Jones was to assemble an array of experts of such competence and diverse knowledge as had never before been gathered under one roof in Washington.

Metals Reserve Company and Rubber Reserve Company, the twins born to RFC on June 28, were to write down on their service records some of the most fascinating and impressive chapters of that agency's history. Metals Reserve had many strings to its bow, with the solution of the critical tin shortage its first victory. Rubber, natural and synthetic, would be the sole problem of the other.

Two days after Metals Reserve came into being, Jones was to learn that he would have to find a source of tin supply and then manufacture

Jones exchanges congratulations with Emil Schram, who succeeds him as RFC chairman, on becoming Federal Loan Administrator.

Jones with Senator Pat Harrison of Mississippi.

Jones with Senator William G. McAdoo of California.

Jones at a Capitol Committee hearing chats with Chairman Henry B. Steagall of the House Banking and Senate Committee.

Above: Jones takes the oath as Secretary of Commerce from Supreme Court Associate Justice Stanley F. Reed. *Below:* Jones (at right) with RFC directors Klossner, Henderson, Schram, and Merriam, discussing national defense plants and stockpiles, in 1940 *(Harris & Ewing)*.

Above: Jones, with President Roosevelt, views 400 planes in the air at one time at the opening of the National Airport in Washington *(Harris & Ewing)*. *Below:* Jones, Wendell L. Willkie, and William S. Knudsen at a wartime luncheon at the National Press Club, Washington *(Harris & Ewing)*.

Above: Orville Wright, Secretary of Commerce Jones, and General H. H. Arnold, Chief of the Army Air Forces, on the 40th anniversary of the Wright Brothers' Kitty Hawk Flight. *Below:* Chinese Ambassador Wellington Koo conferring decorations on Secretary of Commerce Jones and Major General Patrick J. Hurley *(Harris & Ewing).*

Above: Jones, with Secretary of State Henry L. Stimson leaving the White House after the fourth inauguration of Roosevelt. *Below:* Jones, with Senator Walter F. George of Georgia, appearing before the Senate Commerce Committee, asking it to recommend against the confirmation of Henry A. Wallace as his successor as Federal Loan Administrator.

Secretary of Treasury John W. Snyder, left, and New York Stock Exchange President Emil Schram present scroll to Jones on behalf of "alumni" of the RFC.

More than 500 students annually attend colleges and universities on Jones scholarships. Here are a group at Texas A. & M. College.

Above: Fred J. Heyne (left) was Jones' right-hand man for forty-nine years. *Below:* Jones, with Governor James F. Byrnes of South Carolina, and nephew John T. Jones, who succeeded him as president of the Houston *Chronicle*.

Above: Jones with Governor Alfred E. Smith, the 1928 Democratic Presidential candidate. *Below:* General Dwight D. Eisenhower, Mrs. Jones, Mrs. Eisenhower, and Jones in the Jones home in Houston.

this strategic material. When Hitler loosed his cataracts of fire and steel against Holland he had in his possession by May 15, 1940, as one of the first spoils of war, the tin smelter at Arnhem, largest in the Western world.

The United States had long been the world's greatest user of tin, but there was no smelter within our boundaries. Neither were there any tin-bearing ores anywhere in the United States. And Germany had made tin the first and most urgent item in Jones' stockpiling program.

Jones immediately sent an emissary to the Dutch-British controlled International Tin Company, and that concern sent Victor A. Lowinger, one of its ablest technicians to Washington. Lowinger was joined by Dr. Johannes van den Broek, managing director of the N. V. Billiton Maatschappij, principal Dutch tin company, and together they signed the stockpiling agreement with Metals Reserve Company on behalf of International Tin Committee.

When no American firm could be found for the job Jones reached an agreement with Dr. van den Broek's Billiton Company to build and operate the smelter, through an American subsidiary set up for the purpose. Because all the ore would be imported, a Gulf area port was the logical place for the smelter, and Texas City, Texas, was decided upon.

Two Dutch technicians arrived in the United States to assume the company's initial tasks in the building. They left immediately for Galveston. As the Eastern Air Lines plane that carried them approached Atlanta, they were chatting with Eddie Rickenbacker, president of the airline. A few minutes later the plane had crashed, the two Dutchmen were dead, and Rickenbacker seriously injured.

Other technicians were rushed to this country. Construction of the plant got under way in March, 1941, and in April, 1942, a plant with an annual capacity of 50,000 tons of fine tin was in operation. There was on hand a sufficient supply of ore to keep it busy for a year.

That supply had come from Bolivia. Moreover, before the Japanese cut off the supply early in 1942, Metals Reserve had received from the British and Dutch approximately 41,000 tons of fine tin and 13,000 tons of tin ore. With what had come from Malaya, the Dutch East Indies, China, and the Belgian Congo, Metals Reserve had on hand approximately 100,000 tons of tin and tin ore. So precious was tin that after China's ports fell into Japanese hands the Air Transport Command flew it over the 23,000-foot-high Hump of the Himalayas from the Yunnan Province in China to the Assam Province in India and brought it by air to the United States.

There were similar stories in other stockpiling operations. In addition to the full supply of the efficient copper companies that normally had supplied all American needs with a little left over for exports, so great were the defense needs for that metal that Jones dispatched agents to many countries to buy all that was obtainable.

Millions of tons of copper came from South and Central America. Abandoned mines were reclaimed and rehabilitated in Mexico; subsidies were paid.

Nickel was another needed metal, which is not produced in any quantity in the United States, and the stockpiling of this, which like the others began sixteen months before Pearl Harbor, was principally from Canada at our very doorstep and across the world in New Caledonia.

Zinc, the principal war need of which was as an ingredient of cartridge brass, was so much in need that Jones authorized heavy subsidies especially in the tristate Oklahoma, Kansas, and Missouri area and bought 2,000,000 tons of ores and concentrates in Australia, Argentina, Bolivia, Canada, Mexico, and Peru. The construction and restoration of numerous smelters was financed. Mines long closed were reopened; abandoned smelters refitted.

It was with tungsten that Jones and his Metals Reserve Company made the biggest effort to shut out Japan from any metal supplies from Latin America. Not only was it buying every available ton, but North American companies operating in nations to the south were induced to incorporate in their contract of sales to foreign nations a cancellation clause that could be exercised if the United States needed the commodity, and Metals Reserve soon had a contract to purchase the entire supply of Central and South America.

There were many romantic stories in the metals stockpiling such as that of Colonial Mica Corporation, an RFC subsidiary with only ten dollars paid-in capital to buy 5,000,000 pounds of mica and in the scouting for chrome ores, platinum, quartz crystals, arsenic, and other vital materials.

Metals Reserve collected millions of dollars' worth of scrap iron and steel, brass, nickel, and copper. So great was the need that buildings were demolished and bridges, railroad and streetcar tracks, and other installations were bought for their yield of metal. When the United States could not furnish enough, the scrap-gathering campaign was carried to Cuba and the cities of Central and South America.

Of all the corporations created by RFC during the war Jones found the fourth-born of the war corporations—Defense Supplies—the most intriguing. It would be incorrect to call Defense Supplies a special-purpose corporation, although that was the plan when its creation was decided upon. But when its charter was in final form, it was in fact an all-purpose affair.

Jones gave his first thought to it on a hot August day in 1940 when Edward R. Stettinius, Jr., then of the Council of National Defense, came to Jones' office bringing with him Dr. R. E. Wilson, former professor of chemical engineering at Massachusetts Institute of Technology, but at the time president of the Pan American Petroleum and Export Company. Dr. Wilson wanted to discuss the urgent need of a greater production of 100-octane gasoline. There was in the United States, he pointed out, capacity for its production only at the rate of 30,000 barrels a year. That wouldn't be a drop in the bucket if requirements of the proposed expansion of airplane production to 50,000 planes a year, which President Roosevelt had proposed a month before, were carried out.

"We are just now putting together the Defense Plant Corporation, but I don't think its charter is broad enough to handle the gasoline procurement and it probably has enough to do anyway," Jones said. "I will set up a corporation for the purpose, and if the Army and Navy will take the gasoline off our hands later, we will finance the necessary plant expansions in the oil industry and build a stockpile."

When the charter of Defense Supplies came to him a day or two later, he looked it over and then decided to rewrite it to take full advantage of the blanket powers voted by Congress two months before.

When Jones had finished his handiwork, Defense Supplies Corporation had authority to produce, buy and sell, and store critical and strategic materials; to buy or lease land; to engage in the manufacture of arms, ammunitions, and implements of war; to produce or buy railroad equipment, airplanes, aviation training fields and camps; to buy and control transportation facilities in and between American countries in the Western Hemisphere and the United States.

No organization ever surpassed the mushroom growth of the Defense Supplies Corporation. The armed services, which had been chilly when 100-octane gasoline was first offered them, went on to buy more than thirteen billion gallons of it at a cost of two billion two hundred million dollars. Never was it stockpiled. It went straight to air bases and carriers.

Defense Supplies bought more than 200 different commodities, every one of them bearing a "must" label as necessary in preparation and then in the prosecution of the war. In buying, lending, and subsidizing it disbursed nine billion, two hundred and twenty-six million dollars. It made money, except for the subsidies. But Jones, a disbeliever in subsidies all his life, had become the biggest subsidizer in history. Those subsidies aggregated two billion, six hundred million dollars. Wherever possible, purchases were conducted in a business-like manner, but sometimes methods of obtaining and prices paid had to be secondary. Its agents ranged the globe and came back to tell Jones of their exploits in obtaining strangely named commodities in faraway places and under Arabian Nights circumstances.

New industries were constantly being launched, and seemingly each new one created new necessities. New synthetic rubber plants needed millions of gallons of industrial alcohol, and industrial alcohol called for such things as dehydrated potatoes and strap molasses.

Benzol, a by-product of coal-coking, was a necessary ingredient in 100-octane gasoline as well as in styrene and butadiene used in the manufacture of synthetic rubber, and Defense Supplies had to find 200,000,000 gallons of that.

Sometimes the activities were agricultural, and money went to develop the growing of sisal in Haiti, or chicona and abaca elsewhere in Latin America. The corporation backed geological expeditions in its search for minerals, bought mountains of wool, the clip of New Zealand, America, Australia, Africa, Uruguay, and anywhere else it was obtainable. Silk, abaca, hemp, henequen, burlap, jute, cotton, kapok, and every sort of fiber rope and twine were assembled in great quantities.

Defense Supplies arranged for the manufacture of great quantities of penicillin, bought opium, typhus serum, and other medicines. By the time the United States entered the war, Defense Supplies had imported 1,500,000 ounces of quinine, which with that already in the United States was enough for one billion, three hundred and forty-four million five-grain doses.

Quinine was just one of the things to remind the nation how much it depended on such remote countries as Malaya, Java, and Sumatra and which were cut off when those countries were overrun by the Japanese.

Our great supply stores in South America remained open, and Jones saw to it that we had practically a lone hand in purchasing there. On February 16, 1942, he could report to President Roosevelt, "We are buying and will continue to buy every exportable commodity in Latin

America which may be requested by the War Production Board, the Department of State, and the Board of Economic Warfare."

Early in the defense preparations Jones had brought Will L. Clayton in as Assistant Secretary of Commerce and Deputy Federal Loan Administrator. Clayton, a Houston fellow townsman of Jones and long his close personal friend, was head of Anderson, Clayton & Company, the cotton concern. Clayton was quickly put in charge of the overseas procurement activities on Defense Supplies, Rubber Development Corporation, Metals Reserve Company, and eventually the United States Commercial Company.

Defense Supplies was so well managed that it even collected its loan to Russia. In the summer of 1941 President Roosevelt suggested to Jones that Russia be loaned some money to buy military supplies in this country. Jones asked Constantine A. Oumansky, the Soviet Ambassador, to come to his office. Oumansky said the loan should be made to the Amtorg Trading Corporation, its purchasing agency in New York City. He thought they would need 100,000,000 dollars.

"Let's see how far you can get with 50,000,000 dollars," Jones countered.

That was the amount agreed upon. When lend-lease was granted to the Russians in October, 1941, Andrei Gromyko, who by now had succeeded Oumansky as Ambassador wanted us to cancel the loan, Jones refused.

Russia paid it with interest. In return we got 300,000 tons of chrome ore, every ton of which arrived on time. Precious Russian platinum was flown to this country because of the submarine risk. We got also iridium, manganese, and Russian lumber, pig bristles and sheep casings, goatskins, shark livers, horse-mane hair, and goose down, all things for which there was an urgent and special need.

In addition Defense Supplies had the task of getting the German airlines out of their dominant position in South and Central America. It furnished the money for subsidies on meat, flour, butter, coffee, and other foods.

There was one of the wartime corporations whose proficiency and dependability depended upon such techniques as slinking in the dark, operating behind closed doors, and other clandestine methods. This was the United States Commercial Company; in those operations from the time it was formed on March 26, 1942, there was nothing humdrum.

United States Commercial had one plain, simple job. It was to keep away from Germany critical material without a sufficient quantity of which it could not win the war. This called for preventing of the enemy's acquisition of those materials by anticipating his needs in certain cases and getting better-bankrolled operatives there first. But a mite of sabotage, black marketing, and twilight dealings of various sorts were sometimes necessary.

There was no place for bumbling or careless people on the staff of United States Commercial. The demand was for competent men of high character but with sufficient sophistication to know how to carry on negotiations if necessary with men of very low character.

Jones had formed United States Commercial or, alphabetically, USCC at the request of Secretary of State Cordell Hull. At its outset there was one commodity it desperately wished to obtain. That was wolfram. This dark brown metal with its tungstic acid has the highest melting point of any metal. No other metal is an acceptable substitute for it in making armor plate and providing tungsten carbide and fire heads in armor-piercing projectiles.

This country early had driven Germany out of the South American tungsten market, leaving Spain and Portugal as the Nazis' only source of supply. USCC worked always in close liaison and often in partnership with two British agencies, the Ministry of Economic Warfare and the United Kingdom Commercial Corporation, which functioned in a similar shadowy realm for that country.

In its initial deal with United Kingdom Commercial Corporation, USCC agreed to bid 22,000 dollars a ton for wolfram from its former low of a few hundred dollars a ton. Eventually the price went roaring up to 35,000 dollars a ton.

USCC's men contrived ingenious and not always impeccable methods of obtaining Spanish and Portuguese currency for the purposes which were its goal, and a naval vessel dropped anchor at Gibraltar to deliver a plethora of gold coins. Before the end of 1943 victory was in sight in the fight for wolfram. Germany had been forced to discontinue the use of tungsten carbide cores in their armor-piercing projectiles. A little later they found it necessary to forbid the use of tungsten carbide for cutting tools except in armament production.

Together the United States and Great Britain stripped the Iberian Peninsula of wolfram and tungsten concentrates, paying approximately 175,000,000 dollars for a little more than 10,500 metric tons. They spent other millions for "disruptive delays" in material for which Germany had bought and paid. If all of the methods employed would not stand scrutiny under normal commercial rules, they were at least effective in all but bankrupting Germany's foreign exchange holdings in Spain and Portugal.

Jones had made estimates that United States Commercial would lose at least two billion dollars. The cumulative net loss actually was around 172,000,000 dollars. It had paid sky-high prices in neutral countries for raw materials and manufactured goods, some of which we had no need at all but which Germany needed desperately. USCC had vanquished Germany in the black markets too.

The 172,000,000 dollars lost by United States Commercial was more than made back by the 210,000,000-dollar profit of War Damage Corporation. On Tuesday following Pearl Harbor, Jones suggested to President Roosevelt that the RFC create a corporation to write policies that private insurance companies were not prepared to do. Roosevelt gave his approval and War Damage Corporation was chartered four days later.

The corporation started out with 100,000,000 dollars capital. Jones later asked and got congressional approval to increase the capitalization to one billion dollars. The insurance was applicable to buildings, structures, and personal property, goods, growing crops, and orchards, that might sustain damage or destruction from enemy attacks.

The plan was worked out in consultation with insurance companies, and 546 insurance and eighty-three casualty insurance companies took advantage of the provision that they might take a 10 per cent participation in the enterprise, and share in the profit and losses to the extent of 10 per cent.

26

Building Plants and Homes

IN August, 1940, Jones brought about the creation of the Defense Plant Corporation for the purpose of carrying out the directive of Congress to build and operate plants and facilities for the manufacture of war materials. This new corporation was launched by the simple process of calling together the people who had been selected as directors. Jones nominated Schram to be its president, and after that had been voted, he himself accepted the chairmanship of the board just as he did in the case of all the other corporations created under the RFC law for war purposes.

In its lifetime the DPC was to build 2300 plants and equip them with tools and machinery. Its program was gigantic. The magnitude of Defense Plant's activities can be illustrated by the fact that at the end of war its holdings included capacity for manufacturing approximately 50 per cent of the nation's aluminum, 90 per cent of its magnesium metal, 71 per cent of the production of aircraft and aircraft engines, and 90 per cent of the nation's potential for the manufacture of synthetic rubber.

Two months before Jones gave the order for incorporation of Defense

Plant there arrived in Washington, William S. Knudsen. Born in Denmark, Knudsen forty years before had landed at Ellis Island. He was a tall, gangling, awkward young man, but he was able to demonstrate before long a positive genius in the management of machinery and men. He won a reputation at Ford and then at General Motors as the nation's top production man. Knudsen was sixty-one years old when in 1940 he gave up his 300,000-dollar-a-year job as president of General Motors and came to Washington to work for nothing per year as one of the seven members of the Advisory Commission of the Council of National Defense. His prime responsibility was getting production under way.

Anxious as he was to serve his country, Knudsen had misgivings about his fate in the political atmosphere under which the Roosevelt Administration was starting its national defense building. For the President was running for a third term.

"Like Artemus Ward I am not a politician, and my other habits are good," Knudsen jokingly told Jones at their first meeting. "The only thing I try to conceal is that I play the piano."

Knudsen went to work in an office in the Federal Reserve Building. His only staff at the beginning was a stenographer. Of all the heads of executive agencies with whom Jones worked in Washington, he undoubtedly felt the greatest affection for Knudsen and worked most satisfactorily with him.

"I knew of his great reputation in automobile manufacturing," Jones said. "But at our first meeting after it became known that we were to be so closely associated in both the sprouting and the early fruit bearing stages of defense activity I was amazed at his knowledge of the field of manufacturing. He seemed to carry in his head a picture of the whole manufacturing business in the United States and he had a personal acquaintance with hundreds of the men who ran these plants. He knew which would have to be greatly enlarged, which with only a little retooling were ready to go to work."

Of his feelings toward Jones, Knudsen told Norman Beasley, "Jones was the one man in a position of high executive responsibility who knew the pitfalls of politics and how to get around them and who also knew the problems of production and who realized that if we went to war the nation's entire human effort would have to be subordinated to and employed in its prosecution."

When the Federal Reserve Board asked Knudsen, who was its tenant, what it could do to improve his office working convenience, he replied,

"I have just one special request, I want a direct telephone from my desk to Jesse Jones."

Over that telephone, which was later moved to the Office of Production Management, when Knudsen became director general of OPM in January of 1941, Knudsen was to tell Jones of his needs and the various Jones organizations undertook to meet them.

Knudsen's needs included ships, tanks, airplanes, guns, smokeless powder, TNT, and new weapons—things that would have to be manufactured in hundreds of different kinds of plants and then assembled.

The Knudsen-Jones conversations were never long. Knudsen would simply lift the receiver off his telephone and say, "Jesse, I need a plant that is going to cost a lot of money."

Jones would reply:

"All right, send me a confirmation and you won't have to think about it any more."

Knudsen's needs were by no means all that Jones was to fill. Directives came to him from the War and Navy Departments for everything an army and navy must have to meet a mechanized foe on land, sea, and in the air. On April 21, 1941, eight months after Defense Plant and Defense Supplies had been launched, Jones was able to tell the Associated Press' annual luncheon in New York:

> In the period of these few months, more than 14,000 separate prime contracts, probably more that 100,000 subcontracts have been let for the manufacture of everything from a corporal's chevrons to bombers and battleships. These contracts call for the expenditure of $12,500,000,000. Seven hundred and eighty-four defense plants costing more than $2,100,000,000 have been built or are under construction.

At the most critical state of the war DPC plants were located in every state in the Union except North and South Dakota. There were also plants at many points on foreign shores. They represented an investment of nine billion, two hundred million dollars. The program met difficulties not only in building, rebuilding, tooling, and retooling operations, but the trouble of finding men with "know-how." Agencies would suddenly raise their sights and estimates would have to be rearranged. There were lumber and raw material shortages of a baffling nature. There were strikes and labor shortages. There were conflicting directives coming from various agencies. But DPC managed always to keep the program in balance.

There was little difficulty about the orders that came from Knudsen or the army and navy; but when commands began to come from such agencies as the Board of Economic Warfare, headed by Henry Wallace, a tyro on both production and procurement, there were headaches. But Defense Plant Corporation plied its course until military success came. Except in a few cases plants were leased to private companies and Jones concluded agreements with such distinguished lessees as Aluminum Company of America, General Motors, United States Steel, Curtiss-Wright, Republic Steel, Chrysler, Ford, Anaconda Copper Mining, Dow Chemical, United Aircraft, General Electric, Union Carbide and Carbon, Standard Oil, Bendix Aviation, Goodyear Tire and Rubber, Koppers Company, Studebaker, American Rolling Mills, Continental Motors, Mathieson Alkali Works, Packard Motor, B. F. Goodrich, Nash-Kelvinator, E. I. du Pont de Nemours, and the Sperry Corporation.

Jones' final accounting showed that something like half of DPC's expenditures had been in aviation. Its 176,000,000-dollar Dodge-Chicago plant was the largest single industrial plant in the country. It covered 145 acres of ground. Built in this plant were engines for B-29 Superfortresses and B-32 Dominators.

To account for the two billion, six hundred million dollars that Defense Plant spent for aviation land, machines, and equipment were many new plants to build aircraft, engines, and parts.

Into aluminum and magnesium, used principally for airplanes, it put one billion, five hundred million dollars. For forty-five plants to produce high-octane gasoline there went 250,000,000 dollars. It bought and enlarged sixty-two flying schools and provided planes and housing to assist the War Department's pilot training program.

There were 183 plants for steel and pig iron facilities, costing one billion, two hundred and twenty-three million dollars and another billion went to steel companies to finance their privately undertaken expansions. There were fifty-one wholly owned plants for synthetic rubber manufacturing, cost 715,000,000 dollars.

Machine tool expenditures amounted to two billion dollars.

Other millions went for plants and machinery which made bombs, shells, tanks, guns, and other implements of war. The building of ships and dock facilities took many additional millions.

Included in the 335,000,000 dollars that Defense Plant Corporation invested were such projects as the Big Inch and Little Big Inch pipelines to carry petroleum and its products from Texas to the New Jersey-New York City metropolitan area. It financed tugboats and barges for river transportation and bought 400 kitchen cars and 1200 sleeping cars for troop movements. It even bought new buses and streetcars and feeder railroads to carry war materials and workers to and from their places of employment.

Jones could cite many cases of the reasonableness of industry—large or small. United States Steel built the 100,000,000-dollar steel plants for DPC at Homestead and Duquesne, Pennsylvania, at out-of-pocket expense and stipulated on their own motion that no part of the company's general overhead was to be included in the cost. It also built and operated the 200,000,000-dollar steel plant near Provo, Utah, at the request of DPC. In this case a reasonable fee for operation would have been 100,000,000 dollars per year, but in negotiations Jones proposed to B. F. Fairless, the steel company president, that they operate the plant without fee or any other consideration as long as this country remained at war. Fairless and the company's directors readily agreed to this.

Thomas M. Girdler of Republic Steel Corporation and also of Vultee Aircraft Corporation handled in record speed and at a reasonable cost, contracts for buildings amounting to 175,000,000 dollars. Eugene Grace of Bethlehem quickly purchased 20,500,000 dollars of facilities erected by DPC.

Walter S. Carpenter, president of Du Pont, came to Washington when Jones was anxious to buy the company's neoprene plant at Louisville, Kentucky, to speed the synthetic rubber program. Carpenter agreed not only to sell the plant but waived any option of repurchase although the company was anxious to have the plant back at the end of the war.

When Jones suggested to Dr. William H. Dow, president of the Dow Chemical Company, a basis on which he wished the company to build a 60,000,000-dollar plant on the Texas Gulf Coast, Dow readily agreed.

The Aluminum Company of America (Alcoa) built a half-dozen aluminum plants for Defense Plant Corporation which also made advances to the Aluminum Company of Canada for plants. Edward Davis headed Alcoa, and his brother, Arthur, headed the Canadian company, which had to build the Shipsaw Dam in Canada as part of the operation. Jones found the Davis brothers very reasonable men. Especially was this the case of Edward Davis, despite the fact that Jones under a War Production Board directive was to all intents and purposes building up a rival company through its heavy financing of Reynolds Metals Company, and there was some question as to whether the country could absorb the additional output in postwar days.

The Reynolds Metals Company was to become a special favorite of President Roosevelt, who was anxious that Alcoa have a strong rival. This preference led to extended negotiations and large investments.

Defense Plant Corporation lent Reynolds upwards of 42,000,000 dollars for plants in Alabama, Washington, and Kentucky, and for working capital and to pay debts it owed to banks. Reynolds also operated other plants belonging to Defense Plant Corporation that had been erected at a cost in excess of 10,000,000 dollars.

In the negotiations Jones did not deal with Richard S. Reynolds until the final stages. Sam Husbands and others worked out the details. Husbands and Reynolds went together to Jones for his approval of the completed plans.

After Jones had examined the papers very carefully, Reynolds addressed him jokingly:

"You have got some hard traders here, Mr. Jones. They made me scrape the bottom of the barrel for collateral and I have given more security for these loans than I ever gave a bank. I hear you are a harder trader than any of them. Is there anything else you want?"

"Yes," Jones responded. "We want one more thing. We want an Oklahoma guarantee."

"What is an Oklahoma guarantee?" Reynolds entreated.

"Well," answered Jones, "when I was a young man in the lumber business out there, a farmer would go to an Oklahoma country bank for a loan. He would be required to mortgage his prospective crop, a mule or two, and maybe a milch cow or anything else he had. After this was done he was handed a note with all the customary printed conditions, and before affixing his signature he was asked to insert in his own handwriting one more line which read: 'And if I don't pay this note I am a son of a bitch.' "

One industrialist with whom Jones dealt a great deal and who always wanted adequate pay, and Jones thought often more than adequate pay, was Henry J. Kaiser. A big, bald, and breezy man of push and purpose, Kaiser seemed to learn quicker than any other industrialist when War Production Board directives to build facilities were issued to Defense Plant Corporation.

Altogether Kaiser got about 150,000,000 dollars from RFC subsidiaries for his wartime enterprises. Kaiser could never get his costs for magnesium at the Los Altos, California, plant below thirty cents a pound as compared with the eighteen-cents-per-pound cost at the Anaconda Copper Company's Basic Magnesium plant. The Kaiser steel plant at Fontana, California, was not a wartime success. But the RFC had required Kaiser to give the two plants as well as his shipbuilding profits as security, and while he was slowest of all the big wartime borrowers, he did eventually pay the government. In 1956, eleven years after the war had ended, and two years after the RFC had been put into liquidation, the remaining Kaiser debt was paid.

Jones had grave doubts about Kaiser's wartime scheme to build the biggest planes ever constructed, each capable of carrying an entire company of men with their equipment. Kaiser then induced Howard Hughes to join him in the latter venture and won the support of the Cargo Plane Committee and of President Roosevelt. On a directive from the War Production Board, Jones advanced 18,000,000 dollars to Kaiser and Hughes for three such planes, one a prototype and the others for use.

Kaiser was soon out of this project and Hughes, although handicapped by an order that he use no critical war metal, went ahead constructing the prototype of wood.

Jones knew little of what went on at the White House and War Production Board regarding this plane. The WPB ordered him to cancel the contract and then he received a direct order from the White House to reinstate it. The prototype cost more than all three planes had been expected to cost.

Although Hughes once flew the plane, its feasibility remained in doubt. In addition to the 18,000,000 dollars advanced by the RFC, Hughes put 8,000,000 or 10,000,000 dollars of his own money into the project.

Jones' building problems were not confined to the setting up of plants for men and women to work in. There also had to be houses for workers to live in. For this purpose Jones created another corporation under his wide powers, the Defense Homes Corporation.

With 76,000,000 dollars, of which 10,000,000 dollars came from the emergency fund Congress had voted to President Roosevelt, and the balance borrowed from RFC, Defense Homes Corporation built 10,946 housing units in thirteen states and the District of Columbia. In war-crowded Washington, Jones bought the Friendship estate of Evalyn Walsh McLean and built the substantial McLean Gardens. It, like Fairlington—a similar development, and the Meridian Hill Hotel for women war workers, all were sold at a profit at the end of the war.

A distinguishing characteristic of Jones' operation in private life had been the great number of his corporations.

He followed this pattern in the establishment of three large and a half dozen small RFC subsidiaries to fight the depression and another dozen to carry out its responsibilities when for defense and war purposes the RFC became in effect a gigantic war finance corporation.

27

Unnecessary Controversy Over Necessary Rubber

THE public heard more about rubber in the early stages of World War II than any other commodity. This was partly because there had been some delay and uncertainty in getting a synthetic program under way and as a result there was plenty of buck-passing concerning responsibility. Moreover, there were several publicity-conscious people who desired to get in on the program. Also, there was plenty of niggling and needling by Jones' leftist enemies in the Administration.

One of the chief figures in the early defense mobilization said privately in 1940 that the manufacture of synthetic rubber was "too expensive to be considered." Later, after the supply of natural rubber from the Far East had been cut off, the same man, no doubt reflecting the gossip of left-wing Washington, of which he was a part, said that a synthetic program should have been adopted long ago and that Jesse Jones was responsible for the delay.

For some reason the attitude of President Roosevelt about the necessity for adequate supplies of rubber was for a year or more indifferent and dilatory. In May, when France was falling, Harry Hopkins made a random observation to Jones that the President thought some rubber should be purchased. Jones noted this remark and brought up the subject a day or two later in a conversation with the President. He said that there was no law that would permit him to buy rubber. The President merely commented that "maybe you had better ask Congress for the authority." He made no further reference to the subject for a long time.

Jones took the suggestion seriously and secured legislation permitting the RFC to create corporations for the purpose of acquiring critical and strategic material.

Rubber deserved high rank among such strategic and critical materials. Its uses were innumerable. As the army, navy, and air force built up for war, Jones began to hear clamorous evidence of how much the social and economic structure of the nation depends upon rubber for peacetime functions. And the amount necessary to keep armies marching, ships sailing, and planes flying was almost beyond comprehension.

From stethoscopes, amputation strips, and blood-plasma tubing to huge bridge pontoons, the calls were endless. Grindings in take-offs and landing of giant planes took a terrific toll. The speedy and mobile mechanized forces needed tires for ten-wheel trucks, gun carriages, bulldozers, and jeeps. Essential civilian passenger cars and trucks with war's demands were needed more than ever.

Various types of rubber footwear were necessary for the frozen Arctic, the South Pacific jungles, monsoons in Burma, and mountain-climbing in some sectors, and there were many kinds of weather-proof rubber. It was used to de-ice the wings of airplanes. Rubber stills made sea water drinkable when navy planes were forced down and crews awaited rescue. Every battleship needed seventy-five tons of rubber, enough to make 17,000 tires if used for that purpose. To bullet-proof the gasoline tank of a Flying Fortress, 1240 pounds of self-closing rubber were needed; every soldier's gas mask contained a pound of rubber. Rubber-lined, electrically heated suits were needed for high-altitude flying. London asked and received millions of feet of rubber hose to prevent its destruction by fire after blitzes, and the Army Medical Corps asked for 250,000 pounds of rubber per year for adhesive tape alone.

The battle for rubber, after Jones asked Congress for the legislation necessary for its acquisition, fell into three phases. First there was an urgent, almost frantic effort to acquire a stockpile of natural rubber before the Japanese cut off the great supplying centers in Southeastern Asia. Then there was the building of synthetic plants. Finally, there was an effort to bring into production new sources of natural production in South America.

While he was waiting for Congress to enact the legislation permitting the RFC to stockpile rubber, Jones asked A. L. Viles, president of the Rubber Manufacturers Association, to come to see him, bringing along representatives of the major rubber manufacturing companies. Viles came and brought with him Paul W. Litchfield, chairman of Goodyear Tire and Rubber; Harvey Firestone, Jr., vice-president of Firestone; John L. Collyer, president of B. F. Goodrich; William F. McNeil, president of General Tire and Rubber; and F. B. Davis of United States Rubber.

This group told Jones that prior to World War II the United States was consuming more rubber than the rest of the world combined and that 70 per cent of the supply went into tires and inner tubes. Malaya and the Netherlands Indies were the largest producers, but there were British Borneo and Sarawak, Indochina, the Philippines, Latin America, and the Firestone plantations in Liberia. Growth of rubber in this hemisphere, which was its birthplace, had practically ceased.

In rubber, as had been the case in tin, the British and Dutch had to be dealt with. Restrictions against the free flow of raw rubber into the world markets, beginning with the British Stevenson Act in 1922, had resulted in a supply much less than it would have been in a free market. Jones proposed to the rubber men that they and the RFC enter into a partnership. Wary of the pitfalls in a fluctuating market and remembering the crippling losses they had previously taken, the rubber men were hesitant.

They also warned Jones that if he entered the market offering prices even a few cents above the market, rubber growers would hold their stocks in anticipation of yet higher prices. But Jones and the rubber men were so keenly aware of the necessity for action that they finally decided that the RFC would buy and carry the rubber and the industry would pay half of the cost of its carrying and storage.

The next step was to negotiate an agreement with the International Rubber Regulation Committee, which controlled 97 per cent of the world's rubber supply. Jones insisted that there be no delay and from Jones' office Viles called the International Committee's office in London. Before Jones and Viles finished the transatlantic conversation with the cartel's office, they had an agreement that Sir John Hay, Britain's foremost rubber expert, would proceed immediately to the United States. He arrived on June 13.

Congress passed and President Roosevelt had signed the authority for the RFC subsidiary corporations on June 25. Three days later Jones created the Rubber Reserve Company, with RFC Director Howard Klossner as president, and on the same day, June 28, Jones and Sir John completed the agreement for purchase of 150,000 tons of raw rubber.

Jones then went to the White House and told the President, "I have contracted for every pound of rubber the British and Dutch organization will sell. Even if they let me have many times this amount, the natural rubber will not be enough. We are going to have to build a synthetic rubber industry in this country and it will have to be built from the ground up. We ought to get started on it."

Roosevelt disagreed. He said the American rubber corporations were wealthy and ought to do the job. If they didn't, Roosevelt said, and it became necessary, "the government could build the plants in a year's time."

By now it had become evident that the original natural rubber agreement between Jones and the five big companies was not practical; consequently it was arranged for RFC to buy all the raw rubber and sell such as the rubber companies needed at cost plus carrying charges. To speed the program Jones brought Viles and an experienced buyer from each of the five big rubber companies into service with his Rubber Reserve Company.

Despite all that Jones and the American rubber men could do, the rubber came in far more slowly than they had hoped. Sir John kept insisting that 150,000 raw tons was the maximum amount he could sell. On August 15, 1940, a second agreement was made providing for the purchase of an additional 180,000 tons of crude rubber during the year 1941. Jones had great difficulty in increasing this amount, although he testified before a congressional committee later that he warned Sir John that unless a larger supply could be obtained, synthetic production would be undertaken here on a large scale: "I said this to him frequently in as diplomatic a manner as I am able."

When Jones' friend, Lord Beaverbrook, the British Minister of Supply, came to see him to talk about the general war supply situation, Jones complained of the rubber delivery. Beaverbrook put pressure on the cartel. On May 7, 1941, announcement was made of a third agreement with the International Rubber Regulation Committee, which together with the previous agreements provided for the purchase of a total quantity of 430,000 tons of crude rubber. Beaverbrook's help was one of the reasons why when the Japanese struck at Pearl Harbor the amount of rubber that had been received in this country or was en route over the long 9000-mile distance from Singapore to the California harbors amounted to 673,000 tons purchased at a cost of 292,000,000 dollars.

This supply, brought in despite the acute problems of adequate shipping space and shipping schedules, still did not satisfy Jones. He first sent a memorandum to the White House and then called on the President. Jones said that he had come to the firm conclusion that this country would have to build up a source of rubber independent of imports from abroad. Jones told the President that members of the Defense Council believed 100,000,000 dollars ought to be spent as a starter. He himself thought they might get under way for 50,000,000 dollars. Again Roosevelt disagreed, but Jones was obdurate. Finally the President agreed on an initial expenditure of 25,000,000 dollars.

Jones now sent letters to American rubber firms asking them to submit plans for pilot plants. The letters went out on December 4, 1940, a year and two days before the Pearl Harbor attack. In the next few months there were many conferences. There were innumerable obstacles in the path of the Rubber Reserve Corporation, which was to have direct responsibility for the formulation, correlation, and operation of a program.

In the first place, there was not one process of producing synthetic rubber, but many. There was also the fact that there was not just one type of synthetic rubber, but rather a number of types that differed substantially in their properties and applications. The various processes were in a stage of rapid development; yet, with the nation's needs so critical, there was no time for broad research plans to develop the best. The program had to be speculative.

The American rubber men were cooperating fully in the selection of processes, patent rights, and the exchange of technical information. Some of the processes were the subject of heated controversy. There were various chemicals, catalysts, and solvents to be discussed. Butadiene plants, for example, used an alcohol feed-stock, and there was already a clamor for alcohol from many other industries. One by one these difficulties were ironed out.

John L. Collyer of the B. F. Goodrich Company, who had been a pioneer in the development of synthetic rubber for tires, became a frequent Jones consultant. In addition to the big rubber companies, Du Pont, Koppers, Dow, Monsanto, and the Carbide & Chemical corporations were all experimenting either with synthetic rubber or such of its ingredients as butadiene and styrene. So was the Standard Oil Development Company. All were keeping Jones acquainted with their progress.

Late in March, 1941, Jones asked Firestone, Goodrich, and the United States Rubber Company to build four pilot plants, each having a 10,000-ton capacity of the butadiene-styrene type of rubber.

Jones continued his fight for an adequate synthetic rubber supply both at the White House and before congressional committees. On May 8, 1941, he appeared before the Senate Banking and Currency Committee. He explained that while he felt that he had all the necessary authority, he wished to inform Congress of the steps being taken because any large investment in synthetic rubber plants by the government would present major questions of policy for future decisions by Congress. The committee indicated that it was willing to allow Jones to proceed with the rubber problem according to his own judgment of the necessities of the changing situation.

Jones did not consider it necessary to discuss the rubber plans further with the President at this stage, but his discussion with heads of great industrial concerns continued. The Pearl Harbor attack brought a conviction in both industry and government that pooling plans and formula secrets were of little importance in the face of the crisis the nation then faced.

Early in January, 1942, the industrial leaders met with Jones in his office. The session began at ten o'clock one morning, continued uninterruptedly until three o'clock the next morning, then the conferees got a few hours' sleep. At the end of the next session the industrial leaders had made an agreement with Rubber Reserve for pooling of patents and processes and for plants that would produce 400,000 tons of synthetic rubber a year.

At a meeting between President Roosevelt, Prime Minister Winston Churchill, Lord Beaverbrook, and Jones at the White House a day or two later, Beaverbrook asked what the plans for synthetic rubber were. Jones gave him the 400,000 figure. Beaverbrook thought that would be an abundance. Jones at the time had not cleared the 400,000 plan with the President.

The next day he went to the White House carrying a copy of a press release announcing the plan to spend 400,000,000 dollars to produce a minimum of 400,000 tons a year, with the figure possibly running to 500,000 tons. Roosevelt agreed to 400,000 tons but said 500,000 would be too much.

Beaverbrook's belief that 400,000 tons a year would "be a great sufficiency" did not last for forty-eight hours. On Sunday, January 11, Beaverbrook went to Jones' office to tell him that the British, who with the Dutch had controlled the rubber supply prior to the war, would thereafter be dependent upon the United States for its rubber.

Jones and Beaverbrook together put into final form the release of the rubber plans as agreed to by President Roosevelt. The release also disclosed plans to stimulate production of zinc, lead, copper, and tin.

Even though President Roosevelt had cut the plans down to 400,000, Jones' announcement startled the country by its immense size. But Beaverbrook was not satisfied. On January 13 he sent the following memorandum to Churchill, who was leaving Washington the next day to return to London:

PRIME MINISTER
Rubber

On Sunday morning I came to an understanding with Jesse Jones about the production of rubber.

We must persuade him to increase production of synthetic rubber from 400,000 to 600,000 tons per annum.

He has an understanding with me to give us 50,000 tons of synthetic rubber per annum, on the basis of 350,000 tons of production. If production falls short, then Great Britain's share is reduced proportionally.

We have an understanding with OPM to supply us with 25,000 tons of reclaimed rubber in 1942.

I am not sending any reports of raw materials.

Do you want tin?

It is a Jesse Jones business.

Beaverbrook

After Singapore fell to the Japanese on February 15 the goal for synthetic rubber was raised to 805,000 tons per year. Of this 705,000 would be butadiene-styrene. The remainder would be butyl, a Standard Oil product, and neoprene, a Du Pont synthetic.

Charles F. Kettering, whom Jones had asked to form a committee to make recommendations as to procedure, recommended the manufacture of thiacol, which could be produced quickly for rather short-lived tires. It served a purpose while the synthetic plants were being built.

Jones' January 12 statement that some of the factories would be in operation by July, 1943, was considered optimistic by rubber experts, yet one of them was actually constructed and put in operation in 287 days and others did almost as well. It was the greatest and quickest job of construction engineering in history. In two years from the date of the announcement of the program synthetic rubber was being produced at the rate of 700,000 tons a year.

But as the plants went up the natural rubber stocks went down. Three days after Pearl Harbor a ban was clamped down on the sale of new tires and that was quickly followed with the first civilian rationing scheme of the war. Jones was proud that his own state of Texas was first to get its machinery in order for tire rationing.

Despite all earlier efforts to stockpile enough rubber to last until the factories were turning out synthetic production, the demands were pressing upon the supply. This made necessary several further steps.

First Jones turned to South America, where limited amounts were under production but which had never grown, because of the great abundance which in peacetime came from the Far East and the tight controls of the cartel. Jones arranged with the governments of sixteen Central and South American countries to increase their current production. There were also consummated agreements with private interests in Liberia.

Another limited source was scrap rubber. Jones made a contract with four companies that had in peacetime gathered most of the available scrap to carry on intensively for the government. This yielded a substantial amount, but the quality of such reclaimed material was such as to make it usable for only a limited number of purposes.

As new agencies were set up, more and more of them were to have a finger in the rubber pie. These included the War Production Board, Army, Navy, Army-Navy Munitions Board, Office of Petroleum Coordinator, the Department of Agriculture, and of course the Rubber Reserve Company.

To get all the agencies together as much as possible, Jones in May, 1942, inaugurated Monday meetings of all those interested. The meetings brought together such men as General Lucius D. Clay, from the army, Ferdinand Eberstadt for the Army-Navy Munitions Board, Clarence Francis from the Council of National Defense, and representatives from the Navy, War Production Board, Department of Agriculture, and Office of the Petroleum Coordinator. These meetings continued until September, 1942, by which time the selection of processes had been made, plant locations decided, and priority on materials obtained despite the competing claims of other equally urgent war programs. The fifty-one plants decided upon were built by the Defense Plant Corporation. Eighteen of them produced butadiene, five produced styrene, nine produced other chemicals, and nineteen turned out synthetic rubber.

Both tire rationing and gasoline rationing had as their purpose limiting the use of motor vehicles to save rubber. As such measures pinched tighter on civilians there was increased agitation for a survey of the rubber situation. A great part of it came from within the Administration, and, indeed, Secretary of Interior Ickes publicly claimed that he had induced President Roosevelt to order an investigation.

The Jones' Rubber Reserve Company and perhaps all of the other agencies having to do with rubber welcomed a survey hoping that it would acquaint the country of the critical situation and by acquainting the public of these facts bring more willing compliance with the necessary conservation measures.

With great fanfare a committee was appointed, with Bernard M. Baruch as chairman. The other members were Dr. J. B. Conant, president of Harvard University, and Dr. Karl T. Compton, president of the Massachusetts Institute of Technology. The appointment of Baruch for this assignment was not solely because of his public prominence or his knowledge of business and industry. The President had been anxious to provide a task for the man who had been chairman of the War Industries Board in World War I and had chafed somewhat because he had been passed over in earlier appointments in World War II. But the President, in the haphazard manner that had become habitual with him, neglected in this instance to take into consideration the fact that Baruch entertained no friendly feelings toward Jones.

Baruch was most active in the work of the rubber survey committee during its short life between its appointment on August 6, 1942 and the submission of its report on September 10. The official report of what was essentially a superficial survey was prepared by a professional writer selected by Baruch. It took several digs at Jones.

The survey and the preparation of the report was all in such haste as to result in one inexcusable error. The report said that the Jones' Rubber Reserve Company had had the service of only one part-time rubber expert-chemist-scientist. Actually, at the first meeting between Jones and the heads of the big rubber manufacturing companies, they had made their experts, chemists, and scientists available to Jones. Later the oil companies and chemical industries had taken similar action and there was never any lack of the best counsel from these sources.

The Baruch Committee also found that "failure of the responsible officials to request the aid of Russia in setting up our synthetic system is a neglect for which we have not had a satisfactory explanation." Jones in fact had spent more time exploring Russian and German situations with respect to synthetic rubber than the Baruch committee spent in its entire survey of the situation. This early exploration had revealed that the Russians had made no real progress in its manufacture, and while the Germans had done much better they were still far from effective production. He acquired and used the German formulas from the Standard Oil Company of New Jersey and these were improved with experience. To further explore the Russian situation Jones felt would only occasion a needless delay, and his advisers had concurred in this judgment.

However, when the Rubber Director was appointed as a result of the report of the Baruch Survey, this director did send a mission to Russia in December, 1942. The Russians were not cooperative and the Americans returned home in March, 1943, without having seen inside of a Russian plant or having obtained any helpful information.

Perhaps the one constructive suggestion of the Baruch Committee was for the appointment of a Rubber Director, which at that stage of the program proved to have been helpful. The appointment of William M. Jeffers, president of the Union Pacific Railroad, was an excellent one, although he did not meet the Baruch recommendation that he be "a competent operating and manufacturing executive, preferably with experience in the rubber industry."

Jeffers directed the Rubber Reserve Company to do a few of the things the Baruch Committee recommended, but soon found most of them impractical and rescinded them. Jeffers' great service was in capitalizing on the Baruch Committee's almost panicky appraisal of the rubber situation to demand materials for the construction of the plants.

Jeffers remained in Washington eleven months and on leaving wrote to Jones:

> I would be remiss if I did not tell you how genuinely appreciative I am of the understanding and consistent support you have given me in ironing out some of the synthetic rubber problems.
>
> The synthetic rubber program, after all, was your program, and we have succeeded in driving it through. I feel well repaid for the effort.
>
> It has been a great pleasure and a great comfort to have known you better, and I hope that in the years to come our paths will cross often. You are a great fellow.

As for the technical aspects of the synthetic program, the Baruch Committee gave them unqualified approval, and basically the synthetic rubber program remained as Jones and his advisers had established it before the Baruch report. After Jeffers' resignation Rubber Reserve resumed full responsibility for the synthetic program.

When Jones and Jeffers went to Institute, West Virginia, on June 11, 1943, to inspect the completed synthetic rubber plant operated by the Carbide & Carbon Chemicals Corporation and the United States Rubber Company, Jones said:

> The Rubber Survey (Baruch) Committee stated in its report in September, 1942, that, normally to develop an industry as large as this would require a dozen years, and to compress it in less than two years would be an almost superhuman task. I am glad to say that the task has been accomplished in less than two years; just as we are doing many other things necessary to the war effort in a surprisingly short time. Our country is equal to any task and any emergency, and I take pleasure in commending everyone who has had a part in the synthetic rubber program, as well as every other phase of the war effort.

At the end of the war 87 per cent of the rubber being consumed in the United States was synthetic, practically all of it coming from government-owned plants. Had it been necessary, the plants were ready to produce more than a million tons of rubber a year. It was truly one of the great achievements of the war.*

The effort to stimulate the production of natural rubber in Central and South America came close to developing into high comedy because of the interference at this time of Vice-President Henry Wallace's strange creation, the Board of Economic Warfare. This incident is reserved for a later chapter.

* In a statement to the author Raymond Moley, who was well acquainted with most of the people concerned in this chapter said, "In talking to me after the rubber survey committee had submitted its report Baruch said that the President had admitted to him that he and not Jones had been responsible for the delay in getting the synthetic program started."

28

War Within War

AN unforgettable feature of the Roosevelt Administration was the incessant series of feuds and fracases within the official family. To a large degree Roosevelt himself was responsible for this. In the first place, he had brought into his Administration a considerable number of cantankerous individuals who had never before borne the responsibility of getting on in the management of large affairs. The best example of this was Harold Ickes, Secretary of the Interior and administrator of various emergency agencies. There were also plenty of radical dreamers of the Henry Wallace type, for whom all times were out of joint except in their own dreams of a world made over. There was also the great influence of labor chieftains to whom Roosevelt not only felt obligations for services in past elections but whom he wished to retain as future allies of his party.

Roosevelt was also guilty of loose administrative practices such as choosing too many people to be responsible for the same job or by creating agencies with vague and indeterminate functions. This weakness was especially notable in the war years, when scarcely a week passed which did not see the creation of some new super-agency or the appointment of a new coordinator of the uncoordinated.

The impact of such disorderly administrative conditions fell heavily upon all those who were trained by experience to recognize clear lines of responsibility and to work with people accustomed to trained and experienced managers. Two of the victims of these conditions were Jones himself and Knudsen. Jones found conditions tolerable largely because he had made himself indispensable and partly because he had a deft way of warding off attacks upon himself and his various activities. But Knudsen had none of the political astuteness of Jones and relatively little influence in Congress. He had also been the head of a great private corporation that fought many battles with the labor leaders who wielded so much influence with the President and his department heads.

For these reasons the force of the criticism that almost from the beginning fell upon Knudsen was not only very great but it found Knudsen incapable of meeting it without strong White House support. Jones tried very hard to secure that support from Roosevelt. He told the President on more than one occasion of his cooperation with Knudsen and the rare qualities of the former General Motors head.

"No man could have done a better job," Jones told Roosevelt, "and I doubt if anyone could be found who could do so well."

But it was evident that Knudsen's enemies had found the broad highway to the Presidential mind. The labor chieftains had very special grudges against Knudsen. One count against him was the fact that he had blasted Walter Reuther's chimerical 500-airplanes-a-day plan, showing it to be entirely impractical. While the massive practical intelligence headed the OPM, the barrier between the Treasury and the radicals could not be surmounted.

Indeed, Roosevelt had already cut away some of Knudsen's power in August, 1941, by setting up a Supply Priorities and Allocation Board (SPAB) with some authority over the OPM.

Jones told Harry L. Hopkins he knew the campaign was on to drive Knudsen out. "I think it would be a mistake. He is the right man on the right job at the right time."

Jones found Hopkins so noncommittal that he felt that Hopkins was either in favor of Knudsen's replacement or had knowledge that Roosevelt had decided on it to please labor leaders.

On January 13, 1942, the blow fell on Knudsen. A meeting of SPAB was under way, with Vice-President Wallace presiding. Knudsen and Jones, both of whom were members of SPAB's board, were in attendance. A messenger appeared with a note asking Wallace and Donald M. Nelson to come to the White House. Nelson, a former Sears, Roebuck executive, was serving as director of priorities for OPM and executive director of SPAB.

Neither Wallace nor Nelson returned to the meeting. At its close Jones and Knudsen walked out together. Knudsen was in high spirits over his production accomplishments as they parted to return to their offices. Knudsen had just reached his office and seated himself at his desk when a bulletin came over the news ticker announcing that the President had abolished SPAB and superseded OPM with a new agency to be known as the War Production Board. Nelson was named as its chairman. Knudsen sat stunned by the unexpected news.

Jones reached his office and was told that Harry Hopkins at the White House wanted to speak to him immediately. Hopkins related what had happened.

"It was done in a brutal way," he told Jones, "I know it must have hurt Knudsen deeply. Get hold of him at once and ask him not to make any statement. I think we could get the President to give him a commission as a brigadier general to help Under Secretary of War Patterson in his procurement problems."

Jones said he would try, but that he thought Knudsen should be given a commission as high as lieutenant general if he would accept it.

"I have heard Knudsen make two-minute speeches and I have heard him speak for an hour and he is one of the most inspiring speakers I have ever heard," Jones said. "I think personal appearances by him would help anywhere. The bosses would like him and so would the fellows in overalls."

Hopkins said that a rank as high as lieutenant general was out of the question. Jones telephoned to Mrs. Jones to break a dinner engagement and went to Knudsen's residence. Knudsen's wife was in Detroit and he was alone except for the household servants. Jones said later of this visit:

> I never saw so forlorn a man as Knudsen was when he greeted me at his house. He had formed a liking for the President, and the President had repeatedly told him what a fine job he was doing. Now he was no longer directing procurement for "The Arsenal of Democracy," a phrase which he himself had coined. I think he would rather have died than to have been ejected at so desperate a stage of the war.

Jones told him of Hopkins' request not to make any statement to the press: "I know you have been shabbily treated," he added, "but I think you will be happier in the end if you take a high-ranking Army appointment and help push production in that way."

Knudsen was unmovable.

"No, I have done a good job and the President has unceremoniously kicked me out to satisfy labor. I am going back to where I came from—Detroit."

They talked all through dinner. Jones persevered.

"I'd take the brass or braid," he said. "No civilian has ever been commissioned as lieutenant general. You will be out of the line of fire of all this wrecking crew in Washington and can do a better job than the head of any alphabetical agency can do."

Jones felt he was not making much progress. As they finished the meal, Knudsen got up and went to the piano.

He sat there playing and humming sad tunes, a broken-hearted man [Jones put down in a memorandum]. I finally got him to play cards, but his mind was not on it and I put up the deck. At midnight I was tired and wanted to go home and to bed. Suddenly, I picked up the telephone and called the White House for Hopkins. Taking a chance, I said to Harry: "Knudsen will accept a three-star generalship in the Army and report to Bob Patterson to help in promoting production for war." Hopkins contended that no higher rank than the one star, for a brigadier general could be given. I repeated that it would have to be lieutenant general. Knudsen said nothing, doubtless welcoming the fact that a friend was deciding for him.

The next day the three-star appointment came. After the war Jones wrote:

Knudsen's commissioning was one of the finest things that happened to our production program. Bob Patterson told me that Knudsen only had to walk into a plant and say "How are you getting along, boys?" to inspire the greatest effort on behalf of the workers. He flew from plant to plant getting higher production. But he never got over the blow of his cruel dismissal from the civilian post. Valuable as he was in uniform he was never happy in the new job.

Donald Nelson was no Knudsen, but Jones' relations with him as chairman of the War Production Board were amicable and satisfactory.

World War II served to increase rather than diminish Jones' role as an indefatigable settler of other people's problems. These perplexities ranged from labor disputes to financial involvements of the Roosevelt family and even to sparing the time-honored social prestige of the President's home on the Hudson from the shock of having Father Divine and a task force of his cult as next-door neighbors.

On April 1, 1941, with the nation in feverish preparation for defense, 400,000 coal miners, North and South, walked out of their pits. For four weeks the deadlock continued. Northern operators had finally agreed to a one-dollar-a-day increase for miners, but the Southern group remained unmovably against it. They had repeatedly spurned White House entreaties.

On April 28 President Roosevelt turned the negotiations over to Jones. Jones scheduled a meeting in his office with the parties to the deadlocked dispute.

"Has anybody changed his mind?" he asked by way of greeting.

"No!" replied L. Ebersole Gaines, chairman of the Southern Coal Operators Wage Conference. "We've been at it for weeks and I doubt if anyone is going to change."

Then Jones told an anecdote of how Carter Glass once when addressing the Senate said, "I would not like to detain the Senate by telling it how often I have changed my mind in the last 40 years—always in the right direction."

Then for ten minutes Jones took the coal men behind the scenes and told them of the defense preparations that were being made.

He concluded:

> Once we get in our stride, so that labor, agriculture, industry and finance feel that each is being treated fairly, our production for defense will greatly surpass the production of the enemy countries. Labor and industry are the two stars in the world drama being played today. They must cooperate to the end that the limit of production is measured only by the capacity of our machines running on a 24-hour basis. I need not tell you how much that machine is going to need fuel. I need not tell you how disappearing coal stocks are already taking a heavy toll in steel production and beginning to threaten railroad schedules and other production. This is the largest and most serious strike that has arisen to hamper vital manufacturing and other services. Now, gentlemen, I want to tell you bluntly that something has got to be done and done quickly. I am going to turn this office over to you for your use.

A few hours later Operators Chairman Gaines telephoned to Jones: "Mr. Secretary, we have changed our minds. An agreement is being drawn up."

The agreement was announced at the White House at midnight and the next day the soft coal mines began to operate. Jones was scheduled for an address before the annual meeting of the United States Chamber of Commerce the following morning. He went to his office and dictated substantially the same talk he had delivered impromptu to the contesting coal groups.

The most wasteful and troublesome vendetta with which Jones had to contend in all his years in Washington concerned Henry Wallace, the mystic who was at the moment Vice-President of the United States. Nothing weighed upon Jones so much over almost the entire four years of the third Roosevelt term as the efforts of Wallace to project himself into a province that had been given by Congress to Jones.

Jones felt that he had plenty of evidence to sustain his belief that Roosevelt had first picked Harry Hopkins as his successor in the White House and that when Hopkins' health failed he switched his choice to Wallace. Jones believed, too, that in the beginning the President thought he could build up Hopkins or Wallace, until he could get the nomination from a New Dealized Democratic convention. When that plan faded in the face of the open hostility of Democratic leaders to Wallace, he decided to remain in the White House as long as he lived and let the succession go to the Vice-President. That would explain Roosevelt's arbitrary and inflexible demand that the convention in 1940 name Wallace as his running mate. It also, according to Jones, explained the desperate efforts of Roosevelt to increase Wallace's stature by giving him assignments connected with the war effort.

In August, 1941, Wallace had been Vice-President for six months. He had not succeeded in making himself a respected Senate presiding officer and was rarely consulted by Senator Alben W. Barkley, the Senate Democratic leader, or by other members of the Senate. Perhaps no Vice-President had ever been so complete an outsider on Capitol Hill.

In an obvious effort to put him on display to the country as part of the defense and wartime economic machinery, President Roosevelt appointed Wallace at the head of what was announced to be a high "coordinating" agency, the Supply Priorities and Allocation Board. Wallace was an ineffective head of this agency, which itself proved ineffective. It lived six months and was succeeded by the War Production Board.

But even before appointing Wallace chairman of SPAB, the President had named the Vice-President head of the Board of Economic Warfare (BEW), an agency that attracted virtually no attention until Wallace had the SPAB horse shot out from under him. The Vice-President, at SPAB's demise, mounted BEW and rode away in many directions. There was no doubt that Wallace yearned to be President with a great intensity, and had lobbied with the President assiduously to create BEW and to name him its head.

BEW certainly must have looked to Wallace like a heaven-sent opportunity to unveil himself before the country as an attractive Presidential prospect. Franklin D. Roosevelt's positive genius for creating agencies that were bound to overlap, duplicate one another's effort, and run into conflicts of authority was never better illustrated than in the case of BEW. The executive order gave Wallace, or anyone he might designate, authority to duplicate the procurement of critical and strategic materials anywhere in the world. This executive order conflicted with the Congressional Act of June 28, 1940, giving statutory responsibility to the RFC and its subsidiaries in this field. Moreover, to make the confusion still greater, the Roosevelt executive order made RFC the banker of BEW, to pay for the purchases of the Wallace-headed agency.

The President on two occasions had told Jones of Wallace's pleadings for the creation of BEW. Jones had told him that it was unnecessary and Roosevelt agreed. But Roosevelt in the end succumbed to Wallace's insistence and made him its head. The President placed Jones on BEW's board of directors along with Secretary of State Hull, Secretary of the Treasury Morgenthau, Secretary of War Stimson, and Attorney General Jackson. To these later was added the chairman of the War Production Board, the Coordinator of Inter-American Affairs, and the Lend-Lease Administrator. Some of the directors, busy with their own affairs, never attended a BEW meeting and few of them attended more than one or two.

As his second-in-command at BEW Wallace named Milo Perkins, who was, like Jones and Clayton, a resident of Houston. Perkins had been a bag salesman and was a devotee of a religious cult, which he himself established at Houston with no similar "church" anywhere in the United States or the world. He called it the "Liberal Catholic Church of the United States of America." He named his home the "Church of St. Raphael the Ark Angel." It attracted attention because of the two words "Ark Angel" and because Perkins had succeeded in getting his home taken off tax rolls by mounting the stairs to his windowless attic each Sunday and conducting "services." There was no record that he had any "parishioners."

As Assistant Directors under Perkins, Wallace appointed Morris Rosenthal, of New York, who gave his occupation as foreign trader, and Hector Lazo, a Guatemala-born public relations man. His general counsel was Morris Oppenheimer, who had been an ultra-New Deal attorney in Washington. All three were ideological disciples of Wallace.

Jones' personal dealings with Wallace had been fewer than with any other high official in Washington. They had been practically limited to meetings of the Commodity Credit Corporation and at the President's Cabinet table. The strife between them that grew in intensity began over the directives given to Jones' various organizations by the visionary Wallace and his subordinates. Many of these directives the efficient RFC men knew to be highly impractical.

The controversy started over certain innuendoes concerning quinine that emanated from officials of the BEW. These were deeply resented by William L. Clayton, a man well trained in foreign trade whom Jones had put in general charge of the overseas procurement activities of Defense Supplies Corporation.

Clayton had paid special attention to quinine purchases. Despite the fact that the army had on hand several years' supply of quinine sulfate in August, 1941, on recommendation of OPM Clayton bought 2,000,000 ounces. Then on January 15, 1942, Rosenthal, Wallace's assistant director of BEW, recommended to Clayton that more quinine be bought.

This astonished Clayton because the President by executive order had stipulated that all stockpile recommendations should come from the War Production Board. Nevertheless, Clayton started the negotiations, only to receive a reply from the Netherlands East Indies Trade Commissioner that while there was no quinine available for immediate delivery, 2,000,000 ounces could be shipped monthly from March through June, 1942. There now came a countermanding order from WPB that this government had on hand 14,000,000 ounces, or the requirements for the next four years, and that no further stocks should be purchased for the stockpile.

On February 16 another letter came from Rosenthal recommending the purchase of 3,000,000 ounces of quinine. WPB agreed to its purchase, and it was ordered for March and April delivery.

Ten days later, when Thomas K. Finletter of the State Department advised that 2,500,000 ounces of quinine in the bark could be bought in Batavia for prompt shipment, it was immediately purchased. The Japanese got to Batavia before shipment could be made. Clayton had also seen to it that quinine developments got under way in Guatemala and Costa Rica and altogether was very proud of the progress being made.

Wallace soon had 3000 men and women under his strange banner at BEW. The friction between men in the Jones organization and in Wallace's mushrooming BEW grew more intense. Jones was convinced that unsound and radical BEW underlings were merely echoing the voice of Wallace. But time and time again he emphasized to the men in his organization that the winning of the war was the only important business at hand and that they must make every attempt to get along with the Wallace people.

Jones kept careful check, however, and made sure that in no case should the war effort be hampered because of the time that it took RFC to look into some of the BEW directives. He was certain, too, that RFC subsidiaries were carrying out to the letter his instructions to comply promptly when they thought those directives were proper and to reason patiently with BEW when they were not.

There were some particularly aggravating cases, such as a dubious sisal development plan in Haiti. Clayton was sure that the war would be over long before it would begin producing, and that proved to be the case, although Defense Supplies put 1,000,000 dollars in it on BEW's insistence.

There was also the case of the Mexican mahogany. Clayton, Sam Husbands, Chick Fisher, and Howard Klossner all were certain that it would fail, but Wallace men came in with a directive, which Roosevelt had given them power to issue, telling the Jones Defense Supply Organization what to do, and where, and how much to pay and to whom.

The Wallace organization had made an agreement with the Export-Import Lumber Company of Buffalo, New York, for the delivery of 2,500,000 feet of the Mexican mahogany. It was to be produced by the Tehuantepec Lumber Company, which had stumpage rights on land in Mexico. The Tehuantepec Company was controlled by the Resources Corporation International of Chicago.

Early in the negotiations Klossner called attention to the fact that officials of the Resources Corporation were under indictment in connection with the company's stock transaction. Moreover, Klossner pointed out that the Export-Import Lumber Company was a father-and-son partnership, and neither *père* nor *fils* had any experience in the lumber business. His protests to the BEW went unheeded.

The Tehuantepec's troubles were many. The Mexican government objected to the company's operations, which got under way only after intervention by our Ambassador at Mexico City. Then the Mexican government charged it with cutting timber on public lands, and sent troops to stop it. Again the United States Ambassador intervened and work was resumed.

The Export-Import Lumber Company never made a satisfactory accounting of 500,000 dollars advanced to it. It delivered only a small part of the 2,500,000 board feet of logs specified in the contract and this at a price in excess of the estimated cost by 100 dollars per thousand board feet.

In 1945 Lindsay C. Warren, the Comptroller General of the United States, after an investigation of the transaction said:

> The results of the operation proved the irresponsibility and inexperience of the operators and justified the reluctance with which the Corporation

(Defense Supplies) had undertaken the project. It is an interesting sidelight that, for a six-month period during the course of this operation, the senior forestry specialist of BEW was an ex-official of Resources Corporation International and at the time of his employment in BEW, was under indictment for fraud.

The Comptroller went on to discuss another sad deal which Wallace's BEW had forced on Jones' Defense Supplies Corporation:

BEW was also instrumental in involving the Corporation in the leasing of a plantation in Guatemala for the production of cinchona bark. The officials of the Corporation were not consulted during the preliminary negotiations for this lease, and, when they were drawn into them, they expressed reluctance to proceed under the terms agreed upon by BEW.

However, BEW was unmovable and the Corporation paid $1,700,000 for a 30-year lease on a 1,200-acre plantation, planted primarily in coffee, for the purpose of growing cinchona trees and harvesting the bark. The lease was effected April 28, 1943, and was transferred to United States Commercial Company on March 31, 1944.

The plantation was owned by a foreign corporation the majority of the stock of which was seized by the Alien Property Custodian. Before its principal asset was leased to Defense Supplies Corporation, the stock of the plantation owner was quoted at from $1 to $2.50 per share. After $1,700,000 had been paid to this company by the Corporation, the stock had a liquidating value of approximately $58 per share. Presumably, the foreign stockholders were among the beneficiaries of this bonanza.

Original estimates of harvest from this plantation were from 5,000 to 10,000 tons of bark during the first year. Later estimates contemplated that the harvest would be 750 tons. A qualified expert stated that the value of the land, for which $1,700,000 was paid for a 30-year lease, was $60,000.

It was not strange that the Jones-trained men, who wanted contracts made only with reliable firms who could carry out their engagements, looked with disgust on such loose dealing. Their irritation was increased by the fact that the Wallace people were haughty and insolent in negotiations between the two agencies.

One of the most exasperating of these negotiations was on the wild-rubber program in South America. Wallace had persuaded Roosevelt to let him participate in this. The executive order putting the Vice-President's organization into this activity had come six weeks after Douglas H. Allen, an experienced foreign trader in charge of the Jones rubber procurement program, had gone to Brazil and got production under way following the signing of an agreement between Defense Supplies and the Brazilian government.

Wallace and Milo Perkins quickly followed the Roosevelt executive order by setting up an organization duplicating that of Jones' Rubber

Reserve. The effect of this was to give the BEW power without responsibility and the RFC agencies responsibilities without power.

Jones took immense pride in Allen's energy and he was showing high competence in the delicate and difficult effort to procure wild rubber from the tropical jungles of Central and South America.

While Allen was still in Latin America, Jones heard from Howard Klossner that Wallace had proposed that free food be given to the natives in the Amazon Basin.

"And," said Klossner, "he had power under the President's executive order either to do this himself or to order us to do it."

Allen was returning from South America and Jones arranged a luncheon so that he might meet Wallace and perhaps persuade him to abandon this chimerical plan. Milo Perkins, Dean Acheson of the State Department, and Klossner and Clayton from the Jones organization also attended.

Wallace lost no time in revealing his absorption in the idea.

"How many people are there in the Amazon Basin?" he asked Allen.

"No one has taken a census, but the best estimates I have are that there are probably 1,500,000."

"Don't they suffer from an inadequate and unbalanced diet?" the Vice-President pursued. Allen thought that was probably true. But he thought social conditions in some parts of the United States were also deplorable.

Wallace suddenly closed his eyes and put his hands on his forehead. After a moment or two he announced that he had made some mental calculations and believed 350,000 tons of staple foodstuffs would give the Amazon people a more balanced diet. Especially, he said, they should have flour adequately fortified with vitamins. The foodstuffs should be given without cost to all the people there.

Allen replied, "Mr. Vice-President, I talked all this over with Mr. Jones. He felt and I feel we have got to work in a sort of partnership with the governments in the wild rubber area. We are making every effort to respect their sovereignty and national pride. We think they would resent our efforts to reform their customs and habits."

"You are taking the wrong tack in the Amazon," Wallace blurted out.

Allen maintained his good humor and went on to reason that Brazil had at the time an allocation of ships insufficient for that country's import needs and that in the tussle for shipping in which every nation was engaged it would be impossible to get more for Latin America and that there would be no way to get 350,000 tons of foodstuff there.

Wallace's facial muscles twitched, his color purpled, and he shouted, "That will be no problem at all."

Allen had no idea of capitulating, despite the Vice-President's avid interest in the plan.

"Mr. Vice-President," he said, "the people in the Amazon Basin are no different from other peoples. Their greatest incentive to work is their desire to eat. Give a primitive people like that all the food they want free and they will do no work. We will get no rubber."

It was Milo Perkins who finally broke up the conversation by saying, "Henry, I guess we just can't give away food in the Amazon and still get rubber; maybe we had better forget about it."

But Allen was soon disabused of any idea that the Vice-President had given up his dubious plan. Back in Brazil there came one day a cablegram to Allen authorizing and directing him immediately to begin to buy 350,000 tons of foodstuffs, and begin delivering it to the Amazon without delay. The BEW, the cablegram added, was arranging to send an 11,000-ton ship with a full cargo of foodstuffs, including a large quantity of rice.

Allen cabled back that Para, a state at the head of the Amazon, was a large exporter of rice and at that very minute had a large glut. He also believed they did not need any part of the 350,000 tons of food.

The BEW pondered Allen's cablegram and decided to delay food buying until the matter of a more satisfactory cuisine could be integrated with matters of better housing, hygiene, and other "social" considerations. An organizational chart was then drawn calling for the expenditure of 400,000,000 dollars on an Amazon project.

Allen now rebelled. He informed Clayton that his considered judgment was that whatever was done in the Amazon, not enough rubber could be obtained to justify the expenditure of 400,000,000 dollars.

The 400,000,000 dollars was never spent, and the most that came of it was a visit by a Wallace expert to the Amazon where, he reported, he had patiently explained to "leaders" of the Indians in the jungles how to grow spinach, string beans, lettuce, cauliflower, and some rare North American greens. But the natives, accustomed to a diet of corn meal and frijoles, showed little interest in a more balanced diet.

Allen told Clayton that he was receiving directives for the purchase of rubber from BEW that were impossible to comply with because we had entered into a solemn agreement with the government of Brazil that the purchases would be through Banco de Crédito da Borracha, a chosen government agency, which then sold it to the United States f.o.b. shipside.

By now William Jeffers had been appointed Rubber Director, and Allen asked if Jones and Clayton had any objections to his placing the matter before Jeffers. They interposed no objection. Jeffers listened in amazement to Allen's factual recitations of what had been taking place.

"I have no intention of letting our effort to get needed rubber be wrecked by incompetents," Allen said. "If this continues I am going to resign and publish the reason. Leave BEW in this natural rubber program and you will have a national scandal."

"What do you want me to do?" asked Jeffers. "If you are asking me to remove the Vice-President of the United States from a place to which the President of the United States has appointed him, you are giving me quite an assignment. But you are very convincing. I will think it over."

Jeffers did use a directive of his own ejecting BEW from all connection with the natural rubber program. Now that it was again under RFC control, Jones ordered the formation of the Rubber Development Corporation with Clayton as chairman and Allen as president and the directors coming from other government agencies. Thus all friction between the various agencies having a vital interest in rubber was resolved.

Allen moved rapidly to wipe out the unsound elements of BEW's Amazon projects. One of them was for growing cryptostegia, a rubber-yielding plant. This was another undertaking that the Jones organization had remonstrated against, but Wallace had plunged into anyway.

It originally had been BEW's intention to plant 100,000 acres in cryptostegia and to spend 30,000,000 dollars on it. This was cut down to 40,000 acres. BEW produced five and a half tons of rubber there and it cost 6,725,000 dollars or 546 dollars for each pound of rubber.

While Allen was having his trouble with the Wallace people, other frictions were running concurrently between BEW and RFC.

Most of the difficulties between the RFC men and the Wallace zealots grew out of the famous executive order 9128, issued by the President on April 13, 1942. The tenacious, resolute, and power-hungry Vice-President had wangled from Roosevelt an order that permitted the Wallace agency not only to direct the RFC agencies to purchase wherever and whenever and at what price it set, but also to advise the State Department on Lend-Lease agreements.

The flames were fanned to an unprecedented high in January, 1943, while President Roosevelt was in Casablanca. In the absence of the

President, Wallace issued "Order No. 5," stripping RFC of power to buy, stockpile, and sell critical foreign materials, usurping this power for BEW. Jones had no doubt of the illegality of this order in view of the fact that RFC subsidiaries had statutory powers in this field.

Still Jones sought to maintain peace. Wartime was no time for public controversy. Jones and Clayton finally decided that, in an effort to remove dissension-provoking overlapping in purchasing, they would make a supreme effort to reach an understanding with Wallace. In order to do this they were willing, under proper safeguards, to transfer to BEW RFC's United States Commercial Company, which was engaged in preclusive buying in many parts of the world.

Jones and Clayton went to the Vice-President's office, made the proposal, and reached an oral agreement. However, when the time came to reduce the agreement to writing, Wallace wanted additional powers that Jones and Clayton were not willing to grant. There the matter stood on June 29, 1943, when Wallace released a letter to the Senate Appropriations Committee, charging the RFC with "hampering" the war effort and asking Congress to remove RFC as BEW's banker and to hand over a checkbook to BEW.

"It seems to me," Wallace wrote to the committee, "that we could end this wrangling and improve the administrative efficiency so essential to winning this war if program money were appropriated directly to the BEW for its purchase and development of *all* imported strategic material."

President Roosevelt gave evidence of being greatly disturbed by the Wallace letter. It was, he told Stephen T. Early, his press secretary, in flat violation of the Presidential order of August 21, 1942, instructing the heads of government departments and agencies to abstain from critical and controversial public debate on the actions of one another in matters of policy. But at his press conference a few hours after the release of the Wallace letter he refused to comment further than to say that its publication took him by surprise. Even before the press conference the President had instructed Director of War Mobilization James F. Byrnes, whose duties made him a sort of "assistant President" to "get Henry and Jesse together and harmonize their differences."

Jones made this tart reply to the Wallace statement:

> The release given out by Mr. Wallace today is filled with malice and misstatements. He makes two serious charges:
>
> (1) That RFC has failed in the purchasing and stockpiling of strategic and critical materials. The facts are that not more than 10 per cent of our

purchases or commitments for these materials have been initiated by BEW. RFC commitments for foreign purchases have been approximately $3,500,-000,000 of which not more than 10 per cent was originated by BEW. We have actually received and paid for materials to the value of $1,600,000,000, of which less than 5 per cent can be credited to BEW initiative.

(2) That RFC and I have obstructed and delayed programs of development and procurement initiated by BEW. There has been no serious delay by us of any vital program.

I will answer that statement in detail, and be glad to have a committee of Congress investigate the facts.

What he did not stress then (he did later) was that the small percentage of RFC purchases made on directives from BEW would have been purchased by RFC subsidiaries anyway on direction from WPB even if BEW had never been in existence.

His reaction to the invitation to the "peace meeting" at the White House was that he had seen good public servants whom he had brought into RFC traduced by Wallace's reckless statement. There would be no peace until his reply was in the record. At the "peace meeting," which was set for the afternoon of the day following Wallace's attack, Jones was fifteen minutes late.

"I want to give Wallace plenty of time to tell his story to Byrnes before I get there," he told Chairman Charles B. Henderson of the RFC.

Jones' temper was evident when he entered Byrnes' office. To Wallace's greeting, "Hello, Jesse," he made no return. Wallace and Byrnes did most of the subsequent talking.

Jones' first statement to Wallace was, "You have lied about me and about other people in the RFC. I want you to prove the truth of any of the statements you have made."

Wallace made no reply.

"I have read that you are a praying man," Jones said quietly. "If you pray tonight you should ask God to stop you from lying."

To Byrnes' statement that the quarrel was damaging to the Administration, Jones said that he had done no quarreling, public or private. It was soon evident that Byrnes' efforts in the role of peacemaker would be in vain. Jones was firm in his determination that the matter should not be settled until he had answered the Wallace charges one by one. The parley broke up on this indecisive note.

As the "harmonizing" effort was under way at the White House, it was evident on Capitol Hill that Congress was in no mood to grant the broad authority over foreign procurement expenditures requested by

Wallace. Instead, the Senate inserted in the War Agencies Appropriations Bill an amendment further clipping the wings of BEW in foreign purchases. The amendment forbade the use of any funds for salaries or any other purpose in connection with BEW's foreign operations unless the "program and policies" involved had been approved by BEW's board of directors in writing and such writing filed with the Secretary of State. And Senator Wiley, Republican, of Wisconsin, asserted that Wallace as Vice-President was in the legislative branch of the government and his serving as Chairman of BEW, an executive office, was an unconstitutional "merging" of the legislative and executive.

Wallace by now was showing a yearning for a visit of the dove of peace. In a statement a few hours after the meeting in Byrnes' office he said:

> We have talked with Mr. Jesse Jones. He and I have agreed for the time being to continue the present arrangement under which the Board of Economic Warfare is functioning. Preparatory to the Congress reconvening the Board of Economic Warfare will initiate steps through the Budget Bureau which will result in a proposal to the Congress that there be made available to BEW the necessary program funds for the procurement and development of all imported strategic war materials under public purchase so that BEW may be completely independent of RFC. Mr. Jones did not object to this policy decision.
>
> I advised Mr. Jones that in my statement to the press I had no intention to reflect upon his patriotism or his interest in the war effort. I intended to assert that the delays in RFC in acting upon projects had delayed the war effort. I did not intend to create the impression that his personal motive was deliberately or intentionally to delay the war effort.
>
> Our difficulties have had to do with strong differences of opinion with regard to the quantities of various products to be obtained at a given time and place. That there should be differences of opinion may reflect upon the judgment of the individuals involved but such differences do not reflect upon the desire of the individuals to serve their country.

The Wallace statement so worded as to contain what amounted to an apology, nevertheless seemed a childish effort to show that he had emerged as victor in the dispute. His implication that he had been assured that he would no longer have to depend upon the RFC for money was so at variance with the facts as to cause Jones to doubt his responsibility.

And so he issued this statement:

> Mr. Wallace in his statement tonight, repeats that delays in the Reconstruction Finance Corporation have retarded the war effort. This dastardly charge is as untrue as when he first made it.

As for the rest of his statement, Mr. Wallace was not authorized to speak for me. I will continue to speak for myself and, as previously stated, I shall insist upon a Congressional investigation.

On July 5 Jones brought the dispute to a new crescendo in a slashing thirty-page reply to Wallace's twenty-eight pages of charges. The reply took the form of a letter to Senator Carter Glass, chairman of the Senate Appropriations Committee.

In my eleven years as a government official [Jones said in his letter to Glass], I have consistently refrained from any public criticism of other government departments, and reluctant as I am to burden the Congress and the public with a detailed reply to Mr. Wallace, his tirade is so filled with malice, innuendo, half truths and no truth at all, that considerations of self-respect and of common justice to my associates force me to expose his unscrupulous tactics.

Jones took up the Wallace charges one by one and answered them through documentation by letters, memorandums, orders, and signed agreements.

Jones rested his case on the letter to Glass and its accompanying detailed reply to the Wallace charges. He made no effort to talk with President Roosevelt about it. There was no doubt from the reactions in Congress and the country that Jones was the overwhelming victor in the controversy. The inner circle of the White House and politicians generally were of the view that the Wallace fiasco had destroyed any Presidential hopes the Vice-President might have had. It was the most cartooned and commented-on controversy among high-ranking officials during the Roosevelt Administration. Further airing of the controversy on Capitol Hill was choked off by the adjournment of Congress.

Sixteen days after Wallace's charges and ten days after Jones' reply, Roosevelt divested both Jones and Wallace of purchasing authority in the foreign field. An executive order took the United States Commercial Company, which had been financing preclusive buying; the Rubber Development Company, banker for overseas rubber procurement; the Petroleum Reserve Corporation, and the Export-Import Bank of Washington, away from Jones. It left untouched the nine corporations and RFC subsidiaries under Jones' direction that serviced important military and nonwar domestic activities.

But on Wallace the ax fell hard. He was thrown out neck and crop from the domain of economic warfare. The President abolished BEW and transferred its function along with the four RFC subsidiaries to the Office of Economic Warfare headed by Leo T. Crowley.

Jones would have gladly given up the four agencies at any time he had felt they were going into competent hands. Now with these agencies under the direction of Jones' close friend, Crowley, all friction ended.

In identical letters to Wallace and Jones, the President said:

Gentlemen:

I have come to the conclusion that the unfortunate controversy and acrimonious public debate which has been carried on between you in public press concerning the administration of foreign economic matters make it necessary, in the public interest, to transfer these matters to other hands.

In the midst of waging a war so critical to our national security and to the future of all civilization, there is not sufficient time to investigate and determine where the truth lies in your conflicting versions as to transactions which took place over a year and a half ago.

My action today is not intended to decide the question. The important thing is to clear the deck and get on with the war at once. To do this requires a fresh start with new men, unencumbered by inter-agency dissension and bitterness.

I am persuaded that the present controversy indicates that future cooperative active between your two agencies is impossible, and that without full cooperation between you the program of economic warfare cannot be carried out.

I am sure that the American people understand that both of you have attempted to do your duty as you have seen it; but we must go forward without any further public debate as to matters which are now academic as far as winning the war is presently concerned.

I have therefore issued today an executive order of which I am attaching a copy for your information and guidance.

Very sincerely yours,
Franklin D. Roosevelt

Jones issued this statement:

I concur most heartily in the President's determination to have harmony and cooperation between Government officials and agencies in the war effort. The Department of Commerce and the Reconstruction Finance Corporation and its subsidiary corporations engaged in foreign purchases will render every possible assistance to the new Director of Economic Warfare.

The director will find the affairs of all RFC agencies engaged in foreign purchases, as well as the Export-Import Bank, in excellent condition. He will find the organizations functioning with a maximum of efficiency and at a minimum of expense.

The President could not have selected a better qualified man for the important assignment of director of the Office of Economic Warfare than Leo T. Crowley. Mr. Crowley is well and favorably known to the business and financial world because of his able administration of the Federal Deposit Insurance Corporation and as Alien Property Custodian.

Shorn of his war job, Wallace fretted in his inactivity. Sentiment against his renomination for Vice-President grew apace in the Democratic party. Jones had no doubt that Wallace would not be on the 1944 ticket. Arthur Krock relates that Jones told him in February that Senator Truman would be Roosevelt's running mate.

In the spring of 1944 Roosevelt dispatched Wallace on "a good will" tour to China and Siberia. The Vice-President returned just before the party convention at Chicago. Two things were certain by now. The delegates would give Roosevelt the fourth-term nomination that he wanted and they would not give him Wallace as his ticket mate.

If there was one thing on which the convention delegates agreed, it was that Franklin D. Roosevelt would most likely not live out another term and that the man nominated for Vice-President would be President. When that convention adjourned after a series of brawls that would have been disgraceful in peacetime and were enormously more so in war, Roosevelt had his coveted fourth-term nomination. The Vice-Presidential nominee was United States Senator Harry S. Truman of Missouri.

Even Wallace knew that the death wounds to his Presidential ambitions had been inflicted in the offensive he had launched against Jesse Jones.*

---

* Wallace never underestimated Jones' power and influence. Years afterward he said in a statement to the Associated Press on June 2, 1956: "Jesse Jones wielded greater power for a longer period than any human being in the history of the United States. No man so assiduously and successfully cultivated the good will of Congress."

PART VII

The Parting Of The Ways

Fraying Bonds with the White House

THE daily commentator must in his news accounts pinpoint his story and offer as explanation simple and immediate causes of events. The historian, on the other hand, must take into account the great truth that the cause of an important decision or event is neither simple nor single.

That rule of the historian has special meaning when, after several years, he is telling of the final break between Jesse Jones and the President. The explanation cannot be simple because the decision that brought an end to the relationship arose from as subtle and complex a personality as ever lived. Certainly there was no single cause or explanation. The President's explanation of his dismissal of Jones left volumes unsaid.

A consideration of a number of contributing elements and incidents will be helpful in filling in what the President failed to reveal. Taken together, these incidents raised the insistent question why there was no break before and, indeed, how two such dissimilar personalities could ever have worked together so successfully and so long.

We have already seen a part of the answer in earlier chapters dealing with the relationships of Jones with the White House and Congress. For three terms Roosevelt had acted the role of a politician who found it essential to get on with Congress. And the prestige and influence of Jones with Congress continued to be immense. Moreover, as the head of a political party and a great administrative machine, the President was under constant pressure for one thing or another, and Jones was useful in taking from him the responsibility of resisting such pressures. In addition, Jones was dealing with a master's experienced hand with complex matters of finance in which, despite his pansophic pretensions, Roosevelt was a hopeless novice. Therefore, during the Depression years and then the war effort, Jones was literally indispensable.

In 1944 and early in 1945 many of these circumstances were changing. The war was obviously coming to an end. Jones' monumental labors for victory were almost finished, and the prosperity of the country made the RFC unnecessary to the domestic economy. Roosevelt, with nomination and election for a fourth term assured, had obviously reached the beginning of the end of his remarkable political career. His need for the cooperation of Congress in the future would be less.

Roosevelt throughout most of 1944 and up to the day of his death was a very sick man whose capacity for deliberate and sound judgments was seriously impaired. In this weakening illness of the President there came into full play an unpleasant trait that had always been present but held in check—plain jealousy of members of his Administration who received marked public acclaim.

These considerations made it possible for a number of incidents, which might have passed in earlier years, to stir the mind of Roosevelt against his powerful subordinate. Some of these had to do with Jones' reluctance to comply altogether with some of the President's transitory fancies. Some were matters of policy on which Jones directly and openly disagreed with the President. There was, moreover, the long-standing antagonism against Jones among the more radical members of the official family, especially Ickes and Wallace. Their incessant campaign of criticism against Jones was bound to have a mounting effect upon the President, who, while he found prudential reasons for keeping Jones in office, was fundamentally at odds with his ideology and public policies.

One incident that miffed the President was Jones' refusal to agree with Roosevelt's wish to acquire the Empire State Building in New York City. Roosevelt admonished that his request for this be kept highly secret. He asked Jones to make the purchase and try to justify it on the ground that it would provide central housing for many of the federal offices located in New York.

It was a curious request because the purchase would have benefited former Governor Alfred E. Smith and John J. Raskob, both of whom had become Roosevelt's political enemies after the 1928 Presidential campaign, and had become increasingly bitter in their attacks upon Roosevelt's New Deal. Still more strange is the fact that Roosevelt never quite forgave Jones for his refusal to go through with the deal, while Smith and Jones remained warm friends.

Roosevelt first broached the Empire State Building purchase proposal to Jones in July, 1941. The President continued his efforts to have Jones acquire the building for two-and-a-half years.

For a time Roosevelt's intensive effort was difficult for Jones to understand. Roosevelt and Smith had broken during Roosevelt's term at Albany. Smith had walked out of the 1932 convention at Chicago that nominated Roosevelt for President. He had also ruptured a lifetime of party regularity to vote for Landon for President in 1936 and Willkie in 1940.

It was only eight months after Smith had actively supported Willkie against Roosevelt that the President had given Jones an envelope in the White House that had in it a financial statement on the Empire State Building. A confidential memorandum marked "For Jesse Jones" and signed "F.D.R." read:

> I have long felt that it would pay the Federal Government to pull all of the Federal Offices in and around New York City into one central building.
>
> We all know that the Empire State Building is a losing proposition, but on the other side, it is ideally located for a central Federal Office Building.
>
> I wish you would look into this whole subject, without passing it over to any one else or speaking to anyone else about it. We can talk it over next week.
>
> F.D.R.

On top of the typewritten note enjoining secrecy was still another, handwritten by the President, which read: "J. Jones. To put together and justify if possible. F.D.R."

Jones was thoroughly familiar with the Empire State Building. Years before when the old Waldorf-Astoria Hotel began to be outmoded, Jones had negotiated for the purchase of the site for an office building for himself since he had already built several large buildings in New York City. He knew that the Empire State Building was not suited for government occupancy and furthermore that there was a special agency in government—the Public Buildings Administration—whose function it is to provide office space and buildings for government use. If the building was to be acquired by the government Jones believed that it should be bought by that agency and not by the RFC.

However, Jones following the request of the President did make a careful survey of the property, reporting back that because of its great height it was not well adapted to government occupancy and the continuing charge for operation would be much greater than a building of normal height. All of the federal government activities in New York that could be moved into the building would not occupy more than half of its space and the remainder would have to be rented in competition with private business.

Jones reported to Roosevelt that if the government wanted to consolidate all of its offices in New York it should erect a building suitable for its purposes, for materials were much cheaper than when the Empire State Building was constructed.

Furthermore, the construction of such a building would be very helpful in the recovery effort since it would furnish employment and buy materials.

The President replied, "That is probably true, but I would like to do something for Al Smith. He is broke and has an expensive family."

Jones knew a good deal about Smith's finances and he knew that this was not true. The former governor had a 10 per cent interest in the building and was getting a salary of 50,000 dollars per year as president of the Empire State Building Corporation.

Furthermore Smith had told him, "I will get a half million dollar commission if I sell this property for $50,000,000. But my principal interest is to help Raskob get out of the venture. But for attempting this service I never would have talked to Roosevelt about that or anything else. I loathe the man and hold him in utter contempt."

When, after Jones' first unfavorable report Roosevelt insisted that he look further into the matter, Jones again declined to do anything about it. Jones knew by now the real reason for the President's interest in the matter.

In 1928 when Smith was the Democratic candidate for President, he asked his old friend John J. Raskob to be his campaign manager. Smith and Raskob had asked Roosevelt to run for governor of New York, believing his candidacy would help both the state and the national ticket. Roosevelt declined, giving as his reason that he was heavily in debt on the property he had bought at Warm Springs, Georgia. Raskob then told Roosevelt that if he would run he would finance the Georgia property. Roosevelt became the candidate and Raskob paid the pressing Warm Springs debts. Smith lost New York State in his Presidential try, but Roosevelt squeaked through in his gubernatorial race and was himself on the way to the Presidency.

Following the second unfavorable action by Jones, Roosevelt asked that all papers be returned to him. Jones did this immediately and Roosevelt then asked the Budget Bureau to see if the Public Buildings Administration would explore the possibility of purchasing the skyscraper. He got a reply from that agency holding, as Jones had held, that the price of the building was too high and furthermore that it was not suited for government uses.

Now again Roosevelt returned the papers to Jones, asking that he resume negotiations. Jones, still of the opinion that the RFC as an emergency agency should not buy the building and that its purchase would be a misuse of the people's money, did nothing more.

Years later Jones wrote concerning this incident:

> Of all the requests he made of me this was the one that he was persistent about. When I did nothing about buying the building he asked the Director of the Budget, Harold Smith, to try to get the Bureau of Public Buildings to buy it. That agency declined.
>
> I am sure that the President was put out at both that agency and me. I recall that soon Harold Smith called and made a luncheon engagement with me. He brought the Empire State file with him and told me that at the President's request he had conducted the unsuccessful negotiations with the Public Buildings Administration—and that it would probably be back in my lap in a day or two. Sure enough it was.
>
> The file was sent back to me by the President with the request that I try to work out the purchase. I did not like the tone of this note and did nothing further about it.

On another occasion in the course of the war years Jones found it possible to comply with a proposition that was highly personal with Roosevelt but which offered a sound and profitable return to the Treasury. This proposal originated in the fact that in the early 1940's the aristocracy of the Hudson Valley in the vicinity of Hyde Park was shocked to hear that Father Divine, the well-advertised Negro cult leader, had purchased a large estate directly across the river from the President's ancestral home and near Cragston, the enormous countryhouse of the elder J. P. Morgan.

The ink was scarcely dry on this transaction when the patroons of the valley were further shocked to learn that Father Divine, mounting an even bolder social offensive, wanted to buy Crumwold Farms, the 742-acre estate of Archibald Rogers, which directly adjoined the Roosevelt home property. Crumwold was so close that in his boyhood Roosevelt had carried on hollering conversations with his friends, the children of Archibald Rogers. Certainly the President, despite his broad political toleration for all races and creeds, wanted none of Father Divine's didoes disturbing the repose of Hyde Park.

The Hudson's first citizen moved promptly but obliquely at the threat to the formidable social prestige of the east bank. After a Cabinet meeting he suggested to Secretary of Agriculture Claude R. Wickard that the Department of Agriculture acquire the place and use it for reforestation and other experimental purposes.

The President went on to explain that he knew every foot of the ground and that Mr. Rogers had planted thousands of trees on it. Wickard had no funds with which the buy the land. The President then asked Jones to try to arrange the purchase. Jones, too, was familiar with the Rogers estate, which he had seen on trips to Hyde Park.

The President told Jones that he had learned from Joseph P. Day, the New York real estate broker, that the property could be acquired for 150,000 dollars. Jones knew that it was one of the most attractive private estates in the East and a bargain at that price. Also, he sympathized with the President in not wishing Father Divine as a neighbor. Moreover, he knew an affiliate of the Prudence Company, on which the RFC had foreclosed, which could use the profit he felt would surely come if it held the estate for a little while. A profit would help the company pay its debt to the RFC. He informed the company, which immediately concluded the purchase of the well-landscaped acres and its massive granite manor house.

Thus Father Divine got none of his "heavens" any closer to the Roosevelt Hyde Park castle than Krum Elbow, which Howland Spencer, the country squire antagonist of the President, had sold to the preacher in a transaction that appeared to have an element of spite in it.

War came and at the President's direction the army stationed first a company and then a battalion at the Rogers estate to protect the President and such distinguished visitors as Winston Churchill who repaired there. Its thirty houses, the large stone garage where Rogers had kept his blooded horses and his dairy herd, and its boathouse, swimming pool, and fishing pond made it a pleasant place for the soldiers.

The army moved the guard out after the President's death and the property was sold in 1947 for 210,000 dollars, a good profit.

One of the most publicized adventures in all of the Roosevelt period was the so-called Hartford loan to the President's son, Elliott. The incident, so far as Jones' participation was concerned, began on December 14, 1941, a week after the Japanese attack upon Pearl Harbor, when the President called Jones on the telephone.

"Jess," began the President, "Elliott has a serious financial problem that I wish you would help him straighten out. The radio company he has been running in Texas is in trouble. As you know Elliott has enlisted in the Army Air Force and will soon be in the combat zone. Of course, we don't know what will happen to him there and for the sake of his wife and three children he would like to adjust matters as much as possible."

The President went on to explain that Sid Richardson and Charles Roeser, Fort Worth oil men, who knew of the predicament in which Elliott's radio company found itself, were at the White House. Would he, the President asked Jones, talk with Richardson and Roeser at once and see what could be done about Elliott's affairs? Jones asked the President to send them over. He would do what he could for Elliott.

Richardson, who later was to become one of the richest men in the world, and Roeser told Jones that the radio company that the President's son had headed had lost its entire investment capital of 500,000 dollars. Elliott had borrowed 275,000 dollars to buy his stock in the concern. Of this, 200,000 dollars came from John A. Hartford, president of the Great Atlantic and Pacific Company; 50,000 dollars from David G. Baird, a New York insurance man, and 25,000 dollars from Judge Charles Harwood, also of New York.

Neither Richardson nor Roeser had much knowledge of the men who had lent the money nor of the circumstances under which it was advanced. They prepared a letter to Jones telling him that they considered the stock they had bought in Elliott's company as no longer having any value. An examination by a reputable public accounting firm showed that the radio company was insolvent.

Jones reported the facts he had obtained to the President. Again Roosevelt told Jones how Elliott was going into dangerous combat territory and had no money with which to pay his debts. He asked Jones would he, "as a special favor," talk to his son's creditors and see if they would be willing to make any concessions on Elliott's debt. It was a thankless and distasteful task, but Jones felt he could not refuse his assistance.

Elliott Roosevelt's second wife, the former Ruth Goggin of Fort

Worth, confirmed what Jones had been told about their financial plight. She was receiving a small salary from the radio network, which she was attempting to operate in her husband's absence. This and Elliott's army salary, were their sole income. The farm that Elliott had bought, using a small inheritance of his wife's, was mortgaged.

Two weeks after Jones first heard of Elliott Roosevelt's financial involvement he communicated with Hartford, the principal debtor, asking him to visit his office the first time he was in Washington and could conveniently do so. Hartford responded by making a special trip to Washington immediately.

Jones found the chain-store operator affable and "willing to do anything the President wants me to do about this debt." Hartford went on to explain that as long as he lived the 200,000 dollars would not mean much to him and at his death probably 90 per cent of his estate would be taken for taxes.

"Candidly, I would rather not have Elliott Roosevelt's notes in my estate while I am living or after I am dead," Hartford said to Jones.

In March, Hartford again called at Jones' office and an agreement was reached that Jones buy the 200,000 dollars par value radio stock that Hartford held as collateral for the loan, paying 4000 dollars for it. Jones gave Hartford this letter:

Hon. John A. Hartford
New York City, N. Y.

This is to advise you that Elliott Roosevelt and his wife Ruth Roosevelt are aware that I am arranging for the purchase of two thousand shares of the capital stock of Texas State Network, Inc., held by you as collateral, and are very appreciative of your consideration of their financial problems and the fact that you are not embarrassing them by suit or otherwise because of their inability to pay their notes to you aggregating $200,000—Two Hundred Thousand Dollars—which you loaned them to invest in the Texas State Network, Inc. stock.

Jesse H. Jones

March 17, 1942

On April 2, 1942, Jones delivered the radio stock to the President with the following letter:

Dear Mr. President:

The enclosed 2,000 shares of stock in the Texas State Network, Inc. were bought from Mr. John A. Hartford for $4000 and are presented to Elliott and Ruth. Mr. Hartford held the stock as collateral for notes to him given by Elliott and Ruth in the sum of $200,000 which notes were destroyed in my presence. The stock has very little if any present value and Elliott advised Mr. Hartford that since the investment had failed he had no means of paying the notes particularly since he was now in the military service with no prospects as to when he would get out or how he would be able to make enough money to pay the notes and his other debts created for investment in the radio business, all of which was lost.

Sincerely,
Jesse H. Jones

The President was profuse in his thanks to Jones and informed him that he would get the money back quicker that he perhaps thought, since Elliott within a year or so would receive approximately 10,000 dollars in the settlement of the estate of his grandmother, Mrs. Sara Delano Roosevelt. Jones had not expected to receive any repayment. He had named the 4000 dollars he offered Hartford for the stock because this was the largest amount he could give to one person without paying a gift tax. The President's statement that Elliott would be able to pay the amount within a year or so was the last he was to hear on that score for five years.

On July 6, 1942, Jones obtained a release on the 50,000-dollar stock held by Baird by the payment of 750 dollars. Harwood refused to sell his stock. According to the calendar in Jones' office Harwood called there eight different times in March, 1942, and again in April, September, October, and December of that year and in December, 1943, and September, 1944. He insisted that he had been promised a judgeship when he loaned Elliott the money. Failing in the prompt finding of a federal judgeship, he had been told, he said, that he would be given a high commission in the army or navy. He was instead made governor of the Virgin Islands, a post he took but did not regard as an adequate discharge of the promise made him.

Long after the Hartford and Baird settlement, Jones was to learn facts that he had not known when he undertook to handle Elliott Roosevelt's affairs.

Elliott had been introduced to Hartford by G. Hall Roosevelt, a brother of Mrs. Franklin D. Roosevelt. Hartford had never met the President. Elliott called the White House from Hartford's room and put his host on the telephone. Hartford was astonished to receive from the President he had never met, a hearty greeting, "Hello, John." In the course of the conversation the President had said, "While any business you have with my son must stand on its own merits, I will appreciate anything you do for him. When you are in Washington come in to see me."

Jones also learned much later that Hartford, his brother and partner, George, and the Great Atlantic & Pacific Tea Company were being sued by the Federal Trade Commission on anti-monopoly charges at the time of the loan to Elliott and that the Department of Justice was considering a criminal suit against the company and the two Hartfords. Neither the President nor Hartford told Jones of this. Jones felt that the President, at least, was guilty of deception in not informing him of this. Hartford, he thought, may have taken it for granted that the President had informed him of the suit, filed and contemplated. And Hartford also made the United States Treasury instead of himself take the loss, which Jones had distinctly understood he would not do.

Jones wrote of this as follows:

Because of the pending government suit Hartford should not have loaned Elliott the money and the President should not have permitted Elliott to borrow it. Had I known of the suit I would have refused to intercede with Hartford on Elliott's behalf. I had no knowledge of it until long afterwards. But for the suit there perhaps would have been nothing morally wrong with Hartford making the loan to the President's son. I can only surmise Hartford's motives for making the loan. Most of the President's family engaged in whatever money-making enterprises came along, and in some cases it perhaps proved very helpful in White House favors for those who had aided the Roosevelt money-making undertakings.

Moreover the action of the Treasury Department in allowing Hartford a $196,000 bad debt deduction was indefensible. When Hartford sold the collateral to me there was no agreement between us that the purchase of the stock was a cancellation of the debt. I doubt if Hartford made any attempt to collect the loan and the law requires that a lender make every effort to collect before taking a tax loss. Undoubtedly the deduction would not have been allowed except that a member of the Roosevet family was involved. As young as he was there was the probability that Elliott might someday have been able to pay it.

The radio stock passed to Ruth Roosevelt upon her divorce from Elliott Roosevelt and she subsequently recovered some of its value.

Jones, back in Houston, never expected to hear of the 4000 dollars again as far as any Roosevelt was concerned. Five years after he had purchased the stock, he received this peculiarly worded letter:

Hyde Park, New York
July 1, 1947

Honorable Jesse Jones,
Houston, Texas
Dear Uncle Jesse:

It has come to my attention that in the settlement of my affairs in Texas, at the time of my divorce from Ruth, one item which I specifically required to be taken care of, namely the amount of money you advanced in straightening out my affairs on the Texas State Network was never repaid to you.

I am extremely anxious that you should not be out of pocket for any sum advanced, and the purpose of this letter is to inquire the amount of the indebtedness so that I may compute what the principal, plus interest, would be to date in order to settle the account with you.

I presume that a six per cent return on that investment would be agreeable.

Thanking you in advance for your kindness in looking up this matter, and with kindest personal regards, I remain,

Very sincerely yours,
Elliott Roosevelt

Jones sent the following reply:

July 5, 1947

Dear Elliott:

The stock bought from Mr. Hartford cost me $4000. The purchase was made March 3, 1942. The stock bought from Mr. Baird cost me $750. The purchase was made May 2, 1942. Interest to this time at 4% per annum amounts to $991, or a total of $5,741.

With best wishes,

Sincerely,
Jesse H. Jones

Mr. Elliott Roosevelt
Hyde Park, New York

Two weeks later a letter arrived with the check.

An incident that certainly contributed materially to the disintegrating relations between the President and Jones concerned the seizure of the headquarters and main plant of Montgomery Ward during a labor dispute. This long-established mail-order firm, whose plant in Chicago was only one of many over the country, had given offense to the President by ignoring a White House directive to extend a contract with the labor union involved.

Sewell Avery, head of the company, took the position that he had violated no law and that he had not denied any privilege to the union. His company was not engaged in war work and therefore he held that the White House order was illegal.

Roosevelt classed Avery as a prime example of an "economic royalist" and wanted him punished forthwith. From Warm Springs he telephoned James F. Byrnes, Director of War Mobilization, to do it. Byrnes reached for a book of blank directives, which everyone seemed to possess now, and filled out one, directing Jones to take over the Montgomery Ward business and operate it. Of all the distasteful jobs he had ever had in private or public life this was the most distasteful to Jones.

For Jones had known Avery for a long time. He regarded him as somewhat irascible and an arch conservative, but a man of great business ability. A few years before, when the RFC had put 50,000,000 dollars into the Continental Illinois National Bank & Trust Company, Jones had believed Avery the ideal man to pull the bank out of its difficulties, and had sought in vain to induce him to become chairman of the bank's board.

With a perfectly straight face Jones suggested to Byrnes that the job be given to WPB Director Donald Nelson, who came to the government fresh from a job as executive vice-president of rival Sears, Roebuck. If not Nelson, then Jones thought that Harold Ickes, also from Chicago, as cross-grained as Avery but otherwise as different from him as two men could be, would fit the role. But all his efforts at side-stepping failed and Jones was saddled with the job with which he had no sympathy whatever, and from which the zeal of an Attorney General to do the Lord's work partially rescued him.

To Byrnes' emphatic statement that Jones was the only man in Washington "who can handle Sewell Avery," Jones replied, "When Sewell Avery thinks he is right, and he *always* thinks he is right, the man hasn't been born who can handle him."

Attorney General Francis Biddle, Benjamin V. Cohen, and all the convinced and crusading New Dealers wanted a finger in the pie of punishment. Heavy conferences at the White House were followed by more directives to Jones. From experience Jones knew that the effect of directives depended upon the manner in which they were carried out. He therefore picked two sensible men, Under Secretary of Commerce Wayne Taylor and RFC General Counsel John Goodloe, and sent them to Chicago. So that he would know all that was going on, Biddle sent along his executive assistant, Ugo Carusi.

In Avery's office Taylor read the directives. Avery sat gazing out of a window. Suddenly he turned and asked Taylor, "Who gives you your legal advice?"

Taylor replied it came from Attorney General Biddle.

"All I have got to say is that your Attorney General gives damn bad advice," Avery replied.

There were more directives unknown to Jones winging their way to Chicago. The War Labor Board, its dignity ruffled by Rugged Individualist Avery, had alerted the War Department.

Jones' hope that Avery might extend his contract with the union and avoid a show-down was quickly dashed. Avery told Taylor he would do nothing of the sort. Furthermore Avery said he had no intention of turning over his business to the government and that he did not expect to leave the plant unless carried out bodily.

There the matter rested. The next day while Taylor was talking over the telephone with Jones about what the next move should be, a detachment of military police dispatched by the army arrived at the Montgomery Ward offices. On April 27 Attorney General Biddle had arrived in Chicago and, without consulting Taylor or Jones, instructed a major in charge of the Military Police to remove Avery from the buildings. Within twenty-four hours nearly every newspaper in the nation had carried front-page pictures showing two soldiers carrying Avery out of his office.

Out of the welter of directives plus some usurpation, Biddle had emerged in the place Jones had first suggested for Nelson or Ickes. After the soldiers had been in the Montgomery Ward headquarters for a week it was decided at the White House they should be removed so that an election could be held to determine whether the employees wished the union to be their bargaining agent.

On May 8 Jones and Taylor went to the White House for a conference with Byrnes, Biddle, and others. Jones, Taylor, and Byrnes argued that the plant should be returned to its owner if a way could be found. President Roosevelt agreed that if the election showed that less than a majority of the employees wished the union to bargain for them, the case would be ended. The Montgomery Ward management agreed that if the union had a majority, it would continue its contract. The CIO won the election and the government returned the properties to the company. Jones was out of the case.

The White House and the War Labor Board continued to find fault with Avery's management of his business. On December 26, 1944, Secretary of War Stimson took possession of sixteen Montgomery Ward properties in a half-dozen cities. They were to remain in government control for the rest of the Roosevelt Administration and the first six months of the Truman Administration. Then the properties were returned.

A curious incident that concerned the politics of that eventful summer left a lasting impression on Roosevelt's mind. On this occasion it involved the President's eldest son, James.

In June, 1944, Jack Nichols, a former Oklahoma Congressman, and John J. Harden of Oklahoma City, made an appointment to see Jones. Nichols quickly stated their business.

He had been at the White House for breakfast and found the Roosevelt family divided on whether the President should seek another term. Nichols said that he believed that if the President could be assured that James would be appointed Secretary of the Navy in the Cabinet of a successor Democrat, the President would not again be a candidate. Jimmy, said Nichols, was anxious that Jones talk to some of the leaders of the party on this proposal.

Jones replied, "There are some objections to that. In the first place I think that no man fit to be President would make such a crass promise. It ought to be a crime under the Federal corrupt practices act if it is not. Even if these considerations were not involved I still would want nothing to do with the internal politics of the Roosevelt family."

That ended the interview. Jones understood that Nichols had promised to report its result to Jimmy Roosevelt. But he was not to learn of the White House version until some years later when a book by Grace Tully, who had been Roosevelt's secretary, appeared on the market. Indignant, John Harden, who with Nichols had attended the conference with Jones, wrote:

JOHN J. HARDEN
Oklahoma City, Oklahoma

September 20, 1950

Dear Jesse:

Yesterday for the first time I read an excerpt from Grace Tully's book, "F.D.R., My Boss" which I quote:

One evening after the 1944 election while the Boss was giving some dictation, he halted the work and turned to me. In a tone more sad than bitter he said:

"Grace, did you know that a member of my own Cabinet approached my son Jimmy (or he may have meant Elliott) and asked him to come out against me politically?"

He added that he would give me one guess as to the identity of the Cabinet officer. I was startled and shocked by the news and refused to hazard any opinion.

"It was Jesse Jones" he said. . . .

I am sure you remember Jack Nichols and me coming to see you just a few weeks before the convention in 1944 and that Jack told you that he had had breakfast at the White House and that there was a division in the family about the President running again, that Jimmy and his mother were against his running and that if the President could be assured that Jimmy would be appointed Secretary of the Navy that he would not accept the nomination. Jimmy first wanted Jack to talk with Jim Farley but when he advised with me I suggested we talk to you—that Jim Farley was not in the Administration any more and the feeling between him and the President was not good. You told Jack that you would not have anything to do with any such scheme.

When Jack was in Congress he and Jimmy had become good friends.

I remember every detail of this affair and you are free to use this letter in any way you wish.

Sincerely yours,
/s/ Jno. J. Harden

Honorable Jesse H. Jones
Houston, Texas

In political affairs where his interests were concerned Roosevelt bitterly resented opposition. This was especially marked in his attitude toward a conservative movement in Texas which was designed to oppose a fourth term. The members of the group called themselves "Texas Regulars" and several of them were men of very considerable wealth and business importance. Since some of them were old friends of Jones, the President probably entertained the feeling that Jones might have headed off the movement.

Jones, however, could have done nothing of the sort. The movement had gained great headway before Jones heard anything about it. And it was motivated by the profound antipathy for the New Deal, which was prevalent among conservative Texas Democrats who had fought the party battles for many years.

By the time the State Democratic Convention was held, the Regulars were strong enough to outvote the Roosevelt supporters and take complete control. The convention adopted two resolutions of far-reaching importance.

The first of these provided that unless the National Convention restored the rule requiring that two thirds of the delegates must vote for a party nominee, the November Presidential electors named by the State Convention were morally obligated to vote for someone other than the nominee of the national convention. It made the same provision if the national convention failed to seat the delegates sent there by the state convention.

The effect of this would have been to keep Roosevelt off the ballot in Texas unless its terms were met. One of the leaders of the Texas Regular movement was George Butler of Houston, who had married one of Jones' nieces. Seizing upon this fact and wishing to curry favor with the President, some Texans went to the White House in an effort to convince the President that Jones was in sympathy with the Texas Regular movement.

The opposite was true. While Jones would have preferred that Roosevelt abide by the two-term tradition, he had supported him in 1940 because he regarded the differences in political philosophy between Roosevelt and Willkie a matter of Tweedle-dum and Tweedle-dee. He also considered that Willkie was without any governmental experience. Between the 1940 nominating convention and the election he had entered the Cabinet as Secretary of Commerce, as Federal Loan Administrator he headed many of the war agencies, and he was a director in others such as the War Production Board.

Now in 1944 with war at its height he strongly favored the retention of the Administration in power, although he had a great deal higher regard for the ability of Thomas E. Dewey than he had held for Willkie.

Jones went to the White House to talk to the President about the situation including the issue raised by the participation of nephew-in-law Butler in the activities of the Texas Regulars. He had a good many in-laws, he told the President and he made no effort to control their politics. If he were to try, he jocularly told Roosevelt, he would be no more successful than the President had been in controlling Elliott Roosevelt, who after his father announced his desire for Wallace as his running mate in 1940, urged Jones to allow his name to be presented to the convention, and said he would second the nomination. What he had to say, Jones told Roosevelt, would be to no individual but to all the people of Texas.

Subsequently Jones issued a statement designed to clarify his position concerning the movement and the resolutions it had adopted at the state convention. He said in the statement that, while there was no question about the authenticity of the Regulars' majority at the convention or the legality of its proceedings, there was nevertheless a big question about the wisdom of the actions taken there. He felt that the resolutions went much further than some of the delegates realized.

Jones said he himself favored the two-thirds rule for nominating Presidents and Vice-Presidents, but its restoration could not possibly prevent the renomination of Roosevelt. In his statement Jones said:

> It must now be obvious to thousand of Texas voters who did not participate in the State Convention, as well as to some who sat in the councils of that convention that the effect of its actions was to change the rules of the game as we have always known them in Texas, or indeed, as Americans have known them everywhere since this country settled down to the two-party system.
>
> The essence of the two-party system is that the two great political parties shall meet in national convention, name candidates for President and Vice-President and enunciate a platform or charter of its beliefs. The Texas elec-

tion laws, including the one under which the twenty-three electors were chosen by the Texas Democratic Convention, were written in conformance with the fact that for well over a hundred years the elected President of the United States has been a man chosen in national convention by one of the two great political parties. For voters who do not wish to support the nominees of the two major parties other places are provided on the ballot.

No political convention has the authority to deny any qualified voter the right to vote for any candidate he wishes to support, and certainly as it appears today many Texas Democrats will be effectively prevented from casting their votes for the party nominee.

Roosevelt had seemed well satisfied with Jones' statement and a front-page editorial for his Houston *Chronicle* advocating the President's election, which Jones had written after the renomination of Roosevelt and rejection of Wallace at the Democratic National Convention. That convention had seated both the Texas Regulars and the delegates, dividing votes equally between them. The Texas Regular delegates had voted for Senator Harry F. Byrd of Virginia for the Presidential nomination.

At a Texas State Convention in September the Roosevelt adherents regained control and revoked the action of the May convention denying Roosevelt a place on the Texas ballot. Roosevelt was anxious that Jones make a speech in the campaign. Jones had not fully recovered from his summertime pneumonia illness and in October he again was kept at home by a severe cold.

He wrote the radio speech and delivered it on October 31, leaving his sickbed to do so. Fearing that he might not be able to finish it, he took John Goodloe, General Counsel of the Reconstruction Finance Corporation, with him to finish reading it, if he himself were unable to do so. Roosevelt took occasion to thank Jones warmly for the speech, and said he liked the general tone of it very much. Jones sent the formal letter of congratulation to Roosevelt after his election and received this reply:

Dear Jesse:

My warm thanks for your fine note of congratulations. Your good wishes are sincerely appreciated.

Affectionate regards,
F.D.R.

These felicitations, however, are so much a matter of routine in politics that they can hardly be taken as evidence that all was serene in the Roosevelt-Jones relations. Moreover, the determination of the left-wingers to get Jones out of the Administration was now sharpened as the end of the war came in sight by differences of opinion concerning the proper road back to a peacetime economy. Jones' preference was for a return to the conditions of private enterprise as soon as possible, by disposing of the war plants except for those engaged in the making of synthetic rubber. The zealous advocates of government-in-business saw an unparalleled opportunity for socialistic experimentation. Ickes, in fact, had made use of a weekend with the President at Hyde Park to urge that the plants built by Jones be retained and leased to operators on the basis of their agreement to employ a given number of workers. Wallace favored the scrapping of the rubber plants "in the interests of a more balanced world trade."

After the election newspaper speculation began to appear indicating that Jones might be replaced in the cabinet. This was no doubt planted by Jones' enemies.

Hopkins, who had a blunt way of getting at things, told Jones that there might well be a solid basis for the rumors.

"Henry Wallace is begging for your job and he may get it," he told Jones.

Jones replied that he assumed that if the President wanted his resignation he would ask for it. A few days later Hopkins told Jones that Roosevelt would like to give Wallace the post of Secretary of Commerce and leave Jones as Federal Loan Administrator, but that Wallace did not want one without the other.

30

Ite, Missa Est

THE end of Jones' government service came in an almost unbelievable manner.

Only in the strange, whimsical Franklin D. Roosevelt Administration could it have happened as it did.

As the fourth inauguration of Franklin D. Roosevelt approached, Jones was completing his thirteenth year in high government position. Through that period he had carried more responsibilities than any man in Washington, with the exception of Roosevelt. He had been in Washington a year longer than Roosevelt. Roosevelt's three terms had added up to twelve years less a few weeks, to Jones' thirteen.

Jones was now seventy-one years of age. Twice within a few years he had had pneumonia, and, interested as he was in building the sinews of war-making, he had slowed down little. In his office there was a motto for the guidance of himself and his associates which read:

> What we need to do daily is to search our conscience and make certain that we have done nothing to let down our men in uniform.

Jones had taken great interest in seeing that comforts were provided for the new soldiers. On occasion he would go to the Washington Stage Door canteen, a few blocks from his office, put on a long apron, and hand food to soldiers, sailors, and marines.

Jones never had any thought that he would serve out four years in the Cabinet in the fourth Roosevelt term. In truth, as he saw Roosevelt's physical decline he had doubted more and more that the President would serve out his third term.

Jones' relations with Senator Truman had always been agreeable, but he doubted if he would be willing to continue in office if, as seemed more likely every day, the new Vice-President should succeed to the Presidency. Besides, he felt that he had already been away from his interests in Houston too long. He was not worried about a successor in the Commerce Department, for he regarded that office as something for which either Roosevelt or Truman might well find a satisfactory man.

What Jones did consider important was the man who was Federal Loan Administrator. At the beginning of 1945 he felt confident that sometime during the year both Germany and Japan would be overcome. The one big job left for the Federal Loan Administrator and the RFC was the handling of the expanded productive capacity that had come as the result of the war. This had been much on his mind. He told a meeting of the Military Order of the World War:

> This productive capacity properly used can save the world, and improperly applied, become an economic menace. There must be a sound and sensible solution of what to do with government-owned plants. That the government should retain their ownership and operation is unthinkable. It is equally unthinkable that the government's investment should be sacrificed. Government and private business must work together to utilize in peace much of the machinery we have created for war.

Once the policy was set for the disposal of the more than nine billion dollars of government-owned plants, and he was certain that it would have to be set early in the year 1945 and an acceptable man found to succeed him, he would gladly bow out and, as soon as manpower and material became available, he would resume his work on Houston's skyline, which had been both his vocation and his avocation for so many years.

However, it was destined that the story would not end on that happy note.

On Friday, January 19, Jones attended the Cabinet meeting at the White House. The fourth-term inauguration was to be held the following day. The President had not been well and the Cabinet had not been meeting following the election. Jones had not seen the President during that whole period. Now on the eve of the inauguration the deterioration in the President's physical condition shocked him.

The President, however, had pleasantries for several members of the Cabinet, including Jones. He also remarked that while Henry Wallace would no longer be Vice-President, he would still be associated with the Administration, but gave no inkling how. Then he discussed his forthcoming trip to Yalta.

Jones remained to take up some RFC matters with Roosevelt. All of these had been the subject of discussion between them before, but Roosevelt seemed unable to remember anything about them. Nothing was said about Jones' not remaining in the Cabinet.

In his office Jones dictated a memorandum as he often did after a Cabinet meeting. This one read:

MEMORANDUM:

At the Cabinet meeting Friday, January 19, the President stated that he was not going to make any trades on his contemplated meeting with Churchill and Stalin; that he was not going to make any commitments; that he was going to preserve his trading position and that if Stalin and Churchill pushed him for commitments, he would tell them that he wanted time to study their requests and to confer with Congress.

Among other things, he referred to the fact that when President Wilson was taken seriously ill in late 1919, while on a speaking tour in the West, in the interest of the League of Nations, the Secretary of State (Robert Lansing) called a meeting of the Cabinet and that the President resented it very much, and soon after appointed a new Secretary of State, Bainbridge Colby.

He stated that he would be away four or five weeks, and that he would have with him the Secretary of State, and if the next ranking member of the Cabinet, Secretary Morgenthau, wished to do so, the President would have no objection to the Secretary of the Treasury calling a meeting of the Cabinet. In other words that the next highest official of the Cabinet, Morgenthau, could carry on in his absence.

On Saturday morning, January 20, Jones attended the ten o'clock religious services in the White House and at noon proceeded with the official party and stood within a few feet of the President as he took the oath.

At five o'clock that afternoon the White House telephoned to Jones at his office saying that the President wanted to see him at the White House at noon Sunday. A few minutes later a messenger came with this letter:

THE WHITE HOUSE

January 20, 1945

Dear Jesse—

This is a very difficult letter to write—first, because of our long friendship and splendid relations during all these years, and also because of your splendid services to the Government and the excellent way in which you have carried out the many difficult tasks during these years.

Henry Wallace deserves almost any service which he believes he can satisfactorily perform. I told him this at the end of the campaign, in which he displayed the utmost devotion to our cause, traveling almost incessantly and working for the success of the ticket in a great many parts of the country. Though not on the ticket himself, he gave of his utmost toward the victory which ensued.

He has told me that he thought he could do the greatest amount of good in the Department of Commerce, for which he is fully suited, and I feel, therefore, that the Vice-President should have this post in the new Administration.

It is for this reason only that I am asking you to relinquish this present post for Henry, and I want to tell you that it is in no way a lack of appreciation for all that you have done and that I hope you will continue to be part of the Government.

During the next few days I hope you will think about a new post—there are several ambassadorships which are vacant—or about to be vacated. I make this suggestion among many other posts and I hope you will have a chance, if you think well of it, to speak to Ed Stettinius.

Finally, let me tell you that you have my full confidence and that I am very proud of all that you have done during these past years.

With warm regards,

Always Sincerely,
Franklin D. Roosevelt

The Honorable
Secretary of Commerce

The letter had not been given out at the White House and no announcement made there of the impending Cabinet change. The circumstances indicated that the President intended the news to become public on Monday, when he would send the nomination of Wallace to the Senate for confirmation.

Jones was not too much surprised at the manner of his ouster. He had seen Bill Knudsen fired in the same unceremonious and shabby manner. His first feeling was one of relief at being out of government service. He had served fifteen years, in two world wars and the country's most devastating depression.

But the thought that Henry Wallace, of all people, whose fecund mind had brought forth the notion that would have postponed vital tin procurement until he had made sure that every Bolivian Indian workman had a warm meal at midday, would take over as Federal Loan Administrator was a little too much.

There went through his mind the classic contrast between the trim, efficient RFC and Wallace's messy Board of Economic Warfare. No one could think for a minute that Wallace would keep a Jones-blessed board of RFC directors, or that men of the type of Dawes, McCarthy, Couch, Cowles, Schram, Merriam, Fisher, Husbands, and Mulligan would longer have any place there, or want any under Henry Wallace.

Jones had fought for his beloved RFC in season and out. There had been the time of his Wyoming illness. He had got out of bed at Encampment River and come back to recuperate at his desk when Morgenthau tried to move in on RFC. Morgenthau, always envious of Jones, had persuaded Roosevelt to end RFC lending at a time when the need for it was as great as ever, a fact that was soon recognized and its lending resumed.

Jones had envisioned the day when RFC, its work finished, would disappear lock, stock, and barrel. But he wanted its obsequies conducted by the friends of its glorious days. And all its days had been glorious up to now.

Once, when legislation creating RFC was under discussion, Garner had said that "it is easier to lick a depression than it is to kill a government agency once it is launched." Jones, a decade later, had told Garner that once the country's conversion from a war to a peace basis was concluded, RFC would have finished its job. He thought that would take two years after hostilities ceased.

Garner had also said, "Jesse, I myself would have voted for all these powers Congress has given you. But it has given you power it ought to give no man."

Now it was proposed to hand all these powers intact into the hands of Henry Wallace.

Perhaps as a well man Roosevelt would have doubted that the Senate would approve Wallace for the place. But there was also the likelihood that, suddenly confronted with the nomination of a man who had just left the Vice-Presidency by a President who was just entering upon a new term, the Senate might vote confirmation.

There was no doubt in Jones' mind what his course would be, Wallace could be Secretary of Commerce and welcome to it, but he wouldn't get his hands on RFC if Jones could prevent it.

All during the war it had been Jones' habit to go to his office on Sunday morning. Some of his friends in government, knowing this, often paid him visits. On this Sunday Associate Supreme Court Justice Stanley F. Reed stopped by and Jones showed him the Roosevelt letter. Will Clayton, Norman W. Baxter, and two or three others saw it.

The Saturday telephone call asking him to be at the White House at noon and the messenger bringing the letter of dismissal had been so close together that Jones did not know whether the President still expected him to come over. A telephone call by Jones' secretary to the White House got the reply that the President still wished to see him.

The meeting between Roosevelt and Jones took place in the Oval Room where they had often met. Roosevelt, with what Jones thought were the deepest feelings he had ever seen him express, reiterated his thanks for a competent job, which he said he felt had reflected great credit on the Administration in general, and again said he was sorry that he had to ask him to leave.

"I feel that Henry is entitled to about anything he asks to have," Roosevelt said. "He worked like a dog in this campaign. I couldn't give him the place he wanted, Secretary of State, and when I couldn't he asked to be Secretary of Commerce. I just had to give it to him."

Roosevelt shifted his wheelchair around, came closer to Jones, and said, "Jesse, won't you take the post as Ambassador to France? There will be a great reconstruction job there after the war. All the things that you have done here make you the ideal selection for that job. The rebuilding of France is going to be necessary for the welfare of this country and all Europe."

Jones replied that the rebuilding of France was a more formidable job than a man of his age ought to undertake. Then Roosevelt suggested Rome, probably to be followed by appointment to the Court of St. James. Jones replied that he wanted no Ambassadorship and would not leave the country.

Roosevelt then offered him the chairmanship of the Federal Reserve Board, criticizing the manner in which Marriner Eccles was operating it. Jones declined that. Roosevelt now made the final offer. Jones could set up and become the head of an agency that would have to do with the final stages of the war and the readjustment thereafter. As Roosevelt described it, the new organization would have a role closely resembling the ideas Jones had once given the President as the probable job of dismantling for the Federal Loan Administrator and RFC after the war. Again Jones declined, saying he would undertake no new job.

Then Jones asked when Roosevelt desired him to leave office. Roosevelt specified not until his successor was confirmed.

Jones arose and shook hands with the President and bade him good-by.

"It's not good-by: I'll see you when I get back."

Jones replied, "Mr. President, I think it is good-by."

Jones returned to his office and recounted the conversation he had with the President to a few of his trusted associates.

"It would have been better if I had declined to go to the White House after the letter," Jones told them. "I wish I had not seen him for the last time in the condition of physical and mental deterioration he seemed to be in.

"I am sorry for the country that he is going to Yalta to meet Stalin in the condition he is. As I was coming back over here I wondered if he would ever return alive from that trip."

Then Jones remarked that he was going to write a reply to the President's letter, adding, "You fellows may stay here and help me with your literary talents if you wish."

The group in his office grew. Justice Reed, Clayton, Sam Husbands, and Harry Mulligan were among those present. Jones listened to suggestions, but as usual he followed his own inclination as to the kind of reply it would be.

When it was finished someone raised the question of protocol. Could Jones without permission give out the President's letter and reply. Jones joked, "I think the President's letter ended any relation I may have had to protocol."

Then he continued:

> I have great respect for the Presidency and proper respect also for any man who is President. But there is a distinction between the Presidency and the President. The President is a man. My conception of the person of the President is that he is a citizen temporarily in that high office.
>
> Mr. Roosevelt is a citizen. So am I. I know of no good reason why one citizen should not reply to another's communication. I am proud of the record of this agency and of my record with it. The manner of termination was insulting to me. To ask me not to reply to it is asking me to be a little more craven than I could be.

Then Jones dictated this letter:

> January 21, 1945
>
> Dear Mr. President:
>
> Inasmuch as you are sending Mr. Wallace's name to Congress tomorrow, I am releasing your letter to me and my reply.

I have eliminated from your letter any reference to your trip.

With all good wishes for a successful meeting.

Sincerely,
Jesse H. Jones

The President
The White House

When the letter had reached the White House, Bill Costello, Jones' administrative aide, telephoned there, saying that it was Jones' purpose to make the letters public at seven o'clock that night. The White House made no protests and the letters were sent to the press associations, and principal newspaper bureaus.

The following is Jones' reply:

January 21, 1945

Dear Mr. President—I have your letter of today, asking that I relinquish my post as Secretary of Commerce, which carries with it the vast financial and war production agencies within the Reconstruction Finance Corporation and its subsidiaries, so that you can give it to Henry Wallace as a reward for his support of you in the campaign.

You state that Henry Wallace thinks he could do the greatest amount of good in the Department of Commerce and that you consider him fully suited for the post. With all due respect, Mr. President, while I must accede to your decision, I cannot agree with either of you.

You refer very kindly to our long friendship and our splendid relations during all the years, and that you appreciate my splendid services to the Government and the excellent way I have carried out the many difficult tasks during these years. You are also good enough to say that I have your full confidence, and that you are very proud of all I have done during these past years, and that you hope I will continue to be a part of the Government, probably in a diplomatic post.

It is difficult to reconcile these encomiums with your avowed purpose to replace me. While I want to be of any further service that I can, I would not want a diplomatic assignment.

I feel and have felt a great sense of responsibility to the Congress and to you for the proper administration of the laws with respect to the RFC that have been passed in the expectation that they would be administered by me or someone experienced in business and finance.

I have had satisfaction in my Government service because I have had the confidence of the Congress, as well as your own. I have had that confidence because I have been faithful to the responsibilities that have been entrusted to me. For you to turn over all these assets and responsibilities to a man inexperienced in business and finance will, I believe, be hard for the business and financial world to understand.

I appreciate the opportunity you have given me to serve my country through the depression and in time of war. My thirteen years of government service are ample evidence of my desire to be of any assistance I can to the Government. I can best be helpful in the line of my life's work—business and finance—but I seek no job.

With best wishes, faithfully yours,

Jesse H. Jones

Thus Jones announced his own ouster and the news set off more fireworks than had been anticipated. The nation heard of it in Sunday night radio broadcasts and immediately telegrams began pouring in. On Monday the telephone calls were so heavy that the switchboard at RFC was blocked.

Bill Jeffers, out as Rubber Administrator, and back with the Union Pacific, telephoned to say that it was the worst thing that ever happened to the country.

Emil Schram, an old Jones lieutenant, crestfallen, telephoned to Jones. "It's a real calamity."

"But not enough to close the stock exchange," Jones joked.

"I think we will if Wallace gets hold of the RFC," Schram replied.

Senator Harry F. Byrd telephoned to say, "I think we can prevent his confirmation. I have received sheafs of telegrams and I think the country is up in arms."

When an angry Senate met at noon Monday it was very evident that Wallace would not be handed the offices of Federal Loan Administrator and the RFC and its subsidiaries.

Jones might have expected the tribute paid to him by the conservatives, such as that of Josiah W. Bailey of North Carolina, who said:

> Mr. Jones proved to be a faithful servant, and admirable steward. He has handled our money, I think, better than Joseph handled Pharaoh's money back in the days of the great depression in Egypt. Certainly he has done as well. Now that he goes back to private life, he goes with my gratitude and with profound expressions of appreciation.

But even more eloquent than the praises sung by the conservatives was the tribute paid by Senator Elbert Thomas of Utah, a New Dealer:

> I desire to pay tribute to Mr. Jesse Jones, former Secretary of Commerce. I completely endorse everything which the Senator from North Carolina said in regard to Jesse Jones. Not only do I endorse what he said but I should like to add my own type tribute.
>
> . . . Probably Mr. Jones will never read the remarks which we make concerning him, but I should like to have him know that there is gratitude and thankfulness in the hearts of people through the country that has been blessed by his wise administration.

Newspapers attacked the Cabinet change as a "pay-off for Wallace's stalwart service in the fourth-term campaign" and as "a gesture of payment of a political debt and an expression of grudge."

Perhaps typical was this one in the New York *Sun:*

Payment of a Debt

Although not unexpected, the decision of Roosevelt to make Henry Wallace his Secretary of Commerce, and incidentally the new boss of the Reconstruction Finance Corporation, comes as a heavy blow at business confidence in this country. If the inaugural ceremonies of Saturday were quieter and more somber than usual, publication by Jesse Jones of his correspondence with the President has touched off an aftermath of fireworks. The fourth term was scarcely twenty-four hours old before it thus became known that into the hands of the most radical, impractical and idealistic dreamer in his entourage Mr. Franklin D. Roosevelt had placed a large measure of responsibility for the ultimate liquidation of billions of dollars' worth of industrial property now under the control of the Federal government. The man once responsible for plowing under cotton and corn and for the slaughter of little pigs will be in excellent position, when reconversion comes, to plow under quite a substantial amount of private enterprise. So far as private business is concerned, it can be pardoned for wondering whether the wolf has not been appointed to serve as its shepherd.*

Senator Walter F. George of Georgia put in a resolution separating the offices of Secretary of Commerce from that of Federal Loan Administrator. Jones was invited to testify on the proposed legislation. Jones took an ovation from a huge crowd in corridors and hearing room where he appeared before the Senate Commerce Committee at the Capitol on January 24.

The George bill whipped through the House of Representatives by a vote of 400-to-2 and passed the Senate 74-to-12. Then the Senate Committee voted 15-to-5 against a favorable report for Wallace as Secretary of Commerce. But the confirmation finally was lobbied through on March 1 by a vote of 56-to-32.

President Roosevelt at their Sunday conference had asked Jones to remain in office until his successor had qualified. Jones, after finishing the

* Under the heading "Explanation to Jesse Jones," the *Knickerbocker News* of Albany, New York, expressed it in verse pithier than other newspapers had in prose:

Your training has been excellent,
It's made you extra fit,
So now I ask you to get out
For someone lacking it.

Of financial experience
You've surely had a lot
So kindly scram and give the job
To someone who has not.

reply to the President's Saturday letter, had written a letter to RFC Chairman Charles B. Henderson asking immediate acceptance of his resignation as director and chairman of the corporation's five wartime subsidiaries: Defense Plant Corporation, Defense Supplies Corporation, Metals Reserve Company, Rubber Reserve Company, and War Damage Corporation.

To Leo T. Crowley, chairman of the Export-Import Bank, went a letter resigning from its board of trustees. He ended the momentous day by writing a letter turning over to Under Secretary of Commerce Wayne Chatfield Taylor all the functions of the Department of Commerce.

But Jones as Federal Loan Administrator had no deputy. Neither did he have a staff, drawing on the RFC for help as he needed. There was no one to whom he could assign these functions. He remained in this office until March 12, when the President, following the passage of the George separation bill, appointed Fred M. Vinson as Federal Loan Administrator.

Once there came a message to Jones from Roosevelt at the ill-fated Yalta conference. It was by word of mouth and not written. It had been: "Keep your shirt on. We will work something out."

Jones heard no more from the President along this line, nor had he expected to.

His last letter from Roosevelt came on March 24. In cleaning out his desk Jones had found some albums of pictures and a well-written history of the Rogers estate, which at Roosevelt's behest Jones had saved from the hands of Father Divine. He sent these to Roosevelt.

The March 24 letter was merely a cordial seven-line one, expressing the President's appreciation. The noteworthy thing was the signature. Instead of the good handwriting on the hundreds of memos Jones had received was a scrawled "Franklin D. Roosevelt," mute evidence of the decline in the President's physical condition.

Nineteen days later Franklin D. Roosevelt was dead.

PART VIII

Home From The Wars

31

From War to Peace

FREE after thirteen busy years in government service, Jones did not immediately return to Houston. All of the Jones companies there were so well manned that he would have to wait "until one of them could find a place for him," he wrote to John Nance Garner. He was also interested in keeping a front seat while the great drama of war was played out to its final conclusion.

There was another reason more pressing. Both he and Mrs. Jones had been under a physician's care for some time, and his trouble was ultimately destined to end in surgery.

He found a fairly exacting and very interesting job in writing editorials for his Houston *Chronicle*. His topics dealt with both international and domestic affairs. He loved his newspaper and the freedom it gave him to express his views, now that all official restraints were removed. He had once told an annual meeting of the Associated Press that while he had not been able to give much time to the *Chronicle*, he would regard it as honor enough to be its editor and publisher.

Office space was scarce in wartime Washington, but Jones found a satisfactory suite in the Statler Hotel. One room housed Norman Baxter, his long-time editorial assistant, and two secretaries. Another Jones took for himself and installed therein a huge desk, a dining table, and a few comfortable chairs. He entered into his editorial work with zest, and never did an editorial writer find it easier to get grist for his mill. Baxter carried on the research and helped with the writing.

To the luncheon table in Jones' suite came Cabinet members, heads of executive agencies, generals and admirals and other high military officers, foreign as well as American Ambassadors, heads of missions, Supreme Court Justices, Senators and Representatives from both the Republican and Democratic parties, business executives, newspaper and magazine writers, radio commentators, and distinguished private citizens.

The advice these visitors sought and the words of personal praise they brought were a warm reminder that the contribution he had made to public service was well known far and wide and appreciated by the thoughtful people of his generation. Newspapers and magazines after his retirement had been most laudatory of his services and condemnatory of Roosevelt's incoherent action in replacing him. The death of the President so soon after strengthened the opinion that the Wallace appointment had not been made by a clear and untroubled mind. Jones had no doubt but that the verdict of history would be favorable to him.

His happiness was redoubled by the return of his nephew, Lieutenant John T. Jones, Jr., from a German prison camp.

With victory in sight, the major topic in Washington discussions and in Jones' mind was the difficult problem of planning the transition to peace. This subject had concerned Jones almost from the beginning of the war.

As early as 1942 he had said:

> It may be three years or five years or even longer but we must anticipate the day when war materials no longer move down the assembly lines. We will then be confronted with the necessity of a decision of what to do with these plants in which so many billions of dollars are being invested. The wisdom with which we consider and determine the future utilization of these government-owned plants will have a substantial influence on our economic future. It will be a real problem and one that Congress, the executive branch and all the rest of us will have to give serious thought.

Jones at the time of that statement knew, of course, that the total of the building would be huge, but he could hardly have conceived that RFC through Defense Plant Corporation would wind up with an investment of more than nine billion dollars in 2300 plants, most of which would be usable in peacetime.

It was a curious fact that the nation that never got a chance to recover from the Depression and take a fresh breath before war came, very generally held the opinion that it would lapse back into Depression when war guns no longer barked. Jones held no such views as those widely expressed by the prophets of adversity.

"It is just as necessary to prepare for peace as it is for war, Jones told a press conference in 1942. "They both mean work and more work, planning as the scene changes. But there can be no thought that we cannot surmount the difficulties."

To bring about that peacetime planning, Jones in 1942 called together his business advisory council,* a group formed to advise the Department of Commerce on business problems and needs.

In greeting the council, Jones reminded the members that the business opportunities that would appear after the war would be inconceivably varied and attractive. There would be needed by the civilian population a tremendous range of things that were unavailable during hostilities and that much of the purchasing power to move them would be found in the bonds purchased during the years of war. Young and vigorous industries would appear and old ones, such as the railroads, would need vast quantities of new equipment. There would be ready for action, moreover, municipal, state, and federal public works. Finally, there would be the reconstruction of the devastated countries abroad. To accomplish this economic effort in an orderly way, close cooperation between government and private business would be essential, Jones emphasized, and the Department of Commerce with all its facilities would be available to private enterprise.

After the meeting of the council, two of its members, Paul Hoffman of the Studebaker Corporation, and William Benton, a former advertising man, suggested to Jones the creation of a Committee on Economic Development to provide unofficial guidance and information in the mo-

* The Business Advisory Council of the Department of Commerce at that time consisted of 105 of the leading businessmen of the country of whom the following were representative: George M. Humphrey, the M. A. Hanna Company, later Secretary of Treasury; M. B. Folsom, Eastman Kodak Company, later Secretary of Health, Education and Welfare; John D. Biggers, president, Libbey-Owens-Ford Glass Company; Ralph Budd, president, Burlington Lines; Vannevar Bush, President, Carnegie Institution of Washington; Clarence Francis, president, General Foods Corporation; Charles R. Hook, president, American Rolling Mills Company; Thomas B. McCabe, president, Scott Paper Company; W. S. S. Rogers, the Texas Company; John S. Sinclair, executive vice-president, New York Life Insurance Company; Walter C. Teagle, chairman of the board, Standard Oil Company, (N.J.); S. Clay Williams, chairman, board of directors, R. J. Reynolds Tobacco Company; and C. E. Wilson, president, General Electric Company.

mentous years ahead. After some discussion of people to serve as chairman of such a committee, including Owen D. Young, retired chairman of General Electric, Jones persuaded Hoffman to accept the assignment. He argued that since the idea originated with Hoffman and Benton, they were the logical ones to put the plan into effect. They were assigned office space in the Department of Commerce Building for this work. Hoffman remained as chairman of the committee until his appointment in 1948 as head of the foreign-aid activities of the government.

In his numerous addresses during the war years Jones made every effort to dispel the idea that with the government so deeply involved in the business activities incident to war, it would be difficult after victory to restore a genuinely free economy. In one of his speeches he said that while it would be impossible for the government to retire from the scene overnight, he would give the assurance that "no government operation created for war purposes should be maintained a day after its functions have been fulfilled."

He nevertheless made it clear that the great plants and facilities built by the government should be wisely disposed of so that there might not be an accent on monopoly by big business. "The country is better off with smaller units," he said, "even if they are not always efficient." But since twenty of the 1860 plants built by the RFC cost an average of 100,000,000 dollars; eighteen between 50,000,000 and 100,000,000 dollars each; forty-four between 25,000,000 and 50,000,000 dollars; and 224 between 5,000,000 and 25,000,000 dollars, it was obvious that a great part of the government holdings were the sort of operation that only a sizable business could handle.

On September 7, 1944, Jones took the first step toward the disposition of the government's industrial holdings. He asked 376 industrialists operating 586 of the plants owned by the Defense Plant Corporation whether they wished to purchase them. In the negotiations that would be conducted in such sales as might result, Jones expected to use the same team he had used in assigning the plants to the various companies for war work. He felt confident that with such men as Sam Husbands, Harry Mulligan, Howard Klossner, and Jim Dougherty in charge, the interests of the government would be well protected.

However, as we have seen, there was bitter opposition within the Administration to this policy of transition to a free economy. The statists were at work, and not the least of the motives that prompted Roosevelt in replacing Jones with Wallace was his sympathy for the perpetuation of government in business.

With Jones' departure from government, most of his carefully prepared plans for the disposition of the government's holdings were scrapped. Nothing as ludicrous as Wallace's plan to junk the synthetic rubber plants or Ickes' grotesque scheme to retain the many-purposed plants and lease them to operators on the basis of their agreement to employ a given number of workers was of course followed. But war plants were disposed of at prices Jones regarded as ridiculously low.

A steel mill built by the United States Steel Company for the RFC in Utah for 200,000,000 dollars was sold to that company for 25,000,000 dollars. It was put up for sale to the highest bidder when it was certain that no one else but the United States Steel Company was prepared to operate it. Jones would have negotiated this sale instead of putting it up for bidding where there could be only one responsible bidder, and there was no doubt that this company, which made the Utah mill the chief supplier of steel in the West, would have paid a great deal more than it did.

Henry Kaiser, still owing the government 44,500,000 dollars for wartime loans, bought the 100,000,000-dollar Willow Run bomber plant for a nominal 10,000,000 dollars. Kaiser immediately went to the RFC and borrowed 25,000,000 dollars on the plant for which he had paid 10,000,000 dollars. The money was to be used in connection with the manufacture of automobiles. It was a strange loan for the RFC and could have been made only in the post-Jones era there.

From time to time there were rumors that Jones would return to government service under Truman, with whom his relations in war days were pleasant and who after a few months had found Henry Wallace to be an impossible Cabinet member. But Jones was convinced that Truman would not offer him the authority he would have needed to carry out an orderly liquidation, and even if the President had been so disposed, Jones would have declined the offer. He stood firmly by a statement he made at the end of his first summer in private life: "In the future I will attend to my own business, of which I have quite a lot, and which I have been neglecting for thirteen years."

The Thousand Islands had long been Jones' favorite spot for rest and relaxation, and as the summer heat of 1945 came to Washington he went with Mrs. Jones to Cape Vincent for the longest and most restful holiday in three decades. In the autumn Bill Knudsen came to luncheon with Jones in his office in Washington.

"I'm no longer a general, but am now a manufacturer," Knudsen said. "I'm back with General Motors, but somehow that law about going back to work at the same compensation did not work for me.

"Roosevelt told me he was drafting me. At that time I was getting a compensation of 1000 dollars a day from General Motors and I went to work for the government for nothing. Even after I got to be Lieutenant General I got only twenty-two dollars per day. The company isn't paying me as much as it did when I left."

In December the two old friends went together to Houston where Knudsen addressed the annual meeting of the Houston Chamber of Commerce.

Jones went back to Washington and his editorial writing. He was engaged in two other matters in which he had great interest. He was President and Treasurer of the Woodrow Wilson Foundation and principal contributor for the restoration of the Woodrow Wilson birthplace at Staunton, Virginia. His principal collaborator in the restoration of the old manse and the piecing together, fragment by fragment, the books, articles of furniture, clothing and mementos that wove themselves into the life of the university president who became President of the United States, was Mrs. Cordell Hull, wife of the former Secretary of State. Staunton was also Mrs. Hull's birthplace.

Jones had also endowed the Woodrow Wilson School of Foreign Affairs at the University of Virginia. He was the sole contributor of funds for this school for the study of international affairs. He had long wanted to pay a practical tribute to the man who, next to his father, more than anyone else had had the greatest influence on his life.

In his letter to Dr. John Lloyd Newcomb, president of the University of Virginia, offering to establish the school, Jones wrote:

> Such a school would be devoted to the teaching of international relations with emphasis on those aspects of those subjects with which his name will ever be associated.
>
> I cannot pretend to outline the field for such a school and nothing would be further from my thought than to limit the academic freedom of the school or of the university authorities. To illustrate what I have in mind, the teaching might embrace such things as past and present history of American foreign relations, American policies in the foreign field, past and present efforts at international organization, international commerce and its effect on government policy, international law and international justice, negotiation and interpretation of treaties, the practice of diplomacy, et cetera.

There were some schools of foreign service in the United States, but their purpose was the training of young men for careers in foreign service. The purpose of the new school primarily would be to give a knowledge of world affairs, of international law and related subjects as a part of the education of young men who did not contemplate diplomatic careers. He thought it would be especially useful to those who were to enter such fields as law, politics, and journalism.

He chose the University of Virginia because Wilson had been a law student there, and furthermore since its founding by Thomas Jefferson in 1819 it had exercised a great influence on the political thought of the nation.

In March of 1946 Jones was again threatened with pneumonia while on a trip to New York. He went to Le Roy Hospital. Beaverbrook was in New York and he spent long hours with Jones. One day Beaverbrook said, "Jesse, you will never get well on hospital fare."

The Beaver went to the Colony Restaurant and worked out a menu, the food to be sent to his friend three times a day.

What Beaverbrook did not know was that the Le Roy was a private hospital, that Jones was its owner, and that he prided himself on its cuisine.

A month later Jones engaged in a campaign that he thought would surely lose him the affection of his old friend. In a six-column editorial blast, the longest editorial ever to appear in his paper, he opposed the proposed three billion, seven hundred and fifty million-dollar loan to Great Britain. The loan was to be for a fifty-year period, the final repayment date to be in the year 2001, and the interest rate 2 per cent per annum.

His attack created something of a sensation because he had made a substantial loan to Great Britain at the beginning of World War II from RFC funds. He had himself suggested the wartime loan and had overcome the objection of Secretary of the Treasury Morgenthau and other Administration sources to it. His 1946 opposition therefore had the effect of starting a nation-wide debate upon the proposed British loan.

The circumstances of the 1941 loan made by Jones were these:

The dollar position of Great Britain was so unfavorable in 1941 that it was hard pressed to pay for war materials bought here. It had by this time taken over and sold close to one billion, five hundred million dollars of the American holdings of British subjects. The indiscriminate throwing of these securities on the market was driving prices down.

Jones was watching these developments carefully. The case of the American Viscose Corporation, the largest producer of rayon in this country, was a vivid example of what was happening. This profitable concern, owned by Courtaulds, Limited, of London, went on the market and brought less than half of its worth.

On March 20, four days after Sir Edward Peacock, who was in this country as the agent of the British Treasury, announced that he had made arrangements for the sale of Viscose to an investment banking syndicate in Wall Street, Jones wrote to President Roosevelt:

> If the British are required to sell their United States investment on a forced sale basis, they will probably not be able to realize their fair value, and the fact that these investments are hanging over the market will have a depressing effect on the entire market, and in that way adversely affect investments of our own citizens.
>
> Furthermore, the British have made a point of the fact that many of their investments in this country are an important factor in their economic affairs. The income from them is being used to buy our products, and otherwise to provide them with dollar exchange.
>
> I think we all feel that the British should pay as long as they can, and should use their foreign investments to fight the war and buy war supplies. But it may not leave a very good feeling with them if they are forced to sell investments that are vital to their existence.
>
> I suggest that we arrange to lend on these investments at approximately the cost of money to us, and for a period—not too long, that will enable them to sell in an orderly way, and probably save some of these investments by applying the earnings toward interest and liquidation of the debt.
>
> In the case of Viscose, as I understand the deal, it was hurried and forced, the bankers advancing $40,000,000, and agreeing to account to the British for 90 per cent of the sale price over the $40,000,000 advance and their fees of $2,700,000 and expenses estimated at $150,000.
>
> In other words, from the total sale price, after paying the advance and the bankers' fees and expenses, aggregating approximately $43,000,000, the bankers take 10 per cent of any excess.
>
> The Company is in excellent shape with almost $40,000,000 cash on hand and a substantial amount of other liquid assets. Its earnings for the past two years have been approximately $9,700,000 a year. This may have been before income taxes, but even allowing for taxes, the net earnings would be more than $7,000,000 a year.
>
> If the bankers sell the property at, say, $75,000,000, which would not be a big price, the bankers' total fees will be in the neighborhood of $6,000,000, or a net to the British of approximately $68,000,000. The British will be justified in feeling that this is a very big price to pay the bankers, particularly since they are selling their choicest American investments.
>
> If we had loaned $68,000,000 against the property at 3 per cent, the earnings would have paid the interest on the loan and amortized the entire debt in approximately ten years, based upon the last two years' earnings.

Although Jones, principally because of the opposition of Secretary of the Treasury Morgenthau, was unable to save the Viscose Company to its owners, he did obtain from Congress a modification of the Johnson Act prohibiting loans to foreign governments that had defaulted on World War I loans, provided such loans were secured by investments in this country.

Under the law's term the RFC in June, 1941, made a loan of 425,000,000 dollars to the United Kingdom of Great Britain and Northern Ireland. It was to mature serially over a period of fifteen years with interest at 3 per cent. In reality only 390,000,000 dollars of it was drawn.

At the time when the loan of three billion, seven hundred fifty million dollars to the British Labor government was proposed in 1945, the RFC loan was being repaid at a rate to insure its retirement well before the maturity year 1956 when the British would regain possession of American investments having a value of in excess of one billion dollars.

Jones thought the proposed 1945 loan was unbusinesslike. It would be for "fifty-five years," practically two generations, he pointed out, and "that is much too long a time to lend money to a foreign government without security."

He also said that:

> No loan of any kind should be made until all considerations incident to it are determined in advance of the loan. Nothing should be left for future negotiations. In the present loan agreement *empire tariff preference* and the proposal for the expansion of world trade, in which the United States is vitally so concerned, are left for future consideration. The time for these arrangements is before the loan is made. . . .
>
> The British are by no means strapped. It has been estimated that their assets in other countries than ours total some $8,000,000,000, their unmined gold reserves have been estimated to be worth at least $15,000,000,000, and their diamond reserves as much as $8,000,000,000.

Jones suggested that instead of a new loan that an additional one billion dollars be advanced to the British on the collateral put up in 1941, that the interest rate be 2 per cent, and that there be no restrictions on Great Britain as to where the money would be spent.

> If these earnings hold up as they have over the past dozen years, and in all probability they will increase, the loan will be entirely repaid in about forty years, and the British will still own their profitable investments in this country [he argued]. Later, if it is found the $1,000,000,000 is not enough, the Congress will be here to consider an application for more.

Much to his surprise, Jones found that Beaverbrook was on his side in this. An even greater surprise was to find Baruch as an ally. But the Administration pushed the loan through.

In later years Jones was to learn that a large body of public opinion in Great Britain agreed with his views. On November 23, 1949, under the heading, "Mr. Jones Saved Our Treasure—Returns It," the London *Evening Standard* said in an editorial:

> There is a dignified, silver-haired, rich old gentleman living down in Texas in whose honor there ought to be a statue in London. His name is Jesse Jones.
>
> Back in 1941 it was Mr. Jones, then head of the Reconstruction Finance Corporation, who first on the American side became appalled at the way we were selling off our accumulated overseas investments in an all-out effort to beat Hitler.
>
> We had already, in the Whitehall phrase, "disinvested" ourselves of close to $1,400,000,000. The market was low and the prices we were getting were called by many Wall Streeters "criminal."
>
> As far as the United States was concerned, it must stop at once said Mr. Jones. Why not use these valuable investments as collateral for a loan.
>
> We did. And it is thanks to Jesse Jones that we still have in this country a huge dollar asset left—instead of nothing at all. . . . From the start the British taxpayer has never had to pay a single penny to square our account with the RFC.

The final installment of the Jones British loan was paid September 28, 1951, five years earlier than the agreement called for. The British got back the securities. The United States government in the ten years had collected 63,000,000 dollars in interest.

Jones opposed the Marshall Plan, despite his pleasant relations with General Marshall in Washington.

In reply to a communication from former Secretary of War Stimson urging Jones to join a citizens' committee for the Marshall Plan, Jones wrote to Robert P. Patterson, a member of the committee:

> I appreciate the opportunity afforded me to join with you and other estimable gentlemen to support the Marshall Plan. I am as anxious as anyone to help the distressed people in Europe, but not with dollars to be spent recklessly as in the case of the British loan. I think that we should give them food, clothing and medicines to the extent that we can, say for a period of a year, and take another look at the situation then.
>
> I think we should also assist them with agricultural and probably some other equipment, that would enable them to work out their own problems. This part of our assistance to be repaid in materials or otherwise when the recipients are able to pay. I am of course impressed by Mr. Stimson's strong telegram and hold him in high esteem, but must decline his invitation because I do not think the program he outlines is as practical as I believe our course should be. Furthermore, we have only been given generalities as to what the Marshall plan is.

Although this correspondence took place before the purposes of the

Marshall Plan had been clearly delineated, Jones remained convinced that better results both for ourselves and Europe would have come if we had known a little more where we were going before we started on what he ultimately regarded as a great give-away journey.

But he had advocated relief for Europe in numerous speeches before the end of the war and had reiterated that belief in a letter to Beaverbrook on October 30, five days before he received the telegram from Stimson asking him to join the committee for the Marshall Plan. In his letter to Beaverbrook, Jones wrote:

> I am glad to see you so confident that England will rid herself of the Socialist Government. As you so well know, the State cannot take the place of private enterprise.
>
> I am sure that our Congress will vote substantial relief for Europe, and should. My own view is that we should provide the peoples of those distressed countries with the means and facilities of producing their own requirements for a wholesome standard of living. A program that would require work to eat.

On August 15, 1946, there came the great sorrow of the death of his brother, John T., four years his senior. Their relations were close all their lives. Of his brother Jesse Jones wrote:

> There was no nobler man, no finer friend, no more affectionate brother. He thought first of his family and friends, last or never of himself. When we were boys he whipped the boys too big for me with whom I sometimes ran afoul. He started fighting my battles then and he fought them all the days of his life.

In memory and in honor of the brother whose educational opportunities had been no greater than his own, Jones established the John T. Jones Chair of Economics at Austin College, Sherman, Texas.

32

The Last Years

WHEN Jesse H. Jones returned to Houston in 1946, it was with no idea that he was retiring in any sense of the word. The "rest of idleness and the peace of inactivity" had no part in his plans for the remainder of his life.

Jones was now in his seventy-third year. The physical strength that had made possible his strenuous days but had been sapped by two pneumonia sieges had returned and he entered into his activities with delight.

His interest in the *Chronicle* and its editorial policies on foreign and domestic affairs remained acute and continuous. Norman Baxter retained his residence in Washington, and every day he and Jones discussed on the telephone current problems of public policy. This was to last until the death of Baxter six years later.

On his desk the week after he reopened his office in Houston was a happy reminder of his great abiding interest—a blueprint of a projected new building. More followed. His interests expanded as he readjusted himself to the atmosphere of his old life and reactivated old interests and associations.

From the first days of their marriage Jesse and Mary Jones had taken keen enjoyment in what they never thought of as charity, but as "helping people." While this help of other people had been continuous and extensive, it was not until the seventeenth year of their marriage that they were to work out the final plans for the institution in which they had been interested and had discussed between themselves for so long.

In 1937 Mary Jones joined him in creating a foundation for philanthropic purposes—Houston Foundation, Inc. To it they gave the major part of their estate. The earliest bequests provided a polio hospital in Houston, a medical library for the Houston Medical Center, and a public library in Mexia, Texas, Mrs. Jones' birthplace, in memory of her parents. One of the bequests was a surprise to Mary Jones. It honored her and was a 1,000,000-dollar gift by her husband to Rice Institute for the construction of Mary Gibbs Jones College for women students at Rice. Another gift, which surprised the man in whose honor it was given, was Jones' 1,000,000-dollar bequest to the University of Houston to enable it to erect the Fred J. Heyne Classroom Building. When the gift was announced Heyne was completing his forty-seventh year as Jones' right-hand man.

But the principal activities of the foundation, Jesse and Mary Jones stipulated, was to provide scholarships for young men and women—white and colored—who otherwise would have difficulty in completing their education. By the early 1950's they were aiding an average of 500 students a year in both graduate and undergraduate study in fifty institutions of higher learning. They had provided that this average number would be maintained thereafter. In all cases the colleges have selected the students. The foundation contracts with the colleges to provide a given sum each year for five or ten years.

Twenty-three of the schools were in Texas, four in Tennessee, three in each Kentucky and Virginia, two each in Arkansas, California, and Maryland, and one each in Alabama, Georgia, Louisiana, Massachusetts, New York, Nevada, New Mexico, Pennsylvania, Norway, Sweden, and Canada.

There were such scholarships as the ones named for Generals Dwight D. Eisenhower and George S. Patton, Jr., in Texas A. & M., Douglas MacArthur at New Mexico Military Institute, and George Catlett Marshall at Virginia Military Institute; for Fleet Admirals Ernest J. King and Chester W. Nimitz at the University of Texas; Fleet Admiral William S. Halsey, Jr., and General A. A. Vandegrift at Rice Institute, Herbert Hoover at the University of Nevada, William S. Knudsen at the Massachusetts Institute of Technology, John Nance Garner at Trinity University, Lord Beaverbrook at the University of New Brunswick, General Lucius Clay at Georgia Institute of Technology, Cordell Hull

Fellowship in International Affairs at Vanderbilt University, the Carter Glass Professorship in Government at Sweet Briar College, and the Woodrow Wilson School of Foreign Affairs at the University of Virginia.

For Royal A. Ferris, Dallas banker who loaned him 500 dollars, the first bank loan he ever received, Jones established the Royal A. Ferris chair of finance at Southern Methodist University, and for George H. O'Connor, a Washington entertainer whose songs delighted a generation of Washington political figures, he established a scholarship in Georgetown University in the District of Columbia.

The recipients of the scholarships and fellowships enrolled for instruction in agriculture, Christian service, education, business administration, engineering, general subjects, arts, home economics, ceramics, music, medicine and nursing, military, journalism, public affairs, and international relations.

The Negro scholarships were set up at Tuskegee, Prairie View A. & M., and Texas Southern University.

At one time twenty-eight students in Texas A. & M. College, all on Jones scholarships and all wearing military cadet uniforms, lined up for a photograph and sent it autographed to him. At another time eighteen students from all over Texas and all on Jones scholarships paid him a surprise visit in his office.

Jones also gave many achievement awards to students. When Texas A. & M. won the national football championship he gave an engraved gold watch to each member of the team and to the coaches.

Of the 514 students on Jones scholarships in 1953, a representative year, 282 were boys and 232 girls. Nearly every year a boy or girl on a Jones scholarship won the highest scholastic honors in some of the colleges, sometimes national honors.

Among the most rewarding of the scholarships were those set up for Negro girls specializing in home economics at Prairie View University. Mrs. Jones was particularly interested in assisting girls who wished to study for home economics or music.

While most of the Jones scholarships went to the twenty-three selected institutions of higher learning in Texas, his gifts to any single school were the largest to the John Brown School at Siloam Springs, Arkansas, of which he was a principal supporter from the time of its founding. One of the many gifts to John Brown was 50,000 dollars in memory of Jones' parents, William Hasque and Ann Holman Jones. To Peabody College at Nashville, of which he was a member of the Board of Trustees, went 25,000 dollars for freshman scholarships and 50,000 dollars for graduate students. He set up at Prairie View, a Negro college 75,000 dollars—25,000 in agriculture, 25,000 in home economics, and 25,000 for nursing.

Other Jones gifts went to churches, hospitals, homes for the aged, boys' clubs, and many forms of charity. Since Jones was an unconventional philanthropist he gave tens of thousands to help individuals.

After World War II ended, men and material became available and Houston went off on a building surge reminiscent of the one that followed World War I. Jones quickly discovered that he would have to do more building just to accommodate the tenants he already had. The rapid and vast expansion of all manner of business enterprises meant that tenants who had a suite would need an entire floor, and the ones who had three or four floors, the better part of a building.

First cotton and then petroleum had spurred Houston's growth, and now in the latter half of the 1940's the chemical industry came to the forefront. Jones noted the downtown Houston traffic jam, and he built a 1000-car garage for the Rice and Texas State Hotels. Two new sixteen-story Jones structures—the Commerce Bank and the 1114 Texas Avenue Buildings—moved into the skyline. Then there were the fourteen-story addition to the C. and I. Life Building, a twelve-story addition to the Gulf Building, an eight-story addition to the Commerce Building, seven stories to the National Bank of Commerce, five stories to the Kirby-Fashion Building, and an 820-car garage for the National Bank of Commerce and Gulf Buildings and a six-story Capitol and Travis garage building. He also built in the same period the sixteen-story Oil and Gas Building and a five-story garage in Fort Worth.

When General Dwight D. Eisenhower, later to be President, visited him in Houston, Jones told him, "I am happiest when I am planning and building."

His enthusiasm was little diminished from the day long ago when he consummated the lease for the Rice Hotel site. Under the terms of William Marsh Rice's will the land could not be sold. Jones preferred outright ownership, but that was impossible on this ground, the best location in Houston at the time.

All the talk had been of a ninety-nine-year lease. Suddenly Jones said, "I don't want it unless it carries an option for a ninety-nine-year renewal." And he did not sign until assured of 198 years' use of the land.

He was proud of the good relations he had always had with labor.

Once when wages in one of his enterprises went to arbitration, a Jones executive asked the union to suggest an arbiter.

"We would," said the union spokesman, "like to have Mr. Jones act as our arbitrator."

In 1947 Jones wrote to Lord Beaverbrook:

> In addition to lumber, banking, publishing and other activities, I have, for more than 40 years, been building for investment, in Houston, Fort Worth, Dallas and New York City.
>
> With the exception of a general strike in Houston, the early part of this year, by all the crafts, I have never had a strike.
>
> We had a general strike, due largely to the excess of industrial development in this section. The stoppage affected all construction, and after 60 days or so of wrangling between the general contractors, and labor leaders, I was asked by both sides to suggest a solution. In two days the men were back at work with a no-strike agreement for twelve months, and on a fair basis. I have always believed in good wages and good working conditions.

After his return to Houston Jones took special interest in the successive appointments to the Supreme Court. To John W. Davis, with whom he maintained a correspondence as long as Davis lived, he wrote, "I wanted to see you President of the United States. I think I wanted even more to see you Chief Justice of the United States." But when Davis' age precluded that, Jones thought Associate Justice Robert Jackson the best suited for the place. When Chief Justice Vinson died, he hoped for the selection of Jackson, whom he had also favored at the time Vinson was appointed.

He wrote to Jackson at the time: "I have followed your course with great interest and expected you to be Chief Justice. You should have been and probably would have except for old friendships."

Jackson, in an appreciate answer, said:

> I have often told the story that you were the one Cabinet officer of my time who had practical sense about getting along with an Attorney General. You may have forgotten the incident. As we entered the Cabinet meeting, you handed me three pieces of paper. You said the first one "is a question that we would like an opinion on, if we can get a favorable answer. The second one is the answer my solicitor thinks you can make. The third one is the reasons for thinking so. If you can give us the answer we want, write us and opinion and, if you can't just hand these papers back to me." That contrasted with the action of some of the Cabinet members who had a habit of asking for opinions through the newspapers, the result of which was to create frequent conflicts between departments. I don't think all of my colleagues enjoyed the joke.

His interest in national politics was acute and he witnessed with no little anxiety the drift of the Democratic party to the left under Truman. As a consequence in 1948 he announced that for the first time since, when at twenty-two, he supported William McKinley on sound money against Bryan the Democratic candidate in 1896, he would support the Republican national ticket. In announcing for the election of Thomas E. Dewey for President, the Houston *Chronicle* in an editorial said it "must be obvious to all thinking people, that we need a change in our national Administration." He thought that the Democratic party had deserted its ancient states' rights principles, that the South was no longer influential in making its policies and could regain its voice in party matters by the establishment of a two-party system below the Mason-Dixon Line. "We of the South should no longer be taken for granted in our national politics," he said in the editorial he wrote for his paper.

The Republican vote picked up in the Lone Star State that year, but it still registered its electoral vote for the Democratic candidates.

In 1949 Jones induced General Eisenhower to come to Houston and address the annual dinner of the Houston Chamber of Commerce. It had been usual to hold these meetings in the Rice ballroom, with an attendance of about 800 people. When it became known that Eisenhower would be the speaker, there was such a great demand for seats that it was necessary to move the meeting to the Coliseum. There Jones introduced Eisenhower to an audience of more than 15,000 people. When Jones arose to make the introduction, he said the meeting was nonpolitical but a moment later presented Mrs. Eisenhower and commented that she would grace the White House. While the speech of the former AEF Commander was nonpolitical, it marked the beginning of a campaign within the state that culminated in Eisenhower winning Texas support in the 1952 Republican National Convention and in carrying Texas in 1952.

Jones, however, had no part of this campaign. He would have preferred Taft to Eisenhower, although his opinion of Eisenhower was high. It had happened that the contest for the Texas delegation between Eisenhower and Taft was marked with more bitterness than in any other state. Jones, as did many others, believed the fight might split the Republicans so as to give them a lessened chance of winning the election. On June 18, 1952, he wrote similar letters to Eisenhower and Taft. In his letter to Eisenhower he said:

I agree with you that the Democratic party has been in power entirely too long and voted accordingly four years ago. We should not allow other Democrats who feel that way to get too badly divided because of partisanship for you or Bob Taft.

Perhaps both you and Bob could throw a bouquet or two to each other that would obviate the possibility.

Eisenhower replied from Denver:

Dear Jesse:

Thanks for your thoughtful note of June 18th.

As you know, I have entirely avoided personalities and have attempted to strike a balance between necessary criticism of the Democratic administration and clarification of my own position as a Republican.

I am equally convinced that you cannot fight corruption with corruption. Your generous words are heart-warming.

Taft replied:

Dear Jesse:

I certainly did not welcome the Texas fight but, as you know, it came from internal rows in the organization there. If I am nominated, I hope to go out and organize a broad Committee of Democrats for Taft in Texas and give them an outstanding place in the running of the campaign. I will also try to say a few kind things about the General. I understand, however, he is pretty sore, which arises out of the fact that he does not really understand what politics is about.

In December, 1947, the "alumni" of the RFC gave a dinner in New York honoring Jones. From all parts of the nation men who had worked with him in the great lending agency came and crowded the Starlight Roof at the Waldorf-Astoria Hotel.

Herbert Hoover left a sickbed to pay tribute to the man who "never let politics interfere with his concept of public service, which constitutes the mark of a great American."

President Truman through his Secretary of the Treasury, John W. Snyder, sent a message complimenting Jones on "the inspiring part the RFC played in the rescue and stimulation of business during the depression years, and on its magnificent role in the development of critical and strategic supplies for the defense and war programs."

There were also moving personal tributes from former co-workers Snyder, Associate Justice Reed, Wilson McCarthy, and Emil Schram, then president of the New York Stock Exchange.

He told the gathering that a man's most rewarding thing in life is to have the affection of those whose affection he wants:

> You were the ones who were near me in the trying years of depression and war. Such a tribute would compensate for all that was hard and laborious in those years. It is difficult for me to thank you for coming here to honor me. You honored me first and most when you did so faithfully and well the work that was assigned to you by your government.

At this dinner the suggestion was made by Mr. Hoover, Wilson McCarthy, and others that the former RFC chairman write the story of that agency.

This decided him to write his own account of the RFC. To work with him in the thorough job he planned it would be, Jones chose Edward Angly, a native Texan who had been a war correspondent and magazine writer. Jones dug into his files for correspondence and memoranda. He furnished the leads of important transactions, but in all cases he insisted that Angly go directly to them to get additional facts from men who sat on the other side of the table from him. In the three years spent on the book Angly traveled to all parts of the nation and talked to men who had information on RFC dealings. He read minutes of RFC meetings and documents giving the terms on which loans were made.

Jones followed the habit he had pursued for years on any matter in which he was engrossed. He dictated and revised in his office in the daytime and then took his manuscript home for work nights and on Sundays and holidays. After three years of diligent research and carefully considered writing with Angly, the book, *Fifty Billion Dollars, My Thirteen Years with the RFC,* was completed and published in 1951. It was a best seller.

His dedication of the book attested his deep affection for the RFC. He wrote:

> I dedicate this story to the memory of my father, William Hasque Jones, from whom I received the precepts which have guided my life, and to the men and women of the Reconstruction Finance Corporation who rendered a great service to our generation in the depression of the early 1930's and in World War II.

Both Jones and Angly knew that the part of the book that would hold the greatest initial interest and provoke controversy was his evaluation of the men with whom he served in Washington for thirteen years, and especially would this be the case of his reference to Franklin D. Roosevelt.

Jones and Angly weighed particularly these three consecutive paragraphs of Jones' appraisal of Roosevelt:

I do not understand exactly what Secretary of State Dean Acheson meant recently by "total diplomacy," but I understand perfectly what is meant by "total politician"—Franklin D. Roosevelt. He employed all the arts known to politics in getting and holding the confidence of a great majority of the American people and, along with it, the hatred of others—a hatred upon which he capitalized. He changed his tactics whenever politics seemed to dictate, and with no intention of leaving the White House until voted out—or carried out. In his twelve years in the Presidency he never looked back and never explained.

One serious problem with Mr. Roosevelt after the start of World War II in 1939 was that he was always fighting two wars at the same time, the political struggle for the Presidency, which he never lost sight of, and the military conflict. Regardless of his oft-repeated statement, "I hate war," he was eager to get into the fighting since that would insure a third term.

In his first campaign for the Presidency, he charged waste and extravagance in government, and promised economy; but immediately after his inauguration he started spending and spending, and never let up. In the beginning his purposes were undoubtedly high; but as the years went by and the mill seemed to require a new kind of grist to keep him in the driver's seat he never hesitated to provide it and with his famous, "You and I know" on the radio, to tell the people about it.

Despite the certainty that such an observation as this might because of its "news" value distract attention from the meatier parts of the book —the record of RFC—Jones declined to change it.

I have said good things about Roosevelt in this book and I have told of the faults and shortcomings in some of his activities [Jones told Angly]. Unfortunately after the President became thoroughly entrenched in office and came to feel he could hold it as long as he lived, he felt that he could do anything he wanted to.

To err is human, of course, and especially when one is riding high in public opinion as President Roosevelt was. I had a close relationship with him. In that relationship I did not fail to recognize his desire and even determination to bend some factions of our political and industrial life to his wishes. I cooperated with him in every situation that I thought was to the best interests of the country. I felt free to make suggestions to him and he to me with respect to RFC operations, and I recognized him, of course, as President of the United States and never forgot that I was an appointee. When I wrote that our relations were cordial I think it was an understatement.

I could have recited cases in further justification of my "total politician" reference. The things I have written are true and I know of no way to write history except to tell the truth about the living or dead.

The historical importance of the book was just what Jones had wanted it to be, and made it the story of the RFC. There was nothing quite like the RFC in the annals of government. It was as Raymond Moley called it, "the keystone of recovery and the foundation of the war effort."

Ironically, when the book was being printed, the RFC, which had gone untouched by scandal in the testing periods of Depression and war, had fallen into dishonor. The thirteen years of magnificent achievement had been followed by the years of decline, mismanagement, and disgrace.

In the evil days that followed its time of glory RFC had begun making unnecessary and questionable loans. Engulfed in a series of scandals of which the mink coat was the symbol, it had become a haunted palace. The chiselers, moochers, and influence-hucksters who had been kept outside its portals in its better days had moved in.

In the Senate, Senator Willis Robertson of Virginia said, "I had a great many dealings with RFC when Mr. Jones was its head, and there were no loose or ill-considered loans made during that period. I wish we had someone like Mr. Jones at the head of RFC now."

Jones, long before the scandals broke, had written to the Senate Banking and Currency Committee that in times of peace and prosperity there is no need for such an institution as RFC. He suggested that it "be given a decent burial."

> None of the conditions which prompted the creation of the RFC and the various amendments to its powers exist today [he said in his letter addressed to Senator Fulbright of Arkansas]. It is being prostituted by such loans as that to Kaiser-Frazier.
>
> The corporation was created when millions of our people were on short rations, when there was no market for farm products and no demand for anything but a square meal.

But it was not until 1953 that Congress voted to kill it. On October 1, 1954, it passed from the scene. Such liquidating functions as remained were put under the directions of the Secretary of the Treasury.

In the summer of 1952 Jones took what he thought would be his last trip to Europe. It was the fiftieth anniversary of the trip he had made to see the Coronation of King Edward VII and the ending of the Victorian age. And he would, he thought, like "to make a first and last comparison." He wanted to talk to the people and make up his mind on conditions, and resolved to see no heads of states or politicians.

He wanted also to have a ride on the new luxury liner the *United States*, just coming into service. He also wanted a look at the low skyline of Paris "to discourage me from any temptation to pile any more concrete high into the sky."

It was a congenial party. In addition to Mr. and Mrs. Jones, Colonel J. M. Hartfield, Charles Noyes, Miss Ruth Reiber, and Captain T. Reiber went along.

At the close of the trip Jones wrote back to his Houston *Chronicle* a regret that always came to him when he visited Paris: that he had not been able to keep Houston a ten-story town. He also reported the conclusion: "It is time for the United States to slow down on trying to support the world."

As the years went by it became his habit to make fewer trips, stay closer to home.

In his spacious, thoroughly modernized office in one of the first of his ten-story buildings, built nearly a half-century before, the walls were covered with the autographed pictures of the nation's and world's leaders he had known since he first came to Washington in the Wilson Administration. Those walls also attested that he had been one of the most cartooned public men who had ever been in Washington. Most of the cartoonists had been his friends and acquaintances who had sent him the originals. Plaques and scrolls expressing appreciation for some service and framed laudatory resolutions were all about.

On a table lay one of the highest decorations of the Nationalist China government. The citation praised his high war service to China and his support of that government in editorial columns of his newspaper. Near it was the highest decoration the Swedish government ever conferred on a non-Swede—the Commander, with star, of the Royal Order of Vasa. Swedish Ambassador to the United States Erik Boheman flew to Houston to confer this decoration because of "Mr. Jones' interest in Swedish-American Relations and in the Texas Swedish Culture Foundation."

To his office daily came visitors from Houston and from all parts of the world.

Delegations came to confer honors with such frequency that days were arranged for them by his office staff.

A group from Hollywood wished to present a scroll telling him he was selected as "the most fabulous Texan in the most fabulous city in the most fabulous state in the Union."

Then came a unit from the Houston Junior Chamber of Commerce to present him with a certificate of "Honorary Membership." The man with a legend of personal and civic achievement almost unparalleled in this country accepted the honor graciously and told them humorously that "it is possible you have signed up a man who can be of some benefit in the future growth of Houston."

The Knights of San Jacinto filed into his office to make him a member of the order, created by General Sam Houston on the blood-soaked field at San Jacinto. There are only twelve living members of the order and it took some time for a vacancy to occur to which he would be elected. It had been planned ever since Jones got the high monument erected at San Jacinto Battleground.

One day Floyd Jackson, a forty-three-year-old Negro, arrived. He explained to a secretary that the day before he was on a Los Angeles television program and was offered a freakish way to make 1000 dollars. If he would go to Houston, Texas, and shine the shoes of ten millionaires, he would be given 100 dollars for each shine.

Jackson told Jones' secretary that the only Houston millionaire whose name he knew was Mr. Jones. Here, thought the secretary, is a matter Mr. Jones would want to attend to.

In a city where millionaires come in battalions, finding ten of them is not difficult. Jones knew where to find them.

"It's a pretty hot day and you ought not to have to go around hunting millionaires in this kind of weather. I will get them for you," he told Jackson.

Jones called nine of his millionaire acquaintances on the telephone. They were all in his office in twenty minutes. In half an hour more Jackson had shined their shoes and departed.

Joe Didiot came in. Joe needed no appointment, for his association with Jones had been longer than any living man's. It started when Jones came to work in his uncle's lumber yard at Hillsboro in 1892. Joe was working in a rival lumber yard across the street. Like Jones, Joe was born in Tennessee, the son of a highly educated Frenchman who came to America to teach school. Now, sixty-two years later, they had a lot to talk about.

Joe recalled that Jones told him one day, "Joe, I am not going to load lumber on wagons all my life."

Joe also remembered the day Jones founded his first business, the South Texas Lumber Company.

"He called me on Saturday," Joe told a newer Jones friend, "and said, 'I'm in business for myself now.' It was over long distance telephone, the first time I had ever talked to anybody so far away. I thought he was pretty extravagant for somebody just getting into business. He offered me a job. I was there ready to work on Monday."

Years later, when Jones decided to go out of the lumber business and sell his lumber yards and sawmills, he wondered what would happen to

Joe. For Joe had never worked anywhere but in a lumber yard, so Jones kept one lumber yard so that Joe would have a job with him as long as he lived.

In 1950 Jones took the title of publisher, and his nephew, John T. Jones, became president of the Chronicle Company.

"I made John President of the *Chronicle* to give him a start while I was still here, and he is up to the job," Jones explained.

In 1953 Jones had what was up to that time his closest call. An emergency operation for an advanced gall-bladder situation was followed by a nip-and-tuck struggle for life. While his condition was still regarded as critical, his physician came into the hospital room to find the patient with a pad of paper and a pencil. He was computing the aggregate height of his buildings. If all of them were a single structure, his figures showed, it would be 805 stories high, extending into the air 10,525 feet.

"That is not quite two miles high," he observed with evident dissatisfaction.

When he left the hospital he announced plans for an eighteen-story building for the Houston Club, and it rose on the site of the old Bristol Hotel, which had been first of all the buildings he erected.

Jones was still convalescing from the surgery when a proposal was made for the Houston Port Authority to purchase some old wharves owned by private interests. Jones thought the price proposed to be paid for the outmoded facilities was exorbitant, just as in his most bitter fight in Houston he had thought in 1920 that the price for land offered the Harbor Board was exorbitant. He held that if Houston needed more wharfage, it ought to be the most modern. As in the fight in 1920, Jones found himself arrayed against most of the civic leaders of Houston, and many of his personal friends. But again the voters of Houston stood by Jones. He won the hard fight with 74 per cent of the voters on his side, just about the same proportion as in the 1920 fight.

In 1955 there was a celebration to mark Houston's attainment of a population of a million. The city of 40,000 that Jones in 1898 had chosen as a home had grown all over the broad prairie and now ranked twelfth among the cities of the United States. Since the 1950 census it had passed Pittsburgh and Milwaukee. It was also second in tonnage rank among the nation's ports.

The celebration was a happy occasion for Jones, who took the occasion to predict that the second million would be easier to get than the first one. But when a speaker gave him chief credit for the city's growth, he said in reply, "A city like Houston could not be built by one man. It took a lot of people to do it." No other man had worked so hard for Houston, nor had such fierce pride in it.

Arthur Krock on a visit to Houston wrote in the New York *Times:*

> According to Greek legend, old Priam, the last King of Troy, was the city planner who built the topless towers of Illium. And quite as much the consequences of city planning by one individual are the man-made pinnacles of Houston. This modern Priam, in so far as his relation to that phase of the Trojan King's activities are concerned, is Jesse H. Jones, to whose vision and daring can be attributed the massive skyline that thrusts itself between the eyes of the oncoming traveler and the limitless horizon.
>
> The builder of the skyline sits in his penthouse, surveying as did Christopher Wren (and perhaps old Priam above the Scaenan gate), a monument erected to him in his lifetime. Jesse H. Jones is far removed now from the political scene in Washington, where he did more than any federal administrator during the New Deal to employ at a profit the resources of government for the preservation of the capitalist system, while restricting them from stifling the enterprise of the individual.

When Inez Robb, of the International News Service, went to interview him, he spoke with such intense pride of Houston that she said,

"You talk of Houston the way a person usually talks of heaven."

Jones fingered the big elk's tooth at the end of his watch chain, gazed out for a moment at the striking skyline he had created, and replied, "Do you suppose heaven is anything like Houston? Eventually, I suppose I will be lucky just to be inside the pearly gates. But I will be happier there if it is just a mite like Houston."

Early in 1956 Jones was approaching the tenth anniversary of his return to Houston from Washington. They had been busy years and, except for grief at the passing of several old friends, they had been happy years. He was not as strong as he had been before the surgical operation in 1953, but if he was not as robust he was probably not conscious of any failing in health.

On February 22 a thousand of Jones' fellow townsmen crowded into the banquet hall at the Rice Hotel honoring him as the city's outstanding citizen, and twice rose in applause when his initiative and vision in "building Houston" was cited. An old friend, Gus Wortham, in his address said, "Jesse Jones means Houston and Houston means Jesse Jones." Representative Joseph W. Martin of Massachusetts, came down from Washington to join in the occasion and called Jones "one of the greatest Americans of the age."

Jones had felt below par for several days and had been saddened less than a week before by the death of Sam Taub, his close friend for nearly sixty years. But when he rose to respond to the speeches, he seemed the same giant-like and majestic figure that Houston had so long known, and few suspected they were seeing his last appearance at a public gathering. He spoke even more briefly than usual, extending his warm thanks for the honor.

A week later he went to see his personal physician, Dr. B. Weems Turner, and continued these visits until March 20, when Dr. Turner sent him to St. Luke's Hospital for X-rays. Dr. Turner and Dr. M. D. Levy soon decided that an operation for a kidney blockage was necessary. This was performed and on April 10 he went home. But his vitality waned visibly and on May 9 he returned to the hospital for further treatment.

On May 20 Dr. Turner announced his condition was critical. From that time on no hope was held for his recovery. But as life had been unhurried for Jesse Jones, so was death to be. For ten days he slept most of the time, painlessly and peacefully. Mary Jones, John T. Jones, Jr., Fred J. Heyne, Gladys Mikell, or some other member of his family or an intimate business associate was always on vigil at his bedside.

In such a quiet sleep death came at thirty-one minutes past eight o'clock on the night of June 1. It had come unobtrusively and with the calmness and casualness that always seemed to surround Jesse Jones.

Funeral services in St. Paul's Methodist Church, which he had helped to build, were brief and simple. Bishop A. Frank Smith read from the Gospel of St. John's and the Book of Revelations. Dr. Neal D. Cannon, the pastor, read a prayer. Jones had often said that all that need be said on any occasion could usually be said in fifteen minutes, and the services lasted just fifteen minutes.

From the crowded church the casket was carried past thousands who stood with bowed heads in the Main Street he had loved so well. From the church to Forest Park Cemetery, the funeral procession passed over a thoroughfare that had been but a dusty trail when Jones came to Houston.

As the sun sank low on June 4, 1956, Jesse Jones was buried in a grove of trees a few yards from Lake of the Woods chapel. Six miles away stood the skyline he had created; three miles distant was the Houston Ship Channel in which he had brought true the dream of bringing the sea to Houston; and fifteen miles away stood the tall, star-topped San Jacinto shaft he had designed.

Jesse Jones and Houston had said good-by to one another.

An Appraisal

JESSE JONES has been described as the most extraordinary administrator of his time. His achievements, however, were more than those of an administrator. They passed that point where administration ends and statesmanship begins.

The portrait is written in what he did rather than in his statements of what he did or his interpretation of the philosophy that guided him. The record comes through in the decisions he made, the programs he conceived and executed, and also in the unexampled confidence reposed in him by Congress and the business community.

The fame he earned before going to Washington in 1932 will be preserved in Houston as long as the bricks and mortar he laid stand out on that city's skyline and the commerce of the world enters its seaport. But the maturity of his career was in the momentous thirteen years in Washington, years jammed with events that were destined to shape the future history of the nation and the world. In shaping those events Jones played a decisive part. It would be easy to prove that without him the story of those years would be quite different.

So let us scan those years to put in perspective the problems with which Jones had to deal. Then let us see what Jones had to work with and what circumstances in that tumultuous environment helped and hindered his labors. Then let us consider what he carried to his great task in experience and in mental and moral equipment. Finally, there must be considered the reflection of his stature in the powers delegated to him by the Congress of the United States.

The Depression that came so suddenly in 1929 was destined to have a greater impact upon the United States than anything except the Civil War. If we add to that the colossal effect of World War II, the sum total is a veritable revolution. Among the permanent effects of that revolution were widespread alteration in property ownership, a shift in the balance of political power from rural to urban, and an almost incredible increase in the powers and responsibilities of government, notably the federal government.

When the Reconstruction Finance Corporation was created, the capitalist structure in the United States was very ill. It was not suffering, as Marx had predicted, with a malignant degeneration. But its convulsions were such as to provide for Marxists a very plausible argument that the day of doom their prophet had foretold was indeed upon us. There were plenty who, while professing a fervent belief in a free economy, actually entertained in their hearts a lively anticipation of its death. In fact, capitalism might well have died if many of those who rushed to its rescue had been permitted to apply their plans and cures.

However, the panic that fell upon the people of the country was sufficient to induce us all to suffer, indeed to welcome the many strange, irrational experiments conceived by Roosevelt and his more radical advisers. No such group could have attained power in normal times. It is doubtful if Roosevelt could have been elected in normal times. For he actually had little but vast good will, unlimited daring, and an affinity for the unusual. It was Jones' fate to be compelled to carry on in this confused climate. He was a surgeon compelled to operate on a battlefield.

Jones from the first, while he knew that the illness of the nation's economy was violent and dangerous, looked upon the malady as an acute and curable one. He recognized that the root of the difficulty was a defective credit situation, and regarded it as the mission of the RFC to support with the mighty arm of the nation's credit as many of the vital and strategic private enterprises as possible.

Jones, as the earlier chapters in this book recite in some detail, learned the meaning of credit from a rich and diversified experience. He knew it as a borrower and he knew it as a banker and a banker's doctor.

He believed that the RFC had not acted as boldly as the situation demanded in the Hoover Administration. In the Roosevelt Administration Jones' philosophy stood like a mighty fortress against the government expansion of government control over business. To some men who had Roosevelt's ear, Jones was exasperatingly careful with the public money. "The time to collect a loan," he said on one occasion, "is when you make it. Fix the terms so the borrower can pay the loan and you don't have to worry too much about bad debts. If the money is not likely to be paid in a generously allotted time, don't lend it. Make the loan if you can, but remember one of the greatest disservices you can do to a man is to lend him money he can't pay back."

The RFC as an institution was certainly unique in American history and probably in all history. With some extensions and specifications by Congress, it might have done everything that was accomplished by all of the alphabetical agencies of the New Deal. Without doubt, recovery, as far as recovery was attained up to the beginning of the war effort, could have been achieved by Jones with the RFC. And it is certain that recovery in any event could not have been attained without it.

Jones' executive capacity had great breadth as well as depth. His long experience had given him angles of understanding on many divergent business enterprises, from farm management to international exchange. He had a genius for selecting the right men for the many and diverse services his activities required and for winning from them their best energies, their loyalty to him and to the institution which they served. At all times he revealed imagination and a daring that in a lesser man would have been regarded as dangerous irresponsibility. Finally, he saw and put into operation, notably in banking and in railroad management, those underlying and long-range policies that distinguish him in historical perspective as a statesman of high order.

It hardly needs saying, in the light of the range of Jones' labors, that he was a man of great energy and endurance. His physcial endowment was considerable, but even so there were times when his friends feared that he was exacting too much from one body and brain. Indeed, two attacks of pneumonia had warned him that his physical capacities were not unlimited.

His manner of working, however, enabled him to use his energies and hours with efficiency. He never appeared hurried or excited. He knew well when he could actually take time out for sociability or play, and even those moments were not without their place in his plans. He was never diverted by criticism or opposition from his objectives. His capacity for quick judgment saved him long, agonizing hours of indecision.

This manner and habit of working intensified the impression made by his operations. His effort was like a flood pushing ahead—irresistible, tireless, quiet. He cooperated with others when he could; but when conditions made cooperation impossible, he went it alone, screening his real purpose when it seemed wise or daringly announcing it when that seemed more practical. When on a very few occasions he had to fight back at someone like Wallace, he squarely drew a vital issue, fought hard, quickly, and decisively.

We have seen how he succeeded in working with Roosevelt—one of the most disorderly administrators of all time. He granted such demands as he deemed wise or safe, but when Roosevelt wanted something that Jones considered wrong or clearly unwise, he listened, withheld argument, and then contrived an escape by inconspicuous inaction. Roosevelt had apparently never had to deal with this sort of strategy and he found himself powerless to cope with it.

We have also seen the array of opposition that Jones had to meet. There were the purblind bankers and other business executives who were determined to try nothing but practices hallowed by long observance. There were the radicals in the Administration who hated and opposed everything for which Jones stood. There were the callous merchants of influence serving sinister and rapacious interests anxious to get their sullied hands on government money.

Jones was always reserved and suspicious in dealing with Wall Street. As he said over and over, he deprecated the insularity of New York and the Northeast. On the other hand, Wall Street found it difficult to understand this man from Texas whose perplexing lack of orthodox methods was coupled with indubitable power. He was far from the pattern to which they were accustomed. For throughout his life he was a man who worked without partners and with precious few allies.

Jones' consistent refusal to involve himself in partnership arrangements may also explain his disconcerting refusal to recognize the iron curtain that orthodox management creates between the making and the executing of policies. On at least four occasions he was called to tasks that he fondly expected would require his attention only at policy-making board meetings. These were the development of the Houston port, his Red Cross services under President Wilson, the Texas Centennial, and, most important of all, the RFC. In every case he soon found himself carrying a tremendous load of administration. What seemed like part-time diversions turned out to be full-time jobs. In the course of such operations he made his own policies.

This, however, never degenerated into confusion, for as his operations in the RFC grew, he demonstrated an extraordinary capacity to delegate. But this delegation was to people of his own choosing who were always near him and who looked to him for help with their more perplexing problems.

While he was capable of great daring, there were certain risks that he would not accept. Perhaps this accounts for the fact that, despite the prominence of the oil industry in Texas during the period when he was rising as a businessman, and the vast fortunes that were springing up on every side, Jones avoided involvement in the business of oil production. To a degree this suggests the course followed by the elder Rockefeller, whose great fortune was built originally in refining rather than in producing oil. Rockefeller let others take the risk in those booming Pennsylvania fields. He contented himself with spending his money on what he could see and measure. Jones wanted to see accomplishment in brick and mortar rather than in figures in his investment portfolio or on his income tax return.

This disposition meant that he never became known as a mere rich man. In fact, his course meant that his personal fortune was much smaller than it would have been if he had turned to oil. It should also be noted that starting at the age of thirty-nine, when he accepted appointment on the Harbor Board, he gave a major part of his time and energies to the public service. It is an interesting coincidence that Herbert Hoover, who also had shown a capacity to make money, decided at the same age and in the same year as Jones that there were values far beyond the accumulation of wealth. Hoover and Jones entertained great respect for each other and basic agreement on fundamentals.

Jones brought to the RFC an extensive experience in management as well as in banking. Few bankers have a real grasp of the fundamental technique of management. Perhaps that is why there have been so many unfortunate examples of banker-mismanagement of industrial properties and railroads. Jones, on the other hand, had been a manager at the age of fourteen. The patterns that characterized his later dealings were manifested then—quick decisions, reticence, and a judgment that proved itself capable of weighing and appraising the many factors involved in every problem.

Jones throughout his life in business and public affairs had a marked capacity for doing daring, unconventional things. This stood out in all of his financial methods and administrative practices as well as in his handling of his public relations and political activities. In fact, some of his actions carried out under the stress of emergencies might have involved a man of less judgment in serious and most damaging consequences. Many of his actions in his private dealings had counterparts on much larger scale in some of his decisions in the RFC. One example is the story of how he frightened Henry Morgenthau almost out of his wits by getting the Secretary of the Treasury to certify 2000 insolvent banks in 1933 by giving a guarantee that he would make them solvent in six months. Another was the instance when, in 1938, he had the RFC buy 150,000,000 dollars' worth of farmers' notes secured by cotton from the Commodity Credit Corporation, despite the advice of his chief counsel that such an act was not provided for in the law. Later he succeeded in having his action validated by Congress.

Perhaps we can pin down for our use the much-abused term "statesman" by defining him as a public official who not only is able to carry out policies decreed for him by law or other authority, but who by his own dominant influence is able to make lasting policy. Under this definition Jones qualifies in an extraordinary manner. He did more than supply the essential money and credit by which the basic economic institutions were able to revive. He impressed upon them basic and novel patterns of management that assured their solvency and usefulness in later years, perhaps for all time to come. As we have seen, he defined and ultimately helped to establish the conditions under which the banking structure should be reconstructed. One of these, the guarantee of deposits by the federal government, he had believed in and advocated decades before the day when, by the parliamentary strategy of Garner and Senator Vandenberg and despite the stubborn opposition of the President, it became a reality. The other was his insistence, despite the objections of the bankers, and his success in getting more working capital for all banks.

In another field of business, he diagnosed the ailments that afflicted the railroads and, since his help was indispensable, his demands for reform were irresistible. Railway management, which had lived so many years in a deep rut of outworn tradition, entered upon a new era of progress.

In these instances and many others the Jones imprint permanently remains upon the economic structure of the nation.

But beyond any appraisals we have made here, two irrefutable pieces of evidence of the massive stature of Jones will stand in American history.

The first is what happened in the RFC after the departure of Jones.

A period followed that was marked by mismanagement and by the granting of special favors to shabby gentry, who are always a potential danger to any government department with money to spend and privileges to grant. The magnificent history of the RFC ended in the shadows of wrongdoing and incompetence. This fate would certainly have overtaken it, probably in the second Roosevelt term, if Jones had not been in command. For the moochers who live where fumbling management dwells with great accumulations of money were in and around Washington in large numbers in those years. There were also the visionaries who in other departments wasted great sums in the sweet name of welfare. Without Jones the RFC by 1940 would probably have encompassed the Administration in immeasurable scandal, and the name of Roosevelt might have gone down in history with some of the great failures of the past. If such a fate were by some miracle avoided, the war would certainly have seen Wallace and his BEW in charge of our world-wide expenditures. The strange creatures who infested the BEW would have scattered America's substance in every land. Wallace himself would have consolidated his position as Vice-President to a degree that his renomination would have been inevitable. The sad lot of the United States in a moment of victory would have been to have Wallace as President. It was Jones who saved this country from that fate. For the battle in which Jones engaged Wallace's BEW was the beginning of the end of the Vice-President's political career.

In the archives of government there are no sounder documents than the letter written by Jones to Senator Carter Glass on July 5, 1943, when after explaining that generous prices are desirable and often necessary in wartime he blasted the waste of the Wallace's Board of Economic Warfare with this memorable, devastating sentence: "Squandering the people's money even in wartime is no proof of patriotism."

Finally, there is the estimate of Jones that was written in the confidence reposed in him over the years by the Congress of the United States. The measure taken of a man by Congress is a test of very great significance. Congress is a place of great diversity of interests, of philosophies, and of personal abilities. It has men of small account. But it also has men of the highest ideals and attainments. No one can sit many months in that legislative body and not acquire a knowledge of the greed and guile of those who infest a place of power. Indeed, some who have seen that sordid side of life end in cynical despair.

But Congress gave to Jones its highest tribute in allowing him almost everything he asked. Outstanding opposition members like Borah and

Taft paid Jones the tribute of their trust and support. It is doubtful if anyone in history ever had such a measure of Congressional confidence. Certainly Roosevelt enjoyed it only in his first term and in the first months of the war.

It is not in accordance with the great principles of legislation to enact a law such as was passed when Jones was given control of the lending agencies along with the Commerce portfolio. But that was done almost unanimously, because it was Jones who was to hold the two positions. And when, after the departure of Jones and before the confirmation of his successor, the agencies were severed one from the other by an almost unanimous vote. Such expressions are given only once in many generations by free and independent legislatures.

The case of Jones at the bar of history may well close with those votes. For such decisions of a Congress traditionally jealous of power, wherever it exists, constitute the measure of a very great man.

Afterword

THIS book has been completed a few weeks after Jesse Holman Jones "went down into the silences" and at a time when the sense of loss is so heavy for me and those others who were privileged to be close to him in his lifetime.

My acquaintance with Jesse Jones began in wartime Washington in 1917. A friendship developed that continued as long as he lived. He was the most companionable man I have ever known. He had more friends than any man I have ever known. And a goodly percentage of his friends became my friends.

In fifty years as a newspaperman, forty-four of these years in Washington, I, too, have acquired a considerable acquaintance. But Jesse Jones was the most interesting man I have ever known. I never heard a dull utterance from his lips. I also say unhesitatingly—all things considered—I believe him the ablest man I have ever known.

When I told him a few years ago that I was beginning to accumulate material to write a biography, he said in his characteristic way, "It will be interesting to see what you find out or already know that is bad about me. But if you go ahead with any project concerning me, put in the bad with the good."

He was indeed a man with human foibles, frailties, and fallibilities. But his faults were smothered by his virtues. Nor could I find any failures to record, although I had his word that as a youth he was a dismal failure as a cigar salesman. Success was a habit with him, and it is doubtful if he ever suffered a real rebuff in his life, although he had his share of disappointments and what to most men would have been great discouragements. None of these, however, impaired his great optimism or dulled the edge of his friendliness.

Two things about the man always impressed me deeply. These were his extraordinary devotion to his friends and his abiding interest in the welfare of young people. He wanted to help anyone he could. But his great interest was in young men and women who had ability for their foundation and industry for their superstructure. He believed that the top of the ladder was not out of reach of such men and women no matter how humble their beginning; and the great satisfaction of his life came from helping such youth in getting an education.

Jesse Jones' personal letters were warm, often whimsical, sometimes witty. There are some such letters in existence that illustrate his loyalty and understanding. But he was perhaps the greatest telephone user of his day. It was by this method of communication that most of his friends will remember his buoyant words of encouragement or good cheer.

A builder and a doer himself, Jesse Jones' preference always was for other people who did things. At an appearance before a Congressional Committee, an attorney for the committee waved a voluminous report from a so-called Treasury expert before Jones and asked his opinion of it, a question that required five minutes to ask. Jones replied, "I have not read the report. I do not know what the suggestions are. But if I had, I would first want to know about the experience of this man who is making the suggestion. I would want to know whether he is qualified as an expert who has done it or whether he is a fellow who knows how it ought to be done."

The very large proportion of the incidents in this book are matters of my personal knowledge. I have drawn to some extent on his own carefully checked book, Fifty Billion Dollars. *Where I thought it necessary, I have given credit to sources either in the text or footnotes. To all of those who gave me information not obtainable elsewhere I am grateful. Especially am I grateful to his sister, Mrs. Daniel E. Garrett, who gave me so much information about his early years.*

Bascom N. Timmons

Index